COMPETING ON
INTERNET TIME

Lessons from Netscape and Its Battle with Microsoft

MICHAEL A. CUSUMANO
DAVID B. YOFFIE

THE FREE PRESS

THE FREE PRESS
A Division of Simon & Schuster Inc.
1230 Avenue of the Americas
New York, NY 10020

Manufactured in the United States of America

10 9 8 7 6 5 4 3 2 1

Library of Congress Cataloging-in-Publication Data

Cusumano, Michael A.
    Competing on Internet time: lessons from Netscape and its battle
with Microsoft/Michael A. Cusumano, David B. Yoffie.
        p.   cm.
    Includes bibliographical references and index.
    1. Netscape Communications Corporation. 2. Microsoft Corporation.
3. Internet software industry—United States. 4. Competition—
United States. I. Yoffie, David B. II. Title.
HD9696.65.U64N473   1998
338.4'7004678'0973—dc21   98-37653
                                                            CIP

ISBN 0-684-85319-1

The authors would like to dedicate this book to the people of Netscape, whose cooperation and candor made this type of research possible.

David Yoffie would also like to dedicate this book to Joel Friedland, whose tenacious fight against cancer should be an inspiration to us all.

Contents

Preface

THE ORIGINS of this book go back to a casual lunch on the Stanford campus—Thai food eaten outdoors, a sunny and pleasant afternoon—in February 1996. Michael Cusumano, taking a break from classes at MIT's Sloan School of Management and pondering a sequel to *Microsoft Secrets,* had been visiting a few people at Sun Microsystems's JavaSoft Division in Palo Alto. He was asking about how the fast, unpredictable pace of the Internet might affect product planning and the process of product development at leading-edge software organizations, like JavaSoft, Microsoft, and Netscape. He called to chat with a colleague from back home, David Yoffie, who specialized in the strategy of high-technology companies and happened to be living temporarily on the West Coast.

Yoffie was on sabbatical from Harvard Business School. He was visiting Stanford and doing research on Microsoft's ill-fated efforts to build its then-proprietary online network, MSN. He was also spending a day a week at Intel Corporation observing its internal operations, as both a director of the company and a researcher. At the time of the lunch with Cusumano, he had just completed *Competing in the Age of Digital Convergence.* For his next project, he was interested in learning how other companies were dealing with the maelstrom of technologies coming together in the era of superfast personal computers, broadband communication networks, and the rapidly expanding Internet. The two authors exchanged notes and decided to collaborate on a book if the right topic came along. They had known each other since 1985, when Cusumano was a postdoctoral fellow at Harvard Business School and Yoffie an assistant professor. A few years earlier, Yoffie had asked Cusumano to contribute a paper on software development at Microsoft to *Competing in the Age of Digital Convergence*, and Cusumano had asked Yoffie to be a reader and commentator for *Microsoft Secrets.*

Meanwhile, Sun's JavaSoft was in the middle of a public relations boom, but the group was small and still very young. Java was important, but *how* important? There wasn't much strategy and process to analyze yet. The group was still figuring out what to do and how to do it. In addition, Sun executives did not seem to want to be put under a business school microscope. Cusumano went back to MIT and continued work on a book on product development in the auto industry. Yoffie, meanwhile, continued his stint at Stanford, completing a series of cases on Microsoft's MSN and Apple Computer, in addition to a number of articles on digital convergence.

The next event that related directly to this book took place in November 1996. Marc Andreessen, one of Netscape's founders, gave a talk at MIT. Cusumano attended with some graduate students, and one of them brought a tape recorder. (The tape proved invaluable because Andreessen *talks* on Internet time.) Netscape was clearly a central piece of the Internet story. The company was inventing a big part of the future, growing at breathtaking speed, and trying all the while to build complex software products and fight off an awakening giant—Microsoft. Cusumano wrote Andreessen a letter in February 1997 and suggested that he and Netscape might be interested in participating in a book project. This would be like *Microsoft Secrets* but would focus more on how Internet time was affecting the company's approach to product development. Andreessen's office passed the letter on to Suzanne Anthony, Netscape's manager for publishing relations. She liked the idea. Her boss, Rosanne Siino, also liked the idea. Netscape executives approved. Cusumano and Yoffie talked again and expanded the project to include Netscape's strategy and the issues it faced in scaling its organization. The idea went forward.

The next step was a rendezvous at Netscape's Mountain View headquarters in July 1997. One of the first meetings was with president and CEO Jim Barksdale. Cusumano and Yoffie still had to convince him that the book was a good thing to do. He had read *Microsoft Secrets* and wasn't sure he wanted to reveal so much about *his* company to the competition. They argued that Netscape was really attacking the enterprise software market. To do that, the company had to have credibility. If Netscape really had its act together in terms of strategy, technology, and operations, then it would be good—not bad—for the company to get this message out. In addition, Cusumano and Yoffie pointed out that companies usually learn as much as the authors do when they undergo an in-depth study. They learn a lot about what they are doing well and where they are making mistakes. So, if Netscape was not doing all things right, it might learn something. In any case, the authors maintained that everybody should be interested in learning more about whether "Internet time" was a real phenomenon or not.

Barksdale agreed and, to the authors' relief, the interview continued. The first question they asked, though, was perhaps too direct and caught him a bit off guard: "Why will Netscape still be around when we finish this book about a year and a half from now?" This is part of the answer that Barksdale gave:

> Why will? Excuse me. . . . Would y'all like some coffee or something? . . . Well, that's a question you always have with a smaller company. How did Microsoft compete with IBM when they got started? How did DEC compete with IBM when they got started? How did FedEx compete with the Airbornes and UPSs when they got started? The small company has disadvantages and it has advantages. How did the British defeat the Spanish Armada? Because they had smaller, faster, more flexible ships. You depend a little bit on the passion, a little bit on promotion. The fact is that we got our brand known quicker than any other company in history, which was our first strategy. We used the Internet to do that, so now everybody knows who we are. The first and most important reason most companies disappear is they never get invited to the dance. They can't get in to make the sale. We're now invited to every serious bid for Internet software, which is our market.

The rest of this book builds on in-depth interviews with Jim Barksdale, Marc Andreessen, and another 40 or so current and former Netscape executives, managers, engineers, and other employees between July 1997 and September 1998. (See the table of interviews at the end of the book for specific people and dates.) The authors also interviewed another dozen executives, managers, and engineers from other companies, including Microsoft, Intel, Dell, and CNET. Most interviews lasted an hour, though the authors interviewed several people twice, including Barksdale and Andreessen. They recorded and transcribed the interviews and have included as many quotations as seemed reasonable in this book to give the reader a good sense of the conversations and evidence. In addition, the authors reviewed perhaps a thousand pages or more of documents on Netscape's products and policies available through the company Web site. The authors also made extensive use of publications on the company and the industry, as cited in the endnotes.

Netscape required Cusumano and Yoffie to sign a nondisclosure agreement. This gave the company the right to prevent the authors from revealing confidential information that they might have heard in the interviews or while visiting Netscape offices. It also encouraged people to be frank, because they knew they would have a chance to see and approve the use of their quotes. Netscape people then reviewed the final manuscript before the authors sent it off to the publisher. Nearly all the comments received from Netscape were to correct chronological or other factual information or make minor refinements of quotations. Netscape's reviewers mostly agreed with the interpretations in the book. As one senior manager told the authors, "You were tough, but fair." Netscape people did not try to exert any editorial control over the book, even though there were some parts they probably wished were not in the book.

The authors wrote this book because they found themselves drawn to the same topic: *competing on Internet time.* Anyone who wants to know about successful and unconventional companies, technological innovation, and the challenges that high-tech markets pose for managers, engineers, and entrepreneurs probably shares this interest.

Readers do not have to know much about computers and software to understand the arguments in this book. The chapters focus more on strategic, managerial, and organizational issues than on the technology, though some familiarity with the Internet will surely help readers appreciate the pace of change and the kinds of technical and strategic issues that companies competing and living on Internet time face every day. Technical terms that might be unfamiliar to general readers are explained in the chapters where appropriate. Readers can also refer to the index to locate definitions or the meaning of acronyms.

Readers should also be aware that the book does not always tell the story of the battle between Netscape and Microsoft chronologically. Each chapter has a different thematic focus. Chapters 2 and 3 deal with Netscape's start-up and efforts to practice the techniques of what we call "judo strategy," which involved competing with Microsoft on several fronts. Chapters 4 and 5 delve deeper into implementing judo techniques through efforts in product design and software development aimed at increasing leverage versus the competition, as well as making the engineering organization faster and more flexible. Chapter 6, the conclusion, draws lessons from the story for general readers.

Acknowledgments

WE WOULD LIKE to thank, first, Netscape president Jim Barksdale for allowing us to do this book. His cooperation was indispensable. We also realize that it takes considerable courage to put yourself and your organization under a microscope, although, no doubt, it requires even more courage to take on Microsoft. Second, we would like to thank Marc Andreessen for passing on the proposal to do this book and agreeing to spend several hours with us on two occasions. It requires considerable courage for such a young executive to allow outsiders to scrutinize his decisions and actions. Next, we would like to thank Suzanne Anthony, manager of publishing relations for Netscape, as well as her boss, Rosanne Siino. Suzanne was an enthusiastic, though initially cautious, supporter of the project from the very beginning. She easily could have killed the idea herself many times. There were risks for Suzanne in supporting this project because of the amount of potentially sensitive information that we collected.

We need to thank the many current and former Netscape executives, managers, engineers, and other employees who agreed to participate in the project and gave generously of their time. We have listed their names and the dates of our interviews in the back of the book, but want to cite here Jennifer Bailey, Carl Cargill, Desmond Chan, Alex Edelstein, Bill Gargiulo, Larry Geisel, Rick Gessner, Skip Glass, Todd Goldman, Eric Hahn, Julie Herendeen, Mike Homer, Ben Horowitz, Tim Howes, Jerril Jimerson, Roberta Katz, Joy Lenz, Bob Lisbonne, Mike Major, Kandis Malefyt, Mike McCue, Debby Meredith, Lori Mirek, Jon Mittelhauser, Lou Montulli, Tom Paquin, John Paul, Karen Richardson, Todd Rulon-Miller, Greg Sands, Steve Savignano, Rick Schell, Danny Shader, Sharmila Shahani, Ram Shriram, David Stryker, Lloyd Tabb, Mark Tompkins, Aleks Totic, Michael Toy, Jeff Treuhaft, and Bill Turpin for generously donating their time. Susan Walton assisted Suzanne Anthony in the final review process.

Outside of Netscape, many senior executives, engineers, and managers gave us valuable insight into how Netscape and Microsoft operate and what it is like to work with both companies, as well as their perspectives on the browser, server, and portal wars. In particular, we would like to thank Intel chairman Andy Grove, Dell Computer CEO Michael Dell, Microsoft president Steve Ballmer, CNET CEO Halsey Minor, Netscape director John Doerr, and assistant attorney general for the United States Joel Klein for taking time out of their busy schedules to meet with us and share information. We would like to thank Rob Sullivan at Intel for giving us a briefing on the technology early in our research. In addition, we would like to thank Ben Slivka, David Moore, and Max Morris, all currently or formerly of Microsoft, for granting us interviews and talking openly about how competing on Internet time has affected the company. They, along with Steve Ballmer, helped us understand Microsoft's evolution over the last several years as well as provided an alternative perspective on the battle with Netscape. Ben Slivka deserves a special mention because he went much beyond the call of duty by reading and commenting on the entire manuscript with unusual care.

We want to acknowledge the very special contributions of Mary Kwak, research associate at the Harvard Business School. Mary spent endless hours scanning the Internet and analyzing every aspect of Netscape and Microsoft, sending us articles, drafting ideas, and preparing data, as well as reading and editing the entire manuscript—several times. She was delightful to work with and her contributions to the project were invaluable.

We asked the people we interviewed at Netscape as well as a number of colleagues, students, and practitioner friends from Silicon Valley to read the manuscript and suggest changes or improvements. Both authors would like to thank the following people for their time and very helpful comments on all or parts of the manuscript: Desmond Chan (who commented on the entire manuscript with unusual care), Alex Edelstein, Rick Gessner, Ben Horowitz, Lori Mirek, Todd Rulon-Miller, Danny Shader, David Stryker, Mark Tompkins, Debby Meredith, and Karen Richardson, all currently or formerly of Netscape; Nancy Staudenmayer from Duke University (who carefully read the entire manuscript and parts of it *twice*); Adam Brandenburger, Brian Silverman, and Richard Rosenbloom from Harvard Business School; Michael Scott Morton, Scott Stern (who provided detailed suggestions for the Introduction), and Gregory Scott (who also helped us review Netcenter) from the MIT Sloan School of Management; Ben Gomes-Casseres from Brandeis University; Dennis Carter from Intel; Russell Siegelman, formerly from Microsoft and now at Kleiner Perkins (who gave us detailed comments on the entire manuscript); Donna Dubinsky, formerly from PalmPilot and 3Com; Ted Schadler from Forrester Research; Boris Durisin from the University of St. Gallen; Anton Le Roy from Deutsche Bank Securities; Xiaohua Yang from Fidelity Investments; and Terry Yoffie of Newton, Massachusetts.

We would like to thank participants in various seminars for their very helpful comments on early versions of the material. We both presented at the Strategy and Process Seminar at Harvard Business School (February 1998) and the Strategy and International Management Research Seminar at the MIT Sloan School (May 1998). Cusumano also presented at the Organizations Group and the Operations Management Group at the Fuqua School of Business, Duke University (April 1998); the Information Technology Group at the Anderson School of Management at UCLA (March 1998); the Strategy and Organizations Group at the Anderson School of Management at UCLA (March 1998); and the Graduate School of Information Science at the Nara Institute of Science and Technology in Japan (January 1998). Our colleagues at UCLA (especially Marvin Leiberman, Bill Ouchi, Dick Rumelt, Mariko Sakakibara, and Burt Swanson) deserve special mention for hosting two separate seminars and even making an argument about management turnover at Netscape that we came to refer to as "the UCLA hypothesis." Several colleagues at Harvard Business School provided additional feedback and suggestions after our seminar, especially Marco Iansiti, David Upton, Adam Brandenburger, and Steve Bradley.

In addition, we owe special thanks to Bob Wallace, our editor at The Free Press. Bob enthusiastically supported the project from the very early stages—when the book was no more than a one-sentence idea. We greatly appreciated the support of Paula Duffy and other senior managers at Simon & Schuster, as well as the efforts of Bob Wallace's assistant, Caryn-Amy King, the copyediting supervisor, Celia Knight, and other staff at Simon & Schuster who helped produce this book on Internet time.

Separately, Michael Cusumano would like to acknowledge several sources of financial support and assistance for this project. The Dean's Office at the MIT Sloan School of Management provided initial funding with a Creative Research Award in 1996–1997. He especially thanks former dean Glen Urban and former associate dean Tom Allen for their support. The MIT Center for Innovation in Product Development and the Sloan School's International Center for Research on the Management of Technology continued with support for this project during 1997–1998.

John Hauser, Warren Seering, and Rebecca Henderson made this possible. He needs to thank Lisa Breede for transcribing a large number of interview tapes and Annabelle Gawer for helping with reviews of Netscape's server products. Amy Shea helped transcribe some of the interview tapes.

David Yoffie would like to acknowledge the financial support of the Harvard Business School's Division of Research. Dean Kim Clark and Research Director Michael Yoshino offered generous support for this project, including raising the budget several times during the year. As sophisticated users of Netscape technology, the Harvard Business School IT organization provided very useful technical information, particularly on Netscape Calendar and Communicator. Lisa DeLucia, David Yoffie's assistant, helped put the manuscript into its final form and developed some of the graphics for the tables and charts in Chapters 1, 2, and 3. Finally, David Yoffie's wife, Terry, deserves special thanks for putting up with too many weekends in the office and the agony of reading and commenting on early drafts.

Michael A. Cusumano

David B. Yoffie

September 1998

COMPETING ON
INTERNET TIME

Chapter One

INTRODUCTION

Competing in the Age of the Internet

O CCASIONALLY, THE WORLD experiences a technological revolution that changes the way people live and interact. Ancient peoples experienced the emergence of agriculture, irrigation, and civil engineering. These developments led to the creation of cities and urban culture. Medieval peoples experienced the invention of the printing press. This technology gradually made books, magazines, newspapers, and the printed word—information—ubiquitous. Early modern Europeans championed the Industrial Revolution and new fields of science and engineering. New inventions, such as engines and factories, substituted mechanical devices and inanimate power for animal and human labor. Technology then progressed dramatically after the mid-19th century. The world has recently seen, in relatively rapid succession, the emergence of the telegraph, the telephone, radio, automobiles, airplanes, television, and the computer—to name the better-known inventions in communications and transportation.

And now we have the *Internet.* The Internet is a network of computers, tens of millions of them, large and small, around the world. More accurately, it is a *network of networks,* based on a set of software technologies that drive computer hardware to send, receive, and locate "packets" of information traveling a worldwide electronic highway at lightning speed.[1] The Internet has launched a technological revolution that is changing the way individuals, as well as organizations, live and interact. Imagine combining the power of the printing press (and most of the newspapers and magazines on earth) with the power and speed of the telegraph, telephone, radio, television, and computer. Then make this package easy to use and cheap enough for the mass market. You would then have the potential of the Internet in its most usable form, the World Wide Web (known as "the Web" for short).

We are not exaggerating when we say that the Internet and the World Wide Web, with the browser as its user interface, are revolutionizing mass communications, as well as mass networking technology. It is unlike anything we have seen before. The Internet has the potential to link easily and almost instantaneously *every computing device with every database with every person who has access to a communications device (telephone, cable, satellite, etc.).* As a consequence, the Internet is recasting the most traditional organizations, ranging from the U.S. Internal Revenue Service to your local grocery store. Tens of thousands of companies, both large and small, have created Web sites through which you can purchase goods and services or receive valuable (and not so valuable) information. This means that consumers can do common tasks on the Internet, such as ordering groceries or books and searching for stock prices. They can also do far more complex tasks, such as creating ideal travel itineraries, getting investment or medical advice, or holding a videoconference while sharing documents with people around the world. For anyone in the industrialized world, and for many people in developing countries, access to this great wealth of information and services is already available. The cost is usually the price of a personal computer (PC) or a cheaper device like a handheld computer, a TV set-top box, or the new network computer, as well as a local phone call and a charge of a few dollars per month.

THE AGE OF THE INTERNET

To understand the managerial and competitive implications of the Internet, we draw lessons from the experiences of Netscape Communications Corporation, the fastest-growing software company in history. After Netscape's explosion on the scene in 1994, it became synonymous with the Web. One year later, Netscape gained even greater—if unwanted—notoriety when Microsoft Corporation, the world's largest company dedicated to software production, challenged Netscape to a life-or-death battle. Together, these two companies are struggling to control key components of the Internet, including *browsers,* which provide a graphical user interface to the Web; *servers,* which are special software programs that run on powerful PCs or mainframes and deliver, or "serve," information (including pictures or sound) to the browsers; and *portals,* Web sites like Yahoo! and AOL.com (America Online) that aggregate information and become the jumping-off point for users surfing the Web.

It seems hard to believe that Netscape and the World Wide Web were not even on the horizon a decade ago, and the Internet was a little-known curiosity. The Internet began in the late 1960s as an arcane network connecting university and government computers. Scientists wanted to exchange data and electronic mail. Government officials wanted to be able to communicate if a nuclear war caused conventional communications technologies to collapse. The Internet remained the province of these small groups for 20 years. Then, in 1989, Tim Berners-Lee, a British researcher at the European Laboratory for Particle Physics (CERN) outside Geneva, created a system that would make it easier for scientists to use the Internet to share information. Berners-Lee defined the core elements of the Web—a text formatting system (Hypertext Markup Language or HTML), a communications standard (Hypertext Transfer Protocol or HTTP), and an addressing scheme to locate Web sites (Uniform Resource Locators or URLs). Then he built a rudimentary browser.[2] In 1993, a handful of students working for the National Center for Supercomputing Applications (NCSA) at the University of Illinois took Berners-Lee's invention, integrated graphics and multimedia features into the browser, and made it run on mass-market computing platforms, such as Windows and the Macintosh. The result was Mosaic, a wildly popular toy and information access tool. Most of the browsers available today, including Netscape's Navigator and Microsoft's Internet Explorer, have descended in some way from NCSA's Mosaic.

Mosaic launched a wave of innovation that led, in turn, to an ever-expanding technological alphabet soup. People working with the Internet have had to learn new concepts and new vocabularies almost daily. In addition to HTTP and HTML, two other early standards that defined how the Internet could send and receive information were FTP (File Transfer Protocol) and TCP/IP (Transmission Control Protocol/Internet Protocol). Many other standards quickly emerged for sending data and even video pictures and telephone conversations across the Internet. The proliferation of these technologies is testimony to the dynamism of the Web. More important evidence, however, is the explosion of Internet-based software and services in just a few short years. Utilizing the technologies of the Web, some companies have quickly grown to hundreds and even thousands of employees, hundreds of millions of dollars in revenues, and billions of dollars in market value. The "Internet future" has been unfolding so fast that managers in the industry tell us they cannot confidently predict exactly what products and features to build, what technologies to use, or what customers will buy more than six months to a year in advance. Nevertheless, many products that companies want to create, such as new operating systems, browsers, servers, or groupware applications such as electronic mail and electronic bulletin boards, take 18 months or more to design, build, and test.

Life was not like this before! In past decades, many companies extolled the virtues of long-term planning—looking forward five to 10 years into the future. Compared to today, companies also took their time in product development. For example, Microsoft launched an operating system for IBM-compatible PCs, called MS-DOS, in 1981 and only made evolutionary changes in this technology until 1990, when it introduced Windows 3.0. Apple unveiled the Macintosh computer in 1984, and 14 years later, it had yet to deliver any breakthrough changes to its software technology.

Not only has the technology been moving fast, but the number of users has been growing geometrically each year. In 1993, the primary users of the Internet were scientists, professors, and engineers at university and government labs and a handful of corporations. By 1998, there were 130 million users from all walks of life.[3] Web commerce also exploded from nothing in 1993 to $22 billion in 1998, with predictions of hundreds of billions of dollars early in the next century.[4] This rapid expansion of the network is a classic example of what economists describe as "positive feedback loops," "increasing returns," and "network externalities."[5] Behind the jargon, the dynamics are easy to follow. As more people and organizations connect to the Internet, more people and organizations create more tools and applications that make the Internet even more useful. And the more users, as well as tools and applications, there are, the more valuable connecting to the Internet becomes. As a result, more people start connecting, more tools and applications appear, and even more people sign on, ad infinitum. The technology community likes to describe this phenomenon as Metcalfe's Law, which states that the usefulness of a network, like the Internet, grows *exponentially* as the number of users grows.[6] If a company could control a significant piece of the network or the technology, the potential returns would grow exponentially as well.

These competitive dynamics naturally lead managers to race for market share. Companies hope to grab the biggest share of customers, set the standard for the market, and reap huge benefits down the road. This psychology puts a huge premium on speed. This is especially true for firms that are using the Internet or racing to add to its capabilities. In the past, for example, AT&T might have taken a decade to design and build a new telecommunications switch, write the software to make it work, and deploy the new product widely to customers. Similarly, Microsoft and Lotus would spend two to three years just to produce new versions of their desktop applications. Today, Intel upgrades its microprocessors several times per year. Cisco unveils a new communications switch or router almost every month. PC manufacturers, like Dell and Compaq, use new processor technology to launch new computers every few months. And Netscape and Microsoft have been competing to deliver new versions of their browsers and servers as often as the market will absorb them.

COMPETING ON INTERNET TIME

The conventional wisdom about competition in the age of the Internet is that the business world has become incredibly fast and unpredictable, and we need to throw out the old rules of the game. We decided to test this hypothesis by looking in the place where the world was most likely to have changed—the small constellation of companies that are building the new information infrastructure and hope to accelerate the pace of life for everyone else. After more than a year of intensive investigation, we are inclined to agree with some (but not all) of the hype. Some things really have changed because of the Internet, and some traditional forms of business practice have become much less useful than in the past.

For companies competing in the new information economy, the Internet is forcing managers and employees to experiment, invent, plan, and change their ideas constantly *while* they are trying to build complex new products and technologies. The Internet also requires companies to face the reality that competitive advantage can appear and disappear overnight. This is because the Internet makes it possible to organize your business in new ways, to offer new products and services, and to distribute those products and services to tens of millions of people *almost instantaneously* via telephone lines, cable TV networks, and wireless communications. It was the electronic distribution capability of the Internet that allowed Netscape to burst onto the scene in 1994 and, in only a few months, emerge as one of the most serious threats Microsoft had ever faced. This sudden rise to prominence of new companies can and will happen again.

We also found, however, that some of the strategic precepts of the pre-Internet world continue to ring true. Several core elements of competitive advantage—vision, leadership, innovation, quality, barriers to entry, customer lock-in, switching costs, and partner relationships—remain critical to the overall equation for creating a successful company, even in the most turbulent environments. The bewildering pace of the Internet may even put a premium on these old-fashioned virtues. In addition, while the Internet compels managers to speed up several activities, such as product development and product launches, at the same time, other activities, such as *strategic* planning processes, can operate on more "normal" time scales. Microsoft, for example, found that its customary three-year planning cycles worked just fine, as long as you can "pulse," in the words of Microsoft's president Steve Ballmer, and make quick adjustments.

The Internet may be stimulating a revolution in competitive dynamics and some business practices, but it has not revolutionized everything. Some of the new technologies associated with the Internet, such as the new Java programming language, are too immature to be the foundation for many companies, or even a full suite of products. The tyranny of the installed base is also very real. Despite all the hype about the forthcoming supremacy of new devices such as network computers and set-top boxes, PCs running Windows remain the primary access devices for the Internet. Assuming the imminent death of the installed base is a recipe for distraction.

We argue, therefore, that competing on Internet time is about more than just being fast. The apparent compression of time is only one dimension of life in and around the Internet. For us, competing on Internet time is about moving rapidly to new products and markets; becoming flexible in strategy, structure, and operations; and exploiting all points of leverage for competitive advantage. The Internet demands that firms identify emerging opportunities quickly and move with great speed to take advantage of them. Equally important, managers must be flexible enough to change direction, change their organization, and change their day-to-day operations. Finally, in an information world where too many competitive advantages can be fleeting and new entrants can easily challenge incumbents, companies must find sources of leverage that can endure, either by locking in customers or exploiting opponents' weaknesses in such a way that they cannot respond. In short, competing on Internet time requires quick movement, flexibility, and leverage vis-à-vis your competitors, an approach to competition that we define later in this chapter as "judo strategy."

NETSCAPE AND ITS BATTLE WITH MICROSOFT

No two companies better capture the essence of competing on Internet time in a virtual judo match than Netscape and arch-rival Microsoft. Both have moved rapidly to new products and markets, built flexibility into their strategies and operations, and exploited leverage for competitive advantage. Netscape, which is the primary focus of this book, is a particularly powerful model because it has been a catalyst and a driver and could even become a casualty of the new Internet age. Netscape's decision to ship a new browser electronically over the Internet every few months, with "beta," or pilot, versions even more frequently in the early years, made the company an immediate symbol of competing on Internet time. While most established firms have been struggling to change the way they do business, Netscape started with a clean slate. Managers and engineers at Netscape deeply embedded the Internet into the fabric of the company: Netscape designed its human resource systems, strategic planning procedures, product development processes, and product distribution mechanisms with the Internet fully in mind. Netscape also had the advantage of being a recent start-up, with none of the historical baggage that has plagued other companies trying to be fast and flexible in how they operate and compete. As a result, the company was uniquely positioned to capitalize on the market shifts and opportunities created by Internet technology.

Netscape's early history reads like a fairy tale. The company was started in April 1994 by Jim Clark, the founder of Silicon Graphics, and Marc Andreessen, a recent college graduate who had headed up the Mosaic team.[7] The seasoned entrepreneur and the untested computer geek hired half a dozen of Andreessen's former colleagues at the University of Illinois and set about creating software for the World Wide Web. Initially, Netscape's business model called for developing two sets of products—the browser, which would catapult Netscape to fame, and Web servers, which would pay the company's bills.

Netscape Navigator, the company's browser, was a spectacular success. Less than two months after being released in December 1994, it captured more than 60 percent of the market. Navigator owed much of its popularity to the fact that users could get it for free over the Internet. In the public's mind, Netscape became synonymous with software that was innovative, fun, and free. But Netscape was doing more than just giving its products away. Corporate customers who wanted support were happy to pay, which allowed Netscape to generate $80 million in sales in its first full year (see Figure 1.1). The browser accounted for 60 percent of Netscape revenues, with server-based products making up most of the rest. By the end of 1995, Netscape was a fairy tale come true: Less than two years after its founding, the company was valued at $7 billion.

Netscape initially aimed its products at the World Wide Web, but soon became a pioneer in using Internet technology and protocols as the basis for business applications. In 1996, Netscape was an early mover in *intranet* software. These "internal Internet" systems use "open" (i.e., not controlled by any one company) Internet standards and browser technology to support applications such as electronic mail and information sharing behind a corporate "firewall." (The firewall is a software barrer that prevents outsiders or unauthorized users from gaining access to the information on the intranet.) In 1997, Netscape extended its push into

FIGURE 1.1
Netscape Quarterly Results

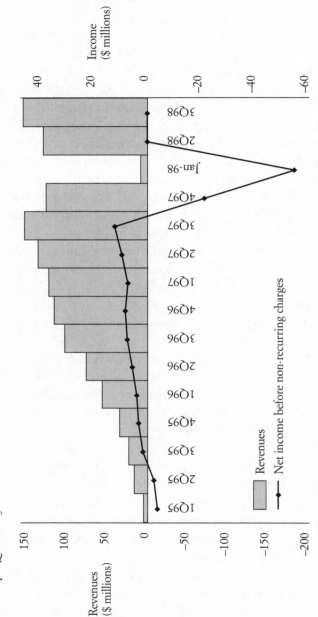

After subtracting one-time charges, Netscape's loss in the fourth quarter of 1997 amounted to $88.3 million. One-time charges also resulted in a loss of $43.8 million in the second quarter of 1997.

Source: Netscape financial reports, press releases.

extranets, which use the same underlying Internet communications technology to connect multiple businesses together over a secure channel. Both moves required that Netscape develop a broad portfolio of increasingly sophisticated products. They also transformed Netscape from a browser company into a growing enterprise software firm, whose sales primarily targeted corporate information systems managers. Unlike Netscape's first customers, the early adopters who loved getting their hands on the latest technology, Netscape's new corporate customers were generally more conservative, with much higher standards for product quality and reliability. The share of revenues represented by corporate sales climbed from 7 percent in 1995 to 41 percent in 1996 and 62 percent in 1997 (see Figure 1.2).

At the same time, Netscape's share of the browser market began a steady decline after peaking at close to 90 percent in early 1996. The primary cause of this decline was, in a word, Microsoft. For much of 1995, Microsoft remained preoccupied with the challenges of bringing out Windows 95. As far as the Internet was concerned, the company seemed to have buried its head in the sand. Most Microsoft employees paid little attention to the Internet, and some had not even heard of Netscape, browsers, or the Web. Not surprisingly, a Web browser was not part of the original Windows 95 product specification.[8] Bill Gates, however, was not ready to be counted out of the game. By the end of the year, he had turned

FIGURE 1.2

Netscape Revenues by Product Category (%)

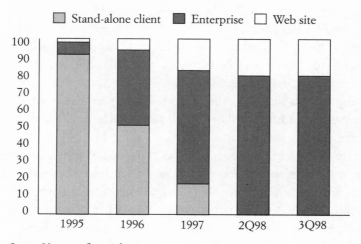

Source: Netscape financial reports.

Microsoft around. On Pearl Harbor Day 1995, he announced that Microsoft was "hard core" about the Internet and planned to "embrace and extend" the Internet across all Microsoft's products. As an opening salvo, Gates promised that Microsoft's Web browser, Internet Explorer, and its Web server would be free to all—not just to noncommercial users.

Netscape's stock promptly fell 28 percent. A classic battle was looming: Netscape and its 700 or so employees were cast as David against Gates's Goliath, which had more than 17,000 employees and almost $6 billion in sales in 1995. Netscape continued to grow at a spectacular rate from the end of 1995 through most of 1997, with 10 quarters of revenue growth averaging 41 percent and 10 quarters of growth in pretax earnings. But with Microsoft attacking aggressively on all fronts, the competition eventually took its toll. At the end of 1997, Netscape was forced to declare a fourth-quarter loss of $88 million, and its share of the browser market had dropped close to 50 percent by the middle of 1998.

Netscape has been trying to regroup since early 1998. The company's management mapped out a new strategic direction, while Microsoft was forced onto the defensive in response to a barrage of state and federal antitrust suits. Questions regarding both companies' futures remained in the autumn of 1998. Yet no matter what happens to Netscape in the future, it will always have the distinction of being one of the fastest-growing start-ups ever. In a little more than three years, the company reached an annual sales rate of more than $500 million. It took Microsoft almost 14 years to reach comparable revenues! In addition, Netscape's browser, Netscape Navigator, has become one of the most successful desktop computer applications in history (see Figure 1.3). After 18 months, Navigator had an installed base of more than 38 million users, making it the world's most popular PC application. By early 1998, users had downloaded more than 90 million copies of Navigator from Netscape's Web site (see Figure 1.4). Netscape's servers attracted less attention, as public interest focused on the drama of the "browser wars." However, Netscape established a solid position in this market as well. By early 1998, it was the leading supplier of Web servers to large U.S. corporations (see Figure 1.5).

We cannot predict, with any certainty, the eventual outcome of Netscape's battle with Microsoft, and we would not bet against Microsoft in any market in which the company takes a serious interest. Nonetheless, we believe there is much to learn from observing what Netscape has done and how it compares and competes with Microsoft. The lessons from Netscape go far beyond the challenges facing a start-up. As Netscape became big, so did its challenges. Many of Netscape's current

FIGURE 1.3

Browser Market Share (%)

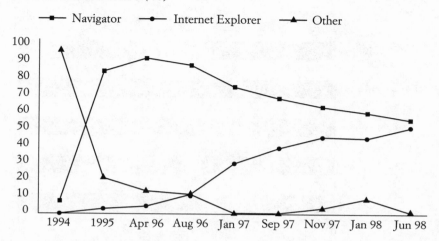

Sources: AdKnowledge, Dataquest, ZD Market Intelligence, and Zona Research.

FIGURE 1.4

Copies of Navigator Downloaded (millions)

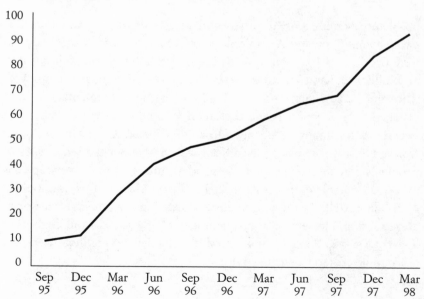

Source: Netscape Web site.

FIGURE 1.5

Web Server Market Categorized by Enterprise Size (%)

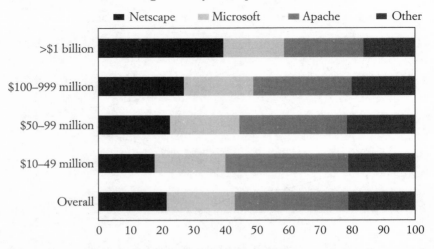

Note: Based on survey of 44,000 Web sites owned by U.S. businesses with annual revenues of $10 million or more.

Source: Adapted from Internet Server Survey, SiteMetrics, April 1998.

problems resemble those of larger companies trying to cope with ultrafast-paced competition and very nimble competitors. Netscape executives also have been worrying about how to respond to intense competition from multibillion-dollar companies, how to manage thousands of employees who must adapt constantly to the Internet, how to maintain a huge installed base of products and customers, and how to solve the puzzle of turning the company's Web site into a money-making machine. In other words, Netscape managers have been worrying about the same types of problems plaguing many enterprises today. And, of course, Netscape has a special dilemma: the Microsoft problem. Microsoft is not only a multibillion-dollar giant with millions of existing customers. Microsoft is also as fast and as nimble as any company of any size. As Bill Gates told *Time* magazine, "I don't think you'd be interviewing me if we were any less nimble. You'd be writing our epitaph."[9]

PLAN OF THE BOOK

This book extracts lessons from Netscape and its battle with Microsoft to help managers learn to compete more effectively on Internet time. We seek to learn from the many things both companies did right, as well as from their mistakes. We have organized the remainder of this book into four main chapters and a conclusion. Each of the following chapters focuses on principles that represent our observations and interpretations of key practices or concepts used at Netscape, and sometimes at Microsoft, to operate and compete (see Table 1.1). These principles do not necessarily represent "best practice" in entrepreneurship, strategic planning, project management, or software engineering. Nor did Netscape or Microsoft implement each of these principles perfectly in every instance. At the very least, however, they represent effective practices that should help many companies become faster and more flexible and exploit strategic leverage.

Chapter 2 explores the lessons of Netscape's start-up phase and the scaling up of a company on Internet time. We suggest that Netscape's early success came from a combination of great vision, experienced people, and a flexible, yet loosely controlled and decentralized organization. In addition, Netscape was the first company to take full advantage of the Internet, enlisting millions of users as a virtual testing organization, transforming its Web site into a virtual distribution channel, and exploiting the press as a virtual marketing organization. Netscape's spectacular success, however, also had its dark side. Netscape did a great job in tapping free external resources, but the company was much less successful in building corporate relationships. At times, Netscape managers seemed so taken by their own accomplishments that they concluded the company could do too many things itself. That arrogance hurt Netscape with potential allies, especially companies that made personal computers and software applications or provided news, financial information, and other kinds of Internet "content."

The next three chapters examine the strategic, technological, and operational dimensions of competing on Internet time. We suggest that firms can prosper in these types of fast-paced and unpredictable environments if they adopt judo strategy, which we are using to describe a philosophy of competition that emphasizes rapid movement, flexibility, and leverage. In chapter 3, we develop principles for competing with judo techniques, and in chapters 4 and 5, we focus on the technical and operational aspects of implementing these techniques.

On the strategic level, we suggest in chapter 3 that firms competing on Internet time must begin by developing a capability to *move rapidly* to new markets and uncontested ground. Particularly for new players, like Netscape, it is crucial to avoid head-to-head combat with industry giants, such as Microsoft and IBM. The second strategic principle is to *be flexible,* giving way to superior force when directly attacked. Netscape had to be

TABLE 1.1

Principles for Competing on Internet Time

Scaling an Organization on Internet Time

- Create a compelling, living vision of products, technologies, and markets that is tightly linked to action.

- Hire and acquire managerial experience, in addition to technical expertise.

- Build the internal resources for a big company, while organizing like a small one.

- Build external relationships to compensate for limited internal resources.

Formulating Judo Strategy on Internet Time

- Move rapidly to uncontested ground in order to avoid head-to-head combat.

- Be flexible and give way when attacked directly by superior force.

- Exploit leverage that uses the weight and strategy of opponents against them.

- Avoid sumo competitions, unless you have the strength to overpower your opponent.

Designing Software on Internet Time

- Design products for multiple markets (platforms) concurrently.

- Design and redesign products to have more modular architectures.

- Design common components that multiple product teams can share.

- Design new products and features for parallel development.

Developing Software on Internet Time

- Adapt development priorities as products, markets, and customers change.

- Allow features to evolve but with frequent synchronizations and periodic stabilizations.

- Automate as much testing as possible.

- Use beta testing, internal product usage, and other measures to improve product and process quality.

---

willing to retreat when confronted with a direct assault that it could not win. The third principle, which is the heart of judo strategy, is to *exploit leverage* that uses the weight and strategy of your opponents against them. Microsoft has a deep commitment to a "proprietary" (the opposite of "open") software architecture, Windows, and to convincing customers to upgrade to the "latest and greatest" version of its operating system and applications. Netscape's judo strategy has been to turn Microsoft's commitments to Windows into a disadvantage by supporting open standards and all the platforms that Microsoft wants to eliminate. These include older Microsoft products (e.g., Windows 3.1) as well as UNIX and Apple operating systems. A problem with judo strategy, however, is that a company's vulnerability increases with its success. As Netscape got bigger, an agile Microsoft used a number of judo moves against Netscape. At the end of this book, we will answer whether Bill Gates or Jim Barksdale is the better judo master.

Chapter 4 analyzes Netscape's attempts to use product design to achieve strategic leverage as well as increase the potential flexibility and quickness of its engineering organization. Netscape's key differentiating skill vis-à-vis Microsoft was the ability to build products that worked on multiple operating system platforms, especially for the UNIX server market. Although cross-platform design had some penalties for productivity and product performance, it allowed Netscape to seek customers that Microsoft shunned. We discuss the specific techniques that Netscape evolved for cross-platform design as well as its experience—more negative than positive—with Java, a cross-platform programming language. We also examine other areas of design strategy, such as how Netscape (and Microsoft) tried to increase the technical and organizational flexibility of their development teams by raising the level of modularity in their products. Both Netscape and Microsoft also used the idea of "parallel development" to overlap design and engineering work in different projects, including the next and the next-plus-one versions of the same product. Parallel development facilitated rapid movement in the marketplace by shortening development cycles and minimizing the intervals between new product releases.

Chapter 5 focuses on Netscape's efforts to increase flexibility as well as innovation and speed in the software development process. We also make many comparisons to Microsoft in order to understand how Internet time may have affected software development techniques. In Netscape's first few years, for example, managers and engineers emphasized the rapid creation of new products and features. As customers evolved from leading-edge Internet users to more conservative corporations, however, the company had to adapt its priorities and engineering culture to place more emphasis on values such as product stability and customer support. Microsoft had to make a similar transition in earlier years but then had to speed up some new projects to compete in Internet markets. Netscape also enhanced its ability to accommodate design changes quickly during a project by following the "synchronize-and-stabilize" process, an approach that Microsoft pioneered in the late 1980s for PC software development. This process allows developers lots of freedom to innovate and experiment during a project but keeps their design changes synchronized through daily "builds" (working prototypes). Product teams then periodically stop in order to stabilize their changes and reevaluate the evolving product. To promote speed and efficiency in managing design changes, Netscape pursued another strategy, test automation, with some, but not complete, success. In addition, Netscape revolutionized the use of beta testing. Like Microsoft, it also adopted a variety of other strategies, such as extensive internal product usage, customer data analysis, and project postmortems to improve products and processes as rapidly as possible.

Chapter 6, the conclusion, explores the implications of judo techniques for competing on Internet time. To some extent, the fast pace of the Internet is slowing; we can see this in the lengthening intervals between new product releases for browsers and servers. Nonetheless, we believe that technologies like the Internet have permanently altered the nature of competition in certain markets and permanently accelerated the flow of information and new products and services around the world. As a result, managers in the age of the Internet must build the capabilities to change quickly all the time.

We begin this final chapter by summarizing the key strategic, organizational, and operational principles that worked together to facilitate movement, flexibility, and leverage. In the process, we distill lessons learned from both Netscape and Microsoft about how to compete effectively on Internet time. The importance of these principles goes well beyond understanding these two companies, however. We believe our principles suggest a more general approach for how companies can be faster, more flexible, and find new sources of leverage in the information economy. In addition, we suggest a number of lessons about what *not* to do when competing on Internet time. Both Netscape and Microsoft made mistakes as they battled for dominance of the Internet. We identify the most serious errors that managers should avoid. Finally, we end with some thoughts about the future of Netscape. In the wake of huge losses at the end of 1997, Netscape has indeed transformed itself. It is pioneering new markets and technologies, such as electronic commerce and application servers, as well as leveraging the browser to build traffic on the Netscape Web site. But the company's success is not completely under its control. Part of its future will depend on the U.S. Department of Justice and its success at limiting Microsoft's dominance of the software industry. Despite this uncertainty, we speculate about how Netscape is likely to fare in three central struggles—the browser wars, the server wars, and the portal wars.

Chapter 2

CREATING THE COMPANY

The Vision, the People, and the Organization

O N MAY 5, 1994, one month after incorporating, Mosaic Communications Corporation opened its doors in Mountain View, California. Four years later, Mosaic Communications had morphed into the half-billion-dollar Netscape Communications Corporation, the fastest-growing software company of all time. This chapter explores how Netscape managers built a company on Internet time. Netscape's success came from its quickness to take advantage of emerging growth opportunities in and around the Internet and from its organizational flexibility. We believe the following principles capture the core lessons of Netscape's spectacular rise:

- *Create a compelling, living vision of products, technologies, and markets that is tightly linked to action.*
- *Hire and acquire managerial experience, in addition to technical expertise.*
- *Build the internal resources for a big company, while organizing like a small one.*
- *Build external relationships to compensate for limited internal resources.*

While most of these principles could apply to any successful start-up, they take on critical importance for companies competing on Internet time. The opportunities associated with the Internet, for example, are almost endless. Without a compelling vision to lead an organization through the fog of possibilities, it would be easy to get lost. In Netscape's case, the company founders, Jim Clark and Marc Andreessen, recognized very early that high-powered, global networks built around Internet (TCP/IP) standards would change the daily behavior of companies and consumers around the world. They planned to capture a large share of the value created by this technological shift by building a universal interface (the browser) for the Internet network, as well as the software delivery mechanism (the server) that would power individual network nodes. This powerful vision gave Netscape an important competitive edge.

Netscape's founders also gave the young company a head start by choosing the right staff. Start-ups are generally alive with young, hungry entrepreneurs who drive their companies to the market through sheer willpower, youthful energy, and new, creative ideas. That youthfulness also helps to explain why most start-ups fail: Exuberance can only get you so far. Clark and Andreessen made a conscious choice to scale the company with a different type of person. They targeted maturity as well as technical expertise. They chose managers and workers who already had start-up experience and in many cases had worked in large companies. To meet the demands of extremely rapid product cycles and constant change, they looked for people who had "seen it before."

As Clark and Andreessen's hiring strategy suggests, Netscape was built as a big company from day one. Most start-up companies scale their systems to meet their current needs. In fact, they usually allow their systems to lag behind their growth. One of the biggest traps for an entrepreneur is to build an organizational structure in advance of sales, profits, and stable cash flow. Far too often, wildly optimistic sales projections do not materialize, the company gets overextended, and everything comes to a crashing halt. So most companies build systems as they need them and replace those systems as they grow. But this approach can be dangerous when you are competing on Internet time: When you grow at "only" 50 to 100 percent per year, you may be able to adapt your systems; when you are growing 50 to 100 percent per *quarter,* you can grow so fast that you are out of touch. Netscape's CEO, Jim Barksdale, was confident that once the rocket engines started, they were not going to flame out. Anticipating spectacular growth, he did not want to follow the traditional entrepreneurial path of rebuilding a company's infrastructure time and time again. Instead, he put in place systems and processes for a "billion-dollar company" while Netscape was still young.

Netscape did many things right in its first few years, and the company took off like a rocket ship as a result. But Netscape's scaling-up strategy was not without flaws. As several former executives reminded us, "Rapid growth hides a lot of sins." Netscape's rocket ship was rising so fast that few insiders worried about the small holes that were appearing in the fuselage. In a different world, many of these problems might have gone unnoticed. But for a company facing a life-and-death struggle with

Microsoft, on top of the challenges of competing on Internet time, the margin for error was slim.

Part of the problem was that Netscape's vision—both of the future and of its own role in that future—became too grandiose. At times, top executives seemed to believe that they could do it all and lost focus as a result. At other times, their preoccupation with ambitious, long-term plans caused them to overlook sources of value, such as their Web site, that were right at hand. In addition, many of the people who were perfect for scaling the company lacked the skills to adapt to the rapid changes of the Internet. Some executives fell into the habits of a pre-Internet age. Turf battles emerged, slowing down decision making and reducing flexibility. And while Netscape managers did a brilliant job of exploiting "virtual" partners such as the press, their confidence (or overconfidence) led them to build weaker ties to "real" partners, who were at least equally critical, such as independent software vendors and leading manufacturers of PCs.

PRINCIPLE *Create a compelling, living vision of products, technologies, and markets that is tightly linked to action.*

The People Behind the Vision

Netscape's vision was the creation of the company's two founders, Jim Clark and Marc Andreessen. The two formed an odd couple, even by the standards of Silicon Valley. In 1994, at the age of 49, Clark was one of the legends of the high-tech world. A high school dropout who joined the navy at 17, Clark was teaching computer science at Stanford by 1979. Three years later, he started a company specializing in advanced computer graphics. Silicon Graphics, Inc. (SGI) went on to make the high-powered workstations that created the special effects for *Jurassic Park.* By 1994, it was well on its way to more than $2 billion in annual sales. Clark, however, had become frustrated with Silicon Graphics's reluctance to pursue the high-volume, low-end consumer market. In February 1994, he stepped down as chairman, walking away from millions of dollars of stock options with the idea of starting again.

Clark had a nimble mind and a willingness to take risks. At the time, he was particularly intrigued by interactive television and consumer electronics. His interest was also piqued by Mosaic, the first widely used browser for the World Wide Web. Out of curiosity, Clark sent an e-mail to Marc Andreessen, one of Mosaic's developers, and soon a partnership was born. The two began by hashing out a number of concepts related to Clark's original interest, interactive TV. As Andreessen recalled, "This was when all the hype about interactive TV was at its peak—it's right around the corner and there will be 10 million subscribers by the end of '94 and all this other stuff. I was pretty excited about it. It took us both a few months to figure out which side of the bread actually had butter on it."[1] Once it had become clear that a full-scale rollout of interactive TV was nowhere in sight, the pair took up other ideas, including an online game service for Nintendo. Finally, Andreessen came up with the winning plan—create a "Mosaic-killing" browser, or "Mozilla" for short. Once Andreessen had laid out his ideas about the future of the Internet and global computing, Clark was hooked. Andreessen would bring the technology, and Clark would bring the money (eventually more than $4 million of his own funds) as well as maturity, experience, and world-class contacts.

Andreessen had been a leading member of the largely student team that created Mosaic at the National Center for Supercomputing Applications (NCSA). Upon graduating from the University of Illinois, where NCSA is based, he headed to Silicon Valley and went to work for Enterprise Integration Technologies, a small Palo Alto software firm. A few months later, Jim Clark's e-mail changed his life. Then 22, Andreessen was a big midwestern kid who dressed in baggy shorts, survived on hamburgers and milkshakes, and frequently indulged a love of pranks. But Clark quickly observed that behind this unpromising exterior, Andreessen combined the intensity of a hardcore programmer with a voracious intellectual appetite. Netscape's general counsel, Roberta Katz, best captured the contrast between the inner and the outer Marc when she described Andreessen as "a 200-year-old man in a 26-year-old's body."

Our meetings with Andreessen gave us an opportunity to observe his intellectual eclecticism firsthand. In addition to technology, he liked to talk about business strategy, philosophy, and history, and he enjoyed bringing together the everyday and the arcane. Andreessen's particular talent seemed to lie in making illuminating connections among the discoveries of other thinkers. Katz recalled sitting at lunch with Andreessen one day and suddenly realizing, "The browser is a map of his brain." She could see that the storehouse of information he had absorbed over the years was organized through a highly personal and often surprising set of cross-references. As a result, conversations with Andreessen were likely to become eye-opening journeys, as he jumped from one unexpected link to the next. At the same time, Andreessen's curiosity was tempered by a mixture of pragmatism and hard-driving ambition. All of these qualities were to prove valuable as Andreessen went about the job of articulating Netscape's vision and tying it to specific product-development projects in an industry where the technology and the market were changing all the time.

Clark and Andreessen were keenly aware that one of the challenges of competing on Internet time is the danger of seeing carefully prepared business plans become obsolete overnight. Therefore, the vision they crafted for Netscape was designed to be a living, moving plan. Three core concepts anchored Netscape's vision—the power of networks, the promise of a universal interface to the Internet from any communications device, and the need for open standards. Just about everything else was open to change. In fact, the fourth element of Netscape's vision, flexibility in implementation, implied a readiness to contemplate new products, new technologies, new partnerships, and new markets as the competitive landscape evolved.

The Power of Networks

Most great companies start with a very simple, powerful vision of their industries and the potential for their firms. Intel, for example, was started by Gordon Moore, Bob Noyce, and Andy Grove to take advantage of Moore's Law, which stated that the number of transistors on a single integrated circuit would double every 18 months to two years. As Grove related in his book *Only the Paranoid Survive:*

> Every start-up has some kind of a core idea. Ours was simple. Semiconductor technology had grown capable of being able to put an ever larger number of transistors on a single silicon chip. We saw this as having some promising implications. . . . When we pondered the question of what we could do with this growing number of transistors, the answer seemed obvious: build chips that would perform the function of memory in computers.[2]

Microsoft owed its start to a similar inspiration. Seeing the power of the microprocessor that Intel invented in 1972, Bill Gates foresaw a world where computers with microprocessors at their heart would be ubiquitous, and there would be a computer on every desk and in every home running Microsoft software. Gates's original insight, which prompted the founding of Microsoft in 1975, dovetailed with the idea that gave birth to Intel: "When you have the microprocessor doubling in power every two years, in a sense you can think of computer power as almost free. So you ask, why be in the business of making something that's almost free? What is the scarce resource? What is it that limits being able to get value out of that infinite computer power? Software."[3]

Clark and Andreessen founded their company with a vision of equal simplicity and power. Just as Moore's Law and microprocessors would change the world for Microsoft and Intel, Clark and Andreessen believed that emerging high-powered, global networks would change how people work, play, and interact with the world at large. Clark initially looked for the future in consumer electronics. But Andreessen convinced Clark that the information superhighway ran through the World Wide Web. On the early Web, a computer novice using a point-and-click browser like Mosaic could check stock prices, look up movie listings, and read newspapers published a continent away. The incurably curious could even watch coffee brew in a Cambridge University common room. Many of these applications were little more than entertaining ways to waste time—in some cases, a great deal of time. Netscape's founders, however, were convinced that much bigger things lay ahead. And they were able to communicate that vision in incredibly compelling ways. John Doerr, one of Silicon Valley's premier venture capitalists and an early Netscape backer, told us about his first meeting with Andreessen a few months after the company was formed:

> I vividly remember Marc sitting in this chair [in the summer of 1994]. Twenty-three years old and he said, "This software is going to change the world." And there was an alignment of the planets, as far as I was concerned. . . . [My friend] Bill Joy once told me, "John, someday you guys are going to back an 18-year-old kid who'll write software that will change the world." And so here's Andreessen, just five years older than 18, and I'd seen Mosaic, the UNIX version of it, running on a Sun Web Explorer in January of that year. Marc earned three dollars and sixty-five cents an hour, or whatever the University of Illinois had paid him, and he posted this thing on the Web, and 2 million people were using it. You would have to be as dumb as a door post not to realize that there's a business opportunity here.

Clark and Andreessen believed that the Web was only the first step toward a networked world. Over the next few years, the development of high-speed, multimedia communications networks would give ever more people ever more rapid access to ever more data. Entrepreneurs would create new ways for people to gather information, form communities, do business, participate in government, and just stay in touch. Andreessen was reluctant to speculate on the form that these changes would take, but he was convinced their impact would be huge. Ten years down the road, he said, "You're going to get megabits of data while you're eating and you are not even going to think twice about it. I don't think we even have the slightest idea of what that's going to mean."[4]

Since the future remained largely opaque, Netscape's vision did not tie the company to any single product or technology. Instead, Netscape defined its mission in terms of providing software that would increase the value of networked communications in the broadest sense. As Roberta Katz explained, "This is a company that deals with communications. For a long time, I think software companies thought of themselves as really in the business of ones and zeroes. What we represent is a fundamental change. It is a new way of thinking about what we do, and it comes from the power of highly scalable networks."

The Promise of a Universal Interface

Clark and Andreessen did not have a blueprint for the networked world. Nonetheless, they believed that the browser had the potential to become a universal interface that would tie the networks of the future together. The browser had two key strengths. First, it could simplify and integrate the management of data and resources, whether located locally on a hard drive or somewhere out on the Web. Consequently, as applications migrated to the network, the browser would replace the operating system (OS) as the primary user interface. Andreessen liked to say that when this happened, the OS would revert to its original role as a set of drivers for devices such as the computer's keyboard and mouse. Or as he wrote in one of Netscape's white papers, "Operating systems become plug-ins under the application."[5]

Second, the emergence of a simple, universal interface would allow the network to grow in size and scope. New devices such as smart phones, televisions, and interactive games could all use the browser to communicate with computers of more traditional types. In Andreessen's words, this was "the Internet's fundamental proposition"—the promise that applications would operate "cross-everything." The browser would be a universal interface that would allow any user to walk up to and use any communications device. This vision applied to both consumers and corporations. As Andreessen told us in the fall of 1997, the browser was just the cusp of the forthcoming user interface revolution:

> There's a big interface shift that's starting to happen, and the browser was the tip of the iceberg. The computer interface for the last 25 years was Windows and the WIMP interface—Windows, Icons, Menus, and Pointers. This is really only suitable for an environment where you're primarily doing it with your local computer and you're primarily dealing with a few files and a few applications. When you get onto the Net, you've got millions

of files and millions of applications and millions of people you're communicating with, and [the WIMP interface] starts to break down. We see this every day because we're getting bombarded with e-mail, the huge bookmark lists, and all the rest of it. It is just going to keep getting worse because the network keeps getting bigger. So there's a big interface change that needs to happen. And then there are other parallel changes that are going to intersect with that—the shift to presumably new forms of devices to hook up to the network to shift to a location-independent user model. The network is a ubiquitous utility. You want it to be like the phone system. You walk up to any phone and you dial, and you walk up to any computer and do whatever you want. So there's going to be a broad-based interface shift.

In order to realize this vision, the browser would have to be everywhere. Ubiquity would be the key to Netscape's success. As Andreessen later noted, this was a tactic straight out of Microsoft's playbook:

> The key to success for the whole thing was getting ubiquity on the [browser] side. . . . It's basically a Microsoft lesson, right? If you get ubiquity, you have a lot of options. . . . You can get paid by the product that you are ubiquitous on, but you can also get paid on products that benefit as a result. One of the fundamental lessons is that market share now equals revenue later, and if you don't have market share now, you are not going to have revenue later. Another fundamental lesson is that whoever gets the volume does win in the end. Just plain wins.[6]

This thinking drove Netscape's early strategy. Rick Schell, a senior engineering executive and early employee, recalled that market share was a top priority from the very first: "Marc had the mindset of, 'Let's get a lot of customers and a lot of users. Let's get millions of these people.' . . . John Doerr [by then a member of Netscape's board] said, 'We need to get 10 million users by the end of the first year of product shipment,' which I think we doubled. We actually got 20, if I remember right. So the goals were pretty ambitious."

Andreessen's underlying assumption was that there would be only one winner in the battle for browsing the Internet. Consequently, whoever got the market share first would reap huge returns over time. As we noted in chapter 1, these kinds of winner-take-all environments can occur when so-called network externalities are present.[7] Although Andreessen had not studied the theory, he had an intuitive feel for the concept of network effects. He understood that if the value of a product depends upon the number of consumers who use it, then one standard usually wins the vast majority of the market. The critical event in such industries is when a market "tips" in favor of one standard over another, giving it a near-monopoly share. For example, in the 1990s the popularity of Windows attracted growing numbers of applications, developers, and support services to the Microsoft platform. Within four to five years, the momentum behind Windows led the personal computer market to tip in favor of Microsoft and away from Apple, IBM's OS/2, and other contenders. As a result, Microsoft reaped the vast majority of profits in the market for operating systems. Andreessen, who was an avid student of business history, hoped that the browser market would tip in Netscape's favor and bring the company equal success. The key was to build market share and create the standard. Profits would eventually follow.

The Need for Open Standards

If ubiquity and "cross-everything" were the fundamental propositions of the Internet, open standards were the building blocks of the networked world. Clark and Andreessen identified the demand for standards as the critical difference between the desktop world and its networked successor. In the desktop world, some degree of standardization was beneficial because the proliferation of a particular product was likely to encourage the creation of complementary goods and services. Workers and companies also benefited from standardization because it reduced training costs and other sources of rigidity. In a networked world, however, standards are not merely desirable; they are essential. Users and platforms have to be able to communicate and interoperate. Otherwise, as far as the network is concerned, they don't exist. Andreessen described the challenge in typically blunt language: "In a networked world, we're headed toward everything being interconnected, and in that world, anything that doesn't talk to everything else [gets killed]."

Standards historically have taken two forms. Open standards like HTML are managed by industry consortia, which make the specifications freely available to all. While this has obvious benefits for consumers, it makes it more difficult for companies to distinguish their offerings from their competitors' wares and encourages customers to switch among solutions as their preferences change. By contrast, proprietary standards are created through the market power of a single firm and remain its private property. Proprietary standards allow companies to lock in customers and generate sizable profits. Ownership of a dominant solution has allowed companies like Microsoft to create captive revenue streams. Netscape's founders, however, believed that this model of competition was bound to fail in a networked world. According to Andreessen, proprietary standards could be the death knell for companies on the Internet: "On an individual desktop basis, companies like Microsoft can play the upgrade game and then they can play the incompatibility game because they can essentially force incompatibility and make you upgrade. In a networked world, if that means things stop communicating with each other, which is exactly what it means, those products actually become less effective in the market."

Flexibility in Implementation

Netscape's vision called for the company to develop universal (i.e., cross-platform) software based on open standards that would add significant value to networked communications. The vision was intentionally broad and ambitious. Andreessen and Clark did not want a niche product, nor did they want to limit the audience, the uses, or the markets that the company's products might serve. But Netscape's founders were not fortune tellers. They had a broad vision about the power of networks, user interfaces, and standards, but they wanted to be practical and flexible in their implementation. About 18 months after founding the company, Clark recalled, "Our initial plan was just to make a browser that was more popular than Mosaic and to build a large installed base of customers as quickly as possible, which we could eventually leverage by selling them other Internet applications."[8] Exactly which applications would be sold, on what kind of networks, was left somewhat undefined. Andreessen, however, knew that he wanted the ideas to be simple and the technology straightforward. Netscape would not fall into the trap of other Silicon Valley start-ups that tried to invent the next great technological revolution. He felt that it was critical to have "a real tight focus on simplicity and a real tight focus on minimizing invention." The standard Andreessen imposed was the "elevator test," an idea he owed to Jim Barksdale: "If you can describe an idea from the eleventh floor of a building to the first floor to a guy who wants to buy your product, then it's probably a good idea."[9]

Rather than follow a narrow technological imperative, Netscape's leaders wanted the company to evolve with customer needs. As Rick Schell recalled:

The mission statement we wrote was broad and didn't even say anything about the Internet. That mission statement hasn't changed in over two years. It said [we would focus on] connecting people and information on networks, with the parenthetical thing being IP [Internet Protocol]-based networks. We didn't restrict ourselves to the Internet or internal networks or anything else. That was a very conscious decision. We believed that there was going to be a blurring of networking going on.

As this blurring of networks took form, Netscape shifted its focus more than once to capitalize on emerging market opportunities. In fact, every year, Netscape's priorities evolved, as the company moved to take advantage of emerging opportunities. But as Roberta Katz commented on this movement, she reminded us that the "big" vision never wavered:

> There's the "big vision," and then there is the more pragmatic implementation of the vision, which changes. So to the extent we've had change, in '95, '96, '97, I put that in the second category. The big vision has not changed that much, and the big vision, the one that I noticed when I first came down here, has to do with the power of networks. . . . The first product [Navigator] was a clear reference to the ultimate scalable network, the Internet, but then you start thinking, "Okay, how else can I use this? Where else can I take advantage of the efficiencies and the strengths that come from a very scalable network?" There's always kind of this overarching vision there, and then the question is, "Okay, in today's marketplace, since we have to make money, what's the best way to do it?"

1995: The Year of the Internet

Katz's question points to the greatest strength of Netscape's vision: It created a tight link between senior management's high-level view of the world and the products they delivered to the marketplace. In 1994 and 1995, Netscape aimed this coupling of long-term purpose with a short-term product focus at the World Wide Web. As Jim Clark told *The New York Times* after founding the company, "I believe that the Internet is the information highway. I'm religious about this."[10] "Mosaic is the future," he informed another reporter, "and you don't need a broadband data highway in the sky to get there."[11] At the time, Clark was not alone in believing that the simple technology of the World Wide Web would quickly turn the Internet into a bustling hub of commerce and community. Analysts predicted that people would abandon printed publications in order to read the latest news online. By publishing on the Internet, news organizations would be able to offer breaking stories mixed with video clips and links to background information. Similarly, retailers would be able to offer a constantly changing product mix and give consumers the convenience of shopping from home. In 1994, market research groups conservatively estimated that $5 billion would be spent annually over the Net by 1998.[12] In addition, the Web was expected to become an increasingly important part of social life, as people began to share interests, news, and gossip online.

Electronic publishers, online merchants, and Internet service providers were all lining up to get a piece of the Internet pie. With the market just emerging, however, Netscape saw an opportunity to "come in below the radar screen" and take control of consumers' surfing habits by making its browser the most popular way to navigate the Web.[13] By the time the online malls were built, consumers would be hooked on driving around in Netscape's car. Moreover, Netscape hoped to convince online merchants to use its server software to run their sites. In this way, consumers using Netscape's browser could be guaranteed an optimal experience online. Although this cheated, a bit, on the promise of purely "open," inter-changeable standards, users of other browsers might find that the road to the mall was a little rough and the stores at the end of the road disappointingly dull.

Netscape released the first beta version of its browser, Netscape Navigator, in October 1994. Two months later, the product was ready to ship. (See Appendix 1 for a chronology, including major product introductions.) Navigator 1.0 was a high-performance, graphics-enhanced browser that was optimized to operate over ordinary 14.4 kbps dial-up connections, an impressive product for the company's debut. But browsers were always only one piece of the vision; servers were an equally important part of Netscape's plans. In conjunction with Navigator 1.0, Netscape delivered a basic server for publishing documents on the Web, as well as a more sophisticated server for electronic commerce. (A complete list of Netscape's products as of mid-1998 can be found in Appendix 2.) Netscape's server software allowed businesses to establish their own presence on the Web. However, in order to jump-start electronic commerce, Netscape also developed a family of turnkey systems that supported the real-time data management and high-volume transactions processing that large-scale sites required. These "Integrated Applications" enabled retailers to create Internet malls and online storefronts, publishers to provide fee-based content online, and Internet service providers to offer subscribers e-mail, chat, and discussion groups.[14]

1996: The Year of the Intranet

As 1995 progressed, Andreessen quickly became convinced that the Internet was developing too slowly to fuel Netscape's ambitions. Growth in

Internet commerce, in particular, was falling short of expectations. Fortunately, another source of business had recently emerged. In early 1995, Netscape management began to notice that most of its revenue was coming from corporate customers who wanted to use Internet technologies to build internal networks, not from corporations seeking a place on the Web. Todd Rulon-Miller, then head of sales, recalled that the first signs of a new market emerged from early, almost accidental customer feedback:

> I think it was the third week of January 1995. The product was on the market for something like 22 days. And one of the sales reps who reports to me asked, "Can these guys pay in Swiss francs?" I said, "Swiss what?! Who's calling from Switzerland?" The second largest bank. What are they going to do with this stuff? Twenty-two thousand browsers for use internally. What are they going to do with that? And I remember Andreessen and I went to an exec meeting and I said, "You know, we're going to get a hundred-thousand-dollar deal from a bank in Europe." And Marc said, "What are they going to do with it?" I said, "I guess they are not doing Internet commerce." That was the first manifestation of an intranet that used a TCP/IP network. They had already figured out that a browser and a Web server could pollinate information. And Marc—I don't know this to be true but I think it was—went to the telesales group, interrogated that rep, came back and said, "We're good in corporations!!!" And that was the birth of an intranet.

After listening to what Netscape's customers had to say, Andreessen concluded that corporations wanted simple, Internet-based technology that could support electronic mail and collaboration, preferably across the many different hardware and software platforms that the typical large corporation had already deployed. Armed with this realization, Andreessen pushed Netscape to turn from the consumer-oriented Internet to intranets, or corporate TCP/IP-based networks. As Greg Sands, Netscape's first product manager, recalled, the choice was simple: "I remember as early as February of '95, having a conversation with Marc where he said, 'Look, we've just got to focus. We've got to pick one group of customers. There's more money behind the firewall than there is outside the firewall.'"

Andreessen's instincts led him to see the growth potential of intranets very early. One year later, everyone was heralding the intranet as the next big thing. In February 1996, a *Business Week* cover story described how companies were using Internet-like networks to streamline their organizations.[15] "Here comes the intranet," it announced, "and it could be the simple solution to company-wide information-on-demand." Among other examples, the article examined online systems that allowed Compaq employees to move money around in their retirement funds and helped Ford engineers on three different continents to cooperate in designing the 1996 Taurus. "When the Internet caught on, people weren't looking at it as a way to run their businesses," said one manager quoted in the story. "But that is in fact what's happening."

Internal corporate networks were nothing new. In 1989, Lotus had pioneered the market for groupware, also known as software for collaborative computing, with the introduction of Lotus Notes. Other players in this market were Microsoft and networking leader Novell. Notes was a sophisticated and highly robust system for e-mail, document sharing, workflow, and group discussions. Like most groupware products, however, it was based on proprietary technology and expensive to install and maintain. Intranets had fewer capabilities, but they were built on open standards, and they were relatively cheap and easy to use. As more and more companies discovered their virtues, analysts expected the market for intranet servers to grow from less than $500 million in 1995 to $4 billion in 1997 and $8 billion in 1998. By way of comparison, in the same period, the market for Internet servers was only expected to reach $2 billion.[16]

Netscape's original business plan had said nothing about electronic mail. Nonetheless, Andreessen was increasingly convinced that the company's future lay in leveraging networks based on open Internet protocols to enable widespread, low-cost messaging and collaboration inside corporations. According to Rick Schell, Netscape managers saw intranets as a giant, untapped market, where suppliers could lock in customers because "switching costs would be higher." As Schell recalled, the thinking ran: "There's an unfulfilled need here. There aren't any open standards–based messaging and groupware platforms, so let's go buy a messaging and groupware company and start building some products to attack that space."

Netscape started to implement this strategy within three months. By late 1995, the vision of intranets, messaging, and collaboration was firmly embedded in product and acquisition plans. Navigator 2.0, which first appeared as beta software in October 1995, integrated mail and newsgroup features directly into the browser interface. In addition, Navigator 2.0 added support for plug-ins (small applications) and Java, the cross-platform programming language recently developed at Sun Microsystems. Plug-ins allowed multimedia information like audio and video files to be displayed within the browser, while Java enabled designers to embed applets or mini-applications, such as stock tickers, in a Web page. However, the real excitement around Java focused on its promise of a future in which developers would "write [the software] once" and applications would "run everywhere," rather than being laboriously rewritten for every operating system a company might use. (We discuss the pluses and minuses of Java in chapter 4.)

As a second-generation product, Navigator moved from being an application to "a real platform that people could actually write applications to," in one manager's words. Marketing executive Greg Sands admitted that, as initially released, the new mail and newsgroup features were "not terribly functional." Nonetheless, they marked an important step for the company. As Sands said, "They were clearly first-generation products, but they were enough to pique people's interest, and there was enough customer pull regarding highly scalable standards-based messaging products that it made it feel like there was a 'there' there."

At the same time, Netscape developers were working on server products to support the intranet features showcased in the browser. In March 1995, Netscape announced two new products: Proxy Server, which sped up access to the Internet by caching information on the local network, and News Server, which allowed corporations to set up secure discussion groups. In November, Netscape added an electronic mail server based on technology licensed from Software.com.

Netscape also made a number of acquisitions in order to support its move into the corporate market. In September 1995, less than six weeks after going public, the company announced its plans to purchase Collabra, a developer of messaging-based systems for information sharing and collaboration. Collabra's award-winning product, Collabra Share, supported group conferencing and information sharing and functioned as a low-cost alternative to Lotus Notes. Although Collabra's code was not based on open Internet standards, the management team and developers brought deep expertise on collaboration and messaging into Netscape. Three more acquisitions followed in early 1996. InSoft brought Netscape experience in audio and video conferencing; Paper Software specialized in three-dimensional graphics and virtual reality modeling; and NetCode built Java-based tools.

By early 1996, Netscape was ready to share its plans with the world. In March, at the company's first Internet Developers Conference, Andreessen declared, "The big story in '95 was that the intranet exploded." In 1996, Netscape planned to ride the intranet wave to the top. The company detailed its vision for this market in a white paper released on the Web in June. This document began by laying out what Andreessen and his product team thought an intranet should be and do. "Simply put," the white paper explained, "a Full Service Intranet is a TCP/IP network inside a company that links the company's people and information in a way that makes people more productive, information more accessible, and navigation through all the resources and applications of the company's computing environment more seamless than ever before."[17]

Netscape's goal was to enable companies to create intranets based on open Internet standards and cross-platform support. These features would allow customers to reap the benefits of vendor independence and a common network environment. SuiteSpot, which debuted in 1996, was the company's first effort to offer customers a complete intranet solution. SuiteSpot bundled together servers for running a Web site, e-mail, newsgroups, various intranet services, and development tools. At the same time, the focus on intranets imposed some cuts in the company's product line. Since Internet commerce was not developing as fast as senior management had hoped, Netscape announced in April 1996 that its Internet commerce projects (the Integrated Applications) would be spun off as Actra Business Systems, a joint venture with GE Information Services (GEIS).

For a short while, Netscape also toyed with taking a more active role in developing software for new Internet devices. Andreessen believed that consumers intimidated by personal computers would flock to "network computers" and other cheaper, simpler devices to surf the Web. According to one highly optimistic study at the time, cell phones, set-top boxes, and other types of consumer electronics would make up 22 percent of the market for Internet access devices by 2000.[18] By 2005, annual shipments of these alternative devices could outstrip personal computer sales.[19] If Netscape wanted its browser to become a truly universal interface for networked information, it would have to develop versions of Navigator that ran on network computers and game players as well as workstations and PCs. This effort, however, would take resources away from the company's campaign to tap the corporate market.

Rather than risk diluting its focus, Netscape chose to spin off the alternative-devices project as a separate firm. In August 1996, Netscape took a major equity position in Navio Communications, a start-up with backing from IBM, Oracle, NEC, Nintendo, Sega, and Sony. Netscape gave Navio exclusive rights to adapt Navigator for consumer devices, and Jim Clark became Navio's chairman. By early 1997, Navio had licensed its browser to a number of manufacturers of network computers and set-top boxes, including IBM, Sun, Tektronix, and Zenith. In May, it merged with a new Oracle subsidiary, Network Computer, Inc.

This restructuring allowed Netscape to pour its resources into becoming a major intranet provider. In October 1996, Netscape upgraded

SuiteSpot, growing the number of server products from six to ten. One of the key additions was Directory Server, which tied together vital network information including names, e-mail addresses, and access rights. This product was the first commercial server to implement Lightweight Directory Access Protocol (LDAP), a potential solution to the problem of multiple incompatible directories that Netscape was pushing as an open standard.

At the same time, Netscape announced Communicator, the latest addition to the Navigator line. Netscape positioned Communicator as a multifunctional, intranet client suite. In addition to the browsing component, which retained the Navigator name, Communicator integrated support for e-mail, newsgroups, HTML editing, conferencing, and in the professional edition, online scheduling. Several months later, Netcaster, a component that "pushed" Web material to the desktop, joined the mix. Netscape sales executives had always encouraged potential customers to buy browsers and servers together. But with Communicator and SuiteSpot, Netscape positioned its products as an integrated client/server solution for the first time.

Netscape's efforts to reinvent itself as an enterprise (corporate) software firm had implications for more than its development and marketing plans. They also had an important impact on Netscape's business and sales model. The beauty of the Internet was that delivering products to customers was extremely cheap. Netscape had built a world-class delivery system simply by creating a site on the Web. Moreover, in 1995 and early 1996, "Netscape's [browsers] were exploding into a vacuum with an insatiable thirst and demand," as the head of corporate sales remarked. A small sales force, supported by a telemarketing team, was conquering the world. But if Netscape wanted to serve an intranet market based on large corporations, it would require huge investments in direct sales and support. From 15 salespeople in early 1995, the sales organization ramped up to almost 800 people in 1998. By early 1997, the costs of sales and marketing made up roughly 47 percent of revenue, with more than half of those costs allocated to the direct sales force.

Initially, these efforts seemed to pay off. By mid-1996, Netscape could record some impressive results. Ninety-two of the Fortune 100 used the company's products. Reports by Forrester Research and Zona Research showed that Netscape held around 80 percent of the Web server market in corporations. Server sales, which were at 100,000 in the second quarter, jumped to more than 1 million by the end of the year. A preliminary study by another independent research organization, IDC, indicated that

Netscape intranet customers could realize a return on investment in excess of 1,000 percent in three months or less.[20]

Nonetheless, Netscape expected the competition to strengthen as Lotus and Microsoft moved to make their products increasingly compatible with the Web. Netscape executives contended that the company's native support for Internet standards gave Netscape products an important advantage over systems that relied on messaging agents and Internet gateways. The company also acquired two more companies as part of its effort to remain on the technological cutting edge. Portola Communications added expertise in high-performance messaging to Netscape's portfolio, while DigitalStyle contributed an award-winning Web graphics tools team. In the long run, however, Netscape sought to stay ahead of the competition by expanding into new markets.

1997: The Year of the Extranet

By late 1996, Andreessen and his small staff of technologists were pondering how to take Internet protocols one step further. They delivered the next installment of their vision in March 1997, in a white paper outlining the concept of the "networked enterprise." The networked enterprise used extranets to go one step beyond the individual-to-firm transactions that already took place over the Web. An extranet consists of intranets that are connected over leased lines or secure Internet connections. It allows companies to give partners selective access to resources behind the corporate firewall. The goal of the extranet is to streamline transactions with customers and suppliers, just as the intranet simplifies operations within a corporation. For example, Chrysler's Supply Partner Information Network connects the automaker directly with more than 12,000 of its business partners.

Extranets could handle a wide variety of processes, including mission-critical applications like order placement and fulfillment. Over time, as the capabilities of extranets grew, Netscape managers expected them to replace traditional high-cost proprietary forms of electronic data interchange. They also expected the availability of a simpler, cheaper technology to drive growth in electronic commerce as a whole. One study estimated that business-to-business electronic commerce would reach $134 billion in 2000, while consumer sales would total $10 billion.[21] According to the Gartner Group, 40 percent of all businesses would conduct electronic commerce over extranets by 2002.[22]

In Netscape's white paper, Andreessen argued that many businesses had already exhausted the efficiency gains that could be created through traditional forms of restructuring and reengineering. Extranets would allow them to create new forms of competitive advantage by building stronger relationships with all of the participants in the supply chain:

> By strengthening their links with customers, partners, suppliers, and distributors in a seamless networked environment, companies can quickly bring to market the precise products and services the customer demands, when the customer wants them. In this way, companies can engage customers and partners in a tight feedback loop to help create new products and services. . . . Businesses that can pull this off will thrive and build large barriers to entry by binding themselves tightly to their customers for life. Businesses that fall behind will struggle to maintain market share in an increasingly brutal competitive environment.[23]

One of the primary challenges businesses faced in building extranets was the prospect of operating in a highly heterogeneous computing environment. Companies would have to support not only their own platforms, databases, and legacy systems (older systems that they continued to use), but those of their partners as well. Netscape believed that its products were uniquely suited to the task of managing this potential chaos. As the white paper explained, Netscape aimed to provide "full capabilities across all platforms—including multiple versions of the same platform." At the core of its approach was the concept of "crossware," or "cross-everything applications." These products were based on open Internet standards and designed to run on demand across networks and operating systems. Crossware could be accessed through the same interface from different client devices and run across different servers "without changing a line of code." Netscape planned to enhance support for crossware in the next-generation releases of both its client and server suites.

Netscape's white paper also underscored the importance of Actra, the joint venture with GEIS, in the company's extranet strategy. Actra wedded GEIS's expertise in business-to-business electronic commerce to Netscape's budding efforts in the consumer space. The new firm sold a suite of products for handling business-to-consumer and business-to-business sales, internal purchasing, and the delivery of fee-based, customized content. Customers for Actra's products, which ranged in price from $75,000 to $250,000, included Wells Fargo, SportsLine USA, and *The New York Times*.

Actra originally offered Netscape the chance to retain a presence in electronic commerce while refocusing its core business on intranet clients and servers. As Netscape entered the extranet market, business-to-business applications moved back to the center of its strategy. In November 1997,

Netscape demonstrated flexibility in implementation, again, by buying out GEIS and reintegrating Actra. Three weeks later, it announced another major acquisition designed to bolster its extranet plans. This time the target was Kiva Software, the award-winning developer of a high-end applications server. The Kiva Enterprise Server tied together the clients, Web servers, and databases that supported processing-intensive activities such as electronic commerce. With this acquisition, Netscape could finally offer the largest corporations a complete Internet, intranet, and extranet solution.

1998: Returning to the Public Internet

In focusing on extranets and electronic commerce, Netscape was, in a sense, returning to its roots. After having de-emphasized the Internet for life within corporate walls, the company's vision was moving back onto the open frontier. Two dramatic developments in 1998 made this clear.

The first was the stunning decision to give away the source code for Communicator, Netscape's crown jewel. On January 22, 1998, the company announced that it would post the Communicator source code on the Web under the aegis of a Netscape developer group known as Mozilla.org. This initiative went far beyond the long-expected step of offering Netscape's browser for free. As *The Economist* observed, it was "the computer-industry equivalent of revealing the recipe for Coca-Cola."[24] Developers would now be able to modify Netscape's code and incorporate it into their own products. In return, they would be required to submit all modifications to Netscape, which would decide which changes to incorporate into the next official Communicator release.[25] In offering up its source code for free, Netscape returned to its original vision of creating an open, universal interface that could leverage the power of the Web. Software developers apparently welcomed this move, downloading some 250,000 copies of the Communicator 5.0 source in the first month. (We discuss the strategic and operational aspects of the decision to release the client source code in more depth in chapters 3 and 4.)

The second change in strategy in 1998 was the commitment to become a major "portal"— a consumer Web site, like Yahoo! and Excite, that aggregates a wide range of content and a multitude of services. Although CEO Jim Barksdale told us in July 1997, "I've told our [media] customers I'm not going to compete with them, and I mean that," in March 1998 he announced that Netscape was "massively expanding in the media area."[26] Suddenly, Netscape's Web site was moving front and center in the company's strategy.

Netscape's home page was already one of the most popular sites on the World Wide Web by default. Every copy of Navigator automatically went to the Netscape site as soon as a user launched the browser. Users could easily override this feature, but relatively few did. As a result, by mid-1997, the company reported that it was receiving more than 100 million hits per day. This traffic allowed Netscape to charge the four major Internet search engine companies a total of $30 million to be featured in turn on Netscape's "Net Search" page.[27] In addition, in return for the rights to co-own and operate Netscape's "Internet Guide," Yahoo! agreed to pay $5 million up front and to generate at least $25 million in advertising revenues over two years.[28] Netscape, however, had done little to preserve the value of its Web site by making it an attractive, surfer-friendly place. In the summer of 1997, Barksdale still believed deeply that media projects were a distraction from Netscape's core enterprise business. As he explained:

> I learned a long time ago that you can get very distracted trying to pick up these niche markets when you've got this huge thing, unless you just stay focused right on it. . . . Risk a little company and it gets a reputation like ours, and boom! It runs over here, tries to do this, and wants to be all things to all people. The next thing you know, it's spread its resources so thin that it can't stay focused on the main thing.[29]

Yet Barksdale did not want to leave money on the table, and the lure of hard cash made the Web site look more and more attractive as 1997 wore on. Netscape had always had some advertising on its Web site, but online advertising was beginning to explode, with analysts predicting that it would reach $7.7 billion by 2002.[30] Initially, Netscape hoped to capture a large piece of this pie by creating an online community around its enterprise software customers. In September, the company relaunched its home page as Netcenter, a business-oriented site offering news, software, and intranet hosting for small firms. By the end of the year, Netscape claimed 2 million subscribers for its free service, compared to more than 10 million for AOL.[31]

Six months later, Netscape took another important step by creating a Web site division. This move signaled that the Internet would be central to Netscape's future business. Mike Homer, who took charge of Netcenter in the reorganization, told us that the new vision was "to provide all the essential services for a consumer online portal," while differentiating the site from competitors through "tight integration between the client [Navigator] and the Web site." While not abandoning its corporate focus, Netscape planned to re-energize its strategic efforts on the consumer front. Netscape would fill in the gaps in its Web offerings and match features, such as free e-mail, that were offered by competitors such as Yahoo!. In May 1998, Netscape also announced a lucrative partnership with Excite, a leading search engine and directory service. In return for the privilege of providing design services and content for Netcenter—and the 19 million unique visitors who passed through its doors in May[32]— Excite agreed to pay Netscape at least $70 million over two years.

Netscape's New Vision

In previous years, Andreessen had evolved Netscape's vision to match the new opportunities he saw on the horizon. In 1998, he reformulated the vision from the ground up for the first time. In the future, Netscape would not be identified as a browser company, an intranet company, or an extranet company. In fact, Netscape would cease to consider itself a pure software company altogether. Instead, it would embrace a new mission that was based on the convergence between software and services.

In a moment of candor in May 1998, Andreessen admitted that he had made huge mistakes:

> We've completely changed—we've made a huge number of changes in the product family, we've made a huge number of changes to the whole customer orientation, and the business strategy is substantially different. I thought [using our Web site] was a distraction. It's kind of funny to think about how many people have had the opportunity to make *billion-dollar mistakes*. There are reasons and explanations for our behavior every step of the way, but there was still a fundamental misunderstanding that I was very guilty of. . . . This is what's so funny about all the cliches . . . about the railroad companies who thought they were in the railroad business and not in the transportation business. . . . In retrospect it looks obvious, but at the time it certainly didn't. I absolutely thought we were a software company— we build software and put it in boxes, and we sell it. Oops. Wrong.

Andreessen now saw Netscape's businesses merging into an integrated set of offerings that ranged from Internet products to Internet services. In our interview in May 1998, he identified "the large-scale provisioning of Internet services that reach out to millions of customers" as the core of Netscape's new mission:

> Now, today there are two different ways in which we do that. One is we provide the software infrastructure and applications that enable businesses to do that. The other is we run the software directly by running our own Web site. Those two pretty different businesses are going to collapse to-

gether in a major way over the next two years because a lot of companies that think today that they're software companies are actually going to look much more like service companies. You see examples of that happening on both the consumer side of the software business and the enterprise side of the software business. When you have a global network in place, when you build a piece of software, it's going to be increasingly likely in the future you're going to deliver the value of that software to your customer as a network-based service, as opposed to putting it in a box and expecting him to install it at his site, in his home, or in his place of work, and run it himself. That implies a different business model; it implies a different approach to sales and customer service. It implies differences in how you develop the products.

In a strategy briefing one month later, company officials described the three pillars that would support the new vision. The first was a set of software products that would provide businesses with a "services-ready infrastructure": the Netscape Application Server (formerly Kiva's Enterprise Server); Enterprise Server, Netscape's high-end Web server; Messaging Server; and Mission Control, Netscape's directory and security services. Engineers designed these core products to be highly scalable, secure, reliable around the clock, and centrally managed. The second pillar of the new strategy was CommerceXpert, a set of packaged electronic commerce applications that Netscape acquired with Actra. The third pillar was Netcenter, the Netscape Web site. This briefing made it clear that the company's server products had replaced the browser as the heart of Netscape's product plans. Nonetheless, Netscape planned to continue to update Communicator. Communicator 5.0 would be the first release based on the work of Mozilla.org.

The Vision in Perspective

Jim Clark and Marc Andreessen deserve credit for recognizing the Internet's power and mapping a path through the confusion of the Web's early years. Andreessen, in particular, played an important role in crafting a vision that served as Netscape's guiding light. It provided clarity and direction at a time when most companies were struggling with the chaotic, rapid changes that permeated the Internet. While Netscape's early competitors stumbled, Andreessen's vision mobilized the company's troops to develop and deliver an impressive range of client and server products in a very short period of time.

Netscape's vision frequently changed form, and the company's leaders reversed a number of key decisions, such as spinning off Actra and sidelining the Web site. Nonetheless, they remained deeply committed to a basic set of core concepts: the power of networks; a single, universal interface; and open standards. These concepts continue to be central to Netscape's vision today. If anything, with the move to integrate Netcenter with the enterprise software business, the company's faith in the power of networks has become even stronger.

Andreessen's vision, however, sometimes ran ahead of the company, ahead of its customers, and ahead of the world. Before the summer of 1997, as chief technology officer, Andreessen was often isolated from developers and managers in the company. This failure to stay in close touch with the people working on the ground may have contributed to his tendency to proclaim that the future had already arrived. Andreessen's initial enthusiasm for Java, for example, led to predictions that were premature. As early as September 1995, he claimed that the combination of Java and a Netscape browser would effectively kill Microsoft's Windows 95. Time and again, Andreessen argued that the browser would relegate the operating system to its original role as an unimportant collection of "slightly buggy device drivers."[33] Yet, as we will discuss in chapter 4, Netscape's embrace of Java was fraught with technical difficulties that may have slowed the company down at a critical time in its battle with Microsoft. Andreessen may be proven right in the long run, but in the meantime, the tight link between vision and action led Netscape's development teams down some questionable roads.

At the same time, Netscape's vision overlooked significant sources of value. It was not until 1998 that the company realized the Web site was a badly under-exploited resource. Ironically, this oversight was due to the failure, among senior executives, to grasp the implications of one of Netscape's founding tenets: In a networked world, everything is connected. Halsey Minor, the CEO of CNET, has been described by some analysts as the most influential person on the Internet. When we interviewed Minor in September 1997, he pointed out that Netscape's vision at that time focused solely on intranets and extranets, ignoring the fact that all the networks—the Internet, intranets, and extranets—are inextricably linked. Netscape could not hope to be a dominant player in the corporate space without retaining its position in the consumer space:

> I was telling people at Netscape nine months ago that you can't be an intranet company. You can't. The problem is that everyone who is on an intranet looks outside the firewall, and if the browser doesn't work out there, then they won't buy it. You can create this thing called an intranet,

but that's not the way the world works, and so you have to have as much critical mass, and probably more critical mass, on the Internet, and then use that to drive a product into the intranet. Netscape abandoned the whole Internet—they abandoned the Internet service providers, they abandoned the computer manufacturers, they made life difficult for the whole independent content provider market.

No one—not Bill Gates, not Marc Andreessen—can have perfect foresight. Mistakes are made all the time. The key question is whether the people and the organization can capitalize on the right observations and make quick adjustments when managers discover that they are on the wrong path. We turn to these issues next.

PRINCIPLE   *Hire and acquire managerial experience, in addition to technical expertise.*

During our first week of interviews at Netscape in the summer of 1997, we were stunned by one extraordinary fact: Netscape had more than 2,000 employees at the time, and the average age was 37! As the head of human resources wryly observed, "Most of us have gray hair." The company was hiring engineers in their late 20s, but most of the marketing, sales, and support hires were in their mid-to-late 30s. Most senior managers were in their 40s and 50s. By comparison, the average age of Microsoft's employees was 27 in the mid-1990s and 34 by 1997, while the average of Intel's 66,000 employees was 33 in 1997.[34] This told us that there was something different about the type of people Netscape attracted and retained.

Hire Experienced Managers Who Understand the Internet and Information Technology

Two characteristics stand out among the people we met at Netscape. First is the prominence of engineers and managers who had previously worked at major companies in computer software, hardware, or communications technology. Second is the expertise of many employees in the development and usage of fundamental Internet technologies. Table 2.1 illustrates the broad range of experience and the familiarity with Internet- or computer-related technologies and business practices that are common among Netscape employees. For example, Netscape hired people who had worked on very early browsers and servers for the World Wide Web, as well as key technologies such as the LDAP directory protocol. It hired

TABLE 2.1

Sampling of Netscape Employees' Backgrounds

Name	Prior Organizations	Prior Technology Experiences
Marc Andreessen	University of Illinois/ NCSA, IBM intern	Mosaic browser architect
Jennifer Bailey	Apple, Dell	Product marketing
Jim Barksdale	IBM, Federal Express, McCaw	Computer sales, marketing, CIO
Carl Cargill	Digital, Sun	Standards strategist
Desmond Chan	Silicon Graphics, Sun	Operating systems, testing
Alex Edelstein	Microsoft, Spry	Microsoft Exchange, Spry browser
Bill Gargiulo	Silicon Graphics	Technical support director
Larry Geisel	Xerox	Applications development manager
Rick Gessner	DigitalStyle	Electronic publishing
Skip Glass	IBM, Kiva	Sales and marketing
Todd Goldman	IBM, Hewlett-Packard (HP)	Networking technology, marketing
Eric Hahn	Convergent, Lotus, Collabra	Groupware, electronic mail
Julie Herendeen	Apple	Product management
Mike Homer	Apple, Go, Eo	Product marketing
Ben Horowitz	Lotus	Product management
Tim Howes	University of Michigan	LDAP developer
Jerril Jimerson	Apple, Go, Ameritech	Marketing
Roberta Katz	Heller Ehrman, McCaw	High-tech legal counsel
Joy Lenz	EDS, Borland	Testing/QA manager
Bob Lisbonne	Claris, Collabra	Product marketing
Mike Major	Henley Group, Ernst & Young	Human resources, consulting
Kandis Malefyt	Silicon Graphics	Human resource management
Mike McCue	IBM, Paper Software	Virtual reality modeling
Debby Meredith	Bell Labs, Metaphor, Logitech, Collabra	Database, groupware

Name	Prior Organizations	Prior Technology Experiences
Lori Mirek	Oracle, Sun, Ameritech, GM, HP	Product management
Jon Mittelhauser	University of Illinois/NCSA	Mosaic browser developer
Lou Montulli	University of Kansas	Lynx (pre-Mosaic browser)
Tom Paquin	IBM, Silicon Graphics	Graphics software
John Paul	OSF, Compaq, Banyan	User interface, server software
Karen Richardson	Collabra	High-tech sales
Todd Rulon-Miller	Tandem, NeXT, Software Alliance	High-tech sales
Greg Sands	Corporate Decisions, Cisco intern	Channel management
Steve Savignano	Digital, Menugistics, Actra	Supply chain management
Rick Schell	Intel, Sun, Borland	Languages, compilers, databases
Danny Shader	Go, Collabra	OEM business development
Sharmila Shahani	HP, Microsoft, General Magic, Kiva	Product marketing
Ram Shriram	Northern Telecom, Sytek, NCD	Networking equipment, browser sales
David Stryker	Intermetrics, Symbolics, Object Design	O-O languages, compilers, databases
Lloyd Tabb	Borland	Compiler, database architect
Mark Tompkins	IBM, Tandem	QA/testing, development manager
Aleks Totic	University of Illinois/NCSA	Mosaic browser developer
Michael Toy	Silicon Graphics	UNIX developer; MS Bookshelf
Jeff Treuhaft	Silicon Graphics	Technical marketing
Bill Turpin	Borland	dBase, Internet development tools

marketing, sales, and general managers with experience at companies like Apple, IBM, Microsoft, and Silicon Graphics—people who knew how to sell software, computers, and telecommunications products. It also hired engineering managers with experience at firms such as Bell Labs, Borland, IBM and Intel—people who knew how to develop software, computers, and telecommunications products, as well as how to manage software engineers.

The strategy of hiring experience started at the very beginning, with Clark and Andreessen's decision to fly out to the University of Illinois to recruit the core Mosaic group—"this team of people, five, six, seven of us, who worked together very well," as Andreessen described them, and "were all wanting to do something, but didn't really know what they wanted to do." Having a team of engineers that had written a browser once before would jump-start the product-development process. As Jim Clark said a week after his Illinois coup, "I know there are a bunch of people looking for gold in the Internet. These guys have already been there and found it."[35] But talented engineers were not enough. Netscape needed experienced managers to scale into a real company. Although Jim Clark initially took the title of CEO, he had made it clear from day one that it was temporary. And while Andreessen was developing an interest in the business side of Netscape, he had no management experience. His first love was conceptualizing problems and delving into the technology. Andreessen later recalled, "[After we hired the Mosaic team], we went out and started hiring management. It was really important to us, at the rate that we were growing, to be able to hire seasoned people who had already done this before. We knew we could do the technology . . . but we knew that we needed people who could build the company."

Andreessen and Clark turned to L. John Doerr, a general partner at Kleiner Perkins Caufield and Byers, for help in creating a world-class management team. Andreessen later credited Doerr with being instrumental in the process of building a company on Internet time: "He was extremely valuable in helping us to recruit the senior management team, all these good people and eventually the CEO. Without him there's no way we would have gotten people [of such high] caliber." Doerr, who holds electrical engineering degrees from Rice and a Harvard Business School MBA, has frequently been described as the most powerful venture capitalist in Silicon Valley. Since joining Kleiner Perkins in 1980, he has championed investments in Compaq, Lotus, Intuit, Symantec, Amazon.com, @Home, and, of course, Netscape. An inveterate big thinker, he aims to create industries, not just firms. As Doerr himself likes to say, he tries to "swing for the fences."[36]

Doerr's distinguishing characteristic is his boundless energy. In the words of Sun CEO Scott McNealy, "John Doerr is the Eveready [sic] Bunny on steroids and hardwired to the Hoover Dam power plant."[37] A live wire, rail-thin and hyperkinetic, he is constantly in motion. The same intensity comes through when Doerr speaks. Ideas pour forth at a dizzying pace, each one voiced with enthusiastic conviction. Given his track record, it is hardly surprising that colleagues and rivals are unanimous in attesting to Doerr's brilliance. Yet, in an industry known for its sharp edges, he remains unpretentious in dress and manner, affable, and unfailingly polite. And despite the long hours he puts in, Doerr's family life remains a top priority. Pictures of his wife and two young daughters dominate his office. He was happy to meet us for dinner, but it had to be late because he insists on being home to put his children to bed.

Doerr's start-up philosophy provided a blueprint for Netscape's first year. Doerr believed that the biggest challenge was creating an effective team and getting the right people. "When you're putting your team together," noted Doerr, "look for really smart people. It's fundamental. . . . Besides smart, look for a combination of experience, drive, commitment, and passion. You don't want all experience—but you also don't want all drive, energy, passion."[38] He told us that there are five critical elements that he tried to foster in Netscape:

The first and foremost is *technical excellence* . . . an attitude that "we're going to be the very best in the field that we're in," and that's important to attract and retain more and better talent. . . . Marc Andreessen provided it, but it was reinforced with the kind of technical talent that Jim Clark was able to attract to the company. The second is *outstanding management*. That doesn't necessarily mean "experienced," but usually it does. . . . The third is *strategic focus on a large and rapidly growing market* because rapidly growing markets provide new ventures with an enormous amount of air cover, and that covers a lot of sins and missteps. . . . Fourth is a reasonable set of *financings*. . . . And fifth and final is a *sense of urgency*. You can detect it when you walk into a place. If they've got that sense of urgency about them, they're going to win because the most precious advantage that a venture has, after its intellectual capital, is its time-to-market advantage, which, frankly, is shrinking in a terrifying way as large companies get a lot more aggressive and more competitive.

Doerr felt that Andreessen, Clark, and the Mosaic team had the foundation for technical excellence, so recruiting outstanding management was his next task. His mission was to build a complete team, including a world-class CEO, in less than 120 days. In our interview, he revealed that his first decision had been whether or not to recruit himself as CEO: "From the beginning, from the day Clark and I shook hands, Jim said he didn't want to run the company. A little-known fact that I've never disclosed to [the current CEO] is that I was very attracted by this proposition and wondering if I ought to step in. But I felt I could get somebody much better than me to run it and set out to do that."

That somebody turned out to be Jim Barksdale, the CEO of AT&T Wireless Services. Doerr's courtship of Barksdale took time: Barksdale agreed to join Netscape's board of directors in the summer of 1994, but he was not yet ready to leave AT&T. While waiting for Barksdale to come around, Doerr and Clark set about recruiting key leaders in engineering, sales, and marketing. Doerr helped pull in at least three people who were particularly important for ramping up the company: Todd Rulon-Miller, Netscape's first head of sales; Rick Schell, Netscape's first head of engineering; and Mike Homer, Netscape's first head of marketing and later the head of Netscape's Web site business.[39]

Rulon-Miller was 43 at the time. A Princeton graduate in liberal arts, he had a distinguished history in sales at IBM, First Data Resources, and Tandem Computer, and as head of North American sales for NeXT Computer under Steve Jobs. He also had experience as the CEO of a start-up. As Rulon-Miller recounted, he was targeted in a manner that was classic John Doerr:

On a Saturday night, I had come home from dinner with my wife. The message light's blinking. So I pick up, my wife just happens to be sitting there, and the message comes on like this: "Hello, Todd, John Doerr. Kevin Compton tells me you can sell ice to Eskimos. We need you at Mosaic. I'm flying in from Atlanta next Tuesday, 9:05, Flight 118, be there. I want to meet you." Bong. And my wife looks at me and says, "What's that," and I said, "I think it's Mission Impossible—I have no idea.". . . I remember going out to the airport, and there was a packed house, and I couldn't find him. Maybe I missed the flight, I thought—this isn't going to work. And then I saw, from a far corner, this darting figure, and he looked like one of the Marx Brothers—with the trench coat, with eyes that were luminescent and an energy I couldn't believe. It was John Doerr. He walked right up to me and said, "Are you Todd?" And I went, "Yes." And that's how I had a first interview. . . . [Jim Clark was there, but] Doerr just sat there fixated on me and said, "Jim, tell him what we're doing." Jim went on about the Internet, Internet commerce, telephone over the Internet . . . you're going to buy books, etc. And then Doerr was the one who really bore down. He just put pinchers on my head. He made me list, name after name, who I'd hire to get into 5,000 retail stores. . . . [Three days later] they made me an offer, and I was on the job the following Monday.

Doerr and Clark's other early targets had similar stories and brought similar attributes to the early Netscape—maturity and experience in companies both large and small. Rick Schell was 45 years old when he joined Netscape. After completing a Ph.D. in computer science at the University of Illinois, he went to work for Intel, where he spent eight years in microcomputer architecture design. In 1987, he left Intel for Sun Microsystems and then Borland, where he worked in computer languages and databases. After a stint at a start-up that was bought by Symantec, he came to Netscape as employee number 60. In Schell's own words, Doerr and Clark brought him on-board "to be adult supervision for a group of about 25 or 28 people in product development."

Mike Homer, the youngster of this group at age 36, had accumulated almost a decade of experience in marketing and technical jobs at Apple Computer before serving as VP of marketing at Go and VP of engineering at Eo, two start-ups that never quite made it. Homer began his career as an application programmer at IBM after graduating from UC-Berkeley. While at Apple, Homer got a high-level view of how to run a company when John Sculley "grabbed me out of the organization and made me his right-hand man. I taught him as much as I could about the technology and sat right next to him for a year." Homer joined Netscape in October 1994 as employee number 69. "At the time," he noted "there were only 40 employees here, but we used to issue the employee numbers based on offers." As in Rulon-Miller's case, John Doerr was the key to getting Mike Homer. Doerr knew Homer from Go, a pen-based computing venture that was one of Kleiner Perkins's more spectacular flops. Homer recalled, "Doerr called me from the trade show floor of Interop in Atlanta in late September. He said, 'I have a great company. It's called Mosaic. Jim Clark is running it—we are ready to launch our product. They don't know how to price it. They don't know how to set up distribution channels. Yada yada yada. I want you to get your ass over here right now.' The rest is history."

The most important hire was clearly Jim Barksdale, Netscape's disarmingly charming CEO. Soft-spoken by nature, Barksdale seasons his drawl with folksy sayings about dogs and front porches that recall his origins in the South. He offers calm as a counter to Silicon Valley's nervous energy; in an industry of manic talkers, he stands out as a listener. At the same time, he has developed a reputation as a fierce competitor, who in John Doerr's words, represents the "gold standard" of start-up CEOs.

Barksdale's work history began in IBM sales, followed by a long stint at Federal Express. As chief information officer and then chief operating officer, Barksdale was instrumental in guiding the company from $1 billion to $7.7 billion in annual revenues. Barksdale got his first real taste of David-and-Goliath warfare as FedEx squared off head-to-head against giant UPS. Moreover, at both Federal Express and McCaw Cellular Communications, which he joined as president and chief operating officer in 1992, he had ample opportunity to master the art of meteoric growth. After AT&T bought out McCaw, Barksdale became CEO of AT&T Wireless Services, rising, in *Time*'s estimation, to "the varsity squad of American management."[40] When Netscape launched its courtship, Microsoft was searching for a president and chief operating officer, and Barksdale was a candidate. Ultimately, John Doerr, Jim Clark, and a 15 percent equity stake in the company proved too much to turn down. For a man of his stature, Barksdale was taking an extraordinary risk.

Barksdale had a very clear sense of his role at Netscape. As he said, "The main thing I do is sell customers. . . . I'm very involved in the sales and marketing and the distribution side of the business, which is more my expertise." In approaching these tasks, he brought an insider's understanding of the business uses of technology and the corporate customer's goals and fears. As chief information officer of Federal Express, he liked to recall, "I probably implemented more software than any CEO of any software company in the world." This track record proved to be a valuable asset with Netscape's move into the enterprise market.

Barksdale was largely responsible for creating the structures that allowed Netscape to enjoy unprecedented growth in its early years, without spinning out of control. He also worked hard at inspiring the Netscape team. Colleagues lauded Barksdale as a natural leader, who was instrumental in attracting top managers to the company and in motivating workers throughout its ranks. At the party following Netscape's initial public offering (IPO), excited employees stood on their chairs to applaud while he led a group cheer, fists punching the air. When Netscape was having difficulty in 1997, he took a page from Lee Iaccoca's book, cut his pay to $1.00, and returned 300,000 options to the option pool.

Netscape managers were also generous with praise for Barksdale's management style, especially in the early days. Current and former employees alike agreed that Jim Barksdale made the company work. After leaving the company, Todd Rulon-Miller described his initial admiration for Barksdale's style:

For the first year, I thought I'd died and gone to heaven. I've worked at companies with great management. . . . I've worked for guys like Steve Jobs, and I couldn't believe Barksdale. This guy had so much grace and style. He had such a good grasp of business and putting his finger on the pulse. Having worked with Steve Jobs, who is extremely tough on people, I couldn't believe a guy who believed in people so much as to give them responsibility and authority and pep talks. . . . He understood sales. I remember going to Steve Jobs, and Jobs would go, "Are you speaking French? Are you talking to me?" But Jim knew my vernacular, he knew the slang, the order of the deal, how to put stuff together. So I have the highest regard for Jim.

Barksdale obviously respected and valued experience in his staff. As he told us, "We've consistently hired more mature managers. Trying to get senior executives was another part of scaling the business up." He was also a demanding boss who set high standards for his people. For example, everyone in the organization knew that "missing your budget is a terminal offense." Barksdale liked to say that he "manages by facts" and demands hard analysis—not just touchy-feely impressions. He drove himself hard and expected the people who worked for him to do the same.

Barksdale was clearly a charismatic leader who provided great maturity and stability during Netscape's hypergrowth. As CEO, however, Barksdale is vulnerable to two criticisms. First, he was a consensus-seeker who prized unity within his team. Not surprisingly, the culture of senior management reflected this antagonism-shy approach, which involved certain risks in an industry characterized by extraordinary turmoil and change. A number of insiders made the point that Barksdale's management style made it difficult for people to air opposing views when there were deep disagreements on the company's direction. On this dimension, Netscape had little in common with other successful high-tech companies, such as Microsoft or Intel, where shouting matches between top managers could sometimes be heard down the halls. Rick Schell, who previously worked at Intel, compared the two organizations and styles after he left Netscape in 1998:

Netscape is a real grown-up company because Jim Barksdale is a real grown-up. . . . But Jim doesn't have the Silicon Valley style. He does not like conflict. . . . He especially doesn't like it in groups. [I remember] at an Intel executive staff meeting, there would be near warfare: people shouting at one another, lots of apparent hostility—you'd think it was anyway. And then Andy [Grove] would gavel them back into order, get some control over the group. . . . There was no fear of conflict. Jim Barksdale just didn't like it. He never did. If there was an argument at an executive staff meeting, that was just a no-no.

A second criticism of Barksdale is the same charge often aimed at John Sculley, when he was at Apple, and numerous nontechnical CEOs at IBM. Like Sculley, John Akers, and Lou Gerstner, Barksdale came out of marketing, sales, and general management. Barksdale was not a technologist, and he did not present himself as a technological visionary. He was not an Andy Grove or a Bill Gates–type of high-tech CEO, deeply involved in defining products and technical direction. Consequently, Barksdale did not make the final decisions on many of the strategic questions driving the company. Instead, he relied heavily on Andreessen (who was often isolated from the day-to-day activities of the company before mid-1997) and to a lesser degree on Mike Homer, Rick Schell, and senior engineering executive Eric Hahn. Barksdale's priorities were marketing and sales, mentoring people, and building the organization. As he told us in 1997, "I have now delivered more software more quickly than anybody on the planet. I must be doing something right. So I don't worry about the things that are working. I worry about the things that aren't working. . . . [The technology] is not my area of expertise. And probably, therefore, I tend to leave it to others to do what they said they were going to do." Alex Edelstein, Barksdale's assistant in 1997, offered an apt summary of the division of labor in Netscape's senior ranks:

> He [Barksdale] has been a key stabilizing force for everyone. Despite all the hypergrowth, there was a sense that he had a strong hand at the wheel. But when it came to product decisions, they were being made by Marc [Andreessen] and Rick [Schell]. Barksdale did not usually make the final call on a product. When it came to product strategy, he just supervised. He wouldn't say, "We are going to bundle this and drop this price." That was almost always worked out between Marc and Mike Homer.

Barksdale had a particularly close relationship with Andreessen and relied heavily on the young engineer to set the company's technology direction. In our interview in July 1997, Barksdale explained that he delegated responsibility for technology and product development because of Andreessen's intelligence, greater technical expertise, and "passion for the product," qualities that Barksdale thought he also saw in Bill Gates:

> Marc is the brightest and quickest person I've ever met. Marc has not proven himself as a big-leagues manager but, if he does that, which I'm confident he will, he will be an absolute killer. Marc brings a passion for the product. The thing that I admire the most about Microsoft is Bill Gates's

passion for the product. . . . His passion for the product has been the glue that held that place together and made it so successful. I don't have the passion for the product. I never will. That's not my field of expertise. I'm trying to bring that passion in with this structure, and I think it will be effective.

Barksdale made it clear that mentoring Andreessen and trying to develop his protegé's managerial and functional skills was one of his top priorities: "I do a lot of coaching of Marc. Marc and I talk a lot, and we spend two hours together every Sunday. I talk to him, listen to him, and counsel him. In addition, we spend a lot of e-mail traffic solving the little bitty things and big things. Marc has changed a lot in the last two years: It's unbelievable how much he's matured."

Barksdale demonstrated his confidence in Andreessen by giving him greater and greater responsibilities. Beginning in the summer of 1994, Andreessen served as chief technology officer for three years. Usually, this meant that he sat off in a corner of the company with a small staff, thinking great thoughts, writing white papers for the Web site, talking with customers, and expounding his views of the world. In many ways, he existed as an outsider within the Netscape organization. In July 1997, Barksdale brought Andreessen into the heart of the company by giving him responsibility for all product development at Netscape. In the spring of 1998, Andreessen also gained control over marketing. As Barksdale told us:

> He's improved at a faster rate than was necessary to do the job he was given, and now we've expanded his job. I'm always struck by Marc's ability to listen and to learn, despite the fact that when you talk to Marc, you have the impression he is so confident that he is not learning. But the fact is Marc is a great absorber of information. And now we've recently given him enterprise marketing. Marc was quick to give me a hundred marketing ideas a day, even though that wasn't his job. So I said, "Fine. I'm going to see how smart you are."

Hire People Who Can Hit the Ground Running

The philosophy of hiring experience applied throughout the organization. The human resources strategy at Netscape was to bring personnel on board with the hope they would hit the ground running. While Netscape had pockets of neglect or inexperience, particularly in areas such as software testing, which we discuss in chapter 5, the typical Netscape employee was thrown to the wolves on the second day of work.

Kandis Malefyt, the head of human resources at Netscape, explained the company's HR philosophy. She was a typical seasoned senior manager, armed with a master's degree in psychology, and experience at RCA, ISI, and SGI. Malefyt started by telling us that Netscape preferred not to hire many green college graduates. Netscape, she said, was looking for people who had not just studied programming or marketing but had actually done it: "You have to know the area you're applying for. It's not a place to come in and learn, yet." To minimize the need for handholding, she explained, Netscape required experience almost across the board: "In the business functions, aside from R&D, we hired people who just knew how to do that stuff. Experienced people. It bucks the common wisdom that, to be in a whole new space, you need people who haven't gotten set in their ways. But it's not true. If you hire the right kind of people, you have this great experience."

With experienced people, Netscape could ask new employees to start working almost immediately. Alex Edelstein described new hires as "aggressive self-starters . . . who were totally type A." Citing himself as an example, he explained, "I had experience, and I jumped right in. I really wanted to make things happen." The Netscape orientation was clearly geared toward an Edelstein-type person. New employees spent their first morning on the job in a briefing. The rest of the process, according to Malefyt, was brief: "You meet all your coworkers, get a buddy, and the manager, hopefully, has got several meetings set up for you to talk with people and get to know things. And then we let you sit and play with your system for a while." After that, the new employee was largely on his or her own, until the next orientation, which took place within six weeks. In general, training at Netscape was minimal.

Rather than invest in long-term training, Netscape managers emphasized the importance of hiring only the best up front. Todd Rulon-Miller, for example, insisted on hiring "A-pluses" for his sales team:

> As venomous as I was about making quarters and hitting revenue notches, if my guys let a B or a C get in the group, I'd go nuts. And they knew it. I just know that B's who hire C's and D's breed politics and administrative negligence. A's hire A-pluses because they want their job to be easier. The early propulsion of Netscape emerged from our esprit, our attractiveness, and our ability to attract great people because we were a lightning rod for the new age. This made it easy to hire at the outset: In the first week I was there, I hired eleven people.

On the engineering side, David Stryker, former head of the core technologies division, was willing to nurture managerial ability in-house, but he also had a nonnegotiable criterion—technical experience and expertise:

In some companies, there is an idea that there are technologists, and then there are managers. I've never found this to work. Most of my managers were promoted from within. They were originally technologists and are now technical managers. I have a lot of experience mentoring people as managers, and I'm good at it. The thing I can't do is turn people who are "a-technological" into the kind of technical experts who can offer me the advice I need to make the rapid-fire decisions we have to make. So management is pretty technical.

Hiring experienced technologists came, quite literally, at a price: Experience was very expensive. Netscape adopted a philosophy of compensation that differed markedly from the approach taken by other start-ups, and by its rival, Microsoft. The philosophy of compensation at Microsoft was to offer very low base pay relative to many of its direct competitors but compensate its engineers and managers with stock options tied to the company's long-run performance. In the 1990s, for example, Microsoft's average salaried worker earned one-third less than the average of his or her Silicon Valley peers in cash compensation, but total compensation was 140 percent of the average due to the appreciation of Microsoft's stock.[41] Microsoft could make this strategy work because the vast majority of hires were people directly out of college with low expectations for cash compensation and a greater willingness to take a (relatively low) risk on Microsoft stock.

Like their counterparts at Microsoft, senior managers at Netscape received relatively low cash compensation, with stock options composing most of their total compensation package. A number of Netscape's top managers even deferred their salaries in 1997 and took no bonuses because of the wealth they accrued from their stock grants prior to the initial public offering. For the rank and file, however, Netscape's philosophy was to be among the leaders in Silicon Valley in cash compensation. If the company wanted to get experienced people in Silicon Valley, where living costs were among the highest in the country, it had little choice. Salespeople naturally had higher cash incentives, while engineers and product marketing managers received relatively more stock. But broadly speaking, Netscape's human resources strategy was "to be competitive with big companies where we want to recruit from, and take salary away as a recruiting barrier," as Malefyt explained. In addition, Netscape offered spot bonus plans and weekends away for completing specific milestones. And to help people cope with their busy lives, Netscape also provided a wide range of on-site services, ranging from ATMs to dentists and a corporate concierge.

Through the summer of 1997, Netscape generally succeeded in its hiring plans and kept undesired turnover to 5 percent per year. (Total turnover was 10 percent.) In July 1997, Malefyt noted with pride that she had never lost an employee to Microsoft. But as the company's performance deteriorated in the second half of the year, turnover began to rise. Among the people we interviewed, several had left by the summer of 1998, including Eric Hahn, the executive VP who led the server division before taking over as chief technology officer; Larry Geisel, chief information officer; Rick Schell, senior VP and, most recently, head of the client product division; Danny Shader, VP of partner and developer relations; David Stryker, senior VP and head of core technologies; and Alex Edelstein, Barksdale's assistant. On the sales side, the losses included Todd Rulon-Miller, senior VP in charge of sales and field operations; Karen Richardson, VP of strategic accounts; and Ram Shriram, the VP who headed OEM (Original Equipment Manufacturer) sales and business development. Jon Mittelhauser, one of the original Mosaic developers, had also departed.

Acquire the Talent, Expertise, and Experience You Cannot Hire

When Andreessen identified new areas to pioneer in his vision statements, he would often call for expertise that was hard to find on the open job market. In these situations, Netscape aggressively acquired expertise in company-size chunks whenever managers could not hire the people they needed one by one. Fortunately for Netscape, its stock had a very high price/earnings multiple through most of this period. Counting only the quarters when Netscape reported positive earnings, the company's P/E ratio averaged over 270 between the day of the initial public stock offering and late 1997. (Over the same period, the S&P 500 P/E ratio averaged in the low 20s.) This gave Netscape tremendous flexibility to use stock to buy other firms.

The most important acquisition of people and talent was the purchase of Collabra in November 1995. Collabra brought deep expertise on messaging and collaboration into Netscape at a critical point. It also contributed a handful of senior managers who took leading roles in the company—to the point that, in our first interview, Debby Meredith, who had served as VP of engineering at Collabra, joked, "Collabra's takeover of Netscape is almost complete." Meredith headed client engineering in 1997 and then went on to report directly to Barksdale in the newly created position of head of customer satisfaction, a role that included responsibility for technical support. Bob Lisbonne, who had been Collabra's VP of marketing, assumed full responsibility for the Navigator/Communicator product line in 1998. Eric Hahn, who had previously started cc:Mail and sold it to Lotus before founding Collabra, ran the server division for two years before succeeding Andreessen briefly as Netscape's chief technology officer.

Another leading figure that Netscape "acquired" was server architect Tim Howes. In 1996, Hahn and Andreessen decided that the company needed a directory product. After reviewing 20 possible solutions, Hahn settled on LDAP, which led him quickly to Howes. Howes had recently completed a dissertation on "scalable, deployable, heterogeneous Internet directory services" at the University of Michigan. Andreessen, who is not easily impressed, described Howes as "very smart." Yet Howes was not just a theorist. He had already led a team that deployed LDAP for the University of Michigan's network. This experience convinced Andreessen and Hahn that the right choice was to acquire both the technology and the people who could take it forward. Netscape hired a number of members of the LDAP team and, at age 33, Tim Howes became one of the key architects of Netscape's server technology.

A third example of acquiring companies in order to get good people was the purchase of Paper Software, which brought Mike McCue, a highly innovative developer, to Netscape. McCue had a colorful background. Living in upstate New York, he had become interested in computers at a very young age. By the time he was 13, he was building video games for a publisher in California. After graduating from high school, he went directly to IBM to work as a programmer for three and a half years. He left IBM in 1989 to start Paper Software, which Netscape bought in 1996. As Alex Edelstein recalled:

> I found Mike McCue in a little company in upstate rural New York. He had come to our attention because he was one of the first people to write to our plug-in API [application programming interface] when we didn't even have the dollars and the people to evangelize and all we could do was really post it to the Web. McCue came to us and said, "I've got this 3-D viewer that plugs right in, here are all these cool things I'm doing with Netscape technology, and here are all the cool things I want to do." And we ended up acquiring the company. . . . One of the reasons it was easy for me to get the acquisition approved is that everyone from myself to Marc to Jim recognized that this wasn't just technology, this was some really top talent. They had vision and we could see that it went beyond 3-D tools. So we brought them in, and Mike started out by making sure that the 3-D stuff worked

and got integrated. But, over time, even as 3-D was starting to become less [important] for Netscape, he was moving on. . . . He and the guys he took from Paper Software . . . were able to take [their ideas] and turn them into something which became very timely, Netcaster.

According to Bob Lisbonne, Netscape's approach to acquisitions made bringing people like Mike McCue into the company its primary goal: "We have almost always acquired people first, technology a distant second, and installed bases and brand equities and revenue streams a very distant third. We've really taken terrific folks from these small companies and put them right in the middle of the most important stuff going on at Netscape."

Experience Is a Double-Edged Sword

It would have been impossible for Netscape to scale so quickly without its depth of management experience. The combination of Andreessen's compelling vision, Barksdale's leadership style, and Doerr's aggressive recruiting attracted so much talent to Netscape in the first 12 to 18 months that success seemed virtually guaranteed. But deep experience in a young company has a dark side as well. For one thing, the people who were great for scaling the organization fast were not always the right people to grow a successful, ongoing venture. In a number of cases, Netscape's seasoned hires were extremely successful at providing structure and maturity in the company's early years, but less capable at adapting to the pace of change on Internet time.

Some of Netscape's managers loved to start organizations from scratch, but were less interested in running them once they had grown. Jim Clark, for instance, recognized the day he founded Netscape that creating new companies, not managing them, was his vocation. In an interview in the spring of 1998, Marc Andreessen noted that Jim Clark was not alone in this respect. Netscape, he said, hired too many people who were great in the early days but not well suited to the demands and discipline of a large corporation with thousands of employees:

We made some bad hiring decisions in the first couple years of this company. In some cases, we just hired the wrong people. . . . There were others who had the wrong skill sets for managing a big company. I can think of one person who was an absolute genius at helping this company get to a $100 million a quarter of sales. If I started a new company today and wanted to get it to $100 million a quarter, I would hire him again in a split second. But I would go into it knowing that he was not going to do more.

He had no intrinsic desire to take it beyond that. He wasn't going to build the organization that was going to take us to $500 million in quarterly sales.

Some veteran managers did a great job at providing structure and maturity but sometimes let their preconceptions get in the way. Competing on Internet time is about having the speed and flexibility to respond to rapid changes in the environment. But some of the seasoned managers had ways of doing things that were not going to change, despite the new environment of the Internet. One executive gave us an example:

> One of the most senior engineering managers in the company came to Netscape with some stereotypes, given his age. . . . He was always adversarial. He would continuously say, "We can't do that," or, "We can't release that." He became widely known in parts of the company as "Dr. No." He was a classic old-line engineering manager. He did a great job early on with so many kids running around developing code to the moon with no schedule and no logic. His basic parental guidance was needed and required.

Another problem linked to Netscape's reliance on highly experienced senior staff was the fact that self-confident overachievers will almost inevitably clash. In Silicon Valley, large egos collide all the time. Yet as long as they all have a chance to air their points of view, engage in debate, and come to a clear resolution, big egos can usually coexist. The combination of very experienced people who had not previously worked together and Jim Barksdale's conflict-avoiding style made resolving the inevitable clash of egos much more difficult. More often than not, Netscape postponed hard problems rather than attack them head-on. As one self-confessed big ego confided, it was generally hard to get consensus on tough issues:

> If you hire experienced, senior people into a company and they all have big egos—and we all have big egos—you've got to do something to get those egos to work together and to function together. When the company is small enough and everybody's running 150 miles an hour and doing their own thing, it's okay because cooperation isn't going to be very helpful anyway. There's not much friction; there's not much need to be territorial. There is also not much time to do teamwork. Let me give you an example: We were supposed to have an executive off-site in Napa. But it got canceled because everybody got busy. Everything had a higher priority. But not getting the executive group to come together as a team was an indicator and a symptom of our problems working together. And Jim [Barksdale's] style contributed to this problem. Developing the management of the company was important to Jim. But trying to work on his own team, to get them to work

together, was not something he was comfortable doing. He couldn't mediate or arbitrate because it just made him very, very uncomfortable.

In the early days of spectacular growth, the consequences of such missed opportunities were lost in the celebrations of success. But when senior managers started to worry about strategic direction in late 1996 and early 1997, these polite, inconclusive discussions and delayed actions produced growing turmoil within the senior ranks. All the senior managers we interviewed who left the company in 1997 and 1998 shared the view that "success was hiding a lot of sins at Netscape." One of the most important of these sins, as one executive noted, was "the lack of great teamwork that would allow for an informed, articulate decision-making process that yielded both strategy and tactics that were best for the company."

As Netscape's success began to wane, turf battles started to emerge. The contest that was best known within Netscape pitted Todd Rulon-Miller, who headed sales, against Mike Homer, who was in charge of marketing at the time. The two executives had been fighting for years. Homer, who came from a decade of experience at Apple and Go, generally looked at the world from a retail perspective. Rulon-Miller, by contrast, had worked at IBM and Tandem, and he viewed sales and marketing from the perspective of reaching a chief information officer in a large corporation. The deep intensity of the feud made it hard for Netscape management to sort out the emotions from the facts, especially as time wore on.

In one such battle in early 1997, Rulon-Miller had several long discussions with Jim Barksdale and the CEO's direct reports about problems looming on Netscape's horizon. Rulon-Miller recognized that selling servers to corporations was a much more difficult task than selling browsers. Netscape, he argued, was badly out-manned in this task compared to IBM and Microsoft, and he forecasted that the bottom line would suffer severely in late 1997, unless the company took corrective action:

By March of 1997, after 90 days of a lot of politicking and barnstorming, I was frankly at wits' end. I said I had an increasing sense of Armageddon. Around the first of April, I told Jim [Barksdale] that I had strong concerns on impending budget decisions. I talked about staff work and working with Peter Currie [the CFO] and Mike Homer, and the long process that we had been through. I suggested to him that I believed that we were possibly headed for a significant downturn. If left unchanged, my belief was that this budget would erode Netscape's software revenue generation capability. I went over with Jim an assessment of the dollars, the sales results from those expenditures and a bunch of different things, and then I gave him some summary points. I said that we are at the burnout phase of current resources. I told him that if our sales model discussion of the last eight weeks was correct, we may be inadvertently choking the engine with this budget. I still held at the time optimism for Q2, but I was concerned about Q3 and Q4.

Rulon-Miller was calling for more sales resources to redress his difficulties in selling enterprise solutions. Homer apparently disagreed vehemently with Rulon-Miller's diagnosis of the problem as well as his prescription. Of course, Homer and Rulon-Miller would generally disagree with anything the other recommended. Numerous meetings took place in the winter of 1997, but none produced a real decision. Rulon-Miller's recommendation for more "feet on the street" probably would not have materially changed the course of events in 1997. In addition, there was a genuine debate about the productivity of Netscape's sales and marketing efforts. On the one hand, sales costs as a percentage of revenues were trending up modestly over the previous three quarters. Moreover, the indirect sales force was producing roughly 40 percent of revenue through the Web site and OEM (PC manufacturer) accounts, and the large telemarketing organization, which had been great at selling browsers, was having less success selling enterprise solutions. As a result, not everyone agreed that adding more expenses was the right thing to do. On the other hand, there were about 750 people in the sales organization, but the majority were in technical support (100), consulting (150), telemarketing (100), or indirect sales (150). This left only 225 to 250 sales people or engineers who actually called on customers all around the world. Not surprisingly, Netscape's direct sales force was dwarfed by Oracle, IBM, and Microsoft, making it very hard for Netscape to compete for many large corporate accounts. No matter who was right on this particular debate, however, Rulon-Miller, the person with the closest, most intimate connection to customers, was signaling real problems selling the products in the field. Unfortunately, the Rulon-Miller/Homer disputes made it hard for Jim Barksdale and the rest of Netscape's management to see the signal through the noise.

PRINCIPLE   *Build the internal resources for a big company, while organizing like a small one.*

A powerful vision and experienced, expert staff are only two of the ingredients that allowed Netscape to scale its organization on Internet time. As revenues exploded in 1995 and 1996, the company was putting up buildings, hiring new people by the boatload, and generating more ideas than any organization could hope to implement. Greg Sands, Netscape employee number 21, remembered that in the early days everything was going so fast "it was chaos. The biggest decision you have to make every day is what not to do. You have 10 things to do and you can only do five."[42] The answer was obvious: The company needed systems and structure to keep it on track.

Build Systems for a Billion-Dollar Company

Barksdale had been through this process before. At both Federal Express and McCaw, he had suffered through the pains of very rapid growth and the problems of continuously changing information and operational systems. He learned one important lesson from those prior experiences: Do not do it again. In what turned out to be a very bold, potentially very expensive move, Barksdale bet that the company was going to be big and went full steam ahead to create large-scale systems for a billion-dollar company. Here's his story, in his own words, from our first meeting in July 1997:

> The trick is to know when do you bring on the bureaucrats. There's a stage in a company's life where it's fine to be loosely controlled. There's another stage where you have to get more and more serious. What you don't want to do is get too serious too soon. That stifles a lot of things. And even when you get serious, you don't want to take the fun out of it. I'll tell you this: At FedEx, I hired more people in a month than I've hired here in a year. So it's all relative to what you've seen. I guess this is why Clark and Doerr came after me: I had experience in growing two businesses—McCaw, which grew extremely fast, as did FedEx. So here's what we did. We're a little bitty company. At the time, we maybe had a hundred people. We were running our first quarter of revenue. I didn't have a CFO because I was trying to hire Peter Currie. And we were in a mess because we were using something called Great Plains accounting. It's an accounting package. It is PC-based, and it's good if you're less than maybe a $10 million company. [At that level], you could run on it and be happy. But we were starting to see this growth. So I said, "Here's what we're going to do. We're going to go out, and we're going to buy either Oracle financials or SAP. That's a $5 million plus or minus purchase. Plus consulting [fees]." [And] we did it in a year. But a year is a long time commitment. I said, "Look—I have been through so many general ledger conversions in my life. . . . I'm not going through another conversion as we get to be a $100 million company. All right? I've been there. I'm going to buy something that's as big as a billion-dollar business needs. If we don't get there, we've got another problem

anyway." So we've done that in several areas. . . . [We also work closely] with Ernst & Young, controlling our revenue recognition, which is a big problem in a software business because you can ship everything the last day of the month. We have E&Y in the midst of our business, where they're involved before we even sign contracts. I don't want them or anybody coming back to me saying, "You shouldn't have recognized this revenue." We have much tighter controls over dollars and head count and those kind of things than you might imagine.

The decision to build systems for a billion-dollar enterprise was bold. In other circumstances, some might have called it foolhardy. Most startups prefer to match organizational commitments to the so-called burn rate—the rate at which a company is spending its cash. To make forward commitments, especially to intangible assets with no resale value, is extremely risky. If sales do not materialize, those investments are gone. But Barksdale was clearly a risk taker. Taking the job as CEO of a small, unproven start-up like Netscape, when he might have been president of Microsoft or some other established powerhouse, was clear proof of his willingness to take risk.

Larry Geisel, the chief information officer, had the job of building an information infrastructure to meet Barksdale's billion-dollar business needs. At 56, Geisel stood out as one of the oldest members of the Netscape team. Immediately prior to coming to Netscape, he had been executive vice president of global solutions delivery for Xerox. His goal was to prevent the information infrastructure from ever limiting Netscape's growth. While he admitted that he had not been completely successful in meeting this objective, he pursued a clear strategy of leaping ahead of current requirements:

> One of the promises I made to JB [Jim Barksdale] when I came here was to never let our infrastructure be an obstacle to growth, and that turns out to be a tough promise to keep. . . . We're overbuilding our infrastructure on a leap of faith. I was looking two years down the road and saying, "If I don't build for that now, I know darn well I'm going to be ripping out this stuff and replacing it. It's costing me a little more now but, if I build it right, I know I won't be holding us back." We built for being a billion-dollar company. That's the best way to express it.

Todd Rulon-Miller also vividly remembered Barksdale's marching orders, and took the same systems approach for sales:

> I think his quote was, "I want the systems in this company to operate like we're a billion-dollar company." And it wasn't bred by arrogance. It was

bred by a thoughtfulness of where we could be, and what the stumbling blocks are. . . . None of it was driven by a spendthrift notion. Jim got there when we were still running on Great Plains on a 486. And we were just entering an $85 million revenue year. Our PC was hemorrhaging. So Jim said, "We buy Oracle financials." People saw us put an Andersen project together that only a large company would do. And I'll tell you, if we'd missed revenue during that timeframe, it would look like a complete mistake. But we weren't going to miss revenue.

These risks paid off. While Netscape might have spun completely out of control, senior management had a good understanding of the operational side of the business, at least in part because the company had installed the sophisticated PeopleSoft and Oracle systems used in Fortune 500 companies. While Netscape was still small, it also installed other large corporate applications, such as Baan for sales force automation, and Scopus for call center and problem tracking. As Todd Rulon-Miller remarked, Netscape was adopting more than technology; it was "installing a thought process and behavior."

Internally, there was a general consensus that Netscape had done an extraordinary job to scale with the growth, but everyone realized that the company still grew faster than its control systems. Debby Meredith, for example, noted in the middle of 1997, "We're still growing quickly, but we're like a big start-up where our size probably exceeds the processes that we have in place, and we're trying to catch up." Roberta Katz, from her perch as the general counsel, put these problems into perspective: "I worry that we need to make sure that our infrastructure is tight. We're filling it in as we go, but we're always a little bit ahead of ourselves as a company. We're always stretching, so there's a little bit of risk that goes with that. We've always been stretching, and we've always managed to make it."

Manage Growth Through Decentralization and Small Teams

Putting systems into place helps keep growth from spinning out of control, but it does not automatically lead to a well-run organization. The biggest challenge for Barksdale and his team was maintaining the intensity, innovation, and flexibility of a small start-up while simultaneously acting like a billion-dollar company. This time, the solution was a familiar one: Continuously decentralize, breaking the structure into smaller and smaller teams, with some of them in a matrix with functional groups. The idea was to operate like a big company, with big-company control systems, but maintain flexibility and creativity as the organization scaled by "creating lots and lots of small teams." According to Rick Schell, when he was heading the client engineering group, "We managed our growth by subdividing the business, subdividing responsibility, getting smaller teams to work in parallel, trying to create small componentized software, then getting those teams to scale."

Like many companies, Netscape started with a simple functional organization, with separate groups for product management (product marketing), engineering (software development), QA (quality assurance or testing), legal, finance, etc. The groups pretty much ran themselves in the first year or two, but formally reported to Barksdale after he became CEO.

Andreessen's role prior to taking charge of the product groups in the summer of 1997 was mainly to provide ideas and inspiration to the development teams. From the earliest days of the company, engineers broke up into small teams, usually of about six people, and enjoyed enormous autonomy. In 1996, Andreessen explained, "We are trying real hard within the engineering team to push down as much responsibility for engineering as we can. Each of the product teams working on the different products is pretty much self-contained and has the ability to make decisions for its product. They actually set their own schedules, and we have a review process where they tell us their schedules."[43]

As the company grew, Barksdale created separate divisions for different product families, as well as for shared components and tools. The first of a series of reorganizations toward a more product-centered organization came in November 1996. Eric Hahn was in charge of running "Project Rifle," Barksdale's plan to "build the gun to fire up the organization." Under this plan, Netscape moved product marketing from a central marketing group into the product divisions, creating integrated teams for product management, development, and testing. Andreessen explained that, when Netscape reached 1,500 full-time people, it was time to make an organizational shift:

> We took our two groups [engineering and marketing], we smashed them together, and we came out with three groups: . . . one that is essentially just the client product; a server group, which is essentially all the server products; and a central marketing group, which does cross-company marketing. Then there's the sales organization. We've become a hybrid organization. And we have three managers, three senior managers, doing what two senior managers had been doing before. So each person has more time to do his job. . . . To the extent that people can accept splitting their responsibilities in half at certain points in time, they can actually become more effective in their roles.

Within the product divisions, Netscape created smaller groupings that managers tended to call "divlets." Divlets varied in size—any group working on a project that was smaller than a division was a divlet—but they were usually run by general managers or engineering team leaders, with titles ranging from vice president to director. Some of the teams built specific product releases. For example, in the server division, at one time or another, each of the server product teams operated as a divlet. Some groups of engineers also built smaller product components that Netscape might or might not tie to a particular release.

During our first interviews in July 1997, Netscape had a separate general manager and development team for Communicator 5.0, which was just starting up. It also had a separate general manager and a team for Communicator 6.0, although managers did not expect to ship this product for at least 18 months. These teams worked in parallel, but on different release schedules. (We will say more about this strategy of "parallel development" in chapter 4.) In addition, the client division had small groups that focused on the browser, the messenger component, the collaborative component, and Netcaster, as well as groups that tailored or created features for particular product versions, such as the standard and professional editions of Communicator. The previous version of Communicator, version 4.0, had utilized approximately 10 feature teams. The feature teams tended to stay together for an entire project because they needed to evolve their features and debug their code until they shipped. Some developers also worked on two or three feature teams.

The thinking behind the divlet approach was to encourage better and faster decision making as well as "generalist thinking." Andreessen and other executives believed that combining the functional groups needed to build a product under a single general manager would enable the product groups to be closer to customers, focus more effectively on specific markets and competitors, and act more autonomously. While the divlets did give the organization sharper focus, Barksdale was still not satisfied. In July 1997, he made another change in the governance structure. He decided to make the product groups report directly to Andreessen, in order to improve communication and tie product planning more tightly to the work of the product groups. During our November 1997 interview, Andreessen explained the rationale behind this move: "Barksdale spends most of his time on either internal operational issues or external sales/customer/partner/PR/analysts. He is the outbound ambassador and has very little time to spend on product issues. He was counting on the product people to do that anyway. We saw the need to have a more well-defined product strategy going forward. So he took the existing product divisions and just had them report to me."

At the same time, Barksdale integrated sales and marketing under one roof. Within that organization, he broke down the divisions into separate geographic sales units for North America, Europe, and Asia, as well as units for OEM sales, the Netscape Web site, technical support, and customer services. Finally, there were small functional staff divisions for finance, legal services, human resources, information systems, and manufacturing operations.

Breaking the organization down into small, flexible groups was good in theory, but by the end of 1997, the performance of the structure was less than ideal. The product divisions had grown large, with huge teams running specific projects. There was also a misalignment between Netscape's emerging strategy and its organization. The independent sales operation, for example, put so much effort into generating new revenues that customer support was lacking. In addition, the Web site was an afterthought in the old organization. If Netcenter was to become a central piece of Netscape's business, it needed organizational focus.

Netscape's organization began to reflect its new vision by the middle of 1998 (see Figure 2.1). Netcenter became a separate division headed by Mike Homer, the former chief of marketing. The Navigator and Communicator product lines, headed by Bob Lisbonne, were placed under Netcenter. Since the standard client product no longer generated revenue, the plan was to make Navigator into a customizable tool that would help drive traffic and revenue to the Web site. At the same time, Barksdale sought to differentiate Netscape from its competitors in the enterprise software market by making customer satisfaction one of his top priorities. In 1998, he assigned Debby Meredith to a new position heading quality and customer satisfaction, reporting directly to the CEO. Andreessen had the remaining product and marketing functions, and sales, again, became a separate organizational unit. In August 1998, Barksdale also hired Barry Ariko, a senior member of Oracle's executive team, to run sales and become Netscape's first chief operating officer.

Mesh Strategic Planning Systems with Tactical Plans

One important system at Netscape was strategic and operational planning. Part of Netscape's success in its first few years was due to its astonishing ability to execute tactically. Todd Rulon-Miller commented, "We were probably one of the best tactically executing companies the world has ever

FIGURE 2.1

Netscape's Organization, August 1998

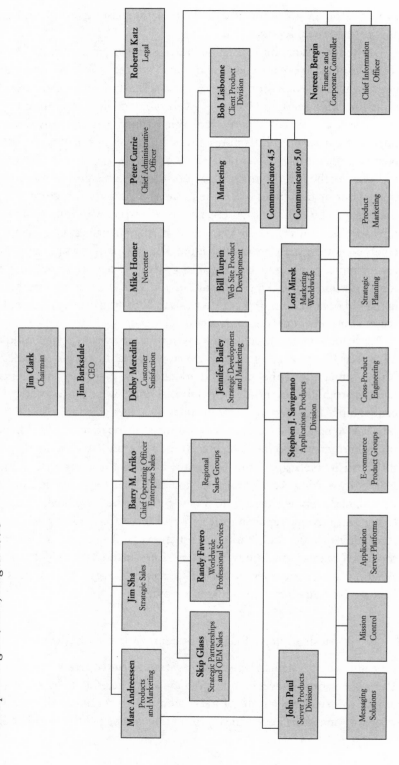

Selected units below the level of the CEO's direct reports have been omitted for greater clarity.

seen." Netscape was second to none in its ability to take a set of short-term ideas, turn them into products, and run like hell. This reflected the fact that Netscape management took the demands of Internet time very seriously. When it came to strategic planning, long term often meant a fiscal quarter or, at most, a year. Unlike many Silicon Valley companies, and in sharp contrast to their counterparts at arch-rival Microsoft, Netscape managers eschewed multiyear plans. Andreessen would lay out sweeping visions of the future, but the planning horizon extended no longer than 12 months. Strategy at Netscape was not about making long-term commitments. Instead, Barksdale defined strategy as "a series of product initiatives against a forecasted market."

The strategy process at Netscape was informal from the start. Barksdale's executive management team would try to meet regularly, usually on Mondays, to talk about current issues. In the early days, they sometimes had meetings on Saturday or Sunday. John Doerr noted, "Barksdale's style is not real rigid, but at the same time has a lot of accountability associated with it. He has short and crisp staff meetings, not for the purpose of having a staff meeting." Once a quarter, there might be an off-site meeting for senior managers, but of these Todd Rulon-Miller observed, "I wouldn't call those agendas rigorous or focused." Netscape also used to hold quarterly "Snake Killer Reviews (SKRs)." The purpose of these meetings was to review thorny issues that were hard to put to bed. Thirty to fifty of the top managers would gather to solve the problem. SKRs got their name from a classic "Barksdalism": "If you see a snake in the organization, you kill it." (After managers incorporated this type of problem solving into their tactical planning, Barksdale discontinued the SKRs in late 1997.)

The real product planning started with Andreessen's technology group, which would prepare a vision statement that recommended specific product features. Since Andreessen's team historically had no line responsibilities, the product groups had to decide on their own the specifics of the next product designs. There were also executive reviews, where people would debate the project status, milestone dates, schedules, resources, issues, risks, and the like. However, the process remained relatively fluid. According to Rick Schell, this was a consequence of operating on Internet time. Netscape managers were making strategic decisions every day as part of a continuous set of routine meetings to refine products:

> When the market is going to change in six months to a year, you can't spend two months worrying about a strategy. So you have to compress the time. It's not that we don't think about our competitors or customers. . . . It's more of a continuous process. . . . We have little "advance planning

meetings," where we talk about technology—[not the] overarching business strategy of the company. During presentations, there's a little bit of
brainstorming, driven by the product teams. In general, our time horizons
are six months to a year.

Microsoft and Netscape Compared: Planning on Internet Time at Microsoft.
We were struck by the very short-term nature of strategic planning at Netscape and wondered if this was truly a function of Internet time or a
unique aspect of Netscape's culture. To explore this question, we interviewed Steve Ballmer, Microsoft's president and the person in charge of
Microsoft's annual strategy process. The question we posed to Ballmer
was whether and how strategic planning was changing at Microsoft after
the Internet became deeply embedded in the Microsoft psyche in 1995.

To our surprise, Microsoft retained a relatively formal and structured
planning process with a three-year horizon. Similar to Netscape, Microsoft ran a series of routine meetings independent of the planning process.
For example, it had an executive committee that met regularly, usually
every three to four weeks. These meetings generally focused on operational and tactical issues and had a formal agenda that the chief operating
officer prepared. Everyone had a chance to give his or her input into the
agenda. Bill Gates then ran a separate executive strategy committee every
three weeks or so, which rarely had a formal agenda. The purpose of these
sessions was to have an open, strategic meeting to discuss high-level issues
on the minds of senior managers, especially Gates. And once a quarter, the
top 50 people in the company would also meet with a fairly formal agenda
for the purpose of general discussion and communication, not decision
making.

The formal planning process began with an annual review in February,
where each business had to present a strategic plan looking out for 36
months. These reviews could be intense. Gates, Ballmer, and others
scrutinized the plans, which included technical and business outlooks. A
vigorous debate usually followed. A few months later, these three-year
strategies would be turned into more tactical annual business and product
plans that generated bottom-up requests for resources. Gates also continued his "Think Weeks." Twice a year, he spent a week reading a wide
range of sources, from doctoral theses to new science. At the end of these
Think Weeks, he usually wrote long memos about his ideas or concerns
for the future direction of Microsoft. Strategic planning at Microsoft had
two other routine attributes: First, throughout the year there were executive retreats on special topics of current interest. And second, at the end of

every year, in December, Microsoft executives identified their top four or five competitors and did an extensive, in-depth analysis with recommendations for action.

The advent of the Internet did not change the basic planning system at Microsoft, but it did augment one of the mechanisms Microsoft used to make rapid adjustments to change. Ballmer called this mechanism a "pulse." He defined a pulse as a time when senior management got together to make course corrections in the strategy that came out of the formal process. He explained:

> You're going to apply one of these [pulses] on top of anything else that's going on at any point in time. Pulses will usually be in response to some competitive factors. Things that don't come out of competitive factors are pretty well addressed through the regular process. . . . Over the last three or four years, we've probably had at least one significant pulse per year. There's usually a lot of people who get all hot and bothered and excited about something. Bill's Think Weeks tend to be a catalyst, or a very specific competitive action or a specific event. Sometimes after Bill's Think Weeks, he says, "Hey look, we're kind of naked. The emperor has no clothes." So the emperor better call an event, tell people how he's dressed, and believe me, whenever that event occurs, the emperor puts on some darned clothes. Of course, we always have to have a strategy in place by the time of the event. . . . Take the Java strategy. Of late, there's been action on the Java front. That was a pulse that occurred, in many ways, last year [1997]. But then a lot of work got done on it again this year. So announcements, events, can be catalysts.

Ballmer's view of strategy on Internet time differed markedly from Netscape's. He was adamant that strategy was strategy and what made Internet time important at Microsoft was the need to pulse more often, take the sharp turns if necessary, but continue to run the business:

> [For me], this whole Internet time thing means it's important to pulse . . . to have a sharp forcing factor that changes direction. The fact is, if your strategy is not right, fix it. Sometimes that takes two pulses instead of one pulse, and sometimes you don't know how to fix it in the first pulse, so maybe it takes a couple or three pulses. But the fact of the matter is, the notion that everything changes every day, the notion that customers really want a new release on everything every three months—that's hogwash. It was hogwash from the beginning, but we play along; we'll play the same game. If Netscape wants to play that you don't have to have quality products, just

beta releases, and there's a community of people that want to play—we better play.

The advantage of Microsoft's approach to strategic planning was the fact that the company had a structure in place to look systematically at its environment and then develop a set of plans both to react to that environment and to try to shape it. By forcing executives to look three years out, the planning process required all senior managers to lay out their business, competitive, and technical assumptions about how the world is changing, and then state the implications of those beliefs. Netscape, by comparison, relied heavily on Andreessen and a small number of very smart people who worked with him to look out into the future. Although Eric Hahn briefly stepped into the role, a few young technologists with a largely technical view of the world generally drove the strategic process at Netscape. Most of Netscape's managers then put their noses to the grindstone and tried to execute.

Some of the differences between Netscape and Microsoft were the differences between a four-year-old company and a 23-year-old company. In addition, Microsoft's planning cycles were driven by its operating system business, which generally required a three-year time horizon. By comparison, Netscape had been scaling at a pace that was unprecedented in the software industry, and it was natural for senior managers to see 12 months as an eternity. Moreover, given that Netscape was releasing products every six months and fighting against Microsoft for its life, short-term considerations were inevitably going to dominate company thinking. After leaving Netscape, Rick Schell reflected on Netscape's strategic planning:

> The Netscape product cycles were typically six months long. And we were getting customer requirements that were changing all the time. The market was moving all over the place. So we were adapting. It did not seem to make sense to have a strategy that you write down to make a decision today about something that's going to occur a year from now, especially in a market you don't understand. At the outset, it wasn't appropriate. Two years into the company, it probably would have been a good thing to have a formal planning process.

In late 1997, Barksdale finally recognized the need for a more systematic, long-term approach. He hired Lori Mirek, a Harvard MBA with a decade of marketing experience at Oracle, Sun, and Hewlett-Packard, to lead corporate marketing and create a new process. Beginning in the fall of 1998, Netscape would start to look more like Microsoft. Mirek was constructing a process to build a 36-month business plan and "detailed market and product marketing plans for the next 18 months." Nonetheless, Mirek's most important priority was to be "fast and agile." She expected the planning process to last less than two months.

PRINCIPLE   *Build external relationships to compensate for limited internal resources.*

It would have been impossible for Netscape management to ramp the company on Internet time without help. The company had some great people, a powerful vision, and an organization geared toward fast growth, but ultimate success depended critically upon a wide variety of external resources and relationships. In fact, Netscape's very success depended on the network externalities or network effects we described earlier in the chapter. This meant that the more customers, partners, and relationships were tied to Netscape's products, the greater their value and the stronger Netscape's long-term competitive position would be.

One of Netscape's greatest skills in the early days was leveraging external resources that allowed the company to act like an organization several times its size. These external assets compensated for Netscape's lack of scale in marketing, financing, and product development. In a sense, Netscape was able to exploit the Internet and other external resources to create a virtual workforce—people outside the organization who were working for free on the company's behalf.

While exploiting external resources was critical to scaling the company on Internet time, Netscape was much less successful in building relationships with individual companies. Netscape invested considerable energy courting independent software vendors, independent content providers, and various distribution partners, such as Internet service providers and computer manufacturers. Yet the company often failed to build deep relationships because potential partners perceived Netscape as arrogant, unwilling to listen, and frequently trying to extract cash for short-term gains.

Create a Virtual Marketing Organization

The biggest problem for any new firm, especially a firm initially targeting a consumer market, is how to get recognized. Until recently, Netscape lacked the resources to launch a big advertising campaign. So rather than spend money directly, Netscape created a virtual marketing organization by leveraging free external resources, namely the press and the Web. Jim Clark was the inspiration behind this strategy. Shortly after starting the company, Clark went to his previous start-up, Silicon Graphics, and brought in PR specialist Rosanne Siino. Initially, Marc Andreessen remembered being confused by this move. "I was like, 'We're a start-up company and we don't need to hire a full-time PR person.' But Jim was like, 'Trust me on this one.'"[44] Later, Andreessen told an audience at MIT:

> Jim [Clark], for employee number 19, wanted to hire a PR person. If this was another company, you would probably think that he was crazy to hire a PR person. I'm like, "We've only got 18 people, and now we're going to hire a full-time PR person?" But what he recognized that I didn't know was that, by then, our phone had started to ring off the hook because the press had started to realize what was going on with the Internet. So they would give us a call. And that turned out to be one of the smartest investments we ever made because he was able to pull our entire strategy, our telemarketing strategy, into a level of brand recognition within a year leading up to the IPO that we got without spending any dollars on traditional marketing.[45]

Even prior to shipping its first products, Netscape had created an enormous amount of hype. Since there were no products to push, Siino started by pushing the people, especially Andreessen and Clark. The story around Jim Clark was easy: Successful entrepreneur makes lightning strike twice. After making Silicon Graphics into a billion-dollar company, Clark would do it again. But Andreessen was the real PR opportunity. As Siino put it, "We had this 22-year-old kid who was pretty damn interesting, and I thought, 'There's a story right there,' and we have this crew of kids who had come out from Illinois, and I thought, 'There's a story there too.'"[46] One of the first articles on Andreessen ran in a local newspaper in California under the title, "He's Young, He's Hot, and He's Here." Five months prior to the shipping of Navigator 1.0, *Fortune* magazine's July 1994 story on "25 Cool Companies" featured a big picture of Andreessen, Clark, and most of the Navigator development team. Mosaic Communications, as it was then known, was squarely on the map.

When Mike Homer came on board to run marketing in the fall of 1994, he pushed hard down the same path. He recalled that one of his earliest goals as head of marketing was to "publicize the hell out of the company and the product":

> We took every opportunity we could to flog the Cinderella story because it was a great PR story. I had learned at Apple that you're blessed if you can get the kind of free visibility that Apple got because the story is a good story. It's amazing. Apple doesn't have to spend nearly as much on adver-

tising as most people. So, we just played it for all it's worth. We trumped up the angle of the boy wonder and the sage of Silicon Valley, Jim Clark.

Despite their relative lack of resources, Homer and Siino generated an enormous quantity of free publicity that served the firm as a virtual marketing machine. By the time Netscape released its first products, it was widely touted as one of the one or two firms likely to survive the inevitable shakeout in the Web browser market. Just about everyone who knew anything about the Internet knew about Netscape, its products, and the people behind their development. In particular, Andreessen had become a folk hero—the next Bill Gates. The press routinely described Andreessen as a boy wonder and a cyberspace star. At the end of 1994, *People* magazine named him one of the 25 most intriguing people of the year, an honor he shared with golf sensation Tiger Woods.[47] Andreessen also appeared on *Time*'s list of 50 future leaders.[48]

However, Netscape's greatest public relations coup was the company's initial public offering of stock. In the spring of 1995, Netscape's management and board made the decision to take the company public, despite cumulative losses of roughly $12.8 million through June 30, 1995. Andreessen recalled:

> Jim Clark came in one day and said he wanted to take the company public, which at first [was] something we were a little bit concerned about because the company was still pretty young. We were still not entirely sure how this was going to play out. . . . The thing that Jim saw very accurately, though, is that there was a really unique opportunity right around the summer of '95 to get a lot of mindshare in the corporate space. What the IPO turned out to be really useful for us for was not even as a financing vehicle, because we were a successful company at that point, but as a marketing event. Because of the general euphoria at the time, it was exactly the right thing to do.[49]

Netscape's initial public offering was a spectacular success. The demand for Netscape shares caused the underwriters to increase the initial issue from 3.5 million to 5 million shares, and the price doubled to $28 the day before the offering. Despite the increase in price, investors placed orders for 100 million shares![50] After the first day's trading, Netscape Chairman Jim Clark had grown his net worth by $544 million; Jim Barksdale's stock was worth $224 million; and board member John Doerr of Kleiner Perkins owned over $256 million in stock. Marc Andreessen, then 24, also did okay, with just $58 million.

The IPO generated more publicity, consumer awareness, and brand equity than most companies could buy. It drove millions of users to Netscape's Web site, and impressed all onlookers, including the corporations that ultimately were going to pay Netscape's bills. Even Andy Grove, the tough-minded chairman of Intel Corporation, looked with awe on the IPO. He commented that part of Netscape's initial success was "a function of their aggressiveness, brazenness and high-profile nature." The IPO, in particular, helped drive the company's early gains:

> That IPO actually propelled them into mass recognition, gave them the brand and the awareness. . . . That IPO was incredible. It was a four-billion-dollar [sic] valuation for a company with, I don't know, twenty-million-dollar revenues, or whatever they had at the time. [Also . . .] Andreessen positioning himself as the next Bill Gates—it has its commercial value. They got a lot of momentum out of it.

Create a Virtual Product Testing Organization

Netscape adopted a similar approach to one of the critical phases of product development—testing the product for bugs. The company only had 115 employees by the end of 1994 and three different product lines in the works. As a result, Netscape was stretched to its limits in staffing development teams. With all the programmers working day and night, Netscape managers could spare few of their staff for the essential job of making sure that their products were free from unpleasant surprises. To expand its pool of testers, Netscape leveraged the community of the World Wide Web. This was a common practice in the noncommercial software world and had played an important role in the development of Mosaic.

Netscape first unveiled its browser as a beta, or preview, release on the Internet in October 1994. By this point, company engineers had finished most of the design work, but there still were a lot of quirks to iron out. By downloading the beta, trying it out, and filing their complaints, customers served, sometimes unwittingly, as Netscape's virtual quality assurance team. One month later, 1.5 million users had given Netscape's Navigator a trial run.[51] Together they put Navigator through a workout that was far more thorough than anything Netscape's stripped-down staff could have devised. From Andreessen's perspective, getting the product out early and getting feedback was invaluable. As he later told students at MIT:

> Kick it out the door. It may not even work reliably. . . . The purpose is to go out and get feedback on it, so the press/analysts community starts writing about it and says you're the leader in the field by virtue of your being there. And also, because you're getting feedback from customers . . . they'll come

back and they will tell you, often in no uncertain terms, what's wrong with it, and what needs to be improved. And that's the most valuable type of input you can really get.[52]

Netscape initially relied on user enthusiasm to keep the virtual testing program alive. Later, it used more tangible incentives to promote the scheme. In October 1995, one month after the beta release of Navigator 2.0, Netscape announced its first "Bugs Bounty." Users who first spotted serious security flaws would receive rewards in cash; those who found lesser problems would receive Netscape merchandise. The company announced the first winners in December 1995, reporting that the bounty had led the number of reported bugs to increase by a factor of nine. By mid-1997, Netscape had given out more than 20 $1,000 cash awards. (But the bugs bounty had some bugs of its own. In June 1997, Netscape reported that a Danish programmer had tried to extort more money out of the company in return for turning over information on a newly discovered security breach. In the end, Netscape programmers found and repaired the problem on their own.)

Create a Virtual Financing Organization

Company finance was the third area in which Netscape's "virtual" strategy reaped large-scale rewards. With Jim Clark's initial investment of $3 million all but spent, the company was running out of money in the summer of 1994. When John Doerr of Kleiner Perkins Caufield & Byers decided to invest $5 million in Netscape, Doerr and company became the virtual finance department. Not only did Doerr help recruit much of the key talent; he was instrumental in generating new sources of equity to keep the company afloat prior to the IPO. Doerr helped manage a private placement of Netscape shares in the spring of 1995 that netted over $17 million. At the time, six companies with interests in Internet publishing—Adobe, TCI, Times Mirror, Knight Ridder, Hearst, and IDG—acquired a total stake of 12 percent in the fledgling firm.

In mid-1995, the company's board, again driven by Clark and Doerr, made the decision to take the company public. The Netscape IPO delivered $130 million in cash and a high-flying stock. This new asset was a powerful tool that allowed Netscape to scale up even more quickly by acquiring companies. Unfortunately, many of these acquisitions never paid off, at least in financial terms. The problem with a virtual finance department is that management sometimes feels as if it is playing with other people's money, rather than its own. Carrying out due diligence and assimilating ventures can also be difficult on Internet time. Flush with a huge valuation in its youth, Netscape generally paid top dollar in its purchases of start-up companies. Moreover, it found assimilating the full value of the acquisitions challenging.

Roberta Katz was positive about Netscape's acquisition strategy, but she admitted that it "has slowed us down in some respects." People also criticized specific acquisitions, such as InSoft as "just plain stupid" and a fiasco that "never amounted to anything." Even the Collabra purchase, which brought some great people into the company, was of questionable value in retrospect because Collabra's technology was, in one manager's words, "totally proprietary" (i.e., not based on "open" industry standards, but tied to a specific platform, in this case Windows). As a consequence, Netscape had to delay the release of a client incorporating Collabra's functionality by a year. The company also turned to another vendor for its first electronic mail server. Two years later, Netscape deemphasized Collabra's focus on groupware. In the end, paying more than $100 million seems like a steep price for the short-lived strategy and a half dozen very good people, several of whom had left the company by mid-1998.[53]

Nonetheless, two of Netscape's acquisitions could still prove instrumental to its future. At the end of 1997, Kiva and Actra brought Netscape technology and management expertise that fit squarely in the heart of the company's future enterprise strategy. Kiva based its high-end application server on open, Internet protocols, and the products fit directly into the Netscape product line. Actra provided Netscape with a high-performance electronic commerce suite that supported high-volume buying and selling online. Together, the two additions had the potential to jump-start Netscape's ability to provide mission-critical intranet and extranet services. Application servers and electronic commerce businesses may not have had an immediate impact on Netscape's revenues or profits—the market for these products was just emerging—but the fit was powerful, and the deals had significant upside potential.

Leverage Partners to Build a Platform

The purpose of the acquisitions was to bring critical skills and technologies in-house. But even if they had succeeded to the fullest extent, Netscape could not have afforded to develop internally all the software that made the Internet, intranets, and extranets run. Instead, Netscape needed partners—partners to write software (independent software vendors, or ISVs) that would plug into Netscape's products, partners to develop content and Web sites (independent content providers, or ICPs) that would take advantage of Netscape's latest technologies, and partners to help distribute Netscape products and make them ubiquitous.

Independent Software Vendors (ISVs). From the start, Netscape relied on outside developers to create complementary products that extended the functionality of Navigator, Communicator, and the Netscape servers. In March 1995, Netscape introduced its Client Application Programming Interface with the beta release of Navigator 1.1. These platform-specific interfaces allowed third-party applications to control the browser. Similarly, the Server Application Programming Interface, which debuted at the same time, allowed developers to customize and extend core server functionality. Intuit was the first major company to take advantage of the new application programming interfaces by integrating Navigator into its market-leading personal finance software, Quicken 96. Customers ordered more than a million copies of Quicken 96 before Intuit even released the product.[54] Netscape also reached similar agreements with Aurum Software (sales force automation), Addison Wesley Interactive (educational multimedia products), and Corel (office productivity suites).

Netscape's plug-in API debuted with Navigator 2.0 in October 1995. By writing to the API, developers could create "plug-ins" or small applications that smoothly integrated multimedia files, like interactive graphics, with images and text. By the middle of the year, developers had released 60 plug-ins and had 70 more in development. Increasingly, the focus was on browser extensions with corporate applications, such as document publishing, spreadsheets, and computer-aided design. Netscape also held developer conferences and offered marketing support to the 12,000 developers working on applications that enhanced its platform. In September 1996, Netscape also unveiled AppFoundry, a collection of reusable business applications and tools developed by ISVs that users could download for free from the Netscape Web site.[55]

By the end of 1996, the company had formalized support for developers within the organization. As Andreessen reported, "We have had roughly 70 people [in developer relations] in the last nine months or so. And we've promoted someone to be in charge of developer relations, so that's an ongoing process for us. We still don't have nearly enough people or enough bandwidth there to cover our weak spot, so we try to target that constituency and build on it. It is something we're in the process of doing right now."[56] Danny Shader, another Collabra graduate, was in charge of this process as the head of developer relations between mid-1996 and early 1998. Armed with an MBA from Stanford Business School, Shader

had worked at Go (one of Mike Homer's former employers) before signing up with Eric Hahn. At Netscape, Shader's strategy was to hire "technology evangelists" who could build the technical notes and supporting
materials that developers required.

Shader noted that Netscape's challenge in developer relations was iden-
tical to Microsoft's: "We had to figure out how to get from one-to-one
[relationships] to one-to-many." By 1997, 35,000 to 40,000 ISVs were
writing for the Netscape platform. One of the keys to providing them with
adequate support was the same solution Netscape had used successfully in
other contexts in the past—go to the Web. Shader's team significantly
expanded the DevEdge program, a Web site extranet dedicated to developers that they "tried to populate with as much online information [as
possible]." To augment the marketing side of developer relations, Netscape also opened an online store in July 1997. Netscape Software Depot
by software.net, as it became known, offered third-party products for the
Netscape platform.

Independent Content Providers (ICPs). ICPs were just as crucial for Netscape as ISVs. The key to Andreessen's vision of making the browser into
a universal interface for the Web was to have independent content
providers optimize their Web sites for Netscape's products. Just as
Microsoft had gained enormous power over the computer industry by
encouraging ISVs to write and optimize their applications for Windows,
realizing Andreessen's vision required ICPs to optimize their content for
Netscape browsers and servers. In fact, one of the company's most brilliant moves had been to push Web sites to display buttons declaring, "This
site best viewed using Netscape Navigator version X." These notices did
more than advertise Navigator—they led directly to Netscape's download
page. As more and more users began to use Navigator, the incentives to
optimize for the Netscape platform increased, and the next turn of the vir-
tuous circle began.

Netscape also built heavily on its relationships with content providers
in unveiling new browser releases. At the launch of Navigator 3.0 in
August 1996, the company announced a long list of partners, including
Amazon.com, CBS Sports, CNN Interactive, and Disney, who had agreed
to support Navigator's latest features. In addition, Netscape matched
Microsoft's promotion of Internet Explorer 3.0 by bundling trial access to
a number of sites that usually charged users a fee. Netscape's partners
included the Gartner Group, *The New York Times,* Quote.com, and
SportsLine USA; Microsoft's list featured ESPNet Sports Zone, Investors
Edge, MTV Online, and *The Wall Street Journal.*[57] Netscape's twist was

that it allowed its partners to deliver interactive Web pages to users' e-mail boxes through a program called Inbox Direct. This innovation allowed Netscape to leverage a feature—the ability to e-mail Web pages with Netscape Navigator—that Microsoft had yet to match.

One year later, ICPs played an important role in launching Netcaster, the push technology incorporated into Communicator 4.0. As Mike McCue, the head of the Netcaster team, recalled, "When we went out and showed the first rickety, horrible prototype of Netcaster, content providers signed up instantly! Within a matter of days, people were creating content for Netcaster and signing up for the press release. Within a couple of weeks, we had signed up something like 30 or 40 companies. And these were the biggest media companies in the world—Time Warner, Disney, CNN." McCue believed that, by optimizing content for Netcaster, Netscape's media partners helped to create an "aura of leadership" around the firm. And as a bonus, he noted, "We actually made money, which helped us out in the quarter."

Leveraging Partners for Distribution. Netscape initially made a splash by distributing millions of copies of its products over the Web. Netscape also built a number of partnerships with hardware suppliers in order to extend the company's reach. In addition, as Netscape moved into the enterprise market, systems integrators and value-added resellers (VARs) became increasingly important elements of the company's distribution system. The growing complexity of its products meant that Netscape could no longer deliver them like shrink-wrapped boxes. Instead, customers required help customizing and installing client/server systems.

Netscape executives took pride in the company's partnerships with distributors. Ram Shriram, then the vice president for OEM sales, told us in August 1997, "We've built a network of partnerships that, to this day, is the single most important part of our sales and marketing strategy, without which we cannot continue our growth or build standards." In particular, PC manufacturers had an important role in Netscape's strategy from the very first. In Shriram's words, the driving goal had been, "Pre-load clients everywhere and pre-load servers everywhere." In November 1994, Netscape concluded its first OEM deal with Digital Equipment Corporation. Digital agreed to distribute Netscape's Web servers on its OSF and NT platforms. In addition, it licensed 600,000 copies of Netscape Navigator for resale. Digital would not only package Netscape's software with the systems it sold; it would also provide documentation, consulting services, and support worldwide.

The Digital deal was important as a vote of confidence in the fledgling firm. Customers who were unwilling to buy from a relative unknown were much more likely to adopt a product backed by Digital's experienced services organization.[58] Soon, other prominent OEMs added their seal of approval to Netscape's product line. Silicon Graphics signed up in January 1995, IBM joined in October 1995, and Hewlett Packard in early 1996. In addition, Netscape concluded OEM deals with a number of software firms, including Lotus; Novell; SCO; SunSoft, the software subsidiary of Sun Microsystems; and Sybase. In Shriram's words, Netscape had a "clean sweep" in the UNIX world.

The UNIX world deals focused on high-powered operating systems for corporations. A separate set of OEMs, led by companies like Compaq, Gateway, and Dell, dominated the market for personal computers. Prior to the release of Windows 95, Netscape was essentially able to charge PC manufacturers whatever it wanted for the browser. Following the Windows 95 launch, as Shriram related, this "got progressively harder to do." With Microsoft giving its browser Internet Explorer (IE) away for free in Windows 95, Netscape looked for clever solutions that could offer revenue to OEMs if they bundled Navigator as well as IE. Shriram described one form of the "bounty model":

> We would let these people put the client on their hard disk. We still won't pay [them] for it. They do it because it's a popular application. The deal is that users would come to the Netscape site, where we offered a series of ISPs [Internet service providers] to whom they could link up, and each ISP got a Web page to talk about the virtues of their service. We then got a bounty from the ISP. We sometimes shared the bounty with them [the PC vendors] and, sometimes where it didn't make sense, we didn't share the bounty.

Despite creative bounties and other programs, the PC manufacturer channel proved difficult for Netscape. The combination of Microsoft's existing relationships with OEMs, the bundling of Internet Explorer with Windows 95, and improvements in IE, made it harder and harder to sell Navigator or Communicator to PC manufacturers.

Netscape's Partnering Strategy in Perspective

Despite an impressive array of programs to build relationships, Netscape developed a very weak reputation as a partner. Prior to 1998, the consensus inside and outside the company was that Netscape was hard to work with, that it was often insensitive to partner requirements, and that the company had failed to build important relationships that could create greater leverage over time. Although there is evidence that Netscape is getting much better, there are important lessons to learn from Netscape's experience.

Partnering Philosophy. Marc Andreessen drove Netscape's attitude toward partnerships. When we first asked him to describe his approach toward alliances, Andreessen told us, "Scott McNealy is fond of saying the only strategic relationship is the purchase order. We don't quite believe that, but it's close." We pushed Andreessen on this philosophy during our May 1998 interview:

> "Partners" is a loaded term. Just partnering with somebody, I guarantee failure. It doesn't matter who you are. Every company operates according to its own self-interest all the time. So having a partnership or a partner relationship without having some economic benefit flowing one way or the other is nothing—it doesn't count. If you have an economic relationship, then you're a customer. So the question to ask is not, "How do we work with partners?" The question is, "How do we work with customers?" Because, when we do a deal with Excite for $70 million, they're now a customer of ours. . . . The reason that Yahoo! is going to say we're a terrible partner is because we never had any relationship with them whereby we would economically benefit as they benefited. The reason that Excite is going to say we're a great partner to work with is because we both will make money. It's not because of partnership—it's because of customer relationships.

For a start-up hungry for cash, Andreessen's philosophy was understandable. But in a highly competitive and fast-moving world, Andreessen's approach toward partnerships was risky. While Netscape expected its partners to be customers, its competitors, particularly Microsoft, took a very different approach. As a consequence, most companies that provided software, content, and PCs lived in fear of Microsoft, but many preferred to work with Bill Gates rather than Marc Andreessen. At least in part, this was because Microsoft had the luxury of investing in long-term relationships without trying to extract cash from potential partners. In fact, the situation was usually the reverse: Microsoft was often happy to throw money at companies if they were aligned with its interests. As Halsey Minor, CEO of one of the largest content providers on the Web, told us in September 1997:

> I may not always like working with Microsoft. I may not like the market power that they have. But Netscape is always trying to extract money out of

the marketplace, and they have not had a cohesive strategy for working with content partners and helping make them more successful on the Web. Netscape tries to suck every dollar they can out of the Web. . . . As a result, there is a lot of antipathy toward Microsoft but, in many quarters, there's a war against Netscape.

Lack of Resources. Beyond the problems created by its partnering philosophy, Netscape faced a genuine dilemma when it came to partnerships. It was a small company overwhelmed by its own success and requests for attention. Most Netscape managers chalked up their weaknesses in developer relationships to simple overload. The company was growing so fast that people felt bombarded with requests every day. There simply were not enough people and time to respond to all the overtures and to nurture all the partnerships. Roberta Katz explained in 1997:

> Early on, a lot of people got upset with us because they couldn't get the attention here that they wanted. Because our name was in the paper every day and because every other thing you thought about was Netscape, there was this presumption, understandable but just incorrect, that we had oodles of people. This is the same time that we were growing from 200 people to 2,000. You can only devote so many people to dealing with partners, all of whom take a lot of time.

Alex Edelstein told a similar story, noting that Netscape "couldn't support all of the newsgroup messages that people were posting. We couldn't take all the meetings at the various levels with all of the companies that wanted to come talk to us and wanted to do deals. And when we did do a deal, we weren't able to support it." As an example, Edelstein cited the case of JavaScript, Netscape's scripting language for the Web. Netscape's practice was to announce the technology, "get something out there on the Net," and then move most of its developers onto the next project, leaving a handful behind to finish up the work. Netscape did not provide "even basic levels of service," which contrasted sharply to Microsoft's long-term approach with developers. "At Microsoft," he noted, "it was taken for granted that you'd never give an API to a developer or partner without having good documentation for it. The documentation might be draft form, but it would still be there."

A number of Netscape insiders commented that the pace of company life was the primary reason for their inability to respond adequately to partner demands. As one former manager explained, "Relationships and partnering take time, focus, and dedication. It's like with your wife. If you don't spend any time with her, she knows you're not a partner. . . . I don't think it was done as deceitful or malice, but it was Internet time and the speed of growth of the company."

But as Intel chairman Andy Grove pointed out, the failure to devote resources to building relationships reflected a choice about priorities. The truth was that partnerships ranked relatively low on Netscape's totem pole. Like many other companies, Intel tried to work with Netscape on several occasions, but Grove found it difficult to get the smaller firm's attention. When we suggested that this might have been due to Netscape's lack of resources, Grove used a simple metaphor to explain why this was not an adequate explanation:

> It's like the following situation: Imagine I'm late to a meeting, and I got caught in traffic. And I'm late to a meeting again, and I got caught in traffic. And I'm late to a meeting a third time, and again, I got caught in traffic. You are sure that I'm telling you the truth—I got caught in traffic—but I never adjusted my departure time for the traffic. So who is at fault?

The Danger of Arrogance. Even as Barksdale committed more and more resources to support independent software and content providers, as well as other partners, Netscape's ambitions often exceeded its ability to execute. By trying to do everything—from building the next great platform for software development to making its products ubiquitous—Netscape risked becoming a jack of all trades and master of none. Yet the company's management and employees had such supreme confidence in themselves during the first few years that they developed a reputation for arrogance. In retrospect, some of them admitted that this had been more than just a question of image. "I think we were too arrogant," commented Alex Edelstein, "The bottom line is that Netscape thought that its stuff was so good, it was enough to just put it out there."

Edelstein was not alone in identifying arrogance as a problem that dogged Netscape in its first few years. Karen Richardson, a Collabra alumna and former VP of strategic accounts, believed that it reflected a lack of discipline within the rapidly growing firm. For example, an important discipline, which Netscape lacked until 1998, was the willingness to say no:

> A lot of the arrogance had to do with the way partners, customers, and potential partners were treated. Everything from do you show up to a meeting on time to attitude. There was also a lack of discipline around telling people what you won't do. . . . We never really had the discipline of being honest and saying, "No, we are not going to do that." So there were

a lot of frustrated customers and partners of Netscape over the years that just felt like they were continually strung along. It's just that Netscape probably tried to do too many things.

Barksdale felt deeply concerned about the danger of arrogance. It was clear that the very thought of it frustrated him. A former senior Netscape manager told us, "One of Jim Barksdale's early pick-ups was that Netscape was an arrogant company. This crosses all realms of partnerships: content providers, Sun, Oracle, whoever. And Jim didn't like to hear that. To his credit, he went about asking questions like, 'Who is arrogant here? What are we doing that is arrogant?' And Jim would then try to personally not be arrogant."

Nonetheless, virtually all our interviews outside the company and many of our interviews inside Netscape confirmed that the perception of arrogance was widespread. This perception emerged fairly early in the company's history. In March 1996, at Microsoft's Professional Developer's Conference, Steve Jobs, a cofounder of Apple and no lover of Microsoft (at least at the time), complained, "Microsoft is treating NeXT the way you'd expect Netscape to treat an independent software vendor. And Netscape is treating NeXT as you'd expect Microsoft to treat us."[59] Jobs's anger meant more than a few days of bad publicity for Netscape. He also threw his support behind Microsoft's ActiveX technology, which competed with the Java platform Netscape endorsed.

We heard numerous direct accounts of Netscape's poor relations with developers and independent content providers. The common theme was that Netscape managers often did not listen well and were slow to respond to partner requests. One former Netscape executive gave us a telling example:

> In 1996, Macromedia came to us and said, "We want to really work with you on developing new multimedia technology." Together, we came up with the idea that they would build something called Fireworks, a set of multimedia Java classes [reusable components] that we would agree to ship. They went off and did a lot of work on Fireworks, and we forgot about it. There was poor communication on both sides. . . . There was poor execution on just what was the nature of the understanding. They ended up putting effort into something that they probably couldn't afford. [Subsequently, Jim Barksdale met with Macromedia's chairman, Bud Colligan, and] they were just incredibly unhappy. Colligan said something like, "We thought you were going to use this. We thought you were going to promote it. We thought you were going to do all this great stuff with it." Jim and I looked at each other and said we'd go back and do some research. No one on our side feels like they made any commitment. It was

like they never talked with us. They didn't do this, and they didn't do that. You end up with another company who is very unhappy with us.

Even some computer makers found Netscape to be arrogant. During our March 1998 interview with Michael Dell, the chairman of Dell Computer, he seemed genuinely puzzled by Netscape. Dell was surprised that Netscape would take sides against PC companies like his own. He also suggested that Netscape had made little effort to understand Dell's business model:

> Netscape was surprisingly arrogant for a company of their size and age and didn't seem to aggressively pursue our business. It was just a number of little things that sent the wrong signal to us. They didn't appear to engage us very heavily in pursuing our business. And there's a complicating factor here: A couple of years ago, Netscape started to align itself with Oracle, IBM and Sun to support the network computer phenomenon, even though their bread and butter counted on the PC.

Captives of the Capital Markets. One very important explanation for Netscape's short-term focus, especially with partners like content providers, was its desire to meet Wall Street's high expectations. Although Andreessen and Barksdale originally wanted to set expectations low, their enthusiasm got the better of them. No one ever likes to admit that they cut corners to make their quarterly numbers. But when you have a high-flying stock and employee loyalty depends on maintaining and increasing the value of your company, the desire to meet Wall Street expectations can become overpowering. Halsey Minor believed that these expectations led Netscape to commit a number of shortsighted strategic mistakes. As an example, he cited Netscape's relationships with the major search engines, which paid a hefty premium to be featured on its NetSearch page. In Minor's words, Netscape's desire to "extract the maximum amount of cash" led it to ignore the big picture—how content providers could help Netscape in its battle with Microsoft:

> This is a small example, but they tried to extract all the money out of search engines [by charging them to appear on Netscape's site]. Next they said, "Great. Let's extract money out of all the content companies." So they launched a new page called "Netscape Destinations." Their idea was to force us to call them up and say, "We want on. We want on," and try to extract the maximum amount of cash. What I would have done for the search engines is I wouldn't have charged them a cent. I'd have made damn sure they were locked up for life as distributors of my product over the Web, and that they were supporting my feature sets. Microsoft can do that

because Microsoft doesn't need the money. But Netscape had allowed these analysts' expectations to be built into their business model, which has forced them to run around and keep cutting short-term deals all the time.

Mike Homer agreed that setting different expectations on Wall Street would have given the company much more freedom of action over the years. When we asked him what he would have done differently during his first four years at Netscape, his first response was:

> Set expectations right. The whole issue of why people think about criticizing Netscape is we let expectations get out of control. Let me tell you a different story of Netscape. Let's say that instead of $80 million in 1995, $345 million in 1996, and $540 million in 1997, we had . . . buried about $100 million on our balance sheet, which we could have done. Didn't quite grow as fast. Then it would have been the $80 million and $250 million, and we would have been swimming in money in 1997. There would have been no issues. People would still be looking at us on a great growth trajectory. And so managing expectations was a huge issue because when people said to us, "Oh, you did $345 million. Could you do $700 million next year?" we kind of said, "Well, I guess so. Let's go for it." And so now, based on where we are, as a $500 million company, people are really disappointed.

Ironically, the original Netscape strategy had been to set low expectations. As Andreessen told students at MIT in 1996, "At the time we went public, Jim [Barksdale] was quoted in *The Wall Street Journal* . . . [as saying] 'If we make a profit, it will have been a mistake.' And the reason was he wanted to make sure that people's expectations were set appropriately low. You don't want to get too far ahead in terms of people's expectations, or you're going to get whacked really hard."[60] Yet, as often happens, management got carried away with their success and promised more than they could deliver.

Netscape as a Partner in the Future

By 1998, Netscape had put significant energy and resources into improving the support it could offer other developers, content providers, and PC manufacturers. Danny Shader, who was in charge of developer relations during much of the period of hypergrowth, believed that Netscape had grown up over the last few years. Partnerships had been "really, really painful" for Netscape in the past, he observed, but "over the year and a half [I was in the job] I went from hearing that Netscape was arrogant and impossible to hearing significantly less about that particular problem." In part, this was due to Netscape's success in bringing a number of people who understood partnerships onboard. The Kiva acquisition was particularly important in this regard.

Skip Glass, a former Kiva employee, took over developer and OEM relations from Danny Shader and Ram Shriram in 1998. While the historical goal of this group had been to "get new revenue from new sources,"[61] Glass's new assignment was to build relationships. He began by borrowing a number of tricks from his 10 years at IBM. For example, he created different tiers of partners, who would get different levels of service, and created product-specific teams to add more expertise to partner interactions. According to Glass, one of his primary objectives was "to reset expectations" and make sure that Netscape no longer would try to be all things to all people. "One of the more important things," noted Glass, is "that we are being much more cognizant of what we can and cannot do. So we are not signing up contracts when we don't have engineers already allocated to deliver against the contract."

Glass also changed internal incentives to align the organization with a partnership strategy. He assigned individual employees overall responsibility for particular relationships, giving them a direct interest in their partners' success. One of the major criticisms that we often heard about Netscape was that it tried to treat every partner like a customer, who should pay for the privilege of working with Netscape. As Skip Glass observed, "If you have a compensation plan that gives incentives [for people to extract cash from potential partners], that's what will happen. But, if you have a comp plan that gives incentives to sell through on the partner's hardware platform, or sell through [in a way] that's in line with your partner's success, that will lead to a different kind of behavior. This has been true since the beginning of 1998."

Although Netscape was just beginning its new approach to partnerships in mid-1998, the company's strategy, incentives, and organizational requirements finally seemed to be coming into alignment. It is easy to forget that Netscape was only four years old, and that some of the tougher problems of managing on Internet time do not always get solved on Internet time. Even CNET CEO Halsey Minor, one of Netscape's toughest critics, believed that Netscape was getting better and would be a more attractive company to work with in the future. As Minor told us in May 1998:

> My problem with Netscape, going way back, was that they never really knew, day to day, the direction of their strategy. As a result, it was very difficult to understand how you work with them. Chasing the revenue is not

always a strategy, at least not a long-term strategy in and of itself. In the past, they had no strategy on the Web other than to figure out how to make money. Now, they do have a strategy, and that clear strategy is to build an asset that will become a portal on the World Wide Web. For instance, my company, CNET, is now their computing channel. In this context, it is far easier to get a deal done in certain areas with Netscape today because it's very clear what they want to do. They want to aggregate people, and they want to look a lot like Yahoo!, Excite, Snap, and others. . . . I might disagree with their strategy, but I'll tell you—it's a heck of a lot nicer knowing where they stand, and it does make them a lot easier to work with.

Minor's comments remind us that growing a company on Internet time requires more than a vision, experienced managers, a flexible organization, and partnerships. If we focus solely on these factors, which are largely under a start-up's control, it is easy to lose sight of the importance of the competitive environment. It is not enough for managers to have a vision for the future. They must also formulate a strategy for dealing with competitors that will give their vision a chance to prevail. In the next chapter, we discuss Netscape's approach to strategy and its evolution over time as the company's mission changed from breaking out of a pack of competitors to surviving a war with Microsoft, the most powerful software company in the world.

Chapter Three

COMPETITIVE STRATEGY

*Using Judo to Turn an Opponent's
Strength into Weakness*

I N FOUR BRIEF YEARS, Netscape management confronted the full array of challenges of competing on Internet time: sudden shifts in technologies and markets, races for market share driven by network effects, the convergence of different industries, and head-to-head battles between start-ups and industry giants. In 1994 and 1995, Netscape's most important strategic objective was to break away from the pack of other would-be browser firms. One year later, the company had to find a way to survive a life-or-death struggle with Microsoft.

In this chapter, we examine Netscape's solution to these problems, an approach we call "judo strategy." We also discuss Microsoft's use of judo techniques in its early competition with Netscape. The purpose of judo strategy is to turn an opponent's strength into weakness. Just like the sport of judo, the "art of hand-to-hand fighting in which the weight and efforts of the opponent are used to bring about his defeat," judo strategy exploits "techniques [that] are generally intended to turn an opponent's force to one's own advantage rather than to oppose it directly."[1] In the world of business, we use the term "judo strategy" to describe a particular way of competing. A judo approach to competition emphasizes the use of *movement* and *flexibility* to avoid unwinnable confrontations and the use of *leverage* to undermine competitors' strengths by turning their historical advantages (installed base, high existing prices, established distribution channels, etc.) against them. Whenever possible, judo strategy seeks to blunt an opponent's will or ability to strike back while avoiding head-to-head struggles with larger, potentially superior firms.

Netscape's intense competitive battles in its first four years demonstrate the power and limitations of judo strategy. We believe that the following principles capture the fundamentals of judo strategy and illuminate the twists and turns of the strategic contest between Netscape and Microsoft:

- *Move rapidly to uncontested ground in order to avoid head-to-head combat.*
- *Be flexible and give way when attacked directly by superior force.*
- *Exploit leverage that uses the weight and strategy of opponents against them.*
- *Avoid sumo competitions, unless you have the strength to overpower your opponent.*

THE CONCEPT OF JUDO STRATEGY

In formulating the concept of judo strategy, we initially took inspiration from work in the field of industrial organization. This branch of economics has long focused on issues such as how market leaders respond when new firms enter their terrain. Writing in the early 1980s, two economists, Judith Gelman and Steven Salop, coined the phrase "judo economics" to describe a strategy that would induce a large incumbent to accommodate the entry of a new player. Gelman and Salop argued that, by making a credible commitment to remain small, a new entrant could render retaliation more costly for the incumbent than it was worth. In other words, a small firm could "[turn] its rival's large size to its own advantage" by presenting the incumbent with a choice between ceding a small slice of its market and spoiling the market by competing aggressively for every last point of share.[2]

While the judo economics literature[3] inspired our thinking, we believe that judo strategy is a much broader idea. Indeed, managers in a variety of settings have employed judo-like techniques for decades. Following the lead of Volkswagen in the 1960s, Toyota and Nissan in the 1970s, for example, adopted a judo-type strategy to build beachheads in the United States against the much larger General Motors, Ford, and Chrysler. Rather than attack U.S. firms head-on, Toyota and Nissan went after the subcompact car, the least profitable segment of the market. None of the big three wanted to introduce low-margin subcompacts and risk customers switching away from their high-margin big cars. Management at GM, Ford, and Chrysler decided that accommodation was better than fighting. In other words, ceding the unprofitable low end to the Japanese seemed a better alternative than cannibalizing existing sales and investments.[4]

Similarly, in 1992, Kiwi International Airlines had to devise a strategy for entry into the airline business without provoking retaliation from the airline giants, such as United, American, or Delta. According to CEO Robert Iverson, Kiwi adopted a classic judo-strategy move by offering low prices and limited capacity: "We designed our system to stay out of the way of large carriers and to make sure they understand that we pose no threat. . . . Kiwi intends to capture, at most, only 10 percent of any one market—or no more than four flights per day."[5] As long as Kiwi had no more capacity than 10 percent of a market and no obvious ambitions to expand, Iverson believed that it was not in the interest of the major airlines to match prices and undermine their existing business. As he explained, "It is absolutely axiomatic in the smaller airline business that if you stay in your niche, you're successful. If you get out, you're out of business."[6]

Sega employed another variant of judo strategy in its battle against Nintendo.[7] At the end of the 1980s, Nintendo was the dominant force in handheld video games. It had captured more than 90 percent of the market for 8-bit systems and sold 40 million copies of the Super Mario Bros. game series. Sega Enterprises, a successful manufacturer of arcade games, had been unable to crack the market for 8-bit handheld systems in the United States. However, it had better luck with a 16-bit system named Genesis. After introducing Genesis in late 1989, Sega had the 16-bit market to itself for two critical years. During this period, Sega's Sonic the Hedgehog became even more popular than Nintendo's Mario. Nintendo delayed bringing out a competing system until September 1991 because it was reluctant to cannibalize its 8-bit franchise. Indeed, Sega priced its product at a relatively high level, one effect of which was to reduce the threat it posed to Nintendo's 8-bit market. This reinforced Nintendo's incentives to cede the 16-bit market, at least for a while.

While these examples demonstrate that judo approaches can apply to a wide variety of industries, we believe that the principles of judo strategy, which emphasize quick movement, flexibility, and leverage, are particularly well suited for competing on Internet time. Not only does the Internet compress time and create a great deal of uncertainty, but many competitive battles on the Internet are "winner-take-all" struggles. If firms are slow to build market positions, they could be locked out of markets for years or decades. In addition, the rapid obsolescence of technology demands high degrees of flexibility. Irreversible commitments down a single path can be suicidal in Internet technologies; there are simply too many rapid-fire innovations and too many unknowns. Finally, the Internet is breaking down traditional industry barriers, wiping out historical barriers to entry, and thrusting start-ups into head-to-head competition with well-established firms. This is true across the board, from Netscape's struggles with Microsoft to Amazon.com's fight with Barnes & Noble or eToys's battle with Toys"R"Us. In these turbulent environments, traditional strategic analyses of core competencies or industry structure will rarely solve strategy problems. Change is simply too rapid and not always predictable: Yesterday's core competency is tomorrow's core rigidity.[8] In this world, judo strategy can be one of the most powerful tools available to managers.

Netscape executed brilliantly many of the core principles of judo strategy, especially in its earliest days. As a start-up, Netscape used *movement* to avoid head-to-head struggles with superior force, especially from competitors in the browser market that had a head start. Where it did attack larger competitors, Netscape specifically chose market segments where it perceived the opponents to be relatively weak and where the newest technology offered customers the highest long-run payoffs. Netscape also learned the art of *flexibility:* Like a good judo master, rather than adhere rigidly to a predetermined path, it ultimately learned to bend to superior force and chose to "embrace and integrate" Microsoft's technology in addition to its own. But most important, Netscape exploited *leverage* by attacking competitors in ways that made it difficult for them to retaliate in kind. In particular, Microsoft's unswerving commitment to Windows allowed Netscape to define itself as the only true "cross-platform" and "open" standard. The last thing Microsoft wanted to do was to make all platforms, such as UNIX, OS/2, or a Java-based operating system or browser, equal partners on the Internet.

We argue in this chapter that, for all of Netscape's skill at judo strategy, it has not been able to parlay those skills into a surefire recipe for long-term success. In part, this has been a problem of execution: The company was not universally proficient at judo techniques or in some key areas of technology strategy and operations, as we discuss in chapters 4 and 5. In addition, at times, Netscape went head-to-head with Microsoft, an approach we describe as sumo strategy. Unlike in a judo match, where the smaller player tries to avoid engaging a bigger and stronger competitor head-on, Netscape occasionally attacked Microsoft and tried to throw it out of the ring. Netscape also discovered some of judo strategy's limitations. Once a company becomes a leader in its field, it becomes increasingly vulnerable to judo moves. In fact, Netscape's browser business and portions of its enterprise strategy have become victims of a superior judo master. We will argue later in this chapter that Bill Gates was a brilliant practitioner of judo strategy and, in many arenas, Gates and Microsoft turned the tables on Netscape. This is why we believe that the moves and countermoves of Netscape and Microsoft illustrate the power of judo strategy for competing on Internet time.

PRINCIPLE *Move rapidly to uncontested ground to avoid head-to-head combat.*

Build a Philosophy Around Using Movement to Avoid Confrontations

From the company's earliest days, Netscape senior management espoused the virtues of using quickness and agility to avoid head-to-head confrontations with Microsoft and the other big guns of the software industry. For CEO Jim Barksdale, the importance of moving rapidly and choosing favorable terrain was more than a strategy—it was a deeply embedded philosophy about how to run an upstart company. Netscape was a minnow facing a whale, and no one was better than Barksdale at fighting these types of battles. He had built his entire career on creating Davids in the land of Goliaths. As chief information officer, and later chief operating officer, at Federal Express, he lived with the potential wrath of UPS and Airborne Express. As chief operating officer at McCaw Cellular, he faced a constant threat from AT&T and the regional Bell operating companies. Barksdale drew lasting lessons from these experiences. As he told us in the summer of 1997, "How did FedEx compete with the Airbornes and UPSs when they got started? The small company has disadvantages and it has advantages. How did the British defeat the Spanish Armada? Because they had smaller, faster, more flexible ships."

Being fast and changing the terms of battle were fundamental principles of Barksdale's strategic philosophy. Barksdale believed strongly that competing on the basis of speed and flexibility gave smaller companies a natural edge:

> I learned, when we were at Federal Express and we were small, competing with much bigger, more established, longer-term companies, that there are certain advantages to being small and quick on your feet . . . don't assume that all advantages go to the larger company. The larger company typically has more difficulty in moving rapidly. Their people are not as fresh and ready to do battle. They tend to have many other irons in the fire that they have to worry about.[9]

By contrast, Barksdale believed that Netscape was geared up to advance rapidly and turn on a dime:

> I don't know how fast this thing is going to grow; I don't know how fast it's supposed to grow. I know that if we get too introspective or think too much about the lessons we've learned in the past, wherever you're from in this company, you will probably cause the group to slow down. So what we

try to do is to run it on a very closed-end set of targets, a very closed-end set of objectives, and a very closed-end set of product releases, and then move again. It is like the marine infantry standing orders: Shoot, move, and communicate.

Barksdale, however, never let movement become an end in itself. His goal was to ensure that Netscape fought battles on its own terrain, not in arenas where Microsoft or IBM had a natural advantage. Inside and outside the company, he was often quoted saying, in his characteristically colorful way, "In the fight between the bear and the alligator, the outcome is determined by the terrain." Another variant on his maxim was: "If Microsoft is a shark, we strive to be a bear and make sure the battle takes place not in the ocean but in the jungle."[10] More prosaically, Barksdale explained:

> Don't go head-on against a larger, more entrenched company across the board. It is a no-win deal—or it is a high-risk deal, although I am sure there have been some stories [where that has worked]. What we chose to do at Netscape was, we went against very specific sectors of our competitors' product lines: primarily their corporate buyers' e-mail and groupware software. That is a relatively smaller part of our competitors' products.[11]

Barksdale's philosophy of being quick, and avoiding head-on battles with entrenched competitors, deeply penetrated the organization, from sales and marketing to engineering and testing. Ram Shriram, who headed up OEM and Web site sales when we interviewed him in the summer of 1997, explained:

> We look at the lessons of history. We see what Novell [another Microsoft competitor] did. The last thing we want to do is to focus our energies on killing [Microsoft] because that's not possible. What we need to do is to make sure we focus on the space where we excel and find other spaces where we can excel and innovate and differentiate ourselves and constantly reinvent ourselves so that we can stay one step ahead of being roadkill.

We heard similar thoughts throughout the organization. Julie Herendeen, one of the first product managers at Netscape, put it another way: "The only way Netscape wins is when we take risks and do gutsy moves vis-à-vis Microsoft and we outflank them. And if we stop doing that, either from a marketing standpoint or a technology standpoint, if we become risk-averse, if we want to take the safe path, we're history." Rick Schell, then the head of client engineering, may have summed it up the best:

We recognized very early on that those folks [Microsoft] were going to be our number one competitor. Jim Clark and I talked about it when Jim interviewed me. Jim Barksdale and I talked about it when Jim Barksdale interviewed me, when he was a member of the board. "Who is the number one competitor?" "Microsoft." "How are you going to beat Microsoft?" "Get out there early, get out way ahead of them. Change the rules on them. Continuously change the rules on them." And that's no secret to them— they know we're doing it.

Move to New Products That Redefine the Competitive Space

One of the earliest examples of Netscape's proficiency in judo strategy was its move to redefine the commercial browser market in ways that neutralized its competitors' strengths. In 1994, interest in the Web was booming, with the number of Web sites more than quadrupling in the first six months of the year and more than tripling in the second half.[12] The phenomenon driving this growth was Mosaic, the point-and-click browser conceived by Marc Andreessen and his NCSA colleagues in early 1993. With its intuitive, button-based interface and integration of images with text, Mosaic became the "killer app" that made the Internet a mass medium. By the end of 1994, 2 million copies of Mosaic had been distributed, and the browser continued to proliferate at a rate of 100,000 copies per month.[13] For all its strengths, however, Mosaic was not an easy program to use. As one analyst put it, "Mosaic right now is a hacker's program. It's very, very buggy; you're kind of thrust into figuring things out. . . . There's a tremendous void for a commercial product that's well documented, easy to use, and won't crash."[14]

At the time, competition for the browser market was expected to be intense. In early 1994, NCSA began to offer licenses for Mosaic, with the first takers being InfoSeek, Quadralay, Quarterdeck Office Systems, the Santa Cruz Operation, and Spry. The price of the license, as of July, was $100,000 up front, and an additional five dollars per copy.[15] In August, Spyglass, an NCSA spin-off that had previously commercialized technology developed at the center, became NCSA's master licensee. By the fall, more than 10 million copies of Mosaic had been licensed to companies including Amdahl, Digital, Firefox, FTP Software, Fujitsu, IBM, NEC, and O'Reilly and Associates.[16] In December 1994, Microsoft joined their ranks.

In August 1994, the Seattle-based start-up Spry became the first company to market a commercial version of Mosaic. At least half a dozen non-NCSA–based browsers were also available, or in the works. In addition to Netscape's Navigator, the competitors included Cello, developed at Cornell; BookLink's InternetWorks; the MCC consortium's MacWeb; O'Reilly and Associates's Viola; and Frontier Technologies's WinTapestry. By early 1995, *PC Magazine* declared that 10 Web browsers were "essentially complete": AIR Mosaic 1.1 (Spry), Cello 1.01a, Enhanced NCSA Mosaic for Windows 1.02 (Spyglass), InterAp 26 (California Software), NCSA Mosaic 2.0, NetCruiser (Netcom), Navigator, Web Explorer (IBM), WinTapestry, and WinWeb (EINet). Three more contenders—InternetWorks, Explore OnNet Mosaic (FTP Software), and WebSurfer (Netmanage)—quickly followed.[17] In April 1995, *Internet World* counted 24 browsers, and by the end of the year, CNET had found 28 browsers worthy of review. Very few of these products, though, had any appreciable market share. Netscape's Navigator had already grabbed more than 60 percent of the market by February 1995, and by the spring of 1996, its share stood at 87 percent.[18] At the same time, Microsoft's Internet Explorer 2.0 had 4 percent of the market, leaving only 9 percent for the other contenders to share.

Netscape's first Web browser, Navigator 1.0, was a very good product compared to many of its competitors. It downloaded Web pages as much as 10 times faster than Mosaic. It allowed Web publishers to design more attractive documents by introducing a number of extensions to HTML, such as a tag for centering text. When used together with Netscape's server software, it promised to safeguard private information through encryption and server authentication. This package of features led reviewers to rate Netscape's browser, consistently, as one of the best products in an increasingly crowded field. *PC Magazine* named it an "Editor's Choice." *Network Computing* awarded it top honors in a six-product review. And after comparing "every major Web surf tool on the planet," *Internet World* found Navigator to be tied for first.[19]

But just having the proverbial better mousetrap was not enough to make Navigator the number-one browser in the world. Netscape was a latecomer to the market, having forfeited the first-mover advantage to Spry, and many of its competitors were close on features. It took several judo moves to help catapult Netscape to the top. First, Netscape moved the battle to unoccupied ground by defining its initial product differently from its commercial competitors. Most of the early products on the market offered a complete stack of Internet tools, including dial-up telephone access as well as a browser and electronic mail. Most developers assumed that consumers required products that would connect them to the Net and provide a full panoply of Internet services. But Netscape sidestepped its inexperience in these areas by offering a simple stand-alone browser, which was initially available only over the Net. While most of the other serious commercial browser contenders distributed their products through retail stores, Netscape focused on relatively sophisticated computer users who already had Internet connections and access to Internet tools.

Moving to redefine the competitive space gave Netscape an early edge that competitors found difficult to match. Like many other companies, first-mover Spry squandered its advantage by failing to meet Netscape's challenge in time. Following Netscape's entry into the market, Spry continued to focus on shrink-wrapped product suites. The Internet seemed so immature that Spry's managers assumed a complete retail solution was the only way to make money. Although they were hardly unaware of Netscape, they believed that the two companies could coexist. Alex Edelstein, Jim Barksdale's assistant in 1997, worked at Spry after leaving Microsoft and prior to joining Netscape. As he explained, "In the early stage, when I got there, it wasn't incredibly clear that there wasn't room for both of us. Netscape in April of '95 didn't have dial-up connectivity at all. So Netscape—even though it had the buzz—was still the province of people who already had a connection. We were in retail land, going through the channel with thousands of units."

Moving to Netscape's model would have violated Spry's basic business assumptions. By the time Spry was ready to make that shift, it was too late. CompuServe bought Spry, and Spry's browser ultimately became a casualty of the Netscape-Microsoft war. As Edelstein looked back on its brief history, he observed: "Spry acted remarkably quickly, and in some cases very astutely, to catch parts of the Internet wave. In the end, they could not evolve their model quickly enough. They were destroyed by Internet time and by the destruction of their business models." Edelstein credited Spry CEO Dave Poole with a strong sense of vision, describing him as "one of the earliest people to capture the browser as a powerful agent of change." Yet, on the strategic front, Poole ultimately fell short. Edelstein concluded: "There is a wonderful story to be written, a tragedy, about these companies that had the vision to form NetManage, FTP Software, Spry and had the vision to build this TCP/IP stuff in the early '90s, when no one else believed, and who almost all couldn't sustain [their businesses]."

Move to New Pricing Models That Competitors Will Not Emulate

The biggest challenge for any start-up is how to price your products. Too aggressive, and you risk leaving money on the table. Too high, and you risk alienating your customers and making yourself more vulnerable to retaliation by your competitors. If you match your competitors' pricing, you may not give your customers any reason to buy. But if you give your product away for free, most people just assume you are crazy. Particularly as a start-up, how do you make money and go public if you don't charge for it?

In the early debates on pricing at Netscape, the marketing team considered charging $99 for the browser and as much as $25,000 for its server software. Ultimately, Mike Homer, the new marketing chief, settled on $1,500 for the Communications Server, and $5,000 for the premium Commerce Server. More important, Netscape's clever pricing innovation was to create a model for browsers that Marc Andreessen described as "free, but not free." In an interview in mid-1995, Andreessen explained the thinking behind this approach:

> [Jim Clark] thought I was a little bit crazy. But we would give it away under specific terms, and to educational institutions for evaluation use. A lot of companies who are going to use it are going to pay for it because, among other things, they want to pay for it. Free software is usually more expensive in the long run for companies to use. It's not a major thing if you have a useful piece of software. It is not too dramatic to make it available to people who are going to pay for it anyway. In addition, we knew that we were going to be doing development in a number of areas and have a range of products. The Web browser was going to be one of these, so in a sense we gave away one so that people could see the others. The third aspect of it—again, an aspect that's pretty unique to the Internet—is we wanted to repeat what happens when you put tools into people's hands on a very broad scale because then they pick them up and do all kinds of great things with them that you would never have thought of.[20]

Getting volume fast meant making bold decisions on pricing. The question was: What did it really mean to offer a product that would be "free, but not free"? Todd Rulon-Miller, reflecting on his time as Netscape's head of sales, remembered an intense debate on this question:

> We had a staff meeting where Andreessen, Homer, and I, and everybody, were saying, What are we going to price this thing for? And we were going to price something for the browser, but Andreessen was arguing hard for free everywhere, only pay if they want to pay. And I was going, "Marc, nobody's going to want to pay. You have to have some teeth in your license to pay after 90 days or whatever." And Jim [Barksdale] was watching this Ping-Pong match and said frankly, "Todd, isn't your sales force in town

next week?" I said, "Yeah." He said, "Let's go in front of them and see what they think." [The sales force was] 30 or 40 guys at the time, not that big. We had this famous meeting, which Barksdale, to his credit, choreographed. He said, "Marc, you give [the big] picture to these guys. Homer, you give your two cents, and then Todd, you can end up with a summary, and we'll see how we vote here." And we had a real donnybrook because Andreessen was a big believer in download it off the Web site for free—that's what he did in college—and it'll all be made up in market share or something. And I kept saying, "Look, I'm a revenue hound. We have to have a good way to make money." That meeting . . . gave all the feedback to Jim. And Jim, at the end of it, as a good CEO did, said, "OK, we're going to have a tight license. Yep, it looks free optically, but it is not. Corporations have to pay for it. Maintenance has to be paid." We sales guys wrote it all down, and I said, "I got that. I can sell that."

The final policy was very creative. Netscape browsers were free for anyone to download on a 90-day trial basis, free for students and educational institutions, and $39 (later raised to $49) for everyone else. At the time, Netscape management had no illusions. Some people would pay after the trial period, and some wouldn't. In effect, the browser would be free. But if the name of the game was volume and market share, "free, but not free" offered the perfect solution.

Netscape could employ this technique successfully because it had two huge advantages compared to its competitors. First, Netscape's original business model anticipated that most of its sales revenue would come from servers, not browsers. And second, Netscape had a significant cost advantage over its rivals. By distributing its product over the Net, and writing the code from scratch, Netscape kept its variable costs close to zero. By comparison, virtually every other competitor at the time had relatively high variable costs in the form of assembling shrink-wrapped software, logistics, and dealer margins to the retailers. Moreover, most of Netscape's competitors (including Microsoft) had licensed technology from NCSA or Spyglass, NCSA's master licensee. While most licensees had to pay five dollars per copy shipped, Netscape escaped the licensing fees.

Consequently, Netscape was able to undercut its rivals on price, even when the browser was not free. As Rick Schell recalled, the company had been prepared for stiff competition. However, Netscape managers soon found that they had overestimated the threat they faced: "Early on, we were tactically worried about Spyglass because they were out trying to establish a similar size customer base, and they claimed that they had millions of customers. In fact, they had OEM licenses that we were also competing for, and they had probably licensed for shipment multiple millions of copies, but nobody was buying it." Instead, buyers were flocking to Netscape and its offer of a high-quality product at a low price.

A number of competitors did try to match Netscape by offering free browsers over the Net. But since most of them relied heavily on retail browser revenues, they had little incentive to push the free option aggressively. In offering versions of their products for free, they risked losing support in the retail channel. Moreover, in many cases, it was simply not in their mindset to give a product away. While free software was an important part of the ethos of the Web, it was an alien notion to most commercial developers. Eventually, of course, the virtues of Netscape's pricing model became too clear to deny. By then, however, for most of the company's competitors, it was too late. Alex Edelstein reflected on his experience at Spry:

> Basically, Spry was too dependent on selling software for revenue. Spry was smart enough to see the browser as an incredible tool, got on board very early, and figured out a very leveraged way to get into the market. But we still, even at the time I left [in July 1995], could not conceive of giving it away, making it a free download on the Net. . . . In the time I was there, we responded to Netscape by reducing our price consistently. We came up with some very innovative stuff where we would make our money by receiving kickbacks for sign-ups. We'd private label it, they'd distribute it, end-users could dial up with a floppy disk and get an ISP [Internet service provider] account, and we'd be a part of the user subscription revenue stream. So we were doing very creative things to try to get it distributed. But in hindsight, I chastise myself for not having the vision to say, "We really have to break the model here, and if we don't start giving away millions of these . . . " Basically, I couldn't see a winning strategy for Spry after a certain point.

Ironically, the strategy of "free, but not free" not only stymied Netscape's competitors, but it probably led to higher revenues than a policy of charging outright for the browser. As Mike Homer remembered, after the release of Navigator 1.0, "the phones are ringing off the hook, and people are paying money. The first quarter, we did $5 million in revenue."[21] "Free, but not free" led to large numbers of trials, and once corporations tried the browser, they were happy to pay Netscape's relatively low price. When Rick Schell reflected on this original strategy, he concluded, "'Free, but not free' was a brilliant stroke. We could charge for client products, but we could get the benefits of being free. . . . That was a no-brainer."

Move to New Methods of Distribution
That Avoid Competitors' Strengths

The battleground for software had been well developed since the emergence of the PC in 1980. Most companies distributed PC software through two channels: a computer OEM channel, where manufacturers like Compaq, Dell, and IBM preloaded software on their new computers; and the retail channel, which included computer and office supply retailers such as CompUSA or Staples, general consumer electronics retailers such as Circuit City, and specialized retailers such as Egghead. Firms gained an advantage in these channels if they had a strong, recognized brand name; a large, experienced sales force; and big co-op marketing budgets. Even more important, retail and OEM distribution depended on building and sustaining relationships over time. It was unusual for new players to break into these channels very quickly. Not surprisingly, the dominant firm in software distribution was Microsoft, with over 80 percent of the world's computers shipping with Microsoft software and Microsoft claiming the largest share of retail shelf space.

Similarly, the methodology for testing software played into the hands of the more established vendors. As we describe in more detail in chapters 4 and 5, traditional software development required significant testing, usually by professional QA engineers inside the company. Software firms also cultivated a carefully chosen external community of beta testers. In 1994 and 1995, observers generally believed that Microsoft had broken the mold by getting 400,000 people to test its new operating system, the forthcoming Windows 95. Testing and distribution went hand in hand. Unless products were high quality and well tested, OEMs and retailers would resist distributing them, since they were often called upon to support the products they sold. These dynamics reinforced Microsoft's stranglehold on PC software: Microsoft could offer more testing, more retailer and OEM support, and more direct support to consumers than any other software company in the world.

In a classic judo-strategy move, Netscape tried to avoid Microsoft's strength and move the battle to new terrain—in this case, the Web. Using the Internet and the Web as its primary distribution channel and as a source of beta testers opened up a new world for Netscape, changing the software paradigm. By posting early versions of beta software on its Web site, Netscape did not have to promise quality, reliability, or support—only a sneak preview into the latest and greatest software for cruising the Internet. Since the people downloading the software already had access to the Internet, they were also the type of people that would be happy to give feedback to Netscape. Relatively sophisticated users could download the product, test it, give the company feedback and, within a few weeks, download a new version and do it again.

Lou Montulli, one of the first Netscape employees (number 9), identified electronic distribution as one of the true galvanizing forces that helped catapult Netscape to its early dominant position:

> I think an incredibly important thing to talk about in this model of the Internet is electronic software distribution. . . . Of all the things that have revolutionized software development here in the last couple of years, that is probably the most galvanizing force because it means increased turn-around, just by orders of magnitude, so that we can release a beta and get immediate feedback. Our beta cycles are a couple of weeks long. That's unheard of. We get amazing amounts of feedback from millions of people and shake out all these bugs very quickly and turn it around.

Move to Emerging Terrain: Intranets and Extranets

While Netscape's innovative tactics offered many advantages, they often had a downside as well. For example, "free, but not free" made it unlikely that Netscape would ever make much money by selling browsers to consumers. Consequently, it needed to find a way to enter the corporate market without starting a war with giants like Microsoft. When Jim Barksdale came on board in January 1995, his solution to this dilemma was to focus the company's sales, marketing, and development efforts on intranets—networks inside corporations, based on Internet protocols.

Barksdale believed, perhaps erroneously, that Netscape had a good shot at dominating enterprise sales of software relying on the open Internet communications standards (TCP/IP). The corporate information systems and operations centers (i.e., the "back office") were areas in which Microsoft was relatively weak. In 1991, Microsoft had declared war on Novell, seeking to displace NetWare as the dominant network operating system. Yet after struggling for years to promote LAN Manager and early versions of Windows NT, Microsoft had barely made a dent in NetWare's installed base. As late as January 1997, NetWare continued to hold 55 to 60 percent of the installed base of corporate servers, with Windows NT held to 20 percent.[22]

Microsoft's real strengths were in the consumer and corporate desktop markets. Thanks to its dominance of the OEM channel and its ability to distribute its operating system on virtually every computer sold, Microsoft was the default choice for PC users. However, Barksdale believed that the corporate back office gave a nimble Netscape an opportunity to avoid Microsoft's dominance. As he told us in the summer of 1997:

> I don't care to compete across the product line of Microsoft. I don't care to compete with them in many spaces where they are entrenched, and certainly probably unassailable, certainly by Netscape. [Those areas are] . . . in the desktop-productivity applications, in operating systems, things that they do particularly well or have a lock on—nobody's going to get the operating system away from them. Every PC shipped in the world has embedded in it the Microsoft operating system with whatever version of Windows they care to sell. . . . But the point is, try not to compete where they're unassailable. . . . In the back-office cross-platform area, they do not have a profound market share. They don't have as much to bring to bear, and they're not as technologically advanced. They also don't have as much mindshare as they do on the individual, particularly the retail PC market, or the business PC market.

In 1995 and 1996, Netscape's strategy for exploiting this opportunity focused on developing intranet software that would compete with Microsoft BackOffice and Lotus Notes. Barksdale believed that these products fell far short of the commanding position that Microsoft had achieved in desktop operating systems. In 1997, however, the company's focus shifted to another emerging arena—extranets. As John Paul, a 22-year veteran of the software industry and general manager of the server division in 1998, explained, the extranet market represented uncontested terrain. In addition, he believed that this was an area in which Netscape's design philosophy gave it an extra edge:

> [We have] a network-services–centric view of the world, not an operating-system–centric view of the world. . . . We think the operating system is less and less important going forward [compared to] creating a network services infrastructure that is secure. The best way [to take advantage of this world] is to focus on extranets. If I want to build an extranet, I need to securely push my IS [information systems] infrastructure beyond the firewall. I can't assume NT is out there. . . . Even if a shop is committed to NT, [Microsoft doesn't] . . . have the solutions. For instance, directory services. Directory services are very important if you're going to build an extranet. You've got to be able to [exercise] control. . . . Who are you going to authenticate? Are they who they say they are? And what access are you going to give them to your extranet? [Microsoft] doesn't have an enterprise directory. They talk about Active Directory; they haven't shipped it. It's planned . . . maybe by the millennium.

The Dangers of Movement

Moving to the high ground and selecting the right battlefield are critical pieces of judo strategy and competing on Internet time. The focus on corporate intranets and extranets was a textbook example of Barksdale's philosophy about moving to terrain where you can potentially have an advantage. Yet too much movement is also dangerous. Constantly searching for uncontested territory can confuse customers and undermine a company's strategic credibility. Put another way, too much movement can look like inconsistency, as well as a lack of focus and a lack of commitment. In our interview with Andy Grove, the chairman of Intel, he likened Netscape to guerrilla fighters living off the land, never engaging the enemy (Microsoft) in direct combat. But Grove also warned against excess movement:

> The battle between Microsoft and Netscape can be described as a guerrilla war against an occupying army. Netscape originally was going after browsers, then going after consumers, and then they changed their strategy to corporations. Then they changed their strategy again. It's almost random. . . . Their advantage comes from their ability to live in the forest, live off the land, be very mobile, and do things that the professional army would never dream of doing. In this regard, Netscape has mounted a very substantial challenge to Microsoft. The guerrilla war has been very effective. The problem is, they're running out of space, munitions, and food. That's what they have done well. The first year to year and a half of their existence, they were seen as very successful.

Internet-addicted consumers may have thrived on the diet of constant change, which brought them several software upgrades each year. Customers investing millions of dollars in Netscape systems, however, were less pleased to hear a Netscape spokesperson blithely declare, "It's the Internet. We have a new business plan every six months."[23] From the perspective of Netscape's enterprise customers, constant movement did not just obscure the company's future strategic plans. It also raised questions about Netscape's ability to focus and execute in the short term. After leaving Netscape, Alex Edelstein suggested that these fears had some basis in fact:

> There was a reliance, which always scares the hell out of me when I hear it, [on the idea that] somehow we have to be more innovative. We have to change the rules. I'm going to strangle the next person who tells me, "We have to change the rules, Alex, that's the only way we are going to beat these guys." Because that is a very valuable tool, but you cannot use it as a crutch, as a replacement, as a surrogate for execution.

Edelstein concluded, "There were hundreds of things we did that were very clever. One of the problems was we just couldn't sustain them."

Another problem Netscape faced was, as Andy Grove suggested, a shrinking open frontier. No matter how fast Netscape moved, it seemed that Microsoft was close behind. As Netscape moved from browsers into intranets and extranets, Microsoft dogged its steps. Eventually, the company would be forced to stop running and take a stand.

Finally, at times, Netscape violated its own philosophy regarding the purpose of rapid movement. Buoyed by their early success, Netscape's managers seemed to believe that they could conquer the world, despite Barksdale's warnings about not swimming with the sharks in the ocean. During 1995 and 1996, Netscape often attacked Microsoft on heavily defended ground. A notable example was the company's effort to define the browser as an alternative operating system. Russell Siegelman, then general manager of Microsoft Network (MSN), remembered sharing a stage at a major industry event with Netscape chairman Jim Clark in the spring of 1995. During their joint session, Clark told the audience that Microsoft was the "Death Star" and that Netscape was developing a full-fledged networked operating system that would make Windows unnecessary and outdated.[24] Throughout the summer and fall of that year, Marc Andreessen was often quoted saying Netscape's technology would relegate Microsoft's operating system to nothing more than "a mundane collection of not entirely debugged device drivers."[25]

Beyond antagonizing statements, some of Netscape's strategic moves were more like the bear walking into the ocean rather than enticing Microsoft, the shark, into the jungle. Pioneering intranets, for example, was a great idea for Netscape as long as the company stayed focused on new applications of open network standards inside corporate firewalls. The decision to converge on e-mail and groupware, however, put Netscape into direct competition with Microsoft and IBM, two of the most dominant players in the history of information technology and two of the most feared competitors of all time. IBM's $3 billion acquisition of Lotus in 1995 signaled clearly IBM's strategic intent to own a large piece of the groupware and e-mail markets. In addition, Microsoft may not have been strong in e-mail and groupware when Netscape attacked, but Microsoft had been investing heavily since the early 1990s to make Microsoft Mail and Microsoft Exchange competitive with IBM's cc:Mail and Lotus Notes.

Rick Schell was one of the senior managers responsible for Netscape's intranet strategy. In retrospect, he admitted that the company's implementation of this move had been a mistake:

The vision was to enable people to do things that they couldn't do before, and you can argue that there weren't effective corporate mail systems that integrate everything. But there were corporate mail systems. You can argue that it's hard to get out and send Internet mail. But you can do it using existing mail technology. It's painful, but it's doable. So we weren't adding revolutionary new capabilities in those areas. We weren't bringing brand new things to the market. We didn't change the rules. And the only way you beat Microsoft is to change the rules. It's the only way. You've got to do it every time. They catch onto the last thing you did to them, and you've got to do something new. . . . That is the way to play judo with them. Right? You're still adapting; they can be great martial artists, and the last martial art you taught them, well don't do that anymore. Learn a new martial art.

PRINCIPLE   *Be flexible and give way when attacked directly by superior force.*

Using *movement* to find unoccupied or favorable terrain is only the first piece of a successful judo strategy. The second element of judo strategy is *flexibility.* At the metaphorical level, flexibility is illustrated by Aesop's "Fable of the Oak and the Reeds":

> An oak which hung over a river was uprooted by a violent storm of wind and carried down the stream. As it floated along it noticed some reeds growing by the bank, and cried out to them, "Why, how do such slight, frail things as yourselves manage to stand safely in a storm which can tear *me* up by the roots?
>
> "It was easy enough," answered the reeds; "instead of standing stubbornly and stiffly against it as you did, we yielded and bowed before every wind that blew, and so it went over us and left us unhurt."
>
> *It is better to bend than to break.*[26]

The same basic principle applies in judo strategy, and in the sport of judo. Effective judo competitors must be constantly prepared to respond to surprise moves. This is particularly important when competing on Internet time, due to the acceleration of technological change. However, the ability to react and respond quickly to the changing landscape of the Internet is only part of the challenge of flexibility. The real challenge is learning how to give way to an attack before fatal injuries occur. In other words, judo players must understand when to carry out a tactical retreat. By *giving way to superior force,* rather than resisting it, a firm in a relatively weak position can enhance its survivability.

The opposite of judo strategy is head-to-head combat, or what we will call "sumo strategy."[27] When sumo wrestlers clash in the ring, then speed, agility, and strategy are crucial. Ultimately, though, a combatant has to be big, strong, and powerful to win. While judo uses your opponent's strength to your advantage, and weight is supposed to be meaningless, sumo has always been "a feat of physical strength," where "weight is a weapon" and weight is "essential to winning."[28] The same is true in business: If a small competitor goes head-to-head or body-to-body in a war of attrition against a large player with deep pockets, the start-up rarely has a chance.

The best model of flexibility in the battle between Netscape and Microsoft was, ironically, Microsoft. Bill Gates made a potentially fatal error in 1994 and the first half of 1995: He did not fully understand the importance of the Internet, and he was slow to recover. By the summer of 1995, Netscape was the big, dominant player on the World Wide Web, and Microsoft was the part of the "old guard" that was far behind. Microsoft, given its size, resources, and inherent strength, might have engaged Netscape and the Internet in a sumo bout, and indeed it later put Netscape on the defensive with a series of sumo moves. However, Microsoft's initial response to the Internet challenge was a textbook example of judo flexibility.

Flexibility at Microsoft: Embrace and Extend

In 1995, Microsoft operating systems shipped on about 90 percent of all personal computers; Microsoft was the most feared company in the software industry; and Microsoft chairman Bill Gates was on his way to becoming the richest man in the world. Yet the movement to knock Microsoft off its throne was gathering speed. Following the explosion of the World Wide Web, Marc Andreessen was widely hailed as the next Bill Gates, and Internet technologies were heralded as the next computing revolution. The software world was abuzz about Java and the possibility of creating open, network-based, cross-platform applications that would make complex operating systems—the foundation of Microsoft's power— a thing of the past. Writing in *Forbes ASAP* in August 1995, influential analyst George Gilder predicted that, together, Netscape and Java would "invert the entire world of software in a way that may permanently displace Microsoft from the center of the sphere."[29]

Microsoft signed a Mosaic license in December 1994, and it planned to release its own browser—Internet Explorer (IE)—together with Windows 95. Nonetheless, it seemed strangely immune to the Internet hype as it carried out final preparations for the August launch of its new operating system and its proprietary online service, MSN. The strongest internal indication that Microsoft was taking the Internet seriously came in May of 1995, when Gates issued a memo titled "The Internet Tidal Wave." In the memo, he proclaimed the dawn of a new era for the industry and Microsoft:

> Our vision for the last 20 years can be summarized in a succinct way. We saw the exponential improvements in computer capabilities would make great software quite valuable. Our response was to build an organization to deliver the best software products. In the next 20 years, the improvement in computer power will be outpaced by the exponential improvements in communications networks. The combination of these elements will have a fundamental impact on work, learning, and play. . . . The Internet is at the forefront of all of this, and developments on the Internet over the next several years will set the course of industry for a long time to come. . . . I have gone through several stages of increasing my views of its importance. Now I assign the Internet the *highest* level of importance. The Internet is the most important single development to come along since the IBM PC was introduced in 1981. The PC analogy is apt for many reasons. The PC wasn't perfect . . . many aspects were arbitrary or poor . . . but companies that tried to fight the PC standard . . . failed, because the phenomena overcame any weaknesses that resisters identified. . . . The next few years are going to be very exciting, as we tackle these challenges and opportunities. The Internet is a tidal wave. It changes the rules. It is an incredible opportunity, as well as an incredible challenge.[30]

Internal debates raged within Microsoft for the six months after Gates's memo. To the outside world, there were only the smallest hints that the company, or senior management, would fully address the Internet. However, within Microsoft, senior executives were gradually coming to the realization that the Internet, with Netscape's Navigator heading the charge, posed perhaps the greatest challenge Microsoft had ever faced. Browsers, servers, increasing bandwidth, and cross-platform programming techniques threatened to make Microsoft's hegemony in PC operating systems obsolete. If users could download Java-written applications on demand, it would no longer matter which operating system they used. Microsoft would lose its lock on consumers, applications developers, and computer manufacturers. Microsoft might be able to stall this trend by continuing to push its own standards, but only for a while. On the other hand, there was no guarantee that Microsoft would thrive if it jumped headlong into the brave new world the Internet had defined. If it prematurely endorsed Internet technologies as the wave of the future, Microsoft might even hasten its own demise.

In order to force a decision on the company's Internet strategy, senior executives turned to a classic Microsoft technique. They announced that a briefing for analysts and journalists would be devoted to the topic in several weeks' time. When Microsoft announces these "days," most of the expected attendees assume that Gates and Microsoft executives will then explain to the world their well-crafted strategy. What many of them don't realize is that Microsoft's leaders are often unsure what they will say right up to the time of the event. But knowing an event is about to take place sets a deadline for the decision and forces Microsoft management to drive to conclusions. It was Steve Ballmer, Microsoft's president and college friend of Bill Gates, who originally suggested Microsoft should have a day on the Internet. When we interviewed him for this book, Ballmer recalled, "I remember saying I want to have an event because we look naked. . . . I first called for the event in July . . . because we were getting our butts kicked, and I was tired of not having a strategy that the field can articulate. That was my only contribution. The rest of the strategy, a lot of other people did . . . "

When Microsoft announced in November 1995 that it would have an Internet "day" the following month, the company's strategy was still under debate. In fact, the architect and general manager of MSN, Russell Siegelman, went on vacation a week before the fateful briefing and did not find out what happened to the company's strategy, or his own operation, until after the fact. But Microsoft did have a strategy by the time December 7, 1995, rolled around. As Gates set the context for the day's briefing, he made it clear that it was a milestone event:

I realized this morning that December 7 is kind of a famous day. Fifty-four years ago or something. And I was trying to think if there were any parallels to what was going on here. And I really couldn't come up with any. The only connection I could think of at all was that probably the most intelligent comment that was made on that day wasn't made on Wall Street, or even by any type of that analyst; it was actually Admiral Yamamoto, who observed that he feared they had awakened a sleeping giant.

Not only had the sleeping giant awakened, but Gates went on to outline one of the most stunning reversals of corporate strategy in recent memory:

So the Internet—the competition will be kind of, once again, *embrace and extend,* and we will embrace all the popular Internet protocols. Anything that a significant number of publishers are using and taking advantage of, we will support. We will do some extensions to those things. This is exactly what Netscape does. They support all the standard protocols, but in the case of things like frame sets or tables or what was called LiveScript [which became JavaScript], they chose to make extensions. Now those extensions can be cloned by someone else. . . . So I have a period of two or three years here of intense enhancement. . . . For Windows, it's very simple. We want to be the best Internet client. A major way that we'll do that is through integration. . . . [For] MSN, we're going to talk about how an Internet online service can fully embrace the idea of the Internet. . . . So this is my summary. Microsoft and the Internet . . . We're hard-core about the Internet. Anything we're focused on, we're generally hard-core, and we are focused on this and therefore, very hard-core. . . . We believe that integration and continuity are going to be valuable to end users and developers, and we think that everybody involved in this needs to take a long-term approach, building up the eyeballs, building up the usage levels, and so that's certainly what we're doing here, and we're very excited about that.[31]

Gates's pronouncement was a stake aimed at the heart of Netscape. The idea that Microsoft would *embrace and extend* the Internet, integrate the Internet directly into Windows, and become "very hard-core" about the Internet was enough to send Netscape's stock reeling. Over the next five days, Netscape's valuation fell by 28 percent. The giant was not only awake, but aware, energized, prepared to reverse course, and if necessary, lose hundreds of millions of dollars to turn its proprietary products, such as MSN, into integral parts of the Internet.

Microsoft's strategy to embrace and extend was Gates's first effort to use judo strategy against Netscape. Rather than a direct assault, Gates demonstrated flexibility by choosing to embrace the Internet and the work that Netscape had done to make it a livelier, more useful place. Gates wanted Microsoft to do its utmost to provide the very best implementation of Internet standards. Over the following months, Microsoft embraced numerous Internet standards, such as HTML, for creating Web pages, and many of the innovations Netscape had pioneered, even if they conflicted with Windows-based technologies. Microsoft licensed Java and abandoned Blackbird, its proprietary multimedia software development tool, once considered the key differentiator for Microsoft's online activities. Microsoft also worked vigorously to play in the standards arenas, moving to position ActiveX, its object-sharing technology, as an open solution.

Gates's instructions to his troops were crystal clear. He repeatedly told Microsoft management that nothing was more important to Microsoft than gaining 30 percent of the browser market, as fast as possible.[32] The emphasis on winning anything less than 50 percent might seem puzzling. Gates, however, clearly grasped the dynamics of the browser wars. He understood that the key to Microsoft's success lay in preventing Web masters from committing en masse to customize their sites for Netscape's Navigator. In the initial stage of the war, Microsoft only needed to gain enough market credibility to convince Web masters that they should wait for a clear winner to emerge before committing irreversibly to either browser. Once Microsoft achieved that goal with the 30 percent threshold, Gates believed that victory would be just a matter of time.

Flexibility at Microsoft: Sacrifice One Child to Protect Another

Perhaps Microsoft's most startling demonstration of flexibility was its willingness to change course on Microsoft Network (MSN) only months after launching the service. As late as the summer of 1995, the prevailing view at Netscape (and indeed, most of the world) was that Microsoft was deeply committed to MSN as *the* alternative to the Internet. Microsoft had designed MSN to compete with AOL and CompuServe as a proprietary platform on which independent content providers would add value. By the time Windows 95 launched, Microsoft was repositioning MSN to be more complementary to the Internet. In fact, Steve Ballmer recalled that Gates was already having second thoughts about MSN: "In 1995, Bill was already thinking maybe we shouldn't even launch MSN; maybe it's off strategy—it's really not right—it's not Internet-based. By 1996, I think he was pretty sure there were other aspects of it [that weren't right]. . . . But sometimes you let things slip—come to market anyway—for whatever the set of reasons. They made sense at the time." Despite Gates's doubts, Microsoft had already sunk several hundred million dollars into MSN and announced that it would commit hundreds of millions more. Ballmer said publicly that Microsoft anticipated MSN and related content investments would lose more than $1 billion during its first three years of operations.[33]

Gates's decision in December 1995 to embrace and extend the Internet had immediate consequences for MSN, including reassigning MSN's technology chief Anthony Bay and his core technology group to the Internet software organization. But MSN still had one huge advantage over the competition: It was the only online service that came bundled with Windows 95 and shipped with 90 percent of the new personal computers sold in the world. AOL and CompuServe had to spend $40 to $80 to acquire each new customer. It was very expensive to offer bounties and ship free disks around the world. In the meantime, MSN could acquire new customers virtually for free.[34]

In March 1996, Bill Gates decided that promoting Internet Explorer was simply more important than protecting MSN's biggest competitive advantage. Gates was willing to sacrifice one child (MSN) to promote a more important one (Internet Explorer). To entice Steve Case, the CEO of AOL, to make Internet Explorer AOL's preferred browser, Gates offered to put an AOL icon on the Windows 95 desktop, perhaps the most expensive real estate in the world. In exchange for promoting Internet Explorer as its default browser, AOL would have almost equal prominence with MSN on future versions of Windows. In announcing this deal on March 12, 1996, Microsoft dealt Netscape a crushing blow. Just one day earlier, Netscape had announced a licensing deal with AOL, which was expected to move the service's roughly 6 million users into the Navigator camp.

Gates later extended his offer to the other online services and the largest Internet service providers, guaranteeing a huge percentage of the home market for Internet Explorer and tough times for MSN. In a conversation about MSN in the spring of 1996, Gates commented:

> We have had three options for how to use the "Windows Box": First, we can use it for the browser battle, recognizing that our core assets are at risk. Second, we could monetize the box, and sell the real estate to the highest bidder. Or third, we could use the box to sell and promote internally content assets. I recognize that, by choosing to do the first, we have leveled the playing field and reduced our opportunities for competitive advantage with MSN.[35]

Russ Siegelman, the original Microsoft champion of MSN and MSN's first general manager, resigned in the wake of these decisions. Siegelman did not doubt Gates, but giving away MSN's last significant advantage was the straw that broke the camel's back. Siegelman did not see any merit in running a business that would continually clash with Gates's desire to win the browser wars.

Tactical Flexibility at Netscape

Flexibility was also a core value at Netscape. From the very beginning, the company had demonstrated the capability to make quick tactical adjustments. Jim Clark set the example for the rest of the company when he founded Netscape. He said at the time, "We don't know how in the hell we're going to make money, but I'll put money behind it, and we'll figure out a way to make money."[36]

Being willing to react quickly to unexpected challenges and opportunities soon became an article of faith. Netscape was very good at making quick, tactical adjustments, particularly in response to Microsoft. Rick Schell described how Netscape senior management viewed flexibility:

We reevaluate what we're doing, strategically, continuously. Is it monthly? Is it quarterly? Is it reexamining everything that we do constantly? I'll give you an example. One of the strategies we had was to dominate every aspect of delivering content—multimedia, 3-D, everything. So we went wild in the beginning of 1996 and bought a couple of companies that were very strong in that space. We've readjusted that strategy to be more oriented toward working with partners and enabling them to attack that space. In mid-course, we said, "Look, we're going after the enterprise. We need to put more of our focus behind the enterprise. But on the other hand, we don't want to lose the content market. How do we go about doing that?" Well, there's a huge ISV market that's developing. We don't need to supply that technology. We can work with partners.

Everyone at Netscape seemed to have an illustration of flexibility or rapid, opportunistic responses to changes in the environment. As just one example, Larry Geisel, the senior VP for information systems, cited Inbox Direct, a mechanism for delivering multimedia content through e-mail. As Geisel recalled, in the summer of 1996, Microsoft was signing up content providers for IE 3.0. In their regular Monday morning meeting, the mood of the executive staff was, "Oh, damn, here we go again. What are we going to do?" One week later, Mike Homer came back to the executive staff and said, "Let me tell you about Inbox Direct. I got 50 content suppliers signed up. We're going to announce this week. Larry, how soon can you make it work?" According to Geisel, "We announced a week later, the site is up in three weeks, and it revolutionized the delivery of content."

The idea behind Inbox Direct was to let consumers register their interests and preferences with a broad array of Internet content providers and receive rich-text e-mail messages directly from Netscape. In that short period of time, Homer had arranged for more than 20 companies to participate in the new service, ranging from American Express and CNET to Excite, *PC World,* Knight Ridder, *The New York Times,* and *U.S. News and World Report.* By the summer of 1998, it had attracted about 1.8 million subscribers.[37] Although Inbox Direct did not generate any revenue for Netscape, it was a classic example of flexibility and movement at the tactical level: Netscape sought to avoid a head-on attack against Microsoft in content. Yet at the same time, Netscape was able to offer something quite different in the same general space.

Strategic Inflexibility at Netscape

While Netscape showed itself to be a master of the quick thrust, it was far less adept at assessing and responding to head-to-head attacks. The key to strategic flexibility is to avoid standing stiffly in the wind when directly assaulted by larger players. The objective is to be flexible, absorbing direct attacks that might otherwise be fatal. Netscape's first real body blow came on December 7, 1995, with Microsoft's announcement that it would "embrace and extend" everything Netscape had done. Yet it would probably be fair to say that most Netscape senior managers did not initially believe that Microsoft could implement its promises as quickly or as efficiently as it ultimately did. Roberta Katz was the only senior member of Netscape management to cite Internet Day as a galvanizing event for Netscape. Katz, the 50-year-old general counsel, reported directly to the CEO and had been recruited by Barksdale to Netscape. Not just a lawyer, she was a cultural anthropologist with a Ph.D. from Columbia and a J.D. from the University of Washington. With her experiences as general counsel of Lin Broadcasting and then McCaw Cellular, she was deeply familiar with the ramifications of fighting a giant like Microsoft. Katz remembered that:

> Microsoft's December 7 announcement was galvanizing in a bizarre way. . . . They tried to make themselves out to be the underdog, which we thought was particularly amusing. It got our attention, though. They tried to claim the high ground. To this day, I laugh when I think about it because they tried to analogize themselves to the U.S. when, in fact, they were very much, in our mind, the aggressor.

Despite her ability to see the humorous side of the December 7 announcement, Katz remembered that the executive staff meeting on December 8, 1995, was one of the most somber meetings in the company's history. Nonetheless, Netscape's initial reaction to Microsoft was not to retreat, nor to bend in the wind. Instead, Netscape and Microsoft often clashed head-to-head as Microsoft aggressively attacked at every turn. Netscape wanted to take a firm stand against Microsoft's frontal assault and give no ground. Mike Homer, then head of marketing and a veteran of battles with Microsoft from his days at Apple and Go, later admitted that he had "an obsession with beating Microsoft."[38] In our interview in May 1998, he continued to maintain that taking a bold position against Microsoft was critical for Netscape:

> When you compete with Microsoft, if you've got a chance, you've got to be bold. They scare the shit out of most people because they make outrageous claims and statements. Take December 7. They were nowhere. They had no strategy. They had nothing. They came out and said, "Vaporware two years later." They've been around for 20 years. Gates is the richest man in the world, right? But from a marketing standpoint, we were never timid. We were bold. When they made claims, we made claims. And it's the only way that we were able to keep up with them at all from a marketing standpoint, because we had no money. . . . We've got PR, and maybe a few clever guerrilla tricks, like the world's biggest Web site. But you've got to be really bold. . . . You have got to market vapor. Don't let their futures be compared to your present, or you get killed. That's what they did to Lotus. That's what they tried to do to us.

Netscape's dilemma was that bold, head-to-head confrontations inevitably moved Netscape onto Microsoft's terrain. Using Jim Barksdale's analogy again, the bear was moving into the ocean, where the shark had enormous advantages. For example, as the two companies went after common distribution channels, such as Internet service providers and online services, Netscape repeatedly lost deal after deal (see Table 3.1). If Netscape got into contests where it had no leverage, Microsoft could simply outbid Netscape with more money, more support, and promises of more to come. Strategic flexibility required that Netscape avoid the head-to-head battles and be willing to do things that Microsoft would avoid. For example, before signing his agreement with Microsoft, AOL's Steve Case had offered Netscape a broad partnership. Case, who preferred Netscape to Microsoft, suggested that AOL run Netscape's Web site in return for using Navigator. But Barksdale showed little interest in the deal. According to Case, "It was a period [when] the press was predicting AOL's doomsday and, I think, Netscape thought AOL would become irrelevant. They thought if they had MCI, AT&T, and Netcom using Netscape, they'd be fine in the consumer space. They had no desire to treat us as a partner; they only wanted to treat us like a customer."[39]

Even more surprising, Netscape later rebuffed opportunities to reengage AOL. As much as half of Microsoft's early market share gains in browsers came from its deal with AOL. Nonetheless, Ram Shriram told us

TABLE 3.1

Head-to-Head Confrontations Between Microsoft & Netscape

	Deal with Netscape	Deal with Microsoft	Details
INTRANET CUSTOMERS			
Chevron	October 1996	March 1997	Chevron replaced Navigator with IE at 25,000 desktops; the major reasons given were price and better integration with Windows 95/NT.
KPMG	January 1997	August 1997	KPMG replaced Navigator with IE at 18,000 desktops; KPMG announced it would create a 500-person practice dedicated to Microsoft enterprise solutions; Microsoft agreed to pay up to $10 million in retraining costs.
ISPs AND OLSs			
America Online	March 1996	March 1996	AOL made IE its default browser; Microsoft put AOL on the Windows 95 desktop.
AT&T WorldNet	August 1995	July 1996	AT&T made IE its default browser; Microsoft bundled WorldNet with Windows 95.
Compu-Serve	March 1996	June 1996	CompuServe chose Microsoft's server platform and browser to move its service to the Internet; Microsoft put CompuServe on the Windows 95 desktop.
MCI	November 1994	March 1996	MCI made IE its default browser with the launch of its dial-up access service.

that four months after AOL signed its deal with Microsoft, Netscape could have recovered half the market share it was about to lose:

> AOL came to us again. AOL's stock was tanking, and it was getting sued by the attorney generals of various states. . . . They were keen to come back to the table and forge a relationship with us. . . . Only two people went on this trip to go see Steve Case—me and Barksdale. Jim and I went there trying to

	Deal with Netscape	Deal with Microsoft	Details
Netcom	March 1996	July 1996	Netcom made IE its default browser; Microsoft bundled Netcom with Windows 95.
Prodigy	November 1995	October 1996	Prodigy made IE its default browser; Microsoft bundled Prodigy with Windows 95.
Sprint	August 1996	December 1996	Sprint made IE its default browser for its new Internet access service.
OEMs AND ISVs			
Apple	August 1995	August 1997	IE became Apple's default browser as part of the deal around Microsoft's $150 million investment in Apple. Apple had already agreed to bundle IE in January 1997.
Intuit	October 1995	July 1997	Intuit preferred Microsoft's ActiveX support and IE's availability as an embeddable component; also, Quicken was designated as a "premier Active Channel" on IE 4.0.
Lotus/ IBM	November 1996	July 1997	Lotus chose to stop bundling Navigator with SmartSuite and Notes due to Netscape's decision to integrate Navigator into Communicator. Previously Lotus bundled both Navigator and IE.

Source: Compiled from various sources, including trade publications, wire service stories, and press releases.

figure out how to make a new AOL user interface with the Netscape browser. [Despite the Microsoft contract], they had some deal that stated, if the desktop got diluted with lots of icons, they were not required to keep Microsoft as the only default. . . . We both came back from that trip and pitched it to Andreessen, the engineering team, and Homer. But we got a very tepid response back at the ranch, saying, "Look, we're all busy. We're going to build this great enterprise software." Netscape was saying, "We're not really interested. Our focus is not consumers, so we're not terribly interested in working with you." We lost another opportunity to take charge of another 10 to 12 million browsers. [Even after we rejected AOL's overtures], AOL asked Netscape if it could take the [browser] source code in whatever form it was available, even as spaghetti code, and turn it over to their BookLink browser team in Boston and have them do something with it. Netscape refused that, too. . . . [During this time], there continued to be an obsession with Microsoft, what I call "mooning the giant." There was an obsession about having to respond to every deal. I think Netscape could have carved for itself a great space on its own, without having to be so focused on them, which of course caused a very strong response from the other side.

Netscape was equally slow to demonstrate flexibility in its technology strategy. Rather than match Microsoft's "embrace and extend" approach, Netscape initially rejected Microsoft's technologies, especially platform-specific frameworks such as ActiveX. The most obvious symbol of Netscape's defiance was Netscape ONE (Open Network Environment), a set of cross-platform standards that the company unveiled in the summer of 1996. Netscape ONE, which posed an alternative to Microsoft's Windows-based approach, incorporated a number of familiar technologies, including HTTP, HTML, LDAP (Lightweight Directory Access Protocol), and Java, along with a free software development kit. Company executives hoped that, by offering free programming tools, they would jump-start development for their platform. In addition, as part of Netscape ONE, Netscape endorsed IIOP (Internet Inter-ORB Protocol), a means of linking software programs that reside on different machines. IIOP and the Common Object Request Broker Architecture (CORBA), on which it was based, competed with Microsoft's Distributed Component Object Model (DCOM) for industry-wide acceptance.

Marc Andreessen made it clear that Netscape would not follow Microsoft's platform-specific route. He wrote in one of his Web site columns, "Netscape ONE is doing for application development what HTML did for information sharing. . . . Like HTML, Netscape ONE works for the entire Internet. Also like HTML, it doesn't assume that you and everyone you want to communicate with use a particular operating system. It isn't Netscape's platform, it's the Internet's platform."[40] More than 50 companies announced that they would support Netscape ONE, including Intuit, Lotus, NeXT, and Oracle.

Netscape ONE was a powerful idea, in principle. According to Ben Slivka, the project manager for Microsoft's early Internet Explorer products, the concept also scared people in Redmond.[41] But trying to build an entirely new platform without embracing Microsoft was too much to expect. Three months later, shortly after the release of Internet Explorer 3.0 led Netscape management to see the first measurable declines in browser market share, the company decided that embracing Microsoft was better than fighting the world's most powerful software company head-on. On October 15, 1996, Netscape announced its "comprehensive strategy to 'embrace and integrate' Microsoft platforms and technology." Netscape told the world that its embrace and integrate strategy would allow customers to protect their existing technology investments in a range of Microsoft products and simplify the migration from Microsoft's legacy systems to Netscape's open client and server solutions. Even technologies once rejected, such as OLE (object linking and embedding) and ActiveX (in essence, the distributed-object version of OLE), would ultimately find at least weak support as part of Netscape ONE.

After October 1996, *embrace and integrate* became an integral part of Netscape's strategy. Netscape became increasingly flexible, working with Microsoft to set standards in areas such as secure electronic transactions while supporting, rather than fighting, Microsoft products, such as Microsoft Mail and Exchange. In our interview in August 1997, Carl Cargill, Netscape's point person on standards, strongly affirmed the company's willingness to embrace Microsoft technologies. When we asked how much flexibility really existed in Netscape's standards strategy, Cargill replied, "Would we switch, or would we remain obdurate and say 'no' and die? Bingo . . . Put it this way, we long ago said we're doing IIOP. But we'll also do ActiveX because the two have to coexist. . . . We can't not really support it. CORBA/IIOP is in the Fortune 500. ActiveX/DCOM will be in groupware. The two have to talk."

Netscape reinforced this open-minded approach in November 1997 when it acquired Kiva. Kiva supported Microsoft's DCOM standard in its application server, which became part of Netscape's product line. Following the acquisition, John Paul explained the extent of Netscape's evolution:

> We're more agnostic when it comes to component models. We haven't backed off of what we think makes a good model: CORBA. On the other hand, we're pragmatic, and customers adopt different technologies. The key here is to offer products that customers can use in their environment. We haven't changed any of our beliefs, in terms of what would make sense. But we're not quite as religious, maybe, as we used to be.[42]

This was true across the board. As times got tougher for Netscape in 1998, Netscape was increasingly willing to bend to Microsoft, rather than stand firm. In the early days, one of Netscape's greatest competitive advantages lay in offering a tightly integrated client/server solution: Navigator and Communicator traditionally worked better than other clients with SuiteSpot servers. However, in February 1998, Netscape reversed course and announced that its new servers would work as efficiently with Microsoft or IBM client software as with Netscape's own. This decision led *PC Week* to proclaim, "Netscape opening up to Windows." It also elicited a positive response from Netscape customers. As one information technology manager explained, "This [strategy] opens up a lot of ideas, but it also makes me less likely to look elsewhere for new products, since Netscape is going to provide me with the broadest range of choices for building applications."[43]

Yet even then, a degree of ambivalence about fully embracing and integrating Microsoft standards remained. In the summer of 1998, the preview release of Communicator 4.5 still did not support Microsoft's ActiveX technology, despite previous assurances. This made it appear that Netscape had not yet fully resolved what Eric Hahn, then chief technology officer, identified as one of the central issues facing Netscape in November 1997:

> What is our interaction with Windows? Does Netscape have a strategy in which Windows customers are compelled to buy Netscape value-added on top of Windows? Or is Windows a fundamental enemy of the company, which it certainly isn't today? . . . I think that's probably the million-dollar question for Netscape. . . . How do you co-opt the Windows franchise in a way that is constructive to the customer, and to Netscape?

PRINCIPLE *Exploit leverage that uses the weight and strategy of opponents against them.*

If he had a lever long enough, and a fulcrum strong enough,
"Give me where to stand, and I will move the earth."
—Archimedes

Movement and flexibility are prerequisites for judo strategy. Exercising these principles is crucial to keeping the competition off balance and preventing competitors from dominating smaller, more vulnerable firms. But speed and agility only buy you time and give you the opportunity to create early-mover advantages before your opponent responds. If you want to do more than just survive an initial confrontation, you need to knock down and ultimately immobilize your opponent. This requires *leverage,* finding ways to use your opponent's weight, history, and larger size against it. As experts in judo attest, "size, weight and power mean nothing in judo, because you employ the efforts of the opponent to defeat him."[44]

In a *sumo* battle between Netscape and Microsoft, size, weight, and power were all in Microsoft's favor. In a *judo* match, however, Netscape management saw three potential vulnerabilities and sources of leverage inherent in Microsoft's position: (1) the installed base of old Microsoft products, such as Windows 3.1 and DOS, which Microsoft wanted to upgrade to its newest operating system; (2) the highly fragmented, hetero-geneous computing environments in most corporations, which Microsoft wanted to kill; and (3) Microsoft's reliance on proprietary technology in an ever-more-open technology world.

Turn Your Opponent's Installed Base to Your Advantage

Once Microsoft became "hard-core" on the Internet, its obvious advan-tage was its dominant share of the PC operating system market. By bundling its browser into the operating system, Microsoft could offer something Netscape could not hope to match: a free browser delivered seamlessly to virtually every new personal computer sold in the world. Microsoft management made no secret of its intentions: As soon as you turned on your new computer, the browser, the operating system, and the computer interface would be inseparable, obviating the need for another application, such as Netscape Navigator.[45]

This strategy had one critical vulnerability: Microsoft required users to upgrade existing computers to the newest and latest Microsoft operating system if they wanted to take advantage of Microsoft's offer. While this did not matter much for the home or consumer user, it was a critical issue for corporations. IT managers liked to upgrade their huge installed base of "old" Microsoft operating systems on their timetables, not Microsoft's. If the newest versions of Internet Explorer came built into Windows 95 or 98, what about all those computer users in corporations that still ran on DOS or Windows 3.1? Jim Barksdale quickly appreciated the scale of this opportunity. He told us, "There are 300 million PC units out there in the world today. About a third of them are running Windows 95; two-thirds of them are running something else. As they continue to develop more prod-ucts in operating systems, Windows 98, Windows 2000, they continue to leave more and more of a trail, so that you have the UNIXification of Windows."

Netscape, in other words, was the only company supporting the *entire* installed base of Windows-based PCs. Marc Andreessen felt passionately about this subject. He argued that only Netscape, and not Microsoft, offered each release of its browser for every operating system on the market. Moreover, Microsoft depended on upgrades for revenues, so it had no incentive to support the old installed base. When we asked Andreessen about the threat of Microsoft's 90 percent market share, and the threat of bundling, he responded:

> Ninety percent of the market isn't Windows. Actually, about 25 percent of the market is Win 95; but 40 percent of the market is Win 3.1, about 10 percent of the market is Windows NT 4.0, and about 5 percent of the market is Windows NT 3.5. That turns out to be four different versions of Windows that are deliberately incompatible with each other. Now people in the industry who watch this tend to discount it. But our business customers who are trying to make all this stuff work don't discount it. It's very serious to them because this stuff doesn't work together. And all you need to do is go into Boeing or go into Lockheed Martin or go into the Department of Defense and ask them what is one of your biggest issues? It's like, "Oh shit!" And then the interesting thing is Win 98 comes out, Win NT version 5 comes out, and they all increase the fragmentation because the stuff that already exists is going to stay there.

Andreessen even went one step further, arguing that Microsoft did not even have the incentive to address this problem, which goes to the core of leverage in judo strategy:

> They [Microsoft] have no interest in pushing the previous version [of their operating systems], no interest whatsoever. Now they make public announcements that sometimes make it sound like some day they may do so, but they never have, and they never will. Microsoft BackOffice, Microsoft Exchange—the latest versions don't run on Win NT 3.5. They don't work. You have to buy Windows NT 4.0. Microsoft is a company like any other. They have a business that they have to protect, and that's operating systems, year in and year out. When you have 90 to 95 percent unit share of all new computers, it's not like you're going to grow your percent share. . . . It would be a crisis if, for some reason, people stopped buying new systems or stopped upgrading as frequently.

When asked about the possibility of Microsoft ultimately merging the various flavors of Windows, Andreessen contended, "It is not in their economic self-interest to do so. They may end up merging Windows 98 and NT, but that does not address the fundamental issue of having your versions deliberately incompatible to the previous one."

TABLE 3.2

Installed Base of Top Four Operating Systems in the U.S. (%)

	1996	1997	1998
DOS	22.2	16.7	11.6
Windows 3.x	49.2	40.2	21.5
Windows 95	9.8	26.8	51.4
MacOS	9.6	9.0	9.2

Source: Adapted from ZD Market Intelligence, Technology User Profile 1996–1998.

An independent analysis of the U.S. market for personal computers largely confirmed Andreessen's analysis (see Table 3.2). While the market was quickly moving to Microsoft's Windows 95 operating system, Andreessen correctly identified a big gap in Microsoft's offerings. Netscape was the only company that could serve the majority of personal computers in the United States because the majority of the PCs in the country had Windows 3.1 or DOS operating systems. American consumers automatically upgraded to Windows 95 when they bought new computers, but corporate customers upgraded slowly. Since Microsoft originally designed Internet Explorer to work only with Windows 95, the vast majority of potential users had to rely on Netscape until they bought a new computer. Microsoft later started releasing Internet Explorer for older Windows operating systems, but only after significant delays. For example, it took Microsoft an extra six months to deliver IE 2.0 for Windows 3.1.

Microsoft's strategy of forcing upgrades also presented Netscape with an opening to sell its vision of the future to corporations. As Mike McCue, Netscape's vice president of technology, explained, the training and upgrade costs involved in moving from DOS to Windows 3.x to Windows 95 and on up the ladder created an opportunity uniquely suited to Netscape:

> They [Microsoft] are going to introduce all this confusion into the market, which gives us an opportunity to say, "Wait a minute. If you're going to change your desktop, well, maybe you should think about a desktop that isn't tied to a particular version of a particular operating system. Maybe you should think about a desktop that looks and works and feels the same across all the different versions of all the different operating systems that

you're running today in your organization." Most IS managers are running like 18 different operating systems today in a large corporation, right? And that includes all the different versions of all the different operating systems, which effectively are different operating systems. So, it's extremely compelling to say, "Hey. . . . You can create an environment that looks, works, and feels the same on your marketing desktops, as well as your engineering desktops, and you can centrally manage it . . . just like a mainframe." Now, you've got something that has immense value. So, Microsoft created a need and confusion, and the opportunity for us to seize. And we did. We're going into sales accounts now, and we're winning deals. . . . [We tell them] you get all the advantages of the Microsoft environment and more.

Rick Schell, while head of client engineering, gave a good summary of the leverage Netscape gained from Microsoft's strategy for Windows:

> [There are] two ways to look at the operating system: the operating system as an asset and a lever; the operating system as a liability. If you focus on the first one, it's a strategy that loses because anything that you do provides Microsoft leverage. . . . If you look at it as a liability, there are situations in which having to either bundle your products with the operating system to make them attractive or trying to convert the customers to use your new operating system because it's an economic imperative for you—that's a liability. Companies don't want to do it. . . . They have to upgrade if Microsoft forces them to. Microsoft holds a gun to their head.

Netscape's strategy to support the entire installed base of client operating systems was, indeed, a significant point of leverage for Netscape in the corporate world. Schell and McCue may have exaggerated the number of operating systems in corporations. Nonetheless, the diverse installed base helps to explain why corporations did not flock to Internet Explorer en masse, even as Microsoft gave the product away and closed the gaps in performance and features. For a long time, unless your company was 100 percent Windows 95 or NT on the desktop, moving to Internet Explorer was simply not an option. Even when Microsoft introduced more versions of Internet Explorer, many corporate IT managers proved to be unwilling to bear the cost of switching. In large numbers of corporations, it would be expensive to install the software and retrain hundreds or thousands of employees to change from Navigator to Internet Explorer.

The weakness of Netscape's strategy is that the half-life of DOS and Windows 3.1 is finite: Over time, more and more companies will migrate away from ancient operating systems like DOS, and the newer versions of Windows with a built-in browser will gain an overwhelming share. The key lesson is that *points of leverage do not last forever, especially when competing on Internet time.* Just like a judo match, opponents may expose weaknesses that are vulnerable to leverage, but only for a few seconds. If you don't use your speed and flexibility to take advantage of them, the opportunities will always disappear.

Turn Your Opponent's Focused Commitments to Your Advantage

In many ways, Microsoft is a highly focused company. It is deeply committed to making Windows the dominant operating system for personal computers, Windows NT the dominant operating system for corporate servers, and Windows CE the dominant operating system for alternative forms of computing, such as palmtops and television set-top boxes. It is Microsoft's top and maybe only priority to convert the installed base of non-Windows machines to Windows. Consequently, it would run contrary to Microsoft's interests to support UNIX or any of the other operating systems that are currently pervasive in the world of big corporations. In fact, the degree of corporate heterogeneity (Table 3.3) may be surprising, given Microsoft's perceived dominance.

Microsoft's solution to this problem of corporate heterogeneity has been to replace older systems with Windows, especially Windows NT. Clearly, NT has momentum and will continue to pick up significant market share. One market analyst predicted that 75 percent of corporate intranets will run on NT by 2001.[46] But the data also suggest that the installed base of legacy UNIX and other systems may not disappear

TABLE 3.3

Server Operating Systems: Forecast 1997–2001
(unit: thousands of licenses)

	1997	1998	1999	2000	2001
Novell NetWare	1,100	1,166	1,236	1,310	1,389
Windows NT Server	1,000	1,300	1,690	2,197	2,856
Total UNIX	650	728	815	913	1,023
Other	850	800	750	710	660
Total	3,600	3,994	4,491	5,130	5,928

Source: Datamonitor, "Servers and the Internet," 1998.

completely, even if NT becomes the dominant operating system in corporations. Conceptually, the picture looks something like Figure 3.1. The
shaded area represents the legacy systems and installed base. From an IT
manager's perspective, this means that NT is clearly the future, but heterogeneity is the present.

In 1998, UNIX continued to handle high-speed, high-volume server
requirements and large-scale multiprocessor networks, as well as recover from system errors much more effectively than NT. As a result, high-
end Web servers and electronic commerce servers tended to be UNIX
machines. Makers of UNIX systems, such as Sun Microsystems, Hewlett-
Packard, and IBM, were also working to evolve their products and might
well extend the effective life of UNIX systems. From Netscape's perspective, therefore, Microsoft's desire to kill corporate heterogeneity, just like
its desire to upgrade the installed base of old Microsoft products, was a
significant point of leverage.

If Netscape delivered equally good solutions across all platforms, it
solved a problem that Microsoft could not address directly. Andreessen
consistently made this argument, dating back to the early days of the company. In October 1996, for example, he gave an interview in which he proclaimed the value of being cross-platform:

> The promise here, the potential which is being delivered, is cross-
> platform—across all desktop operating systems, all server operating sys-
> tems, all non-PC operating systems, and across all the different versions of

FIGURE 3.1

*Conceptual Picture: The Likely Evolution of the Installed Base of
UNIX Versus Windows NT*

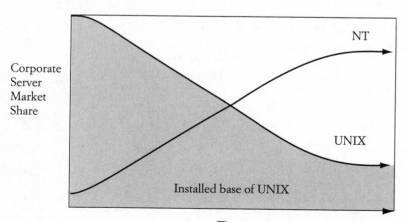

these operating systems. . . . The long-term vision is: It doesn't matter what the operating system is. The operating system should be a plug-in that fits beneath Navigator. . . . It doesn't matter if it's even an operating system that we run today. It doesn't matter if it's a PC or an NC [network computer].[47]

A year later, Andreessen told us the same story Netscape's advantage over Microsoft is simple: "Intranet, extranet, Internet—the Internet's fundamental proposition—cross-platform, cross-device, cross-server, cross-database, going into cross-business applications, cross-mainframe, etc. So, horizontal, as opposed to vertical, and the latest version of everything."

Cross-platform became one of the central mantras in Netscape's strategy, especially after the company went public in 1995. As we will discuss in chapter 4, delivering on this strategy proved to be technically challenging. Cross-platform code generally took more time to design and test. It also usually did not perform as well or as fast as code optimized for a specific platform, such as NT or UNIX. Netscape pinned high hopes on Java to solve these problems because this is an inherently cross-platform programming language. After considerable wasted effort, Netscape engineers realized that Java would not solve their design problems, except for some specific applications. Nonetheless, the cross-platform promise was powerful, particularly in corporate settings. Before serious financial problems emerged in the fourth quarter of 1997, Andreessen claimed the promise was so compelling that Netscape could even win in head-to-head bids against Microsoft. He argued, "We have a natural edge. Anytime we run into Microsoft in a Fortune 1000 account, if we do a decent job of presenting our arguments and actually making the sale and wrapping the services around it and providing it as a solution, we tend to win at a very high percentage of these. So we have a natural advantage there."

Whether or not it had a natural edge, Netscape could offer products that Microsoft would not, could not, and did not want to match. By giving the customer server-based and client-based applications that worked on all operating systems and across heterogeneous systems, Netscape was enhancing the corporate computing environments that Microsoft wanted to kill.

Bob Lisbonne, who was in charge of the project to re-architect the browser client in the summer of 1997, made the argument even more strongly. He argued that the forces driving the Internet and intranets would inevitably increase the heterogeneity of computer systems over time and there was little Microsoft could do to stop it. Moreover, Microsoft's soft underbelly was its basic business model and historical strategy, which he described as a "field of dreams" strategy:

> Their business model [for the Internet] is utterly unchanged. The business model of Microsoft is selling new versions of Windows and selling new versions of Office. That is the economic engine at the company. . . . Now, here's why that doesn't work on the Internet, or why it will prove to be more and more problematic. Corporate customers who have large networks are unable to continue to survive in this field-of-dreams operating-system marketing strategy. By that I mean, "Build it and they will come." People have made transitions very quickly from DOS to Windows 3.0 and Windows 3.0 to Windows 3.1. But anyone with a significant network can't just have an all-anything environment. So the Microsoft strategy is still "all Win 95," or "all Win 98," or "all Office," but it doesn't work very well in a heterogeneous environment. And that would be fine, except for the fact that we think that, almost axiomatically, the Net will bring more diversity in devices. . . . And the reason is not because Microsoft's operating systems are good or bad, it's just that there's one network that people have to connect to. So assume that it's laptops, PCs, workstations, servers, NCs, and ultimately PalmPilots, Segas, Nintendos, and Web TVs, and so forth. . . . The other thing that I think is proving to be problematic for them [and] an opportunity for us is the size of the installed base. It has grown to where Windows itself is balkanizing—we call it the UNIXification of Windows. UNIX sounds like one operating system, but it has many flavors. Windows sounds like one operating system, but it's Windows 3.1, Windows 95, Windows 98, NT 3.5, NT 4.0, NT 5.0, and next year, Cairo, Windows CE— good thing you have tape recorders. So, we support all of those. And not just in marketing data: We ship our software with the same features on all the platforms at the same time. That's because we don't have a vested interest in pushing the latest version of their, or anyone else's, operating system.

Netscape managers realized that Microsoft's strategy of killing heterogeneity with Windows NT would win in many companies. However, they believed that enough corporations would resist the Microsoft message to provide Netscape with a healthy market. As Rick Schell observed:

> Corporations are not going to want to upgrade as often [as Microsoft would like]. They're heterogeneous. But some will do it. There is no doubt about it. There are going to be some customers . . . [who are] going to say, "We're going to go with NT. Our strategy is one operating system across the company, and we have to support many of them. We're going to have one messaging strategy, and we're going to have one company that's our

vendor." That will happen. We're not going to win all the business all the time. Our corporate growth isn't predicated on having 60 or 70 percent market share in that segment. . . . We don't have to do that to be successful.

The Challenges of Exploiting Corporate Heterogeneity as Leverage. As Rick Schell pointed out, Netscape did not have to dominate the corporate market to build a very successful business. But beating Microsoft, as well as IBM, Oracle, and other competitors in the corporate market, will be challenging, even with the leverage of heterogeneity. Some of these challenges will be technical: It is very hard to deliver true cross-platform functionality and performance on Internet time against a highly focused, single-platform company such as Microsoft. In addition, some of Netscape's UNIX products never generated a dime of revenue. During its first few years, Netscape supported every variation of UNIX, regardless of its market potential. Unfortunately, as Desmond Chan, a former senior testing engineer told us, "A lot of the cross-platform binaries had zero market. Zero sales." After servicing the major operating systems, being cross-platform clearly had diminishing returns. As a result, Barksdale downsized a number of these initiatives in 1998.

Even if Netscape overcame the technical and volume problems, it still had to solve other business and strategic challenges. The first of these issues was the pace of change inherent in Internet time. Microsoft has been racing to convert the world to Windows, while Netscape has been racing to enhance the existing installed base of legacy systems and new devices that will attach to the network. In this race, ironically, Netscape— the fast and flexible start-up—has been the tortoise. Microsoft—the large, dominant incumbent—has been the hare. Netscape's vision of a heterogeneous future may win the marathon, but Microsoft's vision of the power of a single standard has been winning the sprints. Even the most optimistic projections (see Table 3.4), which show spectacular growth in new Internet access devices, suggest that Microsoft's home terrain, the world of PCs, will be dominant well into the next century. Even if new devices ultimately become the winners, Microsoft could still have a big share of the operating systems (with Windows CE) and exercise enormous influence. In addition, while UNIX still dominated large corporations running mission-critical applications on very large servers, projections for overall intranet operating systems suggested that Microsoft's NT would dominate the market by 2001 (see Figure 3.2). A truly homogeneous Microsoft environment is years away, but some IT managers have been concluding that it may be better to wait for Microsoft than to bet on the wrong horse.

TABLE 3.4

U.S. Internet Access Device Shipments: 1997–2002 ($ millions)

	1997	1998	1999	2000	2001	2002	CAGR, 1997–2002
PCs	31,478	36,323	41,576	46,397	51,139	55,990	12.2%
Internet Appliances*	1,433	3,634	8,330	16,589	26,439	41,786	96.3%
% of Total Market	4%	9%	17%	26%	34%	43%	

*End-user appliances capable of accessing the Internet, such as set-top boxes, Web-enabled phones, personal digital assistants, and network computers.

Source: Adapted from IDC, "Executive Insights: Death of the PC-Centric Era," http://www.idcresearch.com/F/Ei/gens19.htm, May 1998.

FIGURE 3.2

Worldwide Intranet Server OS Share, 1997–2001

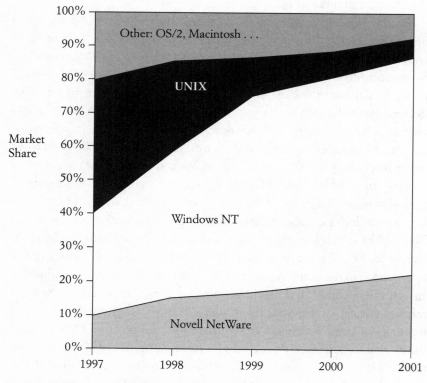

Source: Adapted from Datamonitor, "Servers and the Internet," 1998.

The second challenge was that momentum and perception of momentum, not just market statistics, determine the winners of these races. When Netscape led the charge toward a networked world of non-Windows, non-PC machines, the company could do no wrong. The message of "cross-platform, cross-device" resonated around the world, inside and outside corporations. In a 1996 study by IDC, twice as many respondents named Netscape rather than Microsoft as the company that would be most important to their company's Web-based business, and Netscape's "mindshare" was more than four times as great as IBM's.[48] When Microsoft appeared to grab the momentum back in 1997, fear, uncertainty, and doubt about the future of non-Microsoft solutions began to swell in both corporate and consumer circles. Netscape was the clear winner in mindshare in 1996, but by 1998, Microsoft was 10 times more likely to be nominated as "strategically most important" to the success of corporate Web-based businesses.[49]

The third challenge was that Netscape has to be financially healthy to achieve wide acceptance in the corporate world. If Netscape had focused its strategic initiatives exclusively on the Internet and consumer markets, short-run financial performance would not matter very much. But once Netscape made intranets and the enterprise its primary strategic thrust, concerns about long-run financial stability could overshadow great products and great technologies. No matter how appealing the corporate IT world finds cross-platform products, corporate customers look for signs that you will survive and prosper before they will bet their businesses on your solution. The great attraction of the corporate market is that customers do build their businesses around your solutions, and this makes it very hard to switch at a later date. But these high switching costs make corporate IT customers very conservative and leery of choosing a vendor that may not be around to support them in the future. The old phrase of the 1970s, "You never get fired for buying IBM," emerged because IT managers who bought non-IBM products risked getting fired if their vendor went out of business. The IT managers of the late 1990s have the same dilemma, but the names of the players have changed. Do they take the safe path and choose Microsoft, or do they risk their job on a potentially better, lower cost solution by Netscape?

The final challenge was that Netscape had to count on Microsoft staying the course and not supporting heterogeneous environments. The premise of Netscape's strategy is that Microsoft will remain unwilling or unable to provide cross-platform support, or even full support for its installed base of customers, as their systems age. But even though Microsoft's business model drives it toward upgrading customers to new operating systems and converting legacy systems to Windows, Microsoft has demonstrated amazing flexibility in its battle with Netscape. In the first quarter of 1998, Microsoft surprised the world by delivering a UNIX version of Internet Explorer 4.0. Microsoft's support of UNIX was the moral equivalent of heresy in Redmond. Microsoft also accelerated the introduction of the 4.0 browser for the Macintosh and Windows 3.1. Microsoft still did not deliver server applications to run on UNIX. Nonetheless, Microsoft has managed to take some wind out of the sails of Netscape's cross-platform promise.

Turn Your Competitor's Dominance of [Proprietary] Technology into an Advantage

Microsoft's most powerful competitive advantage has been the ownership of the Windows operating system, which ships on nine out of every 10 personal computers in the world. Microsoft has become one of the most profitable companies in the world because it owns the underlying technology that drives PCs. Through its ownership of the operating system, it controls the critical device drivers (software that connects the hardware and the software) as well as the critical APIs, or application programming interfaces (software that connects applications to the operating system). No one can copy Windows APIs or device drivers, and Microsoft can change them, eliminate them, or upgrade them, whenever it sees fit.

The Internet was the first new technology since the dawn of the PC that could threaten Microsoft's hegemony over future APIs and device drivers. The Internet began as a truly open industry standard: All the relevant technologies were in the public domain. Anyone could copy Internet protocols and integrate them into their own software products. Although individuals and corporations are developing and owning increasing numbers of Internet-related technologies, most key Internet protocols remain open.

Openness is one of the greatest attractions of Internet and intranet protocols for corporate buyers. As long as standards are in the public domain, there are more opportunities for innovation and greater competition. Consequently, it is more difficult for companies like IBM and Microsoft to "hold up" their customers by charging high prices. Open Internet protocols can also level the playing field for suppliers, to some degree, by reducing customers' fears that they will become locked into a single vendor.

Microsoft's proprietary history offered Netscape a powerful lever. Microsoft could never afford to put its existing technology into the public domain. Opening Microsoft's APIs and device drivers would destroy

Microsoft's business model. As Lou Montulli told us, "Microsoft is the antithesis of the Internet, or at least the way the Internet was. Microsoft has changed a great deal, but there is, and probably will always be, this suspicion in people's minds. There still is a large anti-Microsoft contingency, [and] we benefit from it to some degree." In fact, there are thousands of disaffected software developers and Microsoft competitors looking for alternatives to Microsoft. These companies, often called the ABM crowd, "Anybody But Microsoft," were a natural constituency to ally with Netscape.

Netscape has tried to harness this leverage by becoming the guardian of greater "openness." The hope was to shift the rules of the game through two strategies, which we call "open, but not open" and "leverage the Internet." With its "open, but not open" strategy, Netscape sought to mobilize the ABM companies behind standards that Netscape created and Microsoft could not control. In addition, Netscape took a huge gamble by giving away the company's browser source code in 1998. With this move, Netscape hoped to leverage the broad Internet community in support of Navigator over Internet Explorer.

Open, but Not Open. Rick Schell gave us a good overview of how the Internet and open protocols could change the game:

> The shift over protocols upsets the whole field. And it's not a game Microsoft plays very well. They learned the API game. Controlling the API and then controlling the underlying format and then being able to lock people in is great. When you shift to open protocols and open APIs and open standards—oh, my God—I mean, how do we keep control of that? It changes their whole model of the world. Change the model of the world, and they can't participate easily.

The idea was simple: Netscape would promote open standards, which Microsoft would have difficulty matching. What's more, Netscape would become synonymous with openness, placing Microsoft on the defensive. But to make money in an open world, the key is to be "open, but not open." Netscape had to offer customers solutions that appear open, and usually are open, but have very subtle features that are proprietary or difficult to copy. Without these subtle features, Netscape would have limited ability to make money in the long run.

In fact, the dirty secret of the computer industry is that everyone is "open, but not open"; they differ only in degree. Every computer company has proprietary pieces in its solutions, while every company in the industry claims to be "open," including Microsoft and IBM. Bill

Gates likes to say that Microsoft is the most open software company in the world because anyone can write an application for Microsoft's proprietary APIs.

Netscape was, indeed, more open than most technology companies. It published virtually all its innovations and extensions to existing standards, including some of its most important technologies, such as its directory (LDAP) and security or encryption (SSL) technology. In June 1997, Netscape even offered an "Open Standards Guarantee":

> We will adopt the major open standards recommended by the Internet Engineering Task Force (IETF) and other appropriate, vendor-neutral standards bodies, such as the World Wide Web Consortium (W3C), Object Management Group (OMG), ECMA, and others. We will also assume a leadership role in proposing new standards when there is real customer demand and where such standards do not yet exist.[50]

In a Web site column announcing the guarantee, Mike Homer, then head of marketing, explained:

> Netscape was founded on the philosophy that open standards benefit customers by ensuring superior technology and vendor interoperability. Netscape is committed to continuing to deliver all of its products based on open standards . . . both now and in the future. . . . Since its inception, Netscape has successfully driven Internet innovation by building new products, based on Internet standards, with increased functionality over other vendors' proprietary products.[51]

According to Bob Lisbonne, an open strategy might not benefit from the same "lock-in" effects that benefited Microsoft, but it still made sense for Netscape:

> People often ask, how are you going to have the same built-in advantages that Microsoft had in their business? And the answer is, we're not going to. We have all along . . . sincerely believed in an open-standards–based software world, and in open-standards–based competition. If that's really done well and true, it will not afford the lock-in or the increasing-returns advantages that Microsoft has had in desktop operating systems and in Office with the file formats. So, does it mean Netscape will ever be able to just kick back? No. We will continue to have to deliver superior products because customers will be able to switch. But, that's a better world for us, and our shareholders and our customers, than a world where Microsoft, or anyone, owns the customer. Why customers really have stampeded towards intranets has as much to do with the fact that they control their

vendor as with the specific technical advantages of an intranet. And we see that over and over again. So, yeah. It keeps us honest, but we're a young company and we've never been any other way.

We could summarize Netscape's open strategy with following a simple formula: *Netscape's reward = value added to the industry (x) Netscape's share of the industry.*[52] If Netscape could add value to the Internet, intranets, and extranets, and in the process, grow the market and grab share, it could prosper. Netscape has consistently developed new standards that sought to add value to Internet protocols. Netscape has then usually published the specifications and tried to be the first to market with the new protocols. As Andreessen told us, this strategy should work for Netscape, just as it has worked for others in the industry:

> It's the same strategy Cisco employed, and it's the same strategy Oracle employed writing SQL [Structured Query Language]. Sun employed it implementing UNIX. It's basically counting on a very strong underlying growth market . . . for technology that has very much to do with networks, [where] inter-operability and connectivity is critical to the value. The value of a network is absolutely critical on how everything can communicate with everything else. And the minute you try to [become proprietary], it's our assertion that you're taking yourself out of the market. Your products become massively less interesting. It has obvious downsides, but it is the wedge that has driven us into this market. It is the wedge that has resulted in a $600 million run rate after three and a half years, whereas we could not have done it with the proprietary approach.

In addition, by positioning itself as the defender of open standards, Netscape could leverage the deep current of anti-Microsoft sentiment that ran through the computer industry. This animosity had many manifestations. In 1996, for instance, customers and competitors of Microsoft, ranging from IBM and Compaq to Oracle and Cisco, were willing to invest $100 million collectively to create the Java Fund to support start-ups who would use Java to challenge Microsoft's hegemony. In 1998, the Software Publishers Association, a trade group that represents the 1,200 largest U.S. software companies (including Microsoft), announced "competition principles" that directly attacked Microsoft and its "unfair" use of the operating system to dominate competition.

The groundswell of anti-Microsoft sentiment was a natural point of leverage for Netscape, especially in standard-setting bodies. Organizations such as the World Wide Web Consortium (W3C) and the Internet Engineering Task Force (IETF) made decisions to endorse the technologies and protocols underlying the Internet. Negative decisions, in particular, by the W3 or IETF, could kill the adoption of a new technology. The W3C and IETF did not have the power to enforce their decisions. Instead, they owed their influence to their members' confidence that they would not promote a particular company's agenda at the industry's expense. This meant it was essential that all the important players have a chance to participate in the standards process. As Carl Cargill explained:

> You have to play with everybody in the arena, including Microsoft. . . . Standards are an inclusive game, not an exclusive game. The minute you make them exclusive, you're bound to fail. OSF [Open Software Foundation] failed because it was exclusive. UNIX International failed because it was not an inclusive standard. Exclusive standards fail. By saying, "Microsoft can't play inside my arena," you fundamentally screw yourself. So you can't do that. You have to be able to include people.

At the same time, Cargill observed that it was easy for Netscape to build coalitions in support of its standards because Microsoft was the company everyone loved to hate. He commented, "Microsoft's reputation, in many cases, predisposes people to play with Netscape, rather than Microsoft. I have been told, on several occasions, in standardization committees, 'We don't like you very much. But we hate Microsoft more.' Which is not exactly what I had wanted. But at this point in time, it is acceptable to work from that point of view. It gives us a minor lead."

Alex Edelstein also suggested that Microsoft struck fear in the hearts of most software companies. This created a great opportunity for Netscape because, "We get a lot of mileage out of [Netscape's position as an alternative]. Microsoft continues to make enemies to the extent that they continue to expand what they're trying to do. . . . Everyone's terrified of them now, and when Microsoft goes into someone's face, then they're very willing to work with us."

In the first few years of Netscape's history, this strategy was extremely successful. The perception of openness created leverage among customers and throughout the standards bodies. Netscape pioneered many of the standards that have become widely adopted and commonplace on the Internet. By creating open standards around LDAP, and early extensions to HTML, for example, Netscape catapulted itself into the forefront of the industry. Netscape overshadowed Microsoft's role in standard setting in the early years of the Web partly because of Microsoft's limited experience in embracing open standards and partly because Netscape won broad support on its early standards.

On the surface, it would appear that Netscape was pioneering a new form of truly open, standards-based competition.[53] In reality, Netscape was following a more extreme version of "open, but not open." From the early days, Netscape often extended standards into new realms, even if standards bodies did not adopt them. On occasion, Netscape also subtly embedded proprietary features in its products. For example, Netscape created and controlled JavaScript and continued to use its own implementation of JavaScript through early 1998, even though parts of that implementation were at odds with the standardized version. For a time, Netscape also used a version of Java that was not fully compatible with Sun's industry standard.

Netscape also designed some of its client and server products in ways that were classically "open, but not open." Most of Netscape's client software, such as Navigator or Mail Messenger, would work with any server software, and vice versa. Nonetheless, Netscape did some optimization for its own products. Lou Montulli, a senior developer who joined the company to work on the first browser, noted that the tension between openness and Netscape-only features was there since the beginning: "We obviously need to make the features that are client- and server-specific work together. But because we're open-systems–based, we test on every kind of server, not just ours. We don't really do many features at all that are Netscape-server specific. Maybe one or two." From Netscape's perspective, optimization was a good thing, but for customers, it meant higher switching costs. In addition, customers' options decreased when Netscape, as it occasionally did, used non-standard software components. Netscape's calendar and directory servers, for instance, did not conform to broader industry database standards, such as SQL (Structured Query Language, which is used for programming databases) and ODBC (Open Database Connectivity, a standard developed at Microsoft to access databases on different kinds of computers). Consequently, information systems managers could not use alternative databases with these server products.

While these were common industry practices, they drew fire from a number of critics. Netscape also began to suffer from comparisons to Microsoft in the area of standards compliance. When the World Wide Web Consortium released its recommendations for HTML 4.0, for example, it found Internet Explorer 4.0 to be more compliant with W3C specifications than Netscape's Communicator 4.0.[54] These setbacks undermined some of Netscape's credibility and its claim to be the champion of openness.

Andreessen often defended Netscape's record, pointing out that extending standards was not necessarily a violation of openness:

> We innovate. And when we innovate, we publish what we do. The traditional way the Internet-standards process works is that somebody does something and then says, "Look, everybody. Here's what I did." Either it gets added to the standard or it becomes the [de facto] standard. Lots of companies are making innovations in lots of different areas.[55]

> [In reference to JavaScript,] what counts at the end of the day to developers is not whether it's an "official" standard, but that everyone is using it. So I guess that the politically correct way to say it would be to say it has critical mass.[56]

Andreessen, however, did not persuade all the critics.

Netscape, like all technology companies, has walked the fine line that separates open from not open. What Netscape learned the hard way in the last few years was that "open, but not open" is a tricky strategy. Appearances can be as important as, or sometimes more important than, real openness. As more and more observers recognized the "not open" features of Netscape's "open" products, its leverage declined. Cargill summed it up well when he described the standards game as a way to "screw" the competition in implementation:

> The problem is that Microsoft has a reputation in the industry of screwing its partners. The thing that you try to encourage in standards is that you don't screw partners until after the standard is built. You screw them when you start to play implementation games, which is fair game. If you can't implement better than the other person, you lose. You're going to lose anyhow. The idea is that if you all implement the same interface, that [creates] the basis for standards. Microsoft is beginning to catch on to that. When we did the JavaScript standardization, the first question [we were] asked was: "What implementation are you standardizing?" Our response is, "We're not. We're doing an interface specification. We contributed ours. Borland contributed theirs. Microsoft contributed theirs."

Between 1994 and 1997, almost all industry players viewed Microsoft as the enemy of open standards and Netscape as their savior. In 1998, fewer people were certain about who was "screwing" whom.

Leverage the Internet: Give Away the Browser Source Code. By late 1997, sumo strategy had replaced judo strategy as the guiding principle behind the browser wars: Netscape was now competing with Microsoft in a head-to-head war on features. This was a fight Netscape had very little hope of winning. Microsoft could put more developers, more testers, and more marketing and distribution muscle behind Internet Explorer than Netscape could ever match. Netscape's best chance to stem the tide was to return to its judo roots by using flexibility and leverage to offset Microsoft's size and strength. Netscape needed a lever. On March 31, 1998, Netscape found one: It published on the Web the source code of Communicator 5.0, Netscape's next-generation flagship client product.

Source code is the core of any software product; it is the instruction set that defines how the program actually works. For a software company, publishing source code is the moral equivalent of revealing the recipe for Coca-Cola. Netscape's giveaway had only one major condition: Anyone who downloaded the code and modified it had to make his or her modifications available to Netscape and the world. Netscape retained the rights to the Netscape, Navigator, and Communicator brand names and logos, as well as the rights to distribute future products based on the code. But others could now build or distribute their own browsers based on Netscape's source code. And unlike most other free software, Netscape allowed companies to sell products based on the modified or unmodified code. The Mozilla Public License was free forever. Netscape could not change its mind in a few years and phase it out. The license, however, did not prevent Netscape from charging for enhanced or enterprise versions of Navigator and Communicator in the future.

The strategy behind giving away the source code was classic judo. Netscape management recognized that flexibility was critical: Without the resources to fight Microsoft directly, it had to find a creative way to compete. Moreover, leverage was essential. Netscape had to do something that Microsoft would not, or could not, imitate. It also needed huge external resources to offset Microsoft's size and financial strength. Once again, it hoped to find these resources on the Net. Jim Barksdale explained: "The time is right for us to take the bold action of making our client free—and we are going even further by committing to post the source code for free for Communicator 5.0. By giving away the source code for future versions, we can ignite the creative energies of the entire Net community and fuel unprecedented levels of innovation in the browser market."[57] As Tom Paquin, general manager for Mozilla.org (Netscape's brand name and Web site for the source code), told us, the process was off to a good start. Within six weeks of releasing the code, he had found, "lots of new ideas . . . and some are pretty imaginative ideas."

Netscape had returned to its roots. Just like in 1994, when it leveraged the Internet for beta testers, Netscape was trying to leverage the thousands of programmers on the Internet to build the world's largest virtual R&D organization. If successful, it could dwarf the resources of Microsoft. Moreover, Microsoft's decision to tie Internet Explorer more tightly to the Windows operating system in 1998 made it virtually impossible for Microsoft to respond in kind. If Microsoft revealed its source code for Internet Explorer, it would risk undermining its proprietary technology in Windows.[58]

Source code giveaways have worked in the computer world in the past. In 1998, for example, Microsoft, IBM, and Netscape trailed in market share to Apache, free software that ran almost half of all the Web servers on the Internet. Similarly, Linux, a freeware version of UNIX, was a highly popular operating system that ran on roughly 5 million computers around the world.[59] These examples suggested that a free browser could pay off for Netscape, even if the company never charged a penny for the browser again. Navigator and Communicator continued to be powerful brands that could help pull sales of Netscape server software and services available on the company's Web site. But Netscape needed several keys to make the freeware strategy work:

1. Independent developers had to join the party in droves, for the love of money, or for the love of code.
2. Netscape, like Apache and Linux, had to maintain very tight quality control and stewardship to keep the product viable in the enterprise.
3. Netscape had to be able to offer the best version of the revised browser, although independent developers would have access to the same source code and improvements.

One of the greatest challenges for Netscape will be to convince corporate customers that Navigator will be stable. Some IT managers might resist a product that has incorporated code from independent hackers. On the other hand, if Netscape can harness the same kind of spark, creativity, and energy that have produced innovation on Apache and Linux, it has an opportunity to regain the initiative in the browser wars.

Beware That Leverage Can Be Used Against You

Microsoft's past success provided Netscape with a number of valuable points of leverage, which the company aggressively exploited. As Netscape grew and thrived, however, it found that leverage could cut both ways. In 1994, Netscape came into the world with very little baggage. Its history, revenues, and installed base were too meager to give competitors enough of a handhold to bring the company down. By 1997, Netscape had a $500 million annual run rate and a multibillion-dollar market capitalization. This "weight" gave agile competitors such as Microsoft an opportunity to use judo leverage against the master.

Microsoft focused its attack on one of Netscape's greatest innovations, the strategy of making browsers "free, but not free." In 1995, "free, but not free" worked because Netscape was battling against companies that needed revenues to survive. By offering a free or trial version of the product to early adopters, and a $39 or $49 browser to corporate customers, Netscape changed the rules of the game in its favor. Moreover, Netscape's not-so-free browser fueled spectacular growth and a spectacular stock rise. Netscape management believed that any competitive move that undercut its revenue growth in 1996 and 1997 would have had a devastating impact on the stock. A lower stock price would have hurt Netscape's ability to attract and retain personnel as well as to make acquisitions. After Alex Edelstein left Netscape, he reflected on this period:

> Netscape was under intense demand to meet quarterly earnings, and Microsoft wasn't. Microsoft carried out a textbook campaign. . . . You have 20,000 well-seasoned Microsoft veterans, who not only are incredibly smart, but they have just vanquished all the enemies they fought in the last five years. They won all the battles, they own the [desktop] suite market, they own the OS [operating system] markets, and [they have] unlimited resources. . . . You plot out something like Microsoft did, lavish money everywhere, turn the company. Move your best people over to the Internet stuff. Netscape is like the fourth-year West Point student. You have gone public. You have an overvalued stock, and it's incredibly important that you keep earnings momentum. . . . There were times when we were too much like, "It is our God-given right to demand an excise tax on this particular revenue stream" because we have the browser.

Microsoft understood this perfectly: Netscape had become weighed down by its own strategy. By offering a truly free browser, as well as free server software with the purchase of Windows NT, Microsoft was using Netscape's weight against it. Netscape became caught in a classic judo move. It had made a commitment to the world to act like a high-growth company with high-profit potential. That commitment compelled Barksdale and Netscape to maintain revenue growth and margins, which meant powerful disincentives to match Microsoft's policies.

Microsoft's aggressive giveaway of Internet Explorer exposed a key weakness in Netscape's "free, but not free" strategy. Netscape's primary methods of distribution—downloads over the World Wide Web, retail sales, and direct sales to corporations—became less important over time, compared to distribution with new computer sales and online services. Yet these were channels in which Microsoft had a clear advantage. Computer companies shipped almost 100 million personal computers in 1997, growing the installed base of Web-enabled PCs by more than 50 percent. Virtually all these new machines had a Microsoft operating system and a free Internet Explorer browser. Only a tiny percentage included Netscape's Navigator or Communicator. For most PC makers, it was a no-brainer to include Internet Explorer. It cost time and money to remove it. More important, with the exception of a brief period between December 1997 and June 1998, when Microsoft was operating under a temporary restraining order, companies would have had to violate their contracts with Microsoft if they wanted to substitute Navigator for Explorer. But even in the absence of restrictive licensing agreements, PC makers had little incentive to add Navigator. Michael Dell, the chairman and CEO of the world's fastest growing personal computer company, explained his position clearly:

> From our standpoint, the customer is able to get a browser on the Internet for free, so trying to include something with a PC that the customer can get for free is pretty pointless. . . . We actually sell the Netscape browser and, for large customers, we load the Netscape browsers on their machines on a regular basis. We sell them to any consumer who wants to buy it. The problem, of course, is that it will cost $66 [in 1997], and why would you pay $66 for something you can get for free? And perhaps more important, why would a salesperson from Dell spend time on the phone trying to sell something for $66 when the customer can get it for free? I think the question for us is always, if we're going to do something, what are our alternatives, what do our customers want, and which of those allow us to earn the most money for our shareholders? . . . The problem is, if you sit down with the average customer, and you say, "Okay, Mr. Customer, what do you want?" The customer is relatively indifferent with Navigator or IE, and if something is free, he wants it. We see the several million PCs we're going to ship this year as an advertising platform for a company like Netscape. Perhaps they will see that they should, in fact, be paying us to have access to those customers, not the other way around.

Netscape's initial answer to this dilemma was to bundle its products in an effort to add more apparent value and deflect customers from focusing on price. In particular, management decided to stop shipping the Navigator browser as a separate product and integrate Navigator with different applications to create the Communicator suite. As we discussed in chapter 2, the suite included the traditional Navigator browser, but added an e-mail program, collaboration software, an HTML editor, and other applications (also see Appendix 2). Ram Shriram explained why Communicator was an obvious counterthrust to the free Microsoft browser: "We beefed up the client technology to take the high ground so that we're not subject to [customers] searching and replacing individual components of our products for a free product by Microsoft. We figured the higher up the food chain we go, the harder it is for them to start giving away equivalent technology."

Netscape soon discovered, after officially launching Communicator in June 1997, that bundling rarely solves pricing pressures. Unless you are best of class in every category or you offer a better price for the package of products, sophisticated customers will prefer to pick and choose. Bundling worked for Microsoft Office in the early 1990s because Office was close to best of class in each category and, most important, it was much cheaper to buy Office than a separate word processor and spreadsheet from Microsoft, WordPerfect, and Lotus. By the same token, bundling failed when Lotus introduced Symphony, an integrated word processor and spreadsheet, in the mid-1980s because the word-processing program was not as good as alternatives at the time.

Netscape found itself in a similar position to Lotus. It was still trying to sell a more expensive browser (compared to a free Internet Explorer), and corporate customers were not convinced that its mail, calendar, and groupware programs were better than the competition.[60] In addition, bundling put Netscape into conflict with a number of its allies. Intuit, for example, had been shipping the separate Navigator browser with its popular Quicken program. Even though Intuit was fighting for its life against Microsoft, Intuit switched to bundling Internet Explorer with Quicken because it was smaller and more flexible than the bulky Communicator suite. Similarly, IBM and its Lotus subsidiary had also been major distributors of both Navigator and IE. But IBM/Lotus decided to sleep with the enemy and bundle Internet Explorer alone rather than ship Communicator, a program that competed head-to-head with Lotus Notes and cc:Mail. In the end, Netscape's bundling strategy failed to deliver any advantages vis-à-vis Microsoft. In August 1997, two months after the release of Communicator 4.0, Netscape backtracked and made Navigator available as an unbundled product.

Netscape management seemed immobilized by Microsoft's "free IE" judo move. All Netscape's incentives encouraged the company to stay the course, and Microsoft leveraged those incentives every way it could. This is precisely what judo strategy should achieve. Two months after the release of IE 4.0, 15 months after market share started to decline, and almost two years after Microsoft declared war, Netscape managers were still debating what to do. According to Bob Lisbonne, Netscape's internal numbers showed that Navigator and Communicator had been losing one percentage point a month in market share since Microsoft released IE 3.0 in August 1996. These losses were occurring despite the fact that the reviews for Navigator and Communicator were generally comparable to the reviews for Internet Explorer.[61] In November 1997, when we questioned Ram Shriram about pricing and why Netscape did not match Microsoft, he told us:

> We have what I call circuit breakers, where we have some planned decisions we will take based on what happens if market share falls below certain levels. . . . What goes into the decision-making process is obviously the compensating revenue derived through these sources relative to the loss of license revenue in other segments. That's the thought process. If you exclude retail from the equation, the client revenue stream is probably a lot lower today than what we generated last summer. So that proves to me . . . we're not as dependent on client revenue as the company grows. The decision has several facets, but the process is to figure out how important is the pricing decision relative to market share. Is that the single biggest factor hurting market share, or is it the stranglehold on distribution that Microsoft has through its agreements with Windows licensees? In that case, it's irrelevant whether it's free or not. . . . [Making Navigator free] is a subject that has been debated for some time. It won't be decided that quickly or easily.

Two months later, Jim Barksdale capitulated. Going forward, Netscape was abandoning "free, but not free" and would offer all future standard-edition versions of Communicator and Navigator free of charge.

PRINCIPLE *Avoid sumo competitions, unless you have the strength to overpower your opponent.*

From Judo to Sumo Strategy

Most incumbents in the computer software industry lacked the speed, flexibility, or points of leverage to apply these judo techniques against Netscape. But Microsoft was a different story. Following Internet Day in December 1995, Microsoft discovered that it could also be fast, flexible, and a master of leverage. Microsoft has been applying exactly the same approach against Netscape that Netscape was trying to apply against

Microsoft. The winners in such judo matches are easy to predict: Books on judo tell us that if two judo masters of equal skill are in a fight, and one is bigger and stronger, then the bigger player wins. It is that simple.[62]

Microsoft, moreover, was not only good at judo strategy; it was great at sumo strategy as well. Microsoft proved that it could play the 800-pound gorilla as well as be quick and flexible and use leverage to compete on Internet time. Microsoft throws its weight around with the best sumo competitors in the world. In most prior sumo battles, where Microsoft went head-to-head with smaller players, Microsoft crushed its opponents, from Borland and Quarterdeck to WordPerfect. More recently, after years of struggle, Microsoft's efforts have finally begun to pay off in its battle with Novell. By leveraging its historic assets, in particular the operating system and existing customer relationships, Microsoft found that few companies could stay in the ring for very long.

Under these conditions, the right strategy for Netscape was to avoid sumo battles whenever possible; and the right strategy for Microsoft was to look for opportunities to turn the fight into sumo competitions. Unfortunately for Netscape, Gates successfully changed the terms of engagement with his hard-core approach to the Internet, and along the way, he forced Netscape into many unavoidable sumo bouts. The efforts to make the Netscape-Microsoft battle a sumo match was no accident. In April 1996, a senior member of Microsoft's staff stated that "if there was ever a bullet with Microsoft's name on it, [Navigator] is it." He continued, saying that Microsoft's strategy was first and foremost to win and retain browser share by offering users and software vendors a better synthesis with Windows. He also noted that Microsoft would evangelize Web masters and Internet service providers to utilize Microsoft's extensions of Web technology.

An internal 1996 Microsoft memo offered a similar view, proposing a concentrated, no-holds-barred attack on Netscape.[63] It directed managers to achieve "exclusive licensing of Internet Explorer" at the five largest Internet service providers. The plan called for Microsoft negotiators to "break most of Netscape's licensing deals, and return them to our advantage, because our browsers are free." It also pointed out that Microsoft could squeeze Netscape in the corporate world by exploiting Microsoft's Windows licenses. Microsoft's stated intention was, "We should have absolutely dominant browser share in the corporate space. Many of our customers already have a license for Internet Explorer, but don't know it. [The sales force] must make it clear that it does not make any sense to buy Netscape Navigator." Microsoft succeeded on virtually all fronts. Many of the largest Internet service providers around the world stopped supplying Netscape Navigator and started offering Internet Explorer exclusively. It took a U.S. Senate hearing before Microsoft would back off from some of its exclusive deals. Microsoft even threatened its largest single customer, Compaq Computer, with the software equivalent of excommunication, i.e., the loss of its license for Windows, if Compaq replaced Internet Explorer with Navigator.

Microsoft's deals with Apple and KPMG further demonstrated Microsoft's ability to use its sheer power and resources to win head-to-head contests. Apple Computer, for example, was a longtime Microsoft foe and supporter of Netscape. For years, Apple tried every means possible to undermine Microsoft, including asking for help from the Department of Justice and taking Microsoft to the Supreme Court. Microsoft was well known for not delivering Macintosh applications as quickly as it delivered Windows applications. Internet Explorer was no exception. Microsoft did not release the Macintosh version of Internet Explorer until nine months after it shipped with Windows 95. In the meantime, Netscape had been supplying browsers for the Macintosh from day one. But on August 6, 1997, Microsoft won the Apple account by brute force. In exchange for investing $150 million in Apple stock, and promises to deliver key applications to the Macintosh platform, Apple booted out Netscape and made Microsoft the default browser for the platform.

Twenty-four hours later, Microsoft did it again. Seven months earlier, on January 20, 1997, Netscape had announced that KPMG Peat Marwick would become a key reseller of Navigator, Communicator, and SuiteSpot. KPMG also adopted Navigator as the browser for its 17,000 workers. On August 7, 1997, KPMG agreed to throw out Netscape and embrace Microsoft. In exchange for a wide range of services, and more than $10 million in cash, KPMG adopted Microsoft's Internet Explorer for the desktop and Exchange and NT for the server. It also agreed to work jointly with Microsoft to set up a 500-person consulting group dedicated to Microsoft standards and technology. Even though KPMG preferred a cross-platform solution, and standardizing on Microsoft required KPMG to change its hardware and upgrade its software, Microsoft had made an offer that KPMG could not refuse. Netscape fought tooth and nail to hold on to the account, but Microsoft's offer was simply too rich.

From Sumo Strategy to Classical Strategy

By early 1998, Microsoft's combination of judo and sumo attacks was forcing Netscape to find a new way to compete. The company's cross-platform capabilities gave Netscape considerable leverage, especially in the server market, but it was clear that the cross-platform promise alone would not be enough. In addition, a full-fledged sumo strategy was obviously out of the question. Microsoft was simply too quick, too flexible, and too strong.

So Barksdale, Andreessen, and Homer decided to take Netscape back to the basics. The company's new approach exploited both judo leverage and the classical tools of strategy—try to be an early mover in new technologies, exploit your existing installed base of users, then lock in the customer by creating switching costs. Unlike the old strategy, the new strategy did not require a revolution, nor did it require killing or undermining Microsoft or IBM. Instead, the new goal was to grab a reasonable share of two huge industries (enterprise software and Web site portals). Netscape might still have the image of a browser company, but as Bob Lisbonne explained to us in March 1998, the company made a fundamental shift in orientation in 1998:

> We concluded [in early 1998, that] there were two real engines of value creation in the company. One was the Web site business, and the other was our enterprise software business. The way [Navigator and Communicator] supported those two was different. For the enterprise software business, it was creating the great client software that was part of the client-server solution. And for the Web site business, it was driving traffic, and what we call "eyeball hours". . . . We saw the fourth quarter [of 1997] was not going to be a good one, so we seized that opportunity and we turned that lemon into lemonade. We took the client price to zero and exploited its position in the marketplace. We priced it at zero to customers to advance those two businesses.

The new mantra for Netscape managers was to leverage the company's existing assets in order to take part in the Internet's next big phase, which Barksdale called a "land grab." Businesses were rushing to stake out claims on the Web, and Netscape wanted to be an early mover with stakes in the richest turf: enterprise software (intranets and applications), electronic commerce software (Kiva and Actra), and Web site portals (Netcenter). As Lisbonne noted, Netscape management realized they had a relatively unique combination of capabilities to help corporate customers "build, buy, or outsource" software and services. By taking advantage of its installed base of browsers, Netscape could also turn Netcenter into a major portal. Like Yahoo!, Excite, and Microsoft, the plan was to become the home page for as many users as possible, which would attract a large share of Web advertising dollars as well as make Netcenter an attractive site for hosting large corporate accounts. Barksdale believed that this combination of businesses could be a $45 billion market in 2001.

Enterprise and E-commerce Customers. Netscape's new strategy identified "enterprise service providers" (ESPs) as the company's major targets. Andreessen wanted Netscape to distinguish its offerings in this market by adopting what he called a "Mack truck" approach—"very large scale, totally centrally managed, and fundamentally integrated with legacy systems." As he explained to us, enterprise service providers would emerge from the convergence between "Global 2000" companies and Internet service providers:

> Our theory is, basically, that the typical business operating on a global scale in the Internet economy is going to need to be a service provider to its customer base, to its supplier and its distribution base. What traditionally we thought of as IT departments and what traditionally we thought of as ISPs are starting to collide. Your typical IT department has to deal with a world in which they're now responsible for servicing the needs of billions of external customers, as well as hundreds of thousands of internal users. In addition, service providers in the Internet economy are going to need to offer a full range of value-added services [such as e-mail hosting and e-commerce hosting and Web-publishing hosting] on top of what they have traditionally provided—especially people like ISPs or telcos—to be able to stay in the game at all.

Netscape based its ESP strategy on two products it acquired at the end of 1997. The first was the Netscape Application Server (NAS), developed at Kiva. NAS was a high-performance, middle-tier server that tied together legacy database systems and Web-based front ends. Unlike a traditional Web server, it was robust enough to support extremely high levels of transaction processing and mission-critical applications. The second product underpinning Netscape's new strategy was Actra's Commerce-Xpert suite, which the new applications products division handled. These products offered high-end, packaged electronic commerce applications.

Netscape's new strategy was designed to take it out of the "winner take all" world and into markets where the "land grab" metaphor made more sense. The concept was to preempt competitors by moving early and moving fast and grabbing as much business as you can, before others arrive. Steve Savignano, senior vice president and general manager of the applications products division, saw Netscape as having two advantages in this race over potential competitors like IBM and Microsoft. One was the fact that "we have product today that works." The other was Netscape's ability to offer access to a major portal to the Web. As he explained in our May 1998 interview, "I can always sell a Merchant Solution. They're going to pay me a quarter of a million dollars for Merchant Solution. They build a store. Then, what do they do? I put a link to their store on my Web site, and that solution that I provided them is now worth tens of millions of dollars, not hundreds of thousands of dollars." Barksdale agreed that Netscape had clear advantages in this market in 1998: "There are very few products from IBM that have multi-hosting capability and scaling capability like our products. And Oracle is still a year or so away. Microsoft's directory product is two years away, and it's proprietary. They have very immature e-commerce products."

This strategy assumed that competitors such as IBM and Microsoft, which lacked high-end electronic commerce applications in mid-1998, would eventually assemble similar packages. Before that occurred, however, Netscape hoped to build a large, secure installed base. Savignano described how he expected this to happen: "The thing that locks them in is not the technology. The thing that locks them in is the business logic and business rules [customer-specific applications and data added to the product after the purchase]. Where the switching costs come in is that I have connectivity with my trading partners, and I have business rules codified that basically work. If I am a Netscape customer cranking in revenue, why should I change?"

A $20 million deal Netscape signed with Citibank in May of 1998 was the prototype for this strategy: Netscape would not only provide the software infrastructure and e-commerce applications, but also make Citibank a partner on its Web site. As more marquee names, including Ford, Knight Ridder, E*TRADE, and AOL signed on to Netscape's vision in 1998, big corporate customers would build confidence and few would be likely to switch, even if Netscape competitors caught up. Moreover, Netscape was returning to speed as its ultimate advantage. Savignano summed it up this way: "In one sentence, the one word that gives us strategic advantage is speed. It's not something we sit down and say we're going to design ourselves to be faster than everybody else. But if you think about it, we go into new markets, make changes in our product, get to those markets, give customer benefits, and then move on to the next thing faster than anybody else."

The Web Site. The consumer strategy relied on similar logic. Mike Homer, the head of the newly formed Web site division, wanted to build on Netscape's biggest asset, its installed base, and use Netscape's speed to make it happen fast. As Homer told us in May 1998, the new strategy was obvious:

I've got 5 million people signed up for Netcenter, and I've got 70 million Navigator users. I don't give a shit which way the client market share is going. The first guys I'm going to get as members of a site are those 70 million users. By the way, even if our share is 56 percent, I'm still getting five out of 10 new users. Let's say the rate is wrong. Four out of 10? And I have 70 million. So, drawing from that 70 million base is absolutely the first, easiest thing to do. . . . I get 24 million audited visitors to the site itself a month. . . . In the short term, the strategy is: Provide all the essential services for a consumer online portal [to these potential customers] within 60 days. [In the longer run], the point of the strategy is to differentiate, with an integrated Web site and browser services.

With more than half the browsers on the Web using Navigator in the summer of 1998, and a large percentage of those people starting at Netscape's Netcenter by default, Homer saw a natural advantage. His strategy was to exploit the installed base of users and make the Web site easier to use and more feature-rich by building those new features directly into Netscape Navigator. Just as Microsoft gained an advantage from being in the operating system business and then being first to exploit related applications on its platform, Netscape could gain advantages by being the first to utilize browser capabilities that would make its Web site more exciting and accessible to the masses. In the process, Homer noted, Netscape would go "totally head-to-head" with AOL, Yahoo!, and Microsoft: "I don't want to get into, 'Oh, well, they're going head-to-head against Microsoft again.' But we'll be competing with them." And just like the strategy in e-commerce, the name of the game will be land grab and market share. The economics are also simple: the more users, the more advertising dollars, the greater the profits. Or, as Bob Lisbonne told us, Netscape's new value proposition is "driving traffic, and get what we call 'eyeball hours' . . . and then companies pay Netscape, AOL, Yahoo! and others to get access to those eyeballs."

Andreessen saw a huge opportunity to meld together these two businesses. He explained in our May 1998 interview that, "increasingly, Netscape Navigator is going to come preloaded with access to a whole variety of services in a fundamental, easily configured way. . . . It's going to get to the point, within a year or two, that when you install Netscape Navigator, the line between software and services is going to be completely blurred. You are not going to be able to tell the difference." One of the first examples of this integration was what Netscape called "Smart Browsing," a search technology that operated through the browser's location bar. If a user typed a keyword like "sports," rather than a typically lengthy Internet address, the browser would lead to the corresponding Netcenter channel. A more specific keyword like "Ford Ranger" should lead to the appropriate page, while a nearby list of "Related Items" would feature other car-related sites like Chrysler, Toyota, and Chevrolet. In the long run, Netscape executives hoped that these features, plus other ways to personalize a user's Web experience, would prove compelling enough to grow Netcenter and Navigator's installed base. Indeed, Netscape's control over half the browser market could give Netcenter a real leg-up on the competition, if it built special features into its user interface.

No longer relying solely on judo techniques, Netscape's viability and profitability will depend largely on its ability to execute. The challenges will be very real. Netscape has relatively few advantages over Microsoft with its current strategy, other than a small head start. It will simply have to outperform and out-innovate Microsoft to be successful. In addition, as we will discuss further in chapters 4 and 5, it will have to beat other world-class competitors, such as IBM, in the enterprise; master diverse enterprise technologies; and manage two very diverse operations with different skill requirements. Barksdale told us in May 1998, "I'm a media company, and I'm an enterprise software company. Two different businesses." We will return to these challenges in chapter 6.

A Little Help from the Government. Part of Netscape's future will also depend on the U.S. government. On May 18, 1998, the U.S. Department of Justice and 20 states joined forces against Microsoft in the broadest antitrust cases in a generation. In announcing their action, U.S. Attorney General Janet Reno charged Microsoft with using its monopoly power in PC operating systems to "develop a chokehold" on the market for Web browsers and other Internet products.[64] The two lawsuits charged that Microsoft illegally forced personal computer manufacturers to preinstall Internet Explorer and prevented them from modifying the appearance of the IE icon on the Windows start-up screen. They also attacked provisions in Microsoft's contracts with online services and Internet service providers that limited their ability to promote competing browsers. Based on this evidence, the DOJ sought to require Microsoft to offer a version of Windows without IE. Alternatively, they asked the court to order Microsoft to distribute Navigator with Windows. In addition, the plaintiffs sought to limit Microsoft's control over the Windows desktop and to prohibit "exclusionary contracts" with Internet and online service providers.

The DOJ's action could have a material impact on Netscape. Even though Navigator remained free in the summer of 1998, Netscape's share of the browser market will continue to feed the rest of the company's business, especially its Web site. In addition, a favorable ruling in the government's case might make it easier for Netscape to charge for enhanced versions of the browser in the future. As Andreessen told us, "The antitrust action lowers the threshold that we have to get over before OEMs are fundamentally willing to do something that's not in Microsoft's best interest." Some of the benefits of the antitrust case were obvious within weeks, as Microsoft loosened some of the restrictions it imposed on PC manufacturers. In the spring of 1998, Microsoft allowed Gateway 2000, for the first time, to offer IE and Navigator on an equal basis to consumers who chose its Internet access service. IBM announced similar plans. A number of other OEMs indicated that they were studying plans to make Navigator more widely available.

Netscape executives sought to downplay the significance of these events. Roberta Katz, who as general counsel was closest to the issue, resisted characterizing Netscape's part in the antitrust action as a strategic move. Instead, she saw this as an instinctive defensive reaction: "I wouldn't call it part of the strategy. It was during the course of doing business we encountered Microsoft's pressures, and they were of such a nature that we felt obligated to increase the visibility." Katz explained that regulators first approached Netscape in connection with the DOJ's interest in MSN in the summer of 1995. Difficulties the company encountered in distribution and sales by mid-1996, according to Katz, drew Netscape further into the antitrust arena:

> All of a sudden, we were getting pushback from distributors of our products that we hadn't seen before. And they were telling us it was because of their contracts with Microsoft. . . . From Jim [Barksdale]'s point of view, what got him going was when a salesman came in and said we were having trouble with OEMs, based on Microsoft pressure. And he came to me and he said, "This is a violation of the consent decree [that ended an antitrust case against Microsoft in 1995], if nothing else. Look into it."

As Katz began a quiet information-gathering campaign, a number of surprising stories came to light. She recalled: "There were a lot of days when I heard about things that Microsoft did that made my jaw drop. When I started seeing some of these things, at first I didn't believe it. They seemed so far over the line—the things they would do with customers that would harm us." Katz took her evidence to Gary Reback, a Silicon Valley attorney described as "the only man Bill Gates fears."[65] Reback had already gone into battle against Microsoft, filing a brief that urged the court to reject the consent decree that ended its first antitrust fight in

1995. Reback also successfully opposed Microsoft's efforts to acquire financial software maker Intuit. Although his clients often preferred to remain anonymous, many industry observers believed that he represented Borland, Novell, and Sun. In August 1996, he took up Netscape's case.

In a letter dated August 12 to Joel Klein, soon to be the head of the antitrust division at the DOJ, Reback argued that Microsoft was engaging in predatory pricing, making side payments to customers, and tying the distribution of Internet Explorer to Windows 95. Reback claimed that Microsoft provided a three-dollar subsidy per machine to computer makers who refused to distribute competing browsers and offered certain customers five dollars per copy to remove Navigator and replace it with IE. He also quoted in his letter a Microsoft representative telling a crowd of several hundred people, "Our intent is to flood the market with free Internet software and squeeze Netscape until they run out of cash."[66] According to Katz, Netscape's primary role was to make this letter public:

> During the summer of 1996, we highlighted some of the things we had seen in the form of a letter, which we made public. We made the letter public for a couple of reasons. One, we wanted to put Microsoft on notice that we were watching . . . to make clear that Microsoft was doing some really crummy stuff at that point, and we weren't the only ones who were publicly complaining about it. [Another firm] publicly complained about at least one of the things that we cited in the letter. They were trying to change the licensing terms for their workstations, such that you really couldn't use any browser other than theirs to interconnect. But we also referenced other kinds of behaviors that we were seeing.

Joel Klein's version of events mirrored Roberta Katz's recollection. In an interview in the summer of 1998, he told us how he became interested in the case:

> We got a white paper from Netscape and Gary Reback right around the time I took over in the fall of 1996. I decided to put the investigation in the San Francisco office and start an investigation into Section 1 and Section 2 of the antitrust law, and to see whether there were any violations of the consent decree. We started to put resources behind the San Francisco office, and they started the process of collecting data.

Microsoft angrily rebutted Netscape's charges, contending that the decision to release Reback's letter amounted to "a calculated attempt by Netscape to enlist government and the media in its marketing campaigns."[67] Nonetheless, one month later, the DOJ started issuing civil subpoenas for information from Microsoft. Soon Netscape was asked to turn over relevant files. A year later, in October 1997, the DOJ's inquiry bore fruit when regulators charged Microsoft with violating the terms of the 1995 consent decree, which prohibited Microsoft from "tying" separate products to the distribution of Windows. The DOJ argued that Microsoft forced computer manufacturers to install Internet Explorer as a condition of licensing Windows 95. After winning a preliminary injunction from Judge Thomas Penfield Jackson requiring Microsoft to separate Windows 95 and IE, the DOJ broadened its investigation to focus on contracts with online services, Internet service providers, and content partners. In May 1998, these efforts culminated in the filing of the two broad antitrust suits. Although the U.S. Court of Appeals overturned Judge Jackson's preliminary injunction to separate IE and Windows in June, Joel Klein persisted with the larger action.

Katz explained that Netscape's role throughout this process was cooperating with requests for information from the DOJ and ensuring that the facts were heard:

> The legal strategy, if you want to call it that, is simply to educate. Part of the issue on this is that the general public, and I use that term very broadly, does not understand what's happening in front of its nose in terms of the pervasiveness of Microsoft's power. Everyone understands the wealth, but they have not understood the actual and potential power and control. And when it extends to electronic commerce, and when it extends to communications, if we decide as a country, or as a culture, that we want to leave so much control in the hands of one company, fine. But let's do it after knowing the facts. The problem is, people don't know the facts.

Klein noted that he personally did not remember meeting with any lower-level Netscape staff during the investigation, but he did meet with Katz and Barksdale a few times. Klein was impressed with Barksdale's approach: "I met with Roberta Katz a few times, as well as Barksdale. Barksdale meetings were very interesting because he tended to focus more on the policy issues regarding where do you draw the line in the operating system and prevent the operating system from taking over all software. He was more focused on the issues of principle, rather than issues directly related to Netscape in our conversations."

Netscape supported the Department of Justice, but only with one legal staff member, who was not full-time on the case. Outside counsel was leading the efforts. One of Jim Barksdale's clearest instructions to his troops was to keep legal and governmental affairs out of the day-to-day running of the company. Todd Rulon-Miller told us: "I don't think there was ever an internal discussion where we said, 'Let's keep the price on the browser, so the DOJ will stay in the game.' And, by the way, we didn't manage by the DOJ much as a management team. Barksdale made that clear to us. That was a legal problem, and out of bounds. It was a separate set of meetings that was sequestered to just a few people because we had to run our business." Netscape's executive team had enough on its plate without worrying too much about what was happening 3,000 miles away in Washington. In addition to the strategic problems the company had to resolve, the technology side of the business posed constant challenges as well. In the next two chapters, we consider these issues and analyze Netscape's performance when it came to implementing judo techniques by designing and developing software products on Internet time.

Chapter Four

DESIGN STRATEGY

Leverage through Cross-Platform Techniques

T HERE ARE SEVERAL WAYS that a firm can use design strategy to pursue strategic leverage as well as try to increase the potential flexibility and speed of its engineering organization. As we discussed in chapter 3, leverage, as well as rapid movement and flexibility, are the judo techniques that firms competing on Internet time would do well to master. In this chapter, we discuss how Netscape sought leverage by creating products that exploited weaknesses in the competition. More specifically, Netscape targeted older Windows customers and non-Windows markets with its cross-platform designs and built its products around Internet protocols that it either invented or implemented in a way that enabled Netscape to "lock in" customers, at least to some extent.

Netscape's product teams tried to increase their quickness and flexibility primarily by attempting to raise the level of modularity in product designs and creating common components that packaged core technologies important to the cross-platform strategy. Modularity also made it possible to develop in parallel multiple versions of a product (for example, start the 1998 version and the 1999 version at the same time) as well as create new features simultaneously outside of the regular project organization. Parallel development reduced project cycle time by overlapping work, and it enhanced quick market movements by shortening the intervals between new product releases. We believe that the following principles characterize Netscape's efforts in product design as well as key aspects of Microsoft's design approach (except for the emphasis on cross-platform products):

- *Design products for multiple markets (platforms) concurrently.*
- *Design and redesign products to have more modular architectures.*
- *Design common components that multiple product teams can share.*
- *Design new products and features for parallel development.*

While Netscape managers and engineers consciously pursued these design strategies, they did not always implement them perfectly. They had to make decisions on Internet time and they made mistakes on Internet time, both in their technical choices and in how they carried out their decisions. For example, Netscape executives and senior engineers decided to expand the functionality of the browser client (from Navigator to Communicator) before it was sufficiently modular to make these enhancements easily. They ran into technological hurdles when product teams tried to deploy still-evolving technologies like Java and JavaScript too extensively. Netscape also had to back off from overly ambitious plans to restructure its browser code in one fell swoop in order to make it much more modular as well as inherently cross-platform (i.e., Java-based). Finally, Netscape's efforts to create common components in a centralized division proved to be difficult to sustain, technically and politically, as the company portfolio grew larger and more complex. Netscape's engineers and technical executives were slow to identify and correct these problems, although, as we describe in this chapter, they made important course corrections during late 1997 and 1998.

PRINCIPLE   *Design products for multiple markets (platforms) concurrently.*

The Cross-Platform Challenge

As we look at what Netscape achieved during 1994–1998, perhaps the company's most significant source of leverage against Microsoft came from its investment in cross-platform design. Aleks Totic, a member of Netscape's original development team and before that the "Mac guy" on the Mosaic team at NCSA, summarized Netscape's arguments for the benefits of this approach: "The advantage is that your product truly works cross-platform without rewriting. We are able to release on all platforms and it pretty much works the same." The reality was something less than Totic claimed, however. As Netscape's client and server software became more complex in terms of features, it became more difficult to write code that worked equally well across the different platforms, primarily because the application programming interfaces (APIs) differ from platform to platform, among other factors. Complicating matters for Netscape was the fact that Microsoft was also cross-platform, though it was not committed as heavily to this strategy. Microsoft eventually released versions of its browser for other platforms and older Windows versions. Microsoft also released servers finely tuned for Windows NT. Nonetheless, Netscape's commitment to release its products for all platforms quickly into the market and, especially, to release servers for the UNIX market, were key elements that differentiated Netscape from Microsoft in Internet software.

Totic and other Netscape engineers became interested in creating a multi-platform browser even before Clark and Andreessen founded Netscape. The original NCSA Mosaic team at the University of Illinois designed a browser that ran on different operating systems. But they did a "quick and dirty" job. Small teams worked in parallel, competing with each other to finish browser versions for Windows 3.1, Macintosh, and some of the UNIX operating systems. They did not take the time to debug or "stabilize" the product, like a professional software company. They were under no competitive pressure, but were in competition among themselves to build something that worked "most of the time." After founding Netscape, their task with Navigator 1.0 was to do professional cross-platform development that outperformed other browsers on the market. Navigator 1.0 did indeed run on the three platforms successfully, and it quickly became the browser of choice for nearly all desktop computers—Windows, Macintosh, and UNIX. Jon Mittelhauser, another original Mosaic developer, recalled their college days at NCSA and the transition to Netscape:

> We didn't have stress in the sense of pressure. We had competition and fun. We were racing each other so we had all three platforms competing against each other. We had self-induced pressures for time and stuff that, "If I don't work all night, Aleks [Totic] is going to get ahead of me on the Mac. Then I'm going to have to hear him gloat." It felt very similar. It was a different motivation. . . . We didn't really care about quality. We were just cranking out releases and putting in new features. And we did change things between there and when we started here. When we did [Navigator] 1.0, we really said, "Okay, we want to do a cross-platform. We want to do it right. . . . We want to do it with quality." We hired some of these engineering managers who knew how to do things. At NCSA, we never cranked that screw . . . and said, "Okay, we're going to stop adding features. We're going to stabilize. We're going to bug fix." There was no point. We had no outside reason to. So, personally, learning to do that has been a transition. But it's obviously—I'm a logical guy—a necessary one. You're not going to sell a product if you never stabilize it.

Designing products to be truly cross-platform means that developers must write code that does not utilize any interfaces or programming "tricks" specific to a particular operating system or computer hardware platform. Yet many platform-specific APIs or programming conventions exist because they enable programmers to write code that runs faster or handles graphics and memory better than code that uses the "lowest-common-denominator" interfaces. As a result, cross-platform products pose technical challenges that can lead to lower programming productivity and weak product performance compared to platform-specific products.

Cross-Platform Design Techniques

Netscape was by no means the only company to struggle with the cross-platform challenge in software development. In past years, many excellent companies have failed to write true cross-platform code that worked as well as "native" applications (programs written specifically for a particular operating system or hardware platform). In one famous example, IBM and Apple, working together in their ill-fated Taligent joint venture, failed to come up with a cross-platform operating system that worked on both Macintosh or PowerPC and Intel-compatible hardware. Informix, the high-end database software provider, struggled for years to design products that worked equally well across the UNIX and Windows NT platforms. Borland had similar problems trying to create development tools that worked equally well across the Windows and Macintosh platforms. Corel failed to write a cross-platform Java version of its office applications suite. There are many more cases of firms that failed or took years to design good cross-platform code.

Microsoft experienced similar problems in the early 1980s. It used to develop Word and some other applications in a neutral pseudo-code ("p-code") format and then compile it for Windows and Macintosh platforms. This saved time in development, but the code tended to be slow. Mac Word also appeared different from native Macintosh applications since Microsoft tended to favor the Windows user interface (UI) format. In the 1990s, Microsoft continued to have trouble using a single code base across the Windows and Mac platforms for applications such as Word.[1] For Internet Explorer, which Microsoft initially built only for Windows 95, Microsoft chose to create mostly separate code bases for the Macintosh and UNIX versions and to share only some portions of the code between the Windows 3.1 and Windows 95/NT/98 versions.

We learned more about Microsoft's thinking with regard to cross-platform Internet products in an interview with Ben Slivka, the general manager of Microsoft's Windows User Interface group in 1998. Slivka started the Internet Explorer 1.0 team in October 1994 and headed the next two projects as well. He explained why Microsoft developers, including himself, disliked cross-platform design:

> The problems with that pseudo-code–based approach for platforms is that you get this lowest-common-denominator experience. How do you tune things? The different operating systems are just too different. It's a quality/time/space tradeoff thing. We could host all of Windows on UNIX and then it would just run. That would be one way to do it. But there're subtle things, like UNIX doesn't have TrueType fonts, doesn't have color matching, the sound system is weird and different. It doesn't have DirectX [a set of hardware-independent services for graphics, etc.] like we do. We've got these really fancy animation features in IE 3 and IE 4 and I don't even know how to do that on a UNIX box. We don't have the right protocols for printing. How do I print on a UNIX box? It's like they sell you half [of a system]. It's a very primitive thing. . . . On the Macintosh, I've got a one-button mouse. So all those things I did with a two-button mouse on a PC, I can't do. It just kind of goes on and on and on.

During 1996 and 1997, Netscape engineers thought they would solve the problems of cross-platform design by adopting Sun Microsystems's new language, Java. Java promised to make cross-platform programming simple and efficient. As a result, Netscape dedicated significant resources to Java-based development. By late 1997, however, Netscape took a realistic look at Java and reassessed its prospects. Unlike Sun and some other companies in Silicon Valley, we found Netscape to be a practical company, not a highly "religious" company. Andreessen and his senior engineering staff recognized that technologies like Java and cross-platform design are important, but not more important than the business of selling software. Java was not giving Netscape the performance it needed, so Netscape engineers were gradually deemphasizing both Java and the more general cross-platform techniques to make sure that Netscape products were competitive on the Windows platforms.

Over time, Netscape found the lowest-common-denominator approach more and more difficult to sustain for many components in its products. Through Navigator 3.0 and SuiteSpot 3.5, Netscape engineers tailored a relatively small part of the code to particular platforms, probably no more than 20 percent. Communicator 4.0 had a slightly higher percentage of platform-specific code. But two problems emerged. First, as Windows became more important, Netscape engineers could not compromise product performance for the sake of cross-platform design. Poor Windows performance guaranteed a loss of market share. Second, engineers had to design the nontailored code to be truly cross-platform without taking too much extra time in development and testing or overly compromising product performance on any of the other operating system platforms.

By 1998, these problems forced Netscape to alter its design strategy. The Mozilla source-code release of Communicator 5.0, for example, had roughly 40 percent platform-specific code, designed largely to optimize performance for Windows. The precise percentages are difficult to pin down because Netscape did not measure or report this number. Communicator also included huge amounts of cross-platform Java code (as much as one-third of the total product code), with much of this coming increasingly from Sun Microsystems (see Table 4.1). The same general trend was true for servers. Netscape continued to design cross-platform code because UNIX had a relatively large market share. But with Windows NT gaining market share fast, Netscape placed increasing emphasis on optimizing its server products for Microsoft's NT operating system.

Nonetheless, Netscape did appear to have refined cross-platform design techniques to a considerable degree. No PC software company could really match Netscape's expertise here. It helped that the three main platforms Netscape wrote to—UNIX, Windows, and Macintosh—all were relatively "mature." As Mittelhauser admitted, this maturity made Netscape's design and coding tasks a bit easier, compared to what other companies had faced in the past:

> The platforms are not that fundamentally different. . . . Any core routines, like image code and networking code and all that, all entailed abstracting out some comment. . . . To be fair to other companies, one of the things that had happened was that the three platforms had all matured to the point where it was fairly easy to do. I think the development environment and other things had driven the PC and Mac up to where UNIX was. The only things that were slightly contentious issues were memory management, which is fairly easy to abstract. In networking, Windows had finally got in a sockets library that was almost identical to the UNIX sockets library. We wrote our own on the Mac.

Mittelhauser saw another positive factor: The small team of college buddies had few communication problems or conflicts. There were no entrenched teams of Mac versus Windows versus UNIX developers. They were all "hackers" at heart in Netscape, especially in the early days, working together to figure out how to conquer an interesting programming dilemma that was part and parcel of the Internet:

> I think there's another thing that enabled us to do it. . . . We knew each other very well and we didn't have any hidden agendas at that point. We

TABLE 4.1

The Navigator and Communicator Projects, 1994–1997

	Developers	Approximate Code Base	Project Start	Months to: Public Beta	Months to: Final Version	"Final" Release	Person-Months	Estimate of Java Code	Estimate of Netscape Code Delivered Per Person-Month
Navigator 1.0	10	100,000	4/94	7	9	12/94	90	—	1100
Navigator 1.1/1.2	20	150,000	12/94	3	7	6/95	140	—	1100
Navigator 2.0	30	700,000	7/95	4	8	2/96	240	350,000	1500
Navigator 3.0	50	1,000,000	2/96	3	7	8/96	350	400,000	1700
Communicator 4.0	120	3,000,000	8/96	6	11	6/97	1320	1,200,000	1400

Notes:

• Dates of project starts are taken as the same month as the release of the previous product, although the projects had some overlapping.

• Developers is a rough estimate of the number of software engineers that worked on the products more or less full time, for all versions. The estimates exclude QA/testing, product management, other support people, or partner developers not working on-site at Netscape as part of the Netscape product team (such as Java developers at Sun). The numbers tend to reflect peak staffing levels and were clearly lower in the early stages of some projects.

• There were no formal final releases announced of Navigator 1.1 and 1.2. In this table, we take the release of Navigator 1.2 in June 1995 as the end of the Navigator 1.1/1.2 project. This started after the release of Navigator 1.0 in December 1994.

• Months to public beta and release change for Navigator 2.0 if we include Navigator 1.1 as a separate release. A quote from Lou Montulli: "Even though [1.1] wasn't labelled a full point release, it had more than enough features to make it a full rev in today's terms. In many respects, it had more features over 1.0 than 3.0 did over 2.0" (e-mail correspondence, 6 February 1998).

• Public beta refers to the number of months from the start of the project until the first publicly released beta. Most projects had numerous beta releases, with different degrees of completed functionality.

• Navigator 2.0 and later releases onward include large amounts of Java code developed inside and outside Netscape, with increasing amounts coming from Sun Microsystems. Most of this code consisted of the Java virtual machine and some other features, such as for security and Smart Update. The Java code data are extremely crude estimates based on discussions with programmers.

• Most versions of the client also had "point releases" that followed the initial "final release."

Source: Author estimates based on company interviews.

were able to quickly extrapolate past the difficulties and move on, whereas I think [it's more difficult] trying to start a new project at a big company where you have a Mac team and Windows team. . . . We were all just buddies from college and we sat down and said, "Okay, what's different on these platforms. Memory? Okay. So we'll make an X-P (cross-platform) malloc call and you'll write a Windows version and I'll write a Mac version. Okay, what else is different?" And we got past all that pretty quick.

Netscape also did not fall into the trap of trying to use a tool kit to generate cross-platform "front-end" or user-interface code. Before HTML, Java, and JavaScript, this was not very practical to do, and it remains difficult because Internet languages have poor graphics tools. Netscape developers seem to have quickly realized this. At least in part, we can say that Netscape engineers succeeded with cross-platform development because they limited their ambitions. Mittelhauser agreed.

When people say "cross-platform," I think the thing that they do the most is, one, they either try to use one of these tool kits that does [cross-platform user-interface design], or two, they try to make the front end [the graphical user interface] cross-platform. And until Java, there was really no practical way to do that. When we said we were doing it cross-platform, what we said was we're doing 70 percent cross-platform and then we're doing a front-end layer on top. And so we . . . did dialogue boxes the Mac way on the Mac and the Windows way on Windows. But basically everything else we said we're just going to write this in C code. . . . I could compile the image library on a Timex Sinclair, practically, except for memory constraints.

From our interviews, we can summarize the most important concepts or techniques that Netscape programmers followed when designing cross-platform code:

- Avoid platform-specific programming interfaces (APIs) as much as possible.
- Create and maintain a set of APIs that represents an acceptable lowest-common-denominator interface across different platforms. (In other words, create a layer of programming interface abstractions such as the Netscape Portable Runtime, which we discuss in more detail below, and then write code that connects to this layer and not to individual operating systems. Another alternative is to create a layer of "IF" statements or instructions that tell the system what to do if the operating system is X versus Y.)
- Create a set of cross-platform components that connect to this common-denominator layer and that different product groups can share. (This

enables different groups to leverage the investment in successful cross-platform code.)

- Use cross-platform programming languages as much as possible, such as "vanilla" versions of C and C++, as well as inherently cross-platform Internet languages such as HTML, Java, and JavaScript. (This means avoid platform-specific languages such as Assembler or tailored versions of languages such as C and C++.)

- Keep different platform code versions synchronized not by "porting" code in a traditional sense, but by compiling or "building" the code components daily on multiple platforms. (This minimizes different code bases as well as porting code, which usually requires time for some rewriting and debugging.)

- Keep feature sets common across the different platform versions. (This minimizes the creation of different code bases and tailoring work and also supports the common look-and-feel appearance to the user.)

- Tailor to particular platforms those components that are essential to achieve competitive performance levels on the most commercially important platforms. (In other words, allow teams to make at least some changes so products will not perform poorly versus the competition.)

- Do not try to write cross-platform components that developers cannot easily abstract and which might adversely affect users; although try to shift the design of these components gradually over to cross-platform approaches. (An example of this is user-interface components unique to particular platforms, such as the Macintosh toolbars, which often differ noticeably from Windows. Over time, however, engineers can try to introduce more generic user-interface components across different products and write them in a cross-platform Internet language, such as JavaScript or even HTML.)

Balancing Cross-Platform with Platform-Specific Designs

Perhaps the most difficult design decision for Netscape engineers was how much code to tailor to specific platforms. This tailoring also created another potential nightmare: keeping the different teams and code bases synchronized. For example, Netscape organized development teams around components or features, such as mail, news, or Smart Update on the client side. These components were cross-platform: Engineers designed the code to work on different operating systems. But the product teams also contained smaller groups or individual programmers who worked on tailoring products to specific platforms. Netscape tried to make the feature sets as similar as possible across the platforms, but there were still some minor differences, such as certain elements of the user interfaces (like tool bars). As a result, the code bases for some products could diverge fairly widely. Keeping track of all the variations and making sure the engineers tested all the versions and changes properly was no simple task.

There were also strategic reasons for Netscape to reduce the amount of cross-platform code it produced. Most significantly, the Windows platform, especially on the client side, was clearly the dominant standard. In addition, it was becoming increasingly difficult for engineers to keep adding cross-platform code to the growing code base and still make sure that it worked as well as Windows-specific products. There were also declining benefits to cross-platform code on the client as the Mac decreased in importance. To handle the demands of writing good code for the Windows environment, Netscape also hired more Windows developers, and they were not accustomed to thinking cross-platform, nor were they particularly good at it, at least according to Rick Schell, who once managed the client division. Windows developers were very different from the UNIX developers who had founded the company. Schell explained:

In the early days, the design was very good for what it did and the company was very good at doing cross-platform stuff. It's after you have to tack on things, it gets very hard because you can't tack on the code in the completely cross-platform way consistently. After a while, it started to show up. The other thing that happened is there were a lot of compromises made, too, with cross-platform. There was more and more of the business shipped with Windows, and the Mac became less and less of an important platform. A lot of decisions were made that favored Windows. And the mix of developers changed, too. If you ask them, they'd say the reason that the code became less and less true cross-platform code is because there's all those Windows developers that were hired in. And there's some truth in that. UNIX developers pay attention. They had to because, with nine different versions of UNIX, you can't write platform-specific code and have it run. . . . And then it was a nightmare to do multiple versions of Windows development, for anybody. That was one of the reasons we wanted to use Java.

With Communicator 4.0, Netscape also decided to add groupware features, including electronic mail and newsgroups, using design concepts imported from Collabra. The Collabra developers had written their features in C++ for Windows. Netscape had to expend lots of effort "coercing" the designs to be cross-platform, according to Schell. Netscape developers ended up making more of the client code platform-specific, primarily to make sure it ran well on Windows. This meant that they had to duplicate some of the code—write it once for Windows and then again for other platforms. This took significant investment because, according to Debby Meredith and Bob Lisbonne, Netscape developers did not take code directly from the Collabra product line.

On the server side, Netscape developers put more emphasis on cross-platform techniques. Selling to multiple platforms—different UNIX versions as well as Windows NT—was the essence of the market niche that Netscape exploited. Company engineers managed to keep the different UNIX versions pretty much the same, although they clearly optimized the design for the top two or three UNIX versions in terms of Netscape sales (the versions from Sun, HP, and Silicon Graphics). The company allowed some differences with the server versions for Windows NT to optimize performance, though basic features remained fairly common across the platforms. Tim Howes, a VP and chief technology adviser in the server products division, commented on the server versions and differences between the client and the server products:

> We are developing from a single code base, which I think in general is true across Netscape. . . . There are maybe one or two servers that have their code bases diverged a little bit. But that's more out of necessity than out of design—people just moving so fast that they haven't been able to merge back the changes that were made for NT. Definitely a goal of ours is to manage this whole process from a single code base. . . . On the client, you've got a bunch of UI [user interfaces] that changes platform to platform. And you've got the same things that we have on the server side, which are kind of OS-provided services like threading, memory management, I/O [input/output], dynamic linking, and stuff like that. So it's probably a little less for us, although some of that code can take up a bit of room. Some of the security code, for example . . . The UNIX versions are pretty well in synch. UNIX, despite its famous variations, is pretty much UNIX. Between NT and UNIX, there are some differences. They're mostly because we wanted to fit in very well to the NT environment. We don't want to be like a UNIX server running on NT. We want to . . . act like another NT server that you might get from anybody else. So there's some specific code for that. But those are more kind of integration features. In terms of product features, like what can the product actually do, there's not usually any difference between the two.

To keep the code synchronized across different platforms, Netscape developers often had two or more machines, such as one computer that ran Windows and another that ran UNIX. When they checked in their code (see chapter 5), they were supposed to make sure that it would "build" on both machines. Not all developers took the time to build on both platforms, however. UNIX presented an additional problem for developers because it came in as many as nine variations that had minor differences.

Netscape developers in 1997 and 1998 tended to focus their efforts on the most popular UNIX version, Sun's Solaris, and the company no longer made all its products available on every UNIX platform. Netscape developers also created and shared a series of "IF" statements for programming that handled differences in basic operations (though not server-specific features) among the UNIX versions. (For example, the developer might write, "IF IBM, THEN do XXX.") In addition, to deal with variations, Netscape's server developers tried to keep the Windows NT version synchronized with the main UNIX version, although developers needed to keep the NT and UNIX versions on separate code branches to keep from mixing them up (see chapter 5). They might even be on different release schedules. Later on, the developers made any adaptations necessary to run the code on the different UNIX versions. Howes explained how they did this:

> As we go along in a major development cycle, we might try to keep NT and one UNIX platform up to speed on the same code. And then we might port to the other UNIX platforms as we go along. As we get closer to the end, we need to keep more and more UNIX platforms in synch. And we like to keep NT and UNIX in synch. One thing that we've done is that every developer in my group has both an NT and a UNIX machine. When you check in code, you need to make sure it at least makes on the other systems, so the nightly builds don't get broken.

Cross-Platform Components and Abstraction Layer

Netscape also invested in tools and components to make cross-platform development easier. These aids included the Netscape Portable Runtime (NSPR) layer, which both the client and server groups used. The server groups also shared some HTML, Java, and JavaScript components, as well as some of the core Web Server and Directory Server and security code. In addition, the division had some common libraries for handling protocols used in more than one server. Bill Turpin, a Borland veteran and Netscape's vice president of server product development before moving to the new Web site division, estimated that about 20 percent of the code in Netscape's nine server products consisted of these packaged cross-platform components shared among the different products. He outlined the structure of the shared code in the servers:

> Down at the bottom level, there are things called the Netscape Portable Runtime. We call it NSPR, which is in all the servers. Those are just like operating system abstractions for file, print, socket I/O, threading. . . . And above that, about half the servers are based on the Web server code base. . . . One of the things we are doing to make them all common is we have a thing called the Admin Server, which is a cut-back Web Server [that handles setup for the different servers]. And all of our servers are administered though a common set of HTML, Java, and JavaScript forms that run on that Admin Server. And so all Netscape servers . . . use our Admin servers, so they can present a common look and feel. With the 3.0 servers, we integrated the directory into all of them so they share the common users and group definitions. In the future, we are integrating directories even tighter, where we'll store configuration information out in the directory and that sort of thing. So we're doing more and more to make them look the same and operate the same, even though they have different code underneath them.

The philosophy behind the Netscape Portable Runtime layer was simple: create a set of low-level programming interface abstractions for tasks such as memory management and threading (handling different tasks within the same application or on the same processor) that would work on all the platforms for which Netscape built products. The objective was to save time for developers, a goal that the layer achieved. But NSPR, by definition, was a "lowest-common-denominator" interface, and this approach entailed certain disadvantages in performance. Howes recognized this:

> NSPR, the Netscape Portable Runtime, is layered so the basic thing is try to take a set of services and you abstract whether it's the threading model or I/O model or security model or whatever. And you develop this abstraction layer that you can then map onto different things. That's the basic stuff. The question then is, when you choose the model you choose, you make some compromises. It's not exactly like one platform or the other. The place where this probably comes up the most and gives us the most trouble is in the threading and I/O environments that differ across platforms. On NT, for example, there are some primitives that the operating system gives you to make I/O, especially in the context of a threaded application, very, very fast. Some things that would normally take you two system calls, you can do in one—accept and read the first packet, for example. And there's nothing equivalent to that on UNIX, where you're stuck with that kind of select and asynchronous read/write model.

Netscape had to create and maintain a separate team of some six developers to manage the NSPR layer, and they had a difficult job to do. First, they were supposed to serve the entire company, but demands were somewhat different in the client as opposed to the server division. During most of 1996 and 1997, the NSPR team was part of Netscape's core technologies division, which we discuss later in this chapter. After the January 1998 reorganization, however, the developers moved to the application server group that Netscape acquired in the Kiva acquisition. Second, with the decision to give away and license the client code to outside developers, including the NSPR layer, the team took on an additional responsibility to keep the layer current and available for outside developers. Available, however, did not necessarily mean "stable," a software term meaning relatively bug-free. The team faced a continual problem in that Java and JavaScript continued to evolve rapidly. At the same time, frequent changes in the NSPR abstractions led Netscape engineers to complain that the NSPR was an unstable foundation for creating new features. This situation may be inevitable with a rapidly evolving technology like the Internet. Nonetheless, for developers, Tim Howes observed that it was like "trying to build the house while you're still trying to pour the foundation":

> NSPR is still evolving as we speak. It's a bit like trying to build the house while you're still trying to pour the foundation, which makes life kind of interesting. Basically, because performance is so competitive on the server side of things, we have to do whatever it takes to make sure that performance wins. And if that means that we have to change the abstraction layer, we do that. If that means that we need to under-the-covers have completely different implementations of these things, then we do that, too. And if push comes to shove, performance is more important than just anything on the server side. So, for example, in Directory Server right now, we're looking at what we've done. So far, our I/O models have diverged a little bit. We're on different paths for NT and UNIX. And what we'd like to do is bring those two back together under some new abstraction. But we found that, with the existing I/O abstraction that we had, we couldn't leverage the very nice performance characteristics of NT—asynchronous I/O. So we'll just see how much better we can make it. We did an NT-native implementation of that and just IF . . . DIFF-ed around the UNIX stuff.

Penalties for Cross-Platform Design

The difficulties that Netscape faced with the NSPR layer merely reflected the fundamental challenge of cross-platform design: the need to minimize the potential tradeoffs or "penalties." One cost involves the toll on developers, who have to think more about abstractions that cut across different platforms or operating-system versions. A second, even greater, cost is on testers, who have to spend a large amount of time to make sure that features work properly on different platforms and versions of the product. Netscape managers worried relatively little about these first two costs because they were necessary to the cross-platform strategy. It did not matter too much if Netscape had to take a little more time and engineering hours to deliver its products. But a third toll is on the product itself, since developers try not to write too much code that directly takes advantage of conventions particular to one operating system or hardware platform. This means that Java and other cross-platform code (such as UNIX code with many IF statements) usually run slower than code optimized to a particular platform like Windows 95 or NT 4.0 or HP UNIX.

Too much penalty in product performance was something that users were not likely to tolerate for long. As a result, Netscape was optimizing increasing amounts of code for both the client and servers. Nonetheless, Netscape's products still faced some performance disadvantages. In addition, in such a fast-paced market and with such strong competition, Netscape had to be careful about how much more time and people it used to develop new products.

Netscape managers did not estimate how much slower their development teams were because they designed for multiple platforms. From our observations at Netscape as well as other companies, however, we estimated there was at least a 15 to 20 percent time or manpower penalty in development, and an even greater penalty in testing. In other words, developers working on multiplatform components might finish at the same time as a team working on components for only one platform, but they might need 20 percent more people to do the same job. Or a team might use fewer developers but take 20 percent more time. Netscape tended to assign extra people to the cross-platform work, although some projects used both more people and more time. Totic commented on how this issue affected development of the client product:

> Right now, we probably have 10 to 12 people working on Mac-only stuff. But it depends on the feature. Before, we used to have the front-end team . . . but we decided that that's not the way to go. You shouldn't have a front-end team. You should have mail and news teams, which implement mail and news across all platforms, and then somebody usually holds the whole thing together to make sure that mail and news matches with the browser, matches with Mac. . . . The penalty is you do go slower. When you're writing for one platform, there are little API tricks from the [partic-

ular] platform that you can use. [For example,] Mac does not have a socket layer [a connection point such as for writing encrypted code]. I have to write a socket layer myself on top of other networking code. Plus things do differ subtly across platforms. There is porting in that sense. The timers fire off on different frequencies. There might be a bug in Windows, too, that never happens but it does show up on X or on a Mac. Or the Mac is the one with the worst memory problem because we don't have dynamic link libraries. Your application just can't grow indefinitely.

Netscape also had to worry about staffing the different version teams. At one point, only one person was the expert on the Hewlett-Packard version of UNIX for the entire server division, and this person could become a real bottleneck. Another example was the Communicator 4.0 release. One of many reasons for the length of this project was that the client division had trouble staffing the Mac and UNIX teams. This caused the project to fall behind and later put out a "point release" (version 4.02). Michael Toy, release manager for the client products, recalled in our July 1997 interview:

[Version] 4.02 is the thing that we initially set out to do. There're a number of problems. When we started a year ago, we had nobody to work on the Mac. And we had a small Mac team for 3.x and they all said I'm never doing that again. And we had almost nobody to work on UNIX. Those were two completely unstaffed areas and they were not staffed until after our early feature-complete targets. So the Mac and the UNIX releases lagged the Windows release and we never had that problem before. You get a great synergy when all three front ends are in synch because it really helps your cross-platform code get solid fast. If you've only got one platform that's written on top of your cross-platform code, you haven't really shaken the bugs out of it until you run it on a couple of radically different architectures in terms of the way event loops work, in terms of what's fast in the file system or slow, so that you make sure that your architecture scales across the platforms. . . . If I'd been doing Windows only, we would have shipped in early Q2 with fewer features. Since the other releases were hanging out anyway, then more features went into the Windows release and pushed its day out.

Another major penalty came in testing the different versions. For a perspective, we interviewed Desmond Chan, a test manager in Netscape's Proxy Server group during 1995 to 1997 and a veteran tester with experience at MIPS Computer and Sun Microsystems. Chan was also a graduate of MIT. He estimated that testing simply for the seven or so different versions of UNIX took at least double the amount of testing resources compared to testing for one platform. Testing for NT required additional resources. Overall, Chan felt that Netscape should have employed at least twice as many testers as it did when he worked there in order to test all the versions of its software thoroughly.

When Chan worked at Netscape, the company had about one tester for every four developers in the server division. This level was comparable to Sun Microsystems and other companies in Silicon Valley. But Sun and other companies such as Hewlett-Packard tested their operating systems primarily for their own environments. This allowed Sun, for example, to invest heavily in automation, which was also possible because features in its operating system changed relatively slowly. But Netscape was cross-platform in a way that few other companies were. In the early years especially, Netscape committed itself to testing servers on all the UNIX platforms as well as Windows NT. The number of people needed to do testing properly would be less if Netscape had more automation but, as we discuss in chapter 5, it did not have enough people to build a lot of automated test suites. The bottom line was that testing problems persisted. Chan recalled:

> At least in my group, I had four people, including me, and there were roughly 15 developers. . . . You have to perform the same test on every platform. . . . And you just don't know where the code might break, so you have to test other important features on each platform. If it's done by hand, it takes two or three times more time or people resources to do it. If you can automate, most of the testing can be done by machine resources.

For servers, however, much more so than with the client, cross-platform design posed a big risk to the speed of a product. Servers are supposed to be fast, and Netscape could not afford to have products that were noticeably slower than the competition. Howes estimated that platform-specific server code for Windows NT ran at least twice as fast as cross-platform code. This is why Netscape tailored critical portions of its server software for NT and other portions for UNIX. (Some 60 percent of Netscape's server sales in early 1998 were to the UNIX market, and about 40 percent to the Windows NT market.)[2] In addition, Netscape was trying to design more for the Windows NT abstractions. Howes elaborated on the speed issue as well as the importance of continuing Netscape's basic strategy of being cross-platform:

> [Platform-specific code is] certainly in the range of twice as fast. Probably significantly more than that when you combine it with other things we're doing. And that is not to say that NT is twice as fast as UNIX. That's to say

that using the native UNIX-oriented abstractions on NT slows you down versus using the native NT stuff. Does that make sense? So if you use the native stuff on NT and you use the native stuff on UNIX, what each of the respective systems is good at, you could compare performance. I think also that we do have a good shot at bringing these two—as I said, we're branched off now—back together under a common abstraction. . . . Probably what we're going to do is take some aspect of the NT abstraction and see if we can do them in UNIX without losing performance. . . . That's not a general rule, though. There are definitely cases where just the reverse happens. What we try to do in general is to find a level of common ground where one abstraction is different from the other so we can emulate one using the other without losing performance. And trying to do it one way may work. Trying to do it the other way may work better. I'm sure if we didn't have to worry about cross-platform at all, we'd get to go a little faster. But that's really the key to our business model. One of our basic strategies is we're cross-platform, and that's one of the big advantages that we have in the marketplace. And I want to point out that cross-platform for us is not strictly NT and UNIX. There're Macs in there, but it's also NT 3.5, NT 4, NT 5, Windows 3.1, so we're cross-platform even within the Microsoft environment.

The server groups seemed to have less of a problem than the client groups with needing extra developers because the servers used more cross-platform libraries as well as a lot of shared cross-platform components. But the large amounts of shared code added bulk to the server code bases without necessarily increasing functionality, and this bulk slowed down development and testing time. Howes agreed that they probably had up to a 20 percent penalty in development time: "We're set up pretty well to begin with where we've got these cross-platform libraries. Doing the port to a different [UNIX] platform is not that big a deal. We might allocate a week of somebody's time in the schedule to do that—one of our developers. So 20 percent is probably a good number."

Andreessen, as usual, tried to see the big picture perspective on linkages between programmer performance and product performance. Nearly all high-level programming languages have made it easier to write new software at the expense of runtime performance. He saw these as worthwhile and inevitable tradeoffs. Moreover, Andreessen argued that the advantages of creating cross-platform products that easily linked into a network generated more value for customers than speed alone:

I didn't say speed is not an issue. It depends on what you're trying to measure. It used to be our programs were written in machine code, right? And lo and behold, out came structured programming languages [which supported a hierarchical and modular approach to design] like ALGOL and C, and people started writing in these structured languages. And then they started being interpreted by a compiler and it took a performance hit to do that. It benefited forever productivity. And then lo and behold, object-oriented languages came along [which supported the design of computer programs through a hierarchy of classes and reusable modules]. And all of a sudden you started taking additional performance hits there and you benefited in programmer productivity. And then rapid application development environments came along and you took a big hit in performance and got tremendously improved productivity. The same basic thing is happening now with the emergence of cross-platform. There's a danger here of comparing today's cross-platform technologies aimed at the Net versus cross-platform technologies of the past because cross-platform technologies of the past were never driven by a fundamental, large economic opportunity. They tended to be niche products. They tended to be products that were aimed at a very small subset of the market. And so they tended to attract people who architected and developed them and who weren't terribly concerned with large-scale implementation or success. None of them are big. None of them are significant.

Since 1997, Netscape developers have increasingly chosen to reduce the performance "hit" by doing more platform-specific code. Cross-platform code, especially on client software, was becoming less and less important to the company. In any case, according to Andreessen, product performance was not a serious problem. He told us, "the fundamental value simply [comes from] being able to run whatever is out there, no matter what it is. What you do is you take that initial performance hit, to the extent one exists. And then it's the market that decides."

Optimism and Disappointment with Java

Netscape engineers were highly flexible when it came to choosing programming languages for cross-platform design. In the early projects, for example, Netscape wrote all the cross-platform code in the C programming language. AT&T originally had designed this language to work on its UNIX platform, but C has since become a universal programming language. In addition, many of the basic APIs that the NCSA Mosaic and Netscape Navigator teams used for the early browsers came from the UNIX-C environment. Totic recalled, "Originally, all the cross-platform code was written in C. That was the law because C was the only truly portable language." In the 3.0 and 4.0 client projects, Netscape developers relied heavily on C++ (an object-oriented version of C) as well as C. But they did nothing distinctive here: These are the same languages Microsoft used to write all the versions of Internet Explorer.

By early 1997, however, Netscape executives and engineers had become very enthusiastic about Java. As a computing language, Java was object-oriented (modular) and inherently cross-platform. If Netscape could write an entire product in Java, it would eliminate many of the productivity penalties that came from designing and testing cross-platform code. Sun Microsystems's promise with Java was "write once, run everywhere." This worked because, in most cases, developers do not write Java code to run on the APIs of a particular operating system. Rather, they write in a platform-neutral language called "byte code" and to a platform-neutral layer called a "virtual machine" (VM). Internet browsers and some other Internet software include the VM program, which translates or interprets the byte code so that it can run on any operating system. It does not matter whether the machine is a Windows PC, a Macintosh, a UNIX workstation, or a network computer.

The problem with Java is that it has to go through this extra step of being translated or interpreted, so it usually loads and runs more slowly than code written directly for a particular operating system, such as Windows. But Java has other advantages that excited the Netscape engineers. One such advantage was that it helped minimize certain programming errors. Toy pointed out that developers can write good or bad code in any language. Java, however, made it hard for them to break certain useful rules, such as for object abstractions and memory management: "Thinking that a language makes you design better is stupid. You can write really good component software in C and really bad spaghetti code in Java. [But] Java gives you language abstractions that make it hard to break the rules if you decide that these are the rules that we're going to have. It's hard to reach through an interface and do bad things." Rick Schell agreed, particularly with Java's ability to help programmers manage their allocation of memory resources (an especially difficult problem in native Windows programming):

Shifting to Java is helpful because a lot of the problems that you encounter in software have to do with very simple, stupid stuff. Experienced developers should know better, but when you're putting software together, you don't always think about some of these things. And you have to think about some of the stuff, so it takes you away from thinking about other things. And memory management and memory allocation are a pain in the ass.

Most of the stuff that happens in today's commercial software is, "Gee, I've got to allocate something so I can do something for a very short period of time and throw it away" because it's user-interaction based, at least on the client side. It's true on the server side, too, because processes come and go, and they perform tasks, and they go away. So a lot of what happens is resource management. It used to be algorithms were the important thing. Now it's resource management. So the better tools you have to deal with that, the better off you are, and Java provides better tools than conventional . . . language stuff. And the tools are actually remarkably rapid compared to previous generations of stuff.

This enthusiasm for Java led Netscape executives to make a major commitment to developing a Java virtual machine in-house (Sun's VM in 1997 still had many limitations). Netscape would then use this to rewrite in Java at least the Navigator browser and possibly other components in the client. The in-house effort—a Java-based client—became part of the Communicator 6.0 project, code-named "Xena." After Andreessen talked publicly about the idea of a Java browser, the media began referring to this component as "Javagator," or a Java version of Navigator.

During our interviews in July and August of 1997, we talked about the 6.0 project with many executives and engineers. Most remained very optimistic about their potential breakthrough. Four months later, however, we questioned Andreessen about the wisdom of writing a browser and perhaps the entire client in Java, and he agreed that Netscape had "jumped the gun" a bit. Andreessen maintained that Java would still be important for some components, such as the security code or Netcaster. But he confused his own engineers by making public claims about Netscape's plans for Java that were unrealistic. Andreessen probably believed these claims at the time he made them, although this was his response to us in November 1997 when we asked if Netscape had indeed committed to designing a 100 percent Java client:

Of course not. And you know where that actually started? What happened was, when I didn't have this job [as head of product engineering], the best way for me to get attention from our engineers was to go say something in the press that really woke them up. So I went out and said, "All right, the next version of Communicator is going to be written all in Java." And they were fighting a lot of the Java stuff. So I said the next version is all Java. I did a complete 180. And they said, "Okay, we're doing everything in the future in Java." So then I started saying, "Well, wait a minute. This doesn't make any sense. We can't possibly do that." So now they're a little confused.

Andreessen continued to argue publicly that Java posed many advantages. But by fall 1997, he had come to realize that Netscape had to be more careful when making such a critical decision. He discussed where Java might still be useful: "It depends on the project. It depends on the module. . . . But keep in mind Java can be compiled down into Intel machine codes, just like C or C++. So when you look at Java and the implications of Java, it depends on what you're trying to deliver. The ultimate point behind Java for most people is going to what I call 'dynamic on-demand Net-based applications,' where you're going to a Web page, not installing something off the CD-ROM."

Andreessen clearly felt frustrated with the slow pace of Java's evolution as well as the difficulty Netscape engineers had encountered adapting to Sun's Java standards and tools. The 4.05 maintenance release of Communicator, for example, did not fully support Sun's "official" Java Development Kit. In particular, Communicator could not run applets written to the Abstract Window Toolkit standards that, ironically, Microsoft's Internet Explorer 4.01 did support.[3] Of course, having a version of Java that Netscape tailored supported the "open, but not open" strategy. But Netscape was also trying to promote the evolution of the language as an industry standard because it facilitated cross-platform solutions rather than platform-specific solutions (like Windows and NT products). Andreessen, in an April 1998 interview with *PC Week,* reflected on Netscape's efforts to work with Java internally and the engineering problems that remained:

> Java is not yet at the performance, stability, or compatibility level that it needs to be to realize its promise of "write once, run anywhere." We were the first licensee. Starting with [Navigator] 1.0, everyone was pretty happy with the work that we were doing. But starting with 1.1, people started seeing that [Sun Microsystems's] technology was becoming a little more stable, and they started valuing the compatibility more than all the engineering efforts that we were doing. So, during the last 12 months, we were constantly dealing with backdated versions and doing all the work and not getting any credit for it. So we looked at our own internal engineering efforts and realized that the stuff was getting worse, not better. The divergence [between Netscape's Java Virtual Machine and Sun's] was getting worse. We decided that the best thing was to stop doing work with Netscape's Java Runtime [another term for virtual machine] and instead move to a Java API that lets the customers or users pick the Java Runtime to plug in. That said, there are still the fundamental issues of performance, stability, and compatibility. If developers want to create network-centric

applications that can be run on any platform and downloaded over the Net, then Java will be successful, if it can be made to work, which is a large-scale engineering problem. But if developers don't want that, then Java is not right. But the theory is right. Are applications being built in a network-centric world? Absolutely. Do they need different levels of security? Yes. Will there be a wider array of devices on the Net? Sure. But the basic engineering work still needs to be done.[4]

Frustration with Java had begun to spread in the engineering organization in late 1997 and early 1998. As Java, HTML, Dynamic HTML (DHTML), and JavaScript evolved, Netscape engineers had hoped to use these inherently cross-platform Web languages more extensively to develop new components. In particular, Netscape experimented with HTML and JavaScript for multiplatform user interfaces, including generic windows, dialog boxes, and features such as the security manager module. But, as Aleks Totic observed, the immaturity of Java, as well as JavaScript and components built with this language, limited how much Netscape could use the new technology:

> If it [Java] was all the way there, it would be all development, but it's not. There're still a lot of things Java does not do. And when they program code inside Navigator, you essentially can't step through that code. You have to debug it by hand, which is a giant pain in the neck. Everything is on the way. But there are only so many variables you can deal with. I think the longer you're here, you just want to minimize the amount of variables you're dealing with. For example, I used Java, JavaScript, and security, all three, in my last project, and I basically spent 70 percent of my time doing QA for Java, JavaScript, and the security group because I would say, "Okay, this is busted, this is busted . . . " For example, we don't have Java compilers on the Mac that are good enough for our stuff, so they compile all the class files on UNIX and transport it to the Mac.

Totic had also tried to use Java to write the Smart Update code as well as the front-end or user interface for Communicator. Making the UI in Java would eliminate the need to write different end-user interfaces for the different platforms. The problem, however, was that Java still lacked graphical tools to design good user interfaces. Totic admitted that, "Of course, our UI looks like crap. The front-end to make all those sweet widgets and things like that are just really hard in Java now because of the tools. It's just not a mature GUI [graphical user interface]." Within a year, Netscape had abandoned Java for creating user interfaces in favor of C and C++. Developers continued to use Java and JavaScript for Smart

Update because of the way the security features and wrappers for down-loading code worked.

By the middle of 1998, Java was being deemphasized throughout Netscape. The Mozilla 5.0 release did not contain any Java code because Sun provided most of the Java code in the Netscape client and did not permit Netscape to give it away for free. According to Bob Lisbonne, however, enterprise versions of the 5.0 client that Netscape planned to bundle with servers would include Java code as well as the open Java interface.

On the server side at Netscape, programming remained more traditional and there was little debate about Java. The server developers mainly used C for mainstream tasks—"the language of the gods," in the words of Tim Howes. The server group also used some C++ and a little bit of Java and JavaScript, such as in Enterprise (Web) Server. But Java was not ready for the heavy-duty requirements of the enterprise world and, especially, the server market. Howes commented on this decision to adopt Java only very gradually: "I think it's probably going to change more slowly on the server side just because we have higher performance requirements. We have much stricter availability requirements. For us to use Java, it needs to be lightning fast. It needs to be incredibly stable. Our servers stay up for weeks or months at a time. Handling a directory server, for example, is hundreds if not thousands of operations every second. So performance is very important, too."

Use of Java was slowing down, but not dead. Some server applications developers and component groups, such as security, continued to use the language within Netscape (although, according to a product manager in the client division, Todd Goldman, with whom we spoke in July 1998, Netscape's security group had plans to phase this code out within two years). Independent Java developers were also taking Netscape's Mozilla code base and working on their own "Pure Java" browser, this time dubbed "Jazilla" by the high-tech press. In May 1998, Sun's JavaSoft division delivered a new Java plug-in that enabled Java applications to run on Netscape or Microsoft browsers. The new plug-in allowed users to automatically upgrade the Java VMs in their browsers, which was surely a good sign for the future of the language.[5]

In his April 1998 interview with *PC Week,* Andreessen admitted that Java as a programming language had progressed enough for Netscape to end most of its in-house development of Java tools and its own Java VM. Java as an alternative platform to Windows, however, was not progressing so well. In July 1998, at a speech in California, Andreessen announced the formal end to Netscape's plans to work on a browser entirely written in Java, which would have been perfect for a proposed Java operating system. After proclaiming that "Javagator is dead," Andreessen elaborated (facetiously) on his reasoning: "My joke is that a Java Navigator will have a lot of good attributes: It's slower. It will crash more and have fewer features. So you can do fewer things. It will simplify your life." He also complained that supporters of "Pure Java" had not evolved the language sufficiently to use it to build a fast and stable client, and that the only company that had evolved the Java language sufficiently to really use it was Microsoft: "I've always believed Netscape's original mistake was someone actually has to do the work. It's technically possible, but no one is doing the work. The work is to make the Java Runtime stable and fast. There's an opportunity to do that. Right now, Microsoft is doing it."[6]

We should mention that, in mid-1998, one alternative to Java for writing cross-platform applications was Dynamic HTML, an extension of the HTML programming language to handle "dynamic" content, such as interactive screens or video. At various times, Netscape as well as Microsoft (which included support for DHTML in IE 4.0, shipped in September 1997) and the World Wide Web Consortium (W3C) based at MIT have supported this idea. Both Netscape and Microsoft, however, have been reluctant to adopt the W3C industry standards, which are part of a new "open" Document Object Model. The reason is that both Netscape and Microsoft really prefer to be "open, but not open." Microsoft continues to insist on adding extensions that only Internet Explorer 5.0 is likely to support. (IE 5.0 went out as a developer's beta release in June 1998 and should ship in a commercial final version by late 1998.) Netscape, in turn, planned to support the new standard but was not hurrying to have the technology ready even for the Communicator 5.0 release, scheduled for the end of 1998.[7]

PRINCIPLE   *Design and redesign products to have more modular architectures.*

Modular Architectures for Internet Time

The promise of Java was not merely that it solved part of the cross-platform problem. As an object-oriented programming language, it was also an excellent tool to create modular designs. Many Netscape managers and engineers believed that modular designs were essential to make Netscape's engineering organization faster and more flexible when developing new products and features. Not surprisingly, increasing the modularity of Netscape's client product became a major goal in 1997.

Theoretically, a more modular client architecture would improve design flexibility by isolating functions such as HTML rendering for the browser, electronic mail, or the calendar feature within particular modules, rather than spreading these features across many different components. A high degree of modularity would make it possible to keep teams relatively small because projects would need to group together only a few developers and testers around particular features. The small teams could then design, build, and test their components more or less independently. In our August 1997 meeting, Bob Lisbonne explained the underlying logic:

> To succeed in Internet time, to be innovative, to move quickly, it is of paramount importance to have small teams. . . . When our teams grew beyond a certain point, they began to resemble a 200-person three-legged race where, even if you had really fast sprinters, to the extent all their legs were bound, you were guaranteed to have stumbles and slow down through no fault of any particular person or group. So one thing that I'm very committed to is, wherever possible, keeping the team size just as small and as independent as possible. That's why the componentization or the modularization of the product is so key, so that ultimately we can get back to lots of small teams each doing their own thing—doing the right thing—and not getting caught up in one another's efforts.

No one argued about the conceptual benefits of a modular product architecture. The practical problem that Netscape and many other companies faced was how to design modular products or redesign existing products to be more modular without taking too much time or distracting engineers from delivering innovative features. As Netscape engineers evolved the client far beyond the Navigator browser, Communicator became anything but modular. This situation reflected Netscape's priorities. While Netscape engineers did a good job designing products at the *feature level*, they did not take much time to design products at the *system level*. This was true of both the client and the server divisions. Netscape's speed was the culprit: It is extremely difficult to develop a strong system-level architecture when racing forward to create new features on Internet time.

Netscape's individual server products, for example, won many technical awards and were, in a sense, highly modular. But the modularity was an artifact of their separate origins; the servers had separate code bases because many of them came from acquisitions. They were not well integrated in the package (SuiteSpot) that Netscape sold. In the case of Navigator and Communicator, a lack of time and investment in design during 1995 to 1997, a rapid growth period, came back to haunt the company. Of course, the priorities during those years for the client were innovation and time-to-market. Netscape engineers did what they had to do: They shipped new products, with innovative features. By mid-1997, however, Communicator was no longer a separate product like Navigator had once been. The client was now a large and complex system of products built around the browser (i.e., Navigator plus Messenger, Collabra, Composer, Netcaster, Conference, and Calendar, plus some administration tools for IS managers). Adding more features to the client had become time-consuming and technically difficult. Even in versions 4.5 and 5.0 of Communicator, which Netscape released in 1998, the client architecture was still not very modular. Lisbonne made this observation about Communicator 4.0: "By virtue of its architecture, 4.0 required very close coordination among a very large number of people. That is to say, the product's code base did not suitably insulate teams from one another. It was very easy, for example, for a bug in Java to break Netcaster or for a bug in the HTML engine to hold up progress in the mail reader."

To Netscape's credit, its engineers were able to maintain and even improve Communicator's quality and overall stability, despite these architectural issues and despite allocating relatively little manpower to QA (compared to Microsoft). Nonetheless, how well Netscape designed Communicator was an issue that would not go away. Like it or not, Netscape had to continue adding features to the client, and it was important to do this quickly and efficiently. Netscape also had to increase the modularity of Communicator to get away from Lisbonne's "200-person three-legged race" problem.

Architectural design in software is a skill more common among large-scale telecommunications equipment producers like Lucent Technologies or mainframe operating system producers like IBM. Changes in their platform technologies have been relatively slow, and the companies have been able to devote years to planning and evolving their systems. PC software makers, in contrast, are still pioneers and inventors, especially in the Internet space. They generally race to bring new products and features to market. Consequently, they often design early versions of their products in a very incremental and even ad hoc manner. If the product seems to be successful, then they rearchitect later in special projects or over a series of projects. This "incremental" design strategy often proves to be quite useful because PC software companies have to deal with frequent changes in the technology or competitor moves that are difficult to predict. Taking years to plan the "perfect" architecture and then years more to implement it might easily result in a product that is no longer perfect and badly out of date by the time that it ships, if it ever does.

Eventually, though, as Netscape realized with Communicator, even PC software makers have to pay attention to architectures if they want to continue adding complex functions while retaining reliability. This is why, for example, Microsoft took the time to build Windows NT largely from scratch as a new operating system for enterprises, with neat layers and modular subsystems that improved its stability compared to Windows 3.1 or Windows 95. Bill Gates's engineers also restructured the standard Office suite (Word, Excel, and PowerPoint) around shared components.[8] Microsoft did hurry to market with Internet Explorer in the race to catch Netscape in the browser wars. But Microsoft then took extra time to restructure IE 3.0 (which shipped in August 1996, the same time as Navigator 3.0) into tighter modules during late 1995 and early 1996.

Microsoft's efforts to rework its browser architecture required only a few people because managers made the decision early, when the IE code base was small. (Only three or four developers concentrated on the "componentization" work, compared to about 10 lead designers and as many as 60 engineers in Netscape's ill-fated 6.0 project.) The component architecture made it possible for Microsoft to integrate the browser more closely with the operating system for Windows 98 and NT 5.0, pull the browser apart from Windows 98 if necessary, or embed the browser in applications.[9] Microsoft also designed the browser to load into memory only those features that the user wants, which means that Internet Explorer starts up very quickly.[10] In addition, users can customize Internet Explorer relatively easily by reconfiguring the user interfaces and features in the various modules. In contrast, users would need to be able to read and write source code to achieve the same level of customization with the Netscape browser. Netscape made the code available in the Mozilla release, but not many users have the skill or desire to write source code.[11] Ben Slivka from Microsoft identified the re-architecture of IE 3.0 as the critical design decision that helped his company close the gap with Netscape:

IE 3.0 was the key thing because we did the componentized browser. . . . We really made Internet Explorer part of the Windows platform. . . . So we had the URL moniker set of higher level services. There was the WININIT [the HTTP, FTP, and gopher input/output component] lower level set of services. We had the ActiveX scripting stuff. We had MSHTML [the HMTL rendering and parsing component] as a separate component. We had SHDOCVW [shell document viewing component] as a separate component. We had the Java VM as a separate component. We had the security services as a separate component. So all of those things were individually usable by Windows programmers. . . . We had an advantage in that we had people who understood COM, our Component Object Model, and understood the value of component software done correctly. . . . But we made a painful decision in the fall of '95 that we were going to go componentize. And there was kind of a "go, no go" period of time where, like, "Are we going to rip this puppy apart or not?" And one of the motivating factors for componentizing actually was the shell integration we wanted to do in IE 4 and Windows 98. And so we wanted to make a start of it in '95. . . . So that SHDOCVW, the shell document viewer, is exactly because we wanted to get that shell integration. . . . We called it "putting Humpty Dumpty back together again." So we componentized the browser the last few weeks of '95 and the first month or so of '96. Then we had to get it all put back together in order to have a beta release we hoped for March 12, for our PDC, our Professional Developers Conference. And so there were some white-knuckle weeks there where Humpty Dumpty was all on the floor and we're putting him back together and the performance is really bad. It was an exciting time. But that investment was incredible for us.

Slivka also talked at length about the browser competition with Netscape for AOL. As we discussed in chapter 3, Microsoft offered to load the AOL icon and code within Windows to win the deal. Slivka asserted, however, that AOL preferred to deal with Netscape, but Netscape management did not or could not pursue the business aggressively. Netscape did not have the component technology to offer an unbranded browser that AOL developers could customize as easily as IE (although Netscape did provide custom versions of its browser to SGI and others by creating separate code branches). Slivka explained:

We blasted out the browser into a set of components and that's how we got the AOL business. . . . When AOL went to Netscape and said, "We don't want to be in the browser wars. You and Microsoft are going to kill each other, but we want to use your technology," Netscape was apparently fairly dismissive. They were like, "Well, maybe we could do something but you want this personalized to you" and "No, we can't do that." So they [Netscape] were haughty and arrogant and dismissive. By contrast, when the AOL guys came to Microsoft, I said, "I'd love to be your browser. Let me know what I can do." We had this great component story: "You can host the browser in your client. It'll look like your thing and I'll assign developers full-time to support you." So we convinced them that not only was our technology better and we'd give them a better solution, but that we were going to give them great support. And we did. I had a full-time developer and an intern who worked just on AOL integration. . . . The Netscape guys just . . . didn't go get the business. They just weren't aggressive. And they didn't have the component technology to back it up to be able to give that [integrated] experience to AOL.

Evolution of the Navigator/Communicator Product and Projects

Internally, Netscape continued to struggle with the issue of how to evolve the architectures of its products while still creating enough innovative features to attract new customers and retain old ones. Adding the various Communicator functions as well as Java capabilities (with most code imported from Sun Microsystems) also led to enormous growth in the size of the client as well as in the number of developers and time required for each project. We can see this evolution in Table 4.1, which summarizes data on Netscape client projects from 1994 through 1997 (see page 162).

Netscape's developer teams rose from about a maximum of 10 on Navigator 1.0 to 120 on Communicator 4.0, an increase of 12 times. During this period, the code base for the product grew about 30 times (from 100,000 to 3 million lines of code). Excluding Java code from Sun Microsystems, the volume of code Netscape developers wrote increased about 18 times (100,000 to 1.8 million lines). These numbers are very imprecise because they rely on rough estimates of the Java code and do not indicate actual full-time equivalent staffing levels. Nor do they distinguish reused or slightly changed code. With these caveats, and to the extent that delivered code per programmer is at best a very crude measure of performance, the Netscape client teams appear to have been relatively productive compared to older software companies building large-scale systems.[12] Given that Netscape engineers were inventing most of the technology as they went along, leading or matching Microsoft in features, and using half or less than half the number of test engineers that Microsoft employed, their performance was quite impressive.

Nonetheless, under the pressure of competition, Netscape clearly designed and shipped Communicator 4.0 too quickly. The development team did not take the time to rearchitect the product in order to add mail and other groupware features more neatly. Netscape also hurried to add Java and JavaScript components and APIs to the initial browser core. The result was what some developers referred to as "spaghetti code" or "dead code." They called it spaghetti because that was what the architecture looked like: There were intertwining pieces of programming that made it difficult to add new features or design and test modules separately. Spaghetti code was the opposite of neatly defined modules.

During our first interviews at Netscape in July 1997, Aleks Totic complained openly about the code. He concluded that it was "not too bad" because the core features "usually" worked, although we knew that "usually" was usually not good enough for enterprise customers. In Totic's experience, the newly added Java and JavaScript components tended to break most often:

> Our code is generally not too bad. I can still step through most of our code and know what's going on, with the exception of hairy things like the Java VM. . . . It's interesting byte code but that's higher math. . . . It is spaghetti, but it's understandable spaghetti. . . . JavaScript is everywhere. That's the main spaghetti because you have to reflect the whole element of the browser in JavaScript. . . . Most of the code is self-contained spaghetti. Usually the fringes, like the JavaScript part in the layout, are the stuff that gives us the most headaches, too. . . . The core functionality works, but it's the little squeaks everywhere that break.

Even the generally optimistic Michael Toy complained about the poor state of the 4.0 client code base. Netscape released a commercial version anyway in June 1997, trying to preempt Microsoft's forthcoming 4.0 release in September. In Toy's mind, though, this was the price Netscape had to pay for going so fast in the early days of the company:

> We're in a really bad situation with our current code base because we wrote this code three years ago and its major purpose in life was to get us in business as fast as possible. We should have stopped shipping this code a year ago. It's dead. This code should have been taken out back and shot. I'm not proud of this code. If part of our interview process was to show people what our code looked like, people wouldn't come work here. This is like the rude awakening. . . . We're paying the price for going fast. And when you go fast, you don't architect, and so you don't say, "I want those three-years-from-now benefits." You want to ship tomorrow. So we made that decision consciously and now we're paying the price. The problem is that it's hard to get off the boat. [Today] we've got the 6.0 team. They're trying to develop a code base where they can deliver components that can be isolated from the rest of the universe . . . [and do] all kinds of things that you just can't say about our current code base.

Of course, Netscape engineers did not *plan* to write spaghetti code. But it was necessary to plan *not* to write spaghetti code, especially as Netscape lost its focus on the browser market and began taking on other competitors. The temptation grew overwhelming to paste on new components and accommodate new technologies in the attempt to outflank Microsoft in browser and push-technology features, take on the corporate mail and groupware business, deliver cross-platform products, and anticipate new markets, such as for the proposed Java-based network computer. The problems of rewriting Collabra's proprietary code to build these features further slowed down Communicator's progress. In the end, Communicator 4.0 beat Microsoft's Internet Explorer 4.0 to market by only two months and was no more than comparable in features and reliability. Rick Schell recognized this, painfully, in our March 1998 interview:

> Two things are important to know about 4.0. A large part was built on the old code base, which was beginning to run out of steam. But we had no time in the cycle to do much about that because we faced two things. One is we had to make a complete right turn to become an airtight software company, including Enterprise and Messaging. At the same time, we had to get out earlier than IE 4. Now it turns out, we weren't early enough, and you always have to either be first or best. If you're not first by a long shot, you've got to be better, and we weren't either. So, that was unfortunate. We tried to do way too many things with that one release in defense—trying to go into the enterprise, and then we decided, "Oh, we have to defend the turf against IE 4." . . . The [Navigator] 1.0 feature set was probably decided entirely by Marc and two other people. . . . Little bits and pieces [were] grafted on by really bright engineers, who always do that kind of stuff. And they continued to do it with 2.0 and 3.0 and 4.0. And there was always a little room for organic design. . . . To give you a great example: We started out to develop the 4.0 mailer, and the original design objective for that was to be better than Eudora. So it's going to be the best Internet mailer in the business. By the time we shipped that product, we were trying to compete with cc:Mail [from Lotus]. Now that's an entire shift! Are you going here, or are you going there? But we never gave up on this set of features because we just added stuff on along the way. Corporate customers said, "No, we won't take the product unless you do this." So, we simply gave way. It was almost like, if we don't hit it with this one, we're never going to get there. Despite the fact that we pushed really hard not to put everything into the release, it was still a tremendous amount of pressure to continue to expand the enterprise reach of that product.

Schell added that Netscape executives disagreed over the importance of the browser business, which increased the confusion in the development organization. By not having a clear idea what to do with the 4.0 version of the client, Netscape did not focus its limited resources, which can be a fatal mistake for a small company facing a master player like Microsoft. In this case, fatal or not, Netscape to a large degree *allowed* Microsoft to catch up. As Schell noted:

> People have different perspectives on where the business was. There was *a lot* of browser business. There was *a hell of a lot* of browser business. And we say, well, it's only 22 percent of the business in stand-alone browsers. But a lot of the sales were led with browsers. You go find the client. They're using the browsers for universal product capability. And we had a monopoly on the suckers up until Internet Explorer 4.0 came out. . . . It took us a little too long to get [Communicator] 4.0 out. And, unfortunately, Microsoft had a good product by that time.

Problems in Rearchitecting the Client

Netscape executives and technical leaders wanted to solve at least some of the problems they encountered with Communicator 4.0. Once they shipped the first release in June 1997, they adopted three new strategies for developing future generations of the product. First, they decided they would try to "over-design" the architecture. The plan, as devised by Rick Gessner, who joined Netscape in mid-1997 when it acquired his company, DigitalStyle, was to invest heavily in a new architecture that would last for multiple product generations. In the interim, Netscape hoped to build a few new features and release at least one new version of the client product. The second strategy was to restructure the code to make it much more modular, insulating feature or subsystem teams from one another. Third, Netscape would build and stabilize the APIs—the application programming interfaces that constituted pieces of the Netscape ONE platform— before developers built the application code, such as mail or groupware features. Hopefully, the feature teams could then create new features on a more stable code base that was fully debugged.

The decision to refine the APIs before starting to write the application or feature code reflected another of Netscape's bad experiences with the Communicator 4.0 project. Developers built some new features, such as Netcaster (a "push technology" feature like PointCast and Microsoft's Active Channels), using programming interfaces that were still evolving. As a result, they had to ship an incomplete version of the product (4.0) and then continue working to stabilize the feature. They then shipped a "point release" (4.01) with the new feature and followed this with several other point releases to improve stability. Lisbonne recalled the experience:

> One of the things we're trying to do is to bake the platform pieces that we're building on top of earlier, so that you don't have as much a catch-22.

For example, in the 4.0 product, the Netcaster component is built entirely in Java and JavaScript and HTML. And there was a catch-22, as is clear in hindsight. As you might expect, [we had a] rapidly evolving Java, JavaScript, HTML infrastructure, and then built something on top of it in the same release. And that's why the Netcaster piece shipped a little bit after the 4.0 product. Dynamic HTML debuted, and yet we were using it then to build a product. JavaScript 1.1 and 65 new features debuted, and yet we were using it to build the Netcaster product and the object signing in Java and the new JIT [a faster Java VM] and all these new things.

Before Netscape even started the Communicator 4.0 project, however, Toy recalled that the developers realized they should not write any more new features on the old code base. They actually decided to devote two months to reworking the architecture, but failed because this was not enough time. The developers then figured out a temporary solution that got them through the 4.0 project (such as building new features somewhat in isolation from the other features and shipping lots of point releases). But for 6.0, Toy declared, they decided to start over—rework the architecture and then bring in engineers to write the applications (feature) code:

> We're starting all over. They're doing a new thing. And they're laying groundwork and they're not letting regular coders come in because they're building the framework. But what you have to understand is the architecture serves a purpose. That is not the only way to accomplish that purpose. And so you need to go back and say, why are we doing that? We're doing that so that interface changes are predictable, so that modules are unit testable. Well, how can we get those things in our current code base without rewriting it or how can we get some of the benefits of that without rewriting it? With a building full of really bright engineers, solutions to those things come up. I would not have believed a year ago that it was possible to do this [4.0] release. In fact, I stood up a year ago and said, unless we make some serious architectural changes to our code base, we will not ship software based on this code base. It's dead. This code base is dead. And so we spent two months trying to pick the right set of architectural changes to make to the code base and we failed. After two months, we said we just wasted two months. It's not enough time to rearchitect. Everyone said that at the beginning and we just said, "Well, we can only afford two months. What can we do in two months?" We did that and we said, "All right, we failed. Let's solve the problem some other way." We came up with a different solution that got us through this development cycle. Everyone is pretty happy with the results of that solution. And some of the things the rest of the company is picking up.

The 6.0 project illustrated some of the changes Netscape made in its approach to design as well as some practical problems. Netscape started the rearchitecture effort in July 1997 and initially estimated that the effort would require about 18 months and, at the peak, half of the 120 developers in the client product division. Netscape also started work in parallel on a new version of the client to follow Communicator 4.0 more directly, dubbed the 5.0 project. Managers estimated this version would take at least nine months to complete and the other half of the division's staff. In November 1997, Andreessen still described the 6.0 project enthusiastically. This was an effort, he believed, that was both essential and long overdue:

> Actually, it was something that we deferred. The classic engineering mentality is for the next rev [revision of the product] to rewrite what you did on the first rev [revision] because you made some compromises, as you always do. So this time you won't have to make any compromises, God damn it, and your managers won't make you! We fought that impulse for two years and then finally we gave in to it a little bit. . . . What happened was you reach a point where trying to add fundamentally new capabilities to an existing code base just becomes harder and harder and harder. We went through enough pain and trauma on 4.0 where it became apparent that we were going to have to do a reset on some of the stuff. Now, I will say one thing: 6.0 is not going to be a complete rewrite. . . . It's unfeasible to actually rewrite the whole thing in one pass. So there's going to be large parts of it that are going to be carried over. A lot of the core pieces, a lot of the core functions and core engines or modules, will be or are being rewritten.

Andreessen also insisted (much too ambitiously, in retrospect) that the 6.0 project had two goals. One was the architecture rewrite, which became the focus of the project. Initially, however, the goal was to create a new browser core with advanced multimedia and dynamic HTML capabilities. Therefore, Andreessen wanted his engineers to make the client code much more modular than in the previous versions, and he wanted the code to serve as the base for a new browser, including a product for the Java-based network computer that IBM, Oracle, and Sun Microsystems were promoting as an alternative to the Windows-Intel platform. To meet these goals, Netscape developers started restructuring and rewriting the browser code, first in C++ and then in Java (starting with the HTML layout engine). Andreessen continued his explanation during our November 1997 interview:

> Keep in mind there's a goal for 6.0, which actually serves two masters. There's a next-generation Communicator part and then there's also specif-

ically a next-generation kernel or layout/rendering/display engine. We knew that we should do that in a way that it would allow things to be easily componentized so it can be used by many people. We knew it should be highly programmable, and these other things. We knew it should serve as a platform for our future products as well as things the developers do. We debated Java versus C and decided to go with Java because we knew if we wanted to distribute it as an Intel binary we would be able to. If we wanted to distribute it as a Java on-demand thing, we'd be able to do that. And it would be able to be component-ized in either world. But based around that, we're going to emit out of that project an NC browser written entirely in Java. We already announced that. It's basically Magellan [Netscape's next-generation layout engine for the browser, later shipped with the Mozilla code and ported from Java to C++] with the user interface wrapped around it. And that will serve as the heart of 6.0. But then 6.0 has a bunch of other stuff around that, some of which will be written in Java.

Netscape failed to finish a Java browser and failed to carry out the 6.0 client project. Netscape continued with the client modularization effort, but ended up doing this more incrementally. Management reassigned engineers allocated to the 6.0 effort to work on the 4.x code base for a new release, dubbed Communicator 4.5. This team (roughly half of the client product division) worked mainly on enterprise-oriented features and released a beta version in July 1998 that included some bug fixes and performance enhancements. Netscape scheduled the commercial release of Communicator 4.5 for September or October. In parallel, Netscape engineers began working on the 5.0 Mozilla version of the client, whose source code Netscape made publicly available for free. The 5.0 team worked mainly on features related to the browsing functions.

Changes in the Client Technology Strategy

The decision to give away the 5.0 source code as well as to step back from plans to use Java so extensively also led Netscape managers to change their technology strategy for the client. Engineers had to remove or rewrite portions that Netscape was not free to license because other companies (such as Sun Microsystems) owned the code. They also decided to convert a lot of code from Java back to C++. In addition, they had to organize a separate team to figure out how to incorporate features or changes suggested from the community of Internet developers who were now free to play with the Netscape code.

Our interviews with various managers revealed more on the debates behind the 4.5, 5.0, and 6.0 projects. Netscape was continually short of developers and testers, and it was short of money to hire more people. Even apart from the unexpected difficulties encountered in rearchitecting the client code, Netscape did not have enough staff to do a major architecture project and finish the Mozilla release. Consequently, managers gradually pulled more and more developers away from the 6.0 project, making this effort harder to carry out. Managers also pulled people back to fix the 4.x product, which still had bugs and other problems that corporate customers wanted solved. Then the 6.0 project suffered from other setbacks, some of which were part of the rapidly changing world of the Internet.

On the one hand, Netscape engineers were having trouble writing complex features and user interfaces in Java and JavaScript, and they were finding it increasingly difficult to maintain compatibility with Sun Microsystems's Java standards. On the other hand, writing cross-platform code was also becoming relatively more expensive as market shares for UNIX and Macintosh machines dropped. These and other issues prompted Netscape managers to become more practical and regroup. Rick Schell gave us this perspective in our March 1998 interview, after he had left the company:

> The whole 5.0, 6.0 effort went through a lot of permutations and perturbations over the last many months. . . . What they initially wanted to do was rearchitect the browser. . . . And we planned at the time to do as much of that job as we could. Along the way, the project got more ambitious. And along with that, there was this whole pronouncement of what are we going to do with the client and Java, the whole thing. So, that took on a life of its own. And over the course of maybe eight months, different pieces got put into that client. This was all well and good except we never finished 4.0 until 4.05. . . . I attended a private review in early December. It was clear that Netscape couldn't execute on finishing 4.0 . . . given what, at the time, looked like flat quarters for the next two or three quarters.

Schell and other Netscape managers thought they would have a chance to "rebalance" the teams and revise their development plans between January and March 1998. But with a large loss in the last quarter of 1997, time ran out. Barksdale and Andreessen quickly decided to downsize the client team and the internal Java effort. They also encouraged Schell, Stryker, and other executives to take early retirement or move on. The 5.0 effort continued, but Netscape put the 6.0 project "in hiatus." As Netscape's client division regrouped, the engineering leaders decided to continue with the rearchitecting effort, but to do it gradually—in Schell's words, to "overhaul the existing code base a little bit at a time." In April 1998, Lisbonne described the changes to us in more detail, especially their success in salvaging work initially done in Java and porting this code over to C++:

> The 6.0 project, which was code-named Xena and was basically a new Communicator all written in Java, has been shelved. And that's been shelved primarily for technical reasons. The reality was that Java, at least in terms of late '97 early '98, was just not yet up to the task of implementing a product of that complexity. . . . So the question is, well fine, we're not going to do it in Java, how are we going to componentize it? And the answer there is twofold. . . . One is we took the layout engine, which we were writing in Java and is the core of the browser, and we have over the last three months ported it back to C++. In fact, yesterday we released it onto the Net, onto the Mozilla.org site. So that next-generation layout engine work has all been salvaged. We just put it back in C++ and we will plug it into a future version of the client at the right time. And "at the right time" has to do with the second part of the componentization strategy. Working in concert with the Net, we are in an evolutionary incremental way creating more modular interfaces on the existing code base such that, down the road, a future version of the source code we have posted will be able to accommodate in a plug-and-play fashion the engine that was just posted yesterday. . . . Two things must be true in order to plug in a new layout engine. One is you have to have a new layout engine to plug in, and second is your code must accept or accommodate that plug-in. And so we're working on both things in parallel. So componentization we're still doing. The difference is we're doing it in an incremental, evolutionary way on the C++ source code rather than in a revolutionary way all in Java.

Andreessen admitted to us as well that the 6.0 project was simply an effort that went too far. In part, Andreessen must take some of the blame. As chief technology officer, he remained distant from the product teams and, apparently, did not make enough effort to understand what was really going on. To be fair, Andreessen claimed that he was not in a position to do anything about the Java problem until he took direct charge of product development in July 1997. Even then, however, it took him several months to decide what to do. In our May 1998 meeting, Andreessen reflected on the 6.0 project as well as what he had learned about managing the engineering organization:

> The biggest thing I probably learned . . . is don't wait to make the changes that you know need to be made. Make them right away. . . . Up until mid-'97, I didn't have the control to be able to do it. Even through mid- to late

'97, I was willing to give people a bit too much rope. . . . The problem is, of course, if you give people too much rope, they're not only going to hang themselves, they'll hang you in the process. And so, I learned . . . The 6.0 project is a perfect example. I never should have let it get as far as it did. At every single review, I always brought up the Java topic, and there was never a good answer for it. I should have gotten in front of it sooner. I should have just made sure that that was never the case. The other thing was the people running the 6.0 project violated my cardinal rule of how you do product development, which is incrementally. They were trying to do way too much all at once. The project was unbounded in time, had no deliverables even defined. I just didn't kill it soon enough. . . . And 6.0 turned into rocket science, and it was driving me nuts.

Balancing Work on Architectures Versus New Features

We noted earlier that good modular architectures usually require up-front investments in design, and this requirement can pose a daunting challenge for start-up firms, especially those racing to deliver new features on Internet time. As Andreessen and other Netscape managers pointed out, start-up companies do not have the luxury of worrying about long-term investments in architectural development if they have to worry about survival in the short term. Not surprisingly, how much to invest in architectural development became a crucial debate at Netscape with no easy answers. Immature Internet technologies such as Java and JavaScript also added an instability to Netscape's products that made architectural work more difficult.

Restructuring the client using more established design concepts and programming languages would have been a formidable task as well. As we saw in Table 4.1, between 1994 and 1997, Netscape's browser had evolved from around 100,000 lines of code in its first version, built by around 10 developers and a handful of testers and product managers, to the Communicator suite of some 3 million lines of code, built by some 120 developers at the peak as well as some 50 testers and 30 product managers. Rearchitecting the code base using unproven technologies while trying to create new features at the same time could have turned out to be a bottomless pit of expenditures that resulted in nothing to ship. If the effort had continued for months and then years and still failed, Netscape would probably have fallen hopelessly behind Microsoft in the browser market. Indeed, some industry reviewers already gave equal or even higher marks in functionality and quality to Microsoft's Internet Explorer 4.0, compared to Communicator 4.0. Netscape was also struggling to keep its market share in servers, with competition coming from Windows NT as well as IBM/Lotus and Novell.

As Netscape expanded the 6.0 project during the fall of 1997 to include rewriting all the components in Communicator and not simply one layout engine, managers and senior engineers had little choice but to rethink their decision to bet half the client development team on a risky R&D and architecture effort. They still wanted to refine features shipped with the 4.0 product as well as start another version that would add new functions to pull in new customers. Netscape also needed to stabilize the programming interfaces in order to help partners and customers help Netscape by making it easier for outsiders to build features or whole applications to go with the client platform. Even before the decision to absorb the 6.0 engineers into the 4.5 and 5.0 projects, Lisbonne had decided to reduce the 60 or so engineers working on the redesign work and to reallocate most of these people gradually to the building of new applications or feature code. In our August 1997 interview, he recalled their debate on architecture versus features:

> We had a long discussion about it just last night in a leads meeting. I don't believe there is an elegant shortcut that cuts through that tension. The true answer is you have to do both. And what you'd like to do is to be able to spec out what both mean and ask for the resources to do both, and that's what I'm doing. Time in the oven for the platform is more important right now. So, I've staffed the platform piece earlier and more completely than the apps piece. I think that's the right thing to do. But I explained to the apps folks that, if part of the answer is to build a terrific HTML platform that other third parties will want to build on top of, technical elegance is necessary but not sufficient. There must also be volume and an economic motive for these people to do that. And so the way you break out of that chicken and egg is with value, compelling value, in the form of applications that kind of get the thing rolling to begin with. So, you can't also so bias the platform that there's nothing but a great bunch of APIs to download. And that's really a kind of catch-22. . . . Right now, it's roughly fifty-fifty. But we will add more apps people in the coming quarters than platform people.

Lisbonne emphasized that a company like Netscape, which produced a platform product with various features, had to do both. It had to work on product architectures, which customers did not directly see, as well as on features and applications, which customers did see directly. With the 4.0, 4.5, 5.0, and 6.0 projects, Netscape was clearly experimenting and struggling to find the right balance. It was obvious even to managers in client marketing, who usually wanted lots of new features, that the company needed both types of work to proceed in parallel. For example, Julie Herendeen, a product manager for the client, stressed how important it was to have a split of interests and responsibilities within the development team:

> Even on 6.0 . . . we have both engineers and marketing people thinking about both the end-user capabilities as well as the lower-level architecture and the APIs that we would open up to third parties. They're usually different people but on the same team. . . . We'll probably, at least for the midterm, always do both architectural elements or engines and end-user applications. . . . And some engineers really prefer to work on architecture and get to see how that architecture is embodied in an application because that application is being created in their group.

The open Internet standards that Netscape built into its products allowed outside companies or individuals to create applications or plug-ins that made the Netscape browser more functional and thus more valuable. But to build the proper interfaces, which was an architectural issue, Netscape needed engineers who understood architectural standards as well as application needs. Herendeen made this point as well: "I think it would be hard if the application was always being created out there by third parties. And I would argue that it allows you to develop a better architecture if you're actually implementing some application against that architecture because then you're testing your own platform and your own architecture."

Some engineers even wanted to devote *more* than half of the division's resources to architectural work, but this was not really possible. Netscape management had decided to build another version of the client, 5.0, in parallel with the architectural project. The client engineers were also still trying to finish features supposedly shipped with the first Communicator 4.0 release. Michael Toy worried about the pressure to deliver and Netscape's inability to assign hundreds of developers to rewriting features as well as redoing the architecture (which the much larger and richer Microsoft could more easily do in a similar situation). He feared that teams might simply write Java interfaces for some of the modules and then have to go back and rewrite them later in another project: "This is Netscape, and I can easily see, as the crunch for 6.0 comes along, large pieces of code getting interfaces slapped on them and shoved into the 6.0 tree and victory declared and going back and rewriting those in Java later. . . . We have current features that have years and years of engineering. You don't turn right around and pull it out of your hat and we don't have enough money to have a 200-person organization."

Ironically, Netscape servers had the opposite architectural problem. They did not suffer from "spaghetti code." Rather, they were too modular. The architectural challenge was to integrate their look and feel as well as functionality from the viewpoint of the SuiteSpot user. In particular, it was not so easy to combine features that existed in different server products and use them together, such as to create a secure intranet or extranet. Netscape managers also wanted the server groups to share more components but still maintain their traditions of individual technical excellence. Bill Turpin made this observation during our August 1997 interview:

> That is the one difference between us and the client. We have about nine different products, which we collectively call SuiteSpot. Historically, they were a fairly loose collection we called a suite, and we're in the process now of making them into more of an integrated cohesive set of products. It will be one product, with different servers in it. And that is the transition we're working on as we speak. So the [executive] reviews are becoming more where we're looking at the suite as opposed to the individual projects. We are doing a lot more collective planning now on groups of products as opposed to individual products. . . . The Web Server, the Proxy Server, Catalog Server, and Certificate Server, which we have all done ourselves, are all based largely on that initial Web Server code base. But we have acquired several of the others and they are dramatically different code bases. Messaging Server we've acquired. Collabra Server started out as the INN public domain server. Directory Server started out as an LDAPS University of Michigan directory server. So those servers have a lot less in common.

Netscape thus had to balance architectural work with new features even for the servers. Unlike the 6.0 client project, however, Turpin explained that they did the redesigning as part of the regular schedule and as separate work done in parallel teams. They gave priority to creating enough features to feel like they had a new product to ship:

> That [architectural work] is part of the normal schedule. It is mixed in there with the features. And that's tricky sometimes to make the tradeoff between a feature and that thing you need to do for the health of the code base. That is one of the tradeoffs we make at the executive reviews. At the end, you always have to ask yourself, when a customer gets this, are they going to see enough new stuff that they are going to think it is the next-generation product? So we always give a blend of new features in there in addition to any architecture we do.

The relative independence of the different server products and development teams was important both for project management and for marketing. The code that server teams worked with was not closely inter-twined (in contrast to the Communicator 4.0 product). In addition, some customers continued to prefer individual server products or customized packages, rather than the entire suite. Netscape decided to pursue some further integration of the server products and manage them in coordi-nated projects, but continue to sell the servers separately. Turpin elabo-rated:

> We consciously made the choice a year and a half to two years ago to keep the [server] projects pretty uncoupled, so a delay in one project wouldn't cause a delay in another project. We wanted each team to feel like they owned their product, they made their own technology decisions, and they could move as fast as possible. And I think that served us well during that period of time, where speed and getting the new features out was a major push for us. . . . Now that we're trying to build a more integrated suite, we're trying to get all the projects to be more the same time frames, synchronize the betas, etc., so that, when we go to a 4.0 release, all the servers across the board can go 4.0. . . . I think we'll be through this plan-ning process pretty soon, though. And then we'll have every server com-mitted to do a certain set of features and they can go off and implement them individually. We're going to keep each of the product teams individ-ual. What we're trying to do now is agree on the ground rules of the com-mon things each server will commit to do—who owns it, who delivers what to whom. And so we hope to stay fairly efficient in the implementation phase. . . . We will still sell servers individually. Some customers want to buy them that way. But more and more of our revenue is being derived from the suite.

Changes in the Client Business Model

While Netscape managers figured out ways to deal with the architectural problems in their products, the decision in January 1998 to give away the client product created another set of problems. On the positive side, this move stabilized, or at least slowed the decline, in Netscape's browser mar-ket share. Two key issues remained, however: how to manage the techno-logical evolution of the client as well as exactly how many resources to devote to it? Each developer cost between $150,000 and $200,000 per year on average, including benefits and overhead. Testers and product managers cost somewhat less but were still expensive in Silicon Valley. This meant that creating the 4.0 client product over the course of 11 months probably cost Netscape around $20 million for the 120 developers who worked on the project and another $10 million for the 70 or so testers and product managers. This was a lot of money to spend on enhancing a product line that may or may not have much in the way of direct revenues in the future, especially when the company experienced a huge loss in the last quarter of 1997.

Yet Netscape remained committed to evolving the browser and other client features. Formerly, the client product division had been a separate profit center and generated more than enough profits and revenues to fund 250-odd employees in 1997. After January 1998, the division had no direct profits or sales, at least prior to the commercial release of the 4.5 client. Solving this problem of how to fund client development involved a major change in the client business model.

After debating alternatives, Netscape management decided to channel funds to support the client engineers through at least two sources. One was to identify "enterprise" client-server features, create a special enterprise version of the client that would most likely ship with SuiteSpot, and allocate funds to client development that nominally came in through the package sales. According to Lisbonne, this maneuver required "a little bit more complicated bookkeeping." Another source of money would come in the form of "strategic funds" that Netscape management allocated to make sure the client remained competitive, such as to support the newly invigorated Netcenter business. Lisbonne, in our April 1998 interview, explained this evolution in thinking and accounting:

> In terms of a business model . . . client prices are now free. . . . But since changing the business model, we've also rethought how it should be chartered internally. Obviously, you can't have a P&L for a free product. So what we've done is decided to fund CPD [client product division] really in terms of two categories of funding. One is it's funded to do enterprise-related things to the extent those contribute to enterprise client/server revenue and profits. . . . But there's a second category of funding for the client which is, for lack of a better word . . . the "strategic funding" for the client. This basically says it's the senior management's point of view that continued excellence in client software and continued success in proliferating it is of strategic value to the company, even if it's not obvious with the Excel spreadsheet du jour how to track all that in a given quarter. . . . It's quite evident that continued proliferation of the client and the relationship with tens of millions of customers is one of the prime vehicles through which we support our Web site business and, frankly, create new revenue opportunities for the company overall. So we have a chunk of funding that's done under that label and really funds . . . technology and product development

that doesn't directly improve the enterprise revenues but is nonetheless a smart thing for Netscape to do.

Lisbonne admitted, though, that giving the client away did not mean as much of a loss in revenues as one might expect. Individuals tended to download the client for free anyway. And corporate customers usually paid for a client-server "bundle." After January 1998, Netscape was trying to sell the same bundle for the same price while claiming that the client was "free," at least in the standard vanilla version. Special versions or information systems management tools could have separate charges in the future, although most sales would still come with SuiteSpot. (The major client tool was Mission Control Desktop, used for installation of Communicator Pro over networks and customizing the user interface, and for administering network features like Smart Update and Roaming Access.) This repackaging seemed to help corporate customers justify staying with Netscape rather than switching to Microsoft's free Internet Explorer. Lisbonne gave us this account:

> What we did on the enterprise side is we just included the client. . . . Basically, we kept the client/server bundle price the same and told the customer that, instead of it being X for client and "bundle minus X" for server, the whole thing is for the servers, for the client/server bundle, and the clients are free. We had interesting anecdotes happening quite regularly where the customer would say, "I really like your products. They're technically superior. I really like Netscape. It's the vendor I want to work with. I just have this internal political problem with defending the fact that I'm paying money for your client." And so we would say, "Well, fine. We'll give you the clients for free but the total purchase price is the same. How does that sound?" The customers invariably said, "Perfect. That's exactly what I want." So the overall value proposition was fine. It was just we had a little bit of a positioning problem with how we were assessing the price and that's just because Microsoft has been successful in setting an expectation in the market that clients were free.

We described in chapter 3 how Netscape made a decision to link client development more closely with the Web site in May 1998. It moved the entire client product division to become a unit under the new Web site division. The objective was to make sure that new client features drew users to products and services available through the Web site, making it possible for Netscape to charge fees to advertisers or service providers. Andreessen believed that the Web site business alone would create enough revenues to sustain continued development of the browser client, though perhaps with a smaller team than Netscape had used in the past. He explained the strategy for future development of the client code in our May 1998 interview: "We let that team get way too big—way, way, way too big. . . . We're going to link it very tightly with the Netcenter business. The Netcenter business is going to provide the sustainable revenue."

PRINCIPLE   *Design common components that multiple product teams can share.*

The Strategy to Share Components

Only one aspect of Netscape's componentization or rearchitecting strategy was to create modules that smaller, nimbler teams could design and test on their own. A second part of the strategy was to create components that multiple groups could share, in both the client and server divisions. Many managers and engineers referred to these shared components as "core technologies" because they leveraged key technologies that were at the heart of the Netscape platform.

Of course, the concept of modular architectures and shared components is hardly unique to Netscape or the software industry. It is the essence of platform-based design, which we can see in industries ranging from automobiles to consumer electronics to computer software.[13] PC software companies in particular have been adopting object-oriented design philosophies and component reuse strategies for a decade or more. Even Microsoft, which has been more of a follower than a leader in object-oriented design and systematic reuse, has been implementing a similar strategy for years with its applications products and parts of its operating systems. Several Microsoft groups also routinely build components that other groups can share.

In the early and mid-1990s, Microsoft allocated considerable engineering time to creating its Component Object Model (COM) and then redesigning the architectures and code bases of products such as Word, Excel, and PowerPoint as well as Windows and Windows NT. It did this redesign to facilitate component sharing. The Word product unit, for example, builds a text-processing module and a printing module that go into Word as well as Excel, the Office suite, and several other applications that do text processing and printing. The Excel product unit builds modules for doing mathematical calculations and drawing charts that go into Word, the Office suite, and other applications. Microsoft's systems and languages groups provide core technologies to the applications groups, such as the OLE and ActiveX API code and the Visual Basic macro language.[14] Netscape tried to do something similar with its products, as Julie Herendeen described in our July 1997 interview:

> The vision for the company is eventually to have a componentized product. So you'd really have a team around mail. You'd have a team around the browser. You'd have a team around Netcaster. You'd have a team around Communicator Pro. Moving to that architecture, you'd have an engineering lead and a marketing lead for each of those components. Now, what we have is that structure and then one person to try to pull it all together, at least on the standard edition side. . . . If you look further down the line, once we've got the product more componentized, you can see a world where there's a GM [general manager] for mail and a GM for browsing, etc. . . . We would still build a messenger application because another view of the world is, all we do is we create a messaging engine. Then other people can build applications. If we took the platform scenario to the furthest levels, we could provide engines and services, and other folks build applications on top of that. We would still build a messenger, so the e-mail group's goal would still be to create the best e-mail application around.

As we discussed earlier, a serious weakness in Netscape's product set in 1997 and 1998 was that client feature teams shared a lot of code that developers had not sufficiently modularized. The resulting spaghetti code made it nearly impossible to build and test components in independent teams or release the components as discrete chunks of functionality. Resolving this problem required better modularization. With better modularization, it would also become possible to share components more easily and reduce redundant design and testing work as well as de-couple projects. But how to create common components presented another set of managerial and technical difficulties.

One approach that companies have used is to organize a centralized or stand-alone division that builds common components for different product groups. The problem with this strategy, however, is that centralized groups tend to become isolated from the needs of the product teams and to develop their own technical agendas. Another approach is to ask some product groups (as Microsoft does) to build components that other product groups can share. Then at least some product teams will get the components they need. But the problem with this strategy is that the product teams often require extra time or engineering hours to design components that meet the needs of other products as well as their own. Project managers must have the resources, authority, and incentives to have their engineers make this extra effort.[15]

A Division to Build Common Components

The approach that Netscape tried first was to create a separate division to build shared components—the core technologies division. (Netscape later renamed this the strategic technologies and products, or STP, division between October 1997 and February 1998, at which time Netscape disbanded it.) Netscape organized the division in 1996 and made the head of the organization, David Stryker, report to the then-head of client and server engineering, Rick Schell. (Later, when Eric Hahn and then John Paul took over the server division, Stryker continued to report to Schell, who managed the client division only.) Stryker was another veteran: He had worked for more than a decade at Intermetrics, Symbolics, and Object Design and joined Netscape in spring 1996 as an expert in object technologies.

At its peak in 1997, the centralized division had a staff of about 230 people divided into four main groups: Java and JavaScript, protocols, technical publications and usability, and global applications (internationalization and localization). Each group had a general manager as well as a full complement of developers, testers, and product managers. After deciding to cut back on internal Java technology development in January 1998, Netscape merged the core technology groups into various client and server product teams. Before this change, however, Stryker described his mission with great confidence in our August 1997 interview:

> I'm VP of core technology. That means I'm responsible for all the technologies that are shared across our entire product line. That includes the security, libraries, the protocols suites, Java, JavaScript, and a technology called LiveConnect, which is the way you get from JavaScript to elements inside the client and into Java. I'm also responsible for our tools offerings, the most notable of which is Visual JavaScript, just in its third beta release right now. . . . The mission of the group is to provide world-class technology components across the product line, ensuring uniformity of the platform across the product line and providing the tools necessary to grow the market for Internet products, particularly our server products.

Stryker was a major proponent of the effort to rearchitect Communicator. The components that his teams provided to the product groups (which he called "binary deliveries") contained the API code that made modularization and sharing of modules through Internet protocols possible. Stryker admitted to us, however, that redesigning the client turned out to be considerably more difficult than designing application features, and therefore required multiple iterations of designing and redesigning:

I am a leading wave of the effort in the sense that I started this [rearchitec-ture project] a little over a year ago. My binary deliveries embody this new stuff. I had to come first because they [the client product division] couldn't get their stuff done unless the foundation was well enough specified and they had enough confidence in it. Now we've got objectives, both techno-logical and customer requirements objectives, and we know what we're *not* trying to do. So now we go into a phase of design and design again. The real art in it—and there are people who are good at it and there are people who aren't—is picking out the pieces that can sink the ship and doing them down to the atoms. And that'll be 2 percent or 3 percent, but you've got to choose the right 2 or 3 percent. If the architecture is a sensible one and a flexible enough one, the actual building of the application GUI is pretty routine. At the core technology level, it's a lot less routine. You're making architectural choices all the time and the platform components tend to live longer than any particular piece of the application.

One of Stryker's key concerns was not to "over-componentize." Many Netscape developers and teams wanted to be able to test their pieces of code individually, such as a particular server product on multiple hard-ware platforms. Breaking down the products into smaller and smaller pieces facilitated this kind of "unit testing" as well as testing automation because there were fewer components and features, and fewer possible interactions, to test. Developers could also keep separate versions of the code (called "source trees" or "branches") so that they could more easily isolate or trace errors and changes. On the other hand, having too many components placed a burden on the teams importing the code because then they had more components to understand and integrate. Stryker explained this aspect of the problem:

Server guys want to know that 30 days before they go RTM [release to manufacturing] they can take a new drop of the component tree and inte-grate it in and not get blown out of the water. They need to know we've tested it on the 19 platforms. And, in some ways, the client's requirements are less daunting than that because they have fewer individual moving parts than the nine servers. . . . It's easy to go components crazy and say, "Well, I've got these 25 things, each of which could be separate libraries, so I'm going to deliver them all individually and my customers can mix and match." This turns out to be a nonoptimal approach. Your customers want as small a number of packages as they can get by with because what they are really buying is portability and certainty of quality. They don't want to buy into the problem of saying, "Well, I've got four releases. I've got 25 to the fourth possible combinations." . . . So, the first strategy is defining a very small set of large components that can be tested independently of each other. The second strategy is obviously our own source tree for the components that can evolve independently of our customers [the client and server divisions]. A third strategy is specifications for each of the versions detailing what each version of the component hierarchy is supposed to do. The fourth strategy is independent automated test rigs, so that the problem of determining the quality is not proportional to human labor. It's proportional to machine time.

Though the division is now gone, it did play an important role in defining a hierarchy of components. This hierarchy remained central to Netscape's product architectures in both the client and the server divisions. One useful element in the architecture has been the Netscape Portable Runtime layer that we described earlier. Other common components that the core technology division and then other groups built included various Internet APIs or enabling code, as well as services such as security code that made sure, for example, a system can restrict user access. Stryker described the layers:

> There's a hierarchy of components. At the lowest level there's something called the Netscape Portable Runtime. . . . Above that there are things like the security library and the network protocols libraries. Then above those are Java, JavaScript. And above those are things like LiveConnect, the way you call back and forth between Java and JavaScript, so this stack can be tested in basically two groups. There is the part up to but not including Java and JavaScript, and we have some fairly good automated test rigs to go against those. And then there's that stack plus Java and JavaScript and Live Connect. We're building better stuff there but we don't have what we need right now. We have things like the JavaSoft test suite, and some third-party suites. But what we are working on is building our own comprehensive cross-product test suite, particularly for the Java-JavaScript kind of connection where there's nothing you can get from the industry right now.

The core technologies groups provided components and tools to both the client and the server product divisions. Defining what should be "core" was relatively clear when both the server and client product groups used the components. In other cases, one product team would see something good such as security code that the core technologies group provided to another product team, and then they would ask for this as a common component. Stryker explained:

> Nearly all of what I provide goes to both. For example, Java and Java-Script are very much part of the Web Server. All the security libraries go in

essentially all of the products. . . . There are some things that I do that only go into the client. An example of that is I did all the S-MIME (Secure-Multipurpose Internet Mail Extension) development for client-side secure mail. It's properly a client function but is so heavily involved in the security substrate that I ended up doing it in my organization. Plug-ins are another example of a client facility that I handle principally because . . . the hairy part . . . is getting them to interact properly with Java and JavaScript.

But the division and Stryker himself struggled with too many issues. It was never clear how to define core technologies that sat between the client and the server products and still allow the product divisions to retain responsibility for their own product architectures. (This was mainly an issue for the client engineers.) Another problem was how to treat the core technologies groups—as integral partners of the product teams, or as a division of separate units that should design, build, and test components independently. A third problem was how to make sure the core technologies teams did not pursue their own technical agendas, such as to push technologies that the product groups did not really want. A fourth debate took place over what components to develop in-house as opposed to buying from the outside.

Netscape managers never solved their disagreements about what components to build in the core technologies division (and later STP) or in the client and server divisions, as well as how to allocate architectural responsibilities. Historically, the engineers in the product divisions defined the architectures for their products as they wrote code. This was particularly true in the client product division, which had created the first product for the company. In short, the centralized division failed to work smoothly with the client developers to define the architecture, even though, formally, Stryker's boss in 1997 was the head of client development. Core technology engineers also had trouble pulling out pieces that the client and server divisions could easily share. Stryker reflected on the challenges facing his division through August 1997:

> It's an evolving story. The core technology organization originally consisted of a group of client product engineers working on platform capabilities. These capabilities were represented as source files in the client product. As server products were built and needed the same platform capabilities, in terms of security libraries, Java and JavaScript support, and so on, they just grabbed the client source code for these capabilities and added them to the server source code trees. As a result of this highly informal source code delivery process, no testing was done on the platform components before integration with the client and server products, and the same platform

bugs were rediscovered in the different products. It is true that this source code delivery process gave the client and server groups maximum freedom, but it also generated lots of work for them and resulted in inconsistent platform offerings on client and server. We needed to move to a process in which tested binary code, not untested source code, was delivered to the client and server groups.

We can see another side to this debate, too. Bob Lisbonne argued that the division should be no more than a supplier of components, serving not only Netscape but also partners such as Sun Microsystems and IBM. Netscape was in the process of forming a partnership with these two companies in late summer and fall of 1997 to develop Java-related technologies in a new laboratory and use them under license from Sun. In Communicator 4.0 and previous projects, however, the core technologies division built components as part of the regular product teams.

In a sense, the division became stuck in between multiple missions. It also had lots of responsibilities but limited authority. Some managers wanted it to create leading-edge components that moved the Internet architecture forward, in Netscape and in its partners. But the centralized component groups were not independent—again, a product architecture problem. They could not build and test pieces of code separately and then provide debugged and stable components to Netscape's client and server product teams or outside partners. Nor were core technology engineers in a good political position to influence the architectural design work for the client (or the servers). Lisbonne explained his position in our August 1997 meeting:

One of the things we're trying to do is work with David's group more as a supplier of components, to establish more of a consumer-producer contract than to invite them quite to the same table and have them shoulder-to-shoulder in the build process and fixing bugs. By that I mean we expect to take discrete deliveries of certified components of the core technology group. That should help us manage the advances that [Stryker's] group is planning to introduce into our product. And why that will work is because he has multiple other customers for that technology—obviously, our server division, but as we work more closely with them, Sun and IBM as well as third-party developers. There are other people who care a whole lot about the Netscape Java VM. So that's the model that we're working toward. And that, too, is a difference and an improvement over the 4.0 process, where they were an equal part of the team. I don't mean to say they're not a part of the team. But I think formalizing the deliveries—and having QA'd them in his organization and delivered certified components to both the server division and us—will help a lot. The other thing it does, it really enforces some good discipline, which requires the definition of interfaces. Sometimes it shines a bright light on places where those should exist but don't yet. Or it begs questions of backward compatibility that are germane not only to what we're doing internally but to the things that thousands of developers outside of Netscape are doing.

Other problems that the division had to deal with involved changes in protocols or APIs in other companies' operating systems. Netscape itself had to change designs frequently and had some compatibility problems across the first three versions of Navigator. Stryker claimed that Netscape's internal APIs remained relatively stable, although he admitted to problems when connecting to unstable APIs from other companies:

> We try to absorb all those issues in the Netscape Portable Runtime and we get screwed frequently. For example, the differences between NT 3.51 and NT 4 are very large. But that's a problem we solve on the leading edge so that our customers don't have to solve it. . . . I can give you a spectrum. Once we did the first couple of UNIX ports, getting the Netscape Portable Runtime over on average took three or four weeks maybe per new UNIX platform. And typically that three or four weeks was eaten up in the fact that process-threading models are not standard across UNIX. There are a lot of things that are standard but they're not. And certainly the performance statistics are different on each one. At the other extreme, we have so far put five months of time into Windows 3.1 to get its version of the portable runtime working properly. And I still haven't finished it, although it's supposed to be about a week away or two weeks away. We're going to get it, but we had a lot of bumps on the road. It turns out that the first products to use the new version of the Netscape Portable Runtime were server products, and none of those ship on Windows 3.1. Originally, the client group had planned to ship Release 4.0 on the new version of the portable runtime, but by the time the server group had shipped on that version, the client group had decided to stay with the old version. So the uniformity across products we had wanted was not achieved.

To keep track of the many changes he had to deal with, Stryker used to hold two-hour weekly staff meetings. He also required weekly reports from all his managers outlining what was different from the previous week. In addition, everyone communicated very frequently by e-mail. Nonetheless, Stryker complained that the degree of change could make a manager's plans look like "a drunkard's walk":

> It's really tough. . . . The reason that objectives and nonobjectives are so important is that every 72 hours you change your plan. And it can look like

a drunkard's walk if you don't have some way to guide those decisions. But we change our minds a lot, largely because external industry conditions change so fast. I mean, we've got operating system problems, or even at the level of IETF [the Internet Engineering Task Force], they made an unexpected decision on a protocol and, well, it's no use crying about it. You just have to do it.

Diffusing Core Technologies Back into the Product Groups

Netscape ended up disbanding the centralized division in January 1998 and diffusing responsibilities for the core technologies back into the product groups (which had been the original structure). One change moved the security components group, which had been combined with the protocols group, to the server products division and consolidated them with the Directory and Certificate Servers personnel in the Mission Control divlet. Netscape did this because these two servers were very closely related to the security components. Netscape also moved some technical writers, who prepared manuals and help files for the client and server products, to the product divisions. Since the fall of 1997, the company had located most of the technical writers in the centralized division. Netscape also scaled down the Java development group and moved the remaining personnel to the client product division. It also moved the JavaScript group as well as the protocols group (which built the Netscape Portable Runtime layer) to the server products division.

One factor that aided the reorganization involved what common components to create in-house. Netscape managers and engineers debated how much to rely on outside partners, such as the JavaSoft Division of Sun Microsystems. Sun invented the Java programming language and JavaBeans architecture and provided components such as its own Java virtual machine. Netscape had gradually built up a large group for in-house Java development, particularly in the effort to create Netscape's own Java virtual machine and Java Development Kit, which included a components library. Netscape made this internal investment in part because JavaSoft components and tools were not yet suitable for the "industrial strength" programming that Netscape wanted to do. Netscape also wanted to direct the evolution of Java—again, the "open, but not open" strategy.

To reduce its engineering staff, Netscape announced in January 1998 that it was cutting back on internal Java development, both in the form of tools as well as usage of the language. The company let go several dozen developers it had hired specifically to do Java work. Overall, the total downsizing eliminated about 10 percent of Netscape's 3,200 workforce at the time, or about 300 people (including contractors and temporary workers). The reductions affected some 150 of the 1,000 or so engineering staff.[16] Many of these engineers had worked in the core technologies or STP division as well as the Java group within the client product division.

These changes came as no surprise to anyone, however. We first heard of the preparation for the downsizing in August 1997. At this time, Stryker discussed the decision to rely more on JavaSoft and the partnership with IBM for Java components:

> Netscape and IBM and JavaSoft are putting together a Java engineering center where engineers from all three companies will work together to produce a single implementation that Netscape and IBM will ship and that JavaSoft will license to all its licensees. So the long and short is we work pretty closely with them and will ever more closely in the future. . . . There were things that JavaSoft shipped early on that didn't work very well, and we, by and large, made our own versions of those. We're moving back from that. We want commonality and convergence with the industry Java efforts. We've been trying to do that for 14 months. Our value added is in things like the Internet and the Java-JavaScript-HTML triad. Our value added is in reinforcing that triad. It's not in us driving the definition of Java or Java environments forward. We're very happy with JavaSoft handling that problem and following their lead. We don't want to define APIs. We've done it in a very few cases where we're getting killed for competitive reasons for not having it, and JavaSoft wasn't ready. But we're working more closely with JavaSoft. JFC [Java Foundation Classes] is a good example.

We also spoke to Bob Lisbonne in April 1998 about these events. He gave this interpretation of the decision to scale back on Java as well as eliminate the centralized division and reassign its engineers:

> The change in the Java strategy meant that we no longer needed a central Java group because we were no longer going to do our own Java VMs. . . . So that's what happened to Java. Publications [technical writers] we decided to put closer to the product teams, again in the spirit of getting to smaller, more autonomous teams. And internationalization we decided to put closer to the sales geographies, who we thought were in the best position to assess the costs and benefits of incremental localizations. So that leaves JavaScript, which does continue to be a shared technology between client and server, very important to both. But without a central large STP organization, we concluded that we needed to go back to the old model, which is, we'll have one JavaScript group and . . . it will be solid-line to one division and dotted-line to the other. And since for its whole history it had been solid-line into the client division and dotted-line into servers, we just thought it would be healthy this time around to put it in the server division,

dotted-line to client, for all the cultural reasons, to help make the server division think more every day about JavaScript and make those relationships better and physically see these people there and so forth. So that's really where the STP organization went.

When we talked to the head of the server division, John Paul, he admitted that Netscape managers had found it increasingly difficult to decide how to divide up responsibilities and how to allocate new people as the company grew. In addition, the product teams were starting to put up walls and the centralized division was moving further away from the needs of the businesses. Paul commented in March 1998:

> When the company moved to divisions and created a client and server division, there were certain functions that appeared to be valuable to be shared. And basically, Eric [Hahn, then head of the server division] and Rick [Schell] divided them up between themselves, trying not to do a lot of accounting back and forth, and said, "I'll take care of this. You take care of that." It wasn't very effective because there weren't good business decisions being made. As an example, we would be growing. I was probably adding 30 to 50 employees a quarter. And how did you allocate those employees to different product lines or businesses within your business? I would listen to everyone tell me about what they wanted to do and then we would add six writers to the writing group. But after that, they would get dispersed into places that weren't aligned with what our business was attempting to do. So, to me, the dismantling of STP was to bring the resources closer to the business decisions so they could be more properly allocated and decided upon. Organizations create walls. They were also isolated from the market so they weren't hearing customer requirements.

Rick Schell saw the move as more political. The division general managers wanted more control than was possible with a centralized group building key shared components: "It was a political move. And the sad thing is to use the word political in this context. . . . But it was a political move. It's hard to maintain those things when you have divisions because, in typical divisions, general managers want complete control over everything and anything." Schell also believed that Stryker was not particularly good at the maneuvering necessary to maintain such a position: "I don't think Dave had the political skills . . . to work his customer. The organizations were his customers. I think he would have done better with outside customers where he knew what their agenda really was. Often an outside customer will tell you more of what the problem is and what they expect from you than an inside customer will. An inside customer just gets pissed off when you don't deliver."

The January 1998 reorganization also eliminated the separate 5.0 and 6.0 client divlets, and merged the developers (temporarily) into one group. Instead of dividing up people by projects, Netscape retained the divlet idea of having small teams within the divisions but created new groups. One was around the enterprise version of the client. This group included Communicator Pro, with groupware features such as e-mail and group calendars. It also had the Mission Control Desktop tool for information systems managers. Another divlet was for the browser and features closely related to this component. A third divlet was the Web site, which evolved into Netcenter. Later in 1998, the Web site divlet became the new focus of the division, and client development moved to become a division within this division, with Lisbonne reporting to Mike Homer.

Andreessen viewed the decision to dissolve the STP division and create new divlets as a classic case of centralization versus decentralization. He commented in our May 1998 interview that, in the fast-paced environment in which Netscape operated, organizing in a way that required too much matrix-type coordination was bound to fail. He claimed that they quickly realized the centralized structure was a mistake:

At the pace that we're moving, the implementation difficulties inherent with any cross-functional or cross-divisional thing that requires coordination are just best avoided. And this is, of course, the classic tension between centralization and decentralization. I will, in a minute, knee-jerk to decentralization whenever I think I can. In STP, we tried for a little bit more centralization than we probably should have. And what was interesting about the STP experience was that people who were put in the position of being in the central groups, because they argued for it to be that way, quickly realized that they were wrong and quickly realized they actually didn't want it to be like that. They were going to be very unhappy. What happened was we had had the worst of all worlds before. We had large central groups that were not disciplined and had gotten too big and were doing things that were not appropriate to the mission that we were supposed to have—people who were supposed to be their internal customers. So then, when we took those central groups, with their heads, who were very strong advocates of the central groups, and we actually made them subject to discipline and constraint and direction setting and goal setting and budget setting by their internal customers, it became clear that they were still too big. It became clear that they were still out of control. And it became clear that the function of running such a central group was actually not going to be that much fun after all. It meant that you really had to pay attention to what your customers wanted. So, fine. Boom. Blow that up. We've been much happier ever since. . . . Up until March of '98, I don't think we've ever made a mistake taking something that had been centralized and making it decentralized.

PRINCIPLE   *Design new products and features for parallel development.*

Another strategy that depended on modular designs and potentially enhanced speed and flexibility in delivering new products is *parallel development*—simultaneously running multiple projects working on the next and "next-plus-one" versions of a product as well as new features or bug fixes "off-line" from formal projects. Both Netscape and Microsoft used this approach. It was especially useful when new products required 18 or 24 months to develop and test, but the company wanted to introduce new products at shorter intervals, such as every nine or 12 months. In this situation, Netscape and Microsoft would split up their development teams and have them work on the next release of a product as well as the release after that.

Microsoft, for example, used parallel teams to introduce new versions of Internet Explorer quickly into the marketplace, even though projects gradually required more engineering hours and people. According to Ben Slivka, the IE 2.0 and 3.0 projects both started in June 1995. Microsoft shipped IE 2.0 in November 1995 and 3.0 in August 1996. IE 2.0 was a minor release and only had four or five developers, whereas 3.0 included a major rearchitecting effort. Microsoft then started the IE 4.0 project in February 1996, six months before shipping IE 3.0. These IE teams, including developers, testers, program managers, and product managers, grew from merely a dozen people for IE 1.0 to several hundred for IE 4.0.

In Netscape's case, parallel projects tended to stress scarce manpower resources since the company did not have Microsoft's ability to hire as many developers and testers as it needed. Parallel development could also waste time if the technological choices did not work out (as in Netscape's decision to overhaul the client code and use Java extensively in 1997) or if the market or the competition changed course too radically. Nonetheless, both companies used parallel development and combined this approach with more or less modular component architectures and synchronize-and-stabilize development techniques.

Parallel Development in the Client and Server Groups

Rick Schell, in our first interview with him in July 1997, explained the logic of parallel development and how it fit into Netscape's strategy of creating componentized products with frequent releases and electronic upgrades:

> We put the first products together reasonably rapidly. We created the frameworks for . . . assembling pieces. We didn't use as much rigor as we could have because of the time frames we were operating under. Now we're moving to more parallel development, so that we can do more things component-based. . . . Increase the cycles at the beginning and then overlap the cycles, and overlap them in terms of full product releases and then do smaller product releases frequently. One of the advantages we've got is we can update software electronically.

Netscape director John Doerr also recalled that the initial decision to create two parallel teams stemmed from the belief that Netscape would need to put out releases very frequently: "The fundamental decision was we were going to build two parallel technical organizations. We have two VPs of engineering, not one. . . . So there's a blue team and a gold team because we thought we'd have to rev the product every six months." Soon, however, this structure became too confusing. While Netscape divided up the client developers and marketing staff by project, it tried to keep management more centralized. When this proved cumbersome, Netscape broke up marketing and engineering into divlets for each release and ran them in parallel.

Parallel development for the Navigator client began with the 1.0 and 2.0 projects. Work on version 2.0 started before the engineers had finished 1.0. After the emphasis had shifted to 2.0, the 1.0 group continued its work, putting out two point releases, Navigator 1.1 and 1.2. The early years were chaotic but productive, according to Todd Rulon-Miller: "They had enormous process problems because they double-timed their engineering schedules. . . . Navigator 2.0 was almost parallel to Navigator 1.0 at the time." Netscape also launched the Communicator 4.0 project before shipping Navigator 3.0, though it had to pull people back from 4.0 to help when Navigator 3.0 fell behind.

We discussed the advantages and disadvantages of parallel development, as well as the need to give priority to the most immediate release, with Bob Lisbonne in August 1997. He was then struggling to protect his people working on the 6.0 project from "poaching" by more immediate projects: "Another problem with 4.0 was that we were running late in 3.0, and we took developers off of 4.0 to help keep the 3.0 project on track. And that was very easy to do. All the folks worked in the same organization. It's natural. If the organization's top priority is to ship 3.0, then rational behavior produces that reallocation." Michael Toy insisted that the next release got top priority: "The rule at Netscape is the release that's going out the building gets the attention, and this is the release that's going out the building."

Of course, developers cannot move to a new project full-time until they fix the bugs in the current release on which they are working. People finish at somewhat different times, so developers and testers will tend to "slide" into the next project. In this sense, most releases have some *overlapping.* The 4.0 client team, for example, moved gradually into maintenance releases and then the 5.0 release, while a separate group of engineers gradually formed and increased the core of the 6.0 team. This overlapping is different, however, from *parallel* scheduling and development.

Netscape's most ambitious and ill-advised parallel effort was the attempt to rearchitect the client code base in the 6.0 project, which we described earlier. Although Netscape did not finish modularizing the client, as an intermediate measure, the engineering teams "froze" certain parts of the code to enable the 4.5 and 5.0 project teams to work in parallel. That is, they agreed to treat certain components as stable and not change them for relatively long periods of time and be very careful about making changes and informing potentially affected groups when changes occurred. Lisbonne commented on this strategy:

> One of the things we've done is we're working on a 4.5 release that will ship in the fall before 5.0. . . . We modularize it just by freezing certain sections of the product. . . . Now, the shortcoming is that you can't advance all parts of the product simultaneously. But, in this particular case, that expedient was fine because what we wanted to get done in the fall timeframe had to do with messaging and a bunch of enterprise-related features. So we just basically broke off a team to go do that while other folks are working on 5.0.

Of course, Netscape encountered other problems in working on two versions simultaneously when features and technologies were changing so quickly. Engineers were frequently changing different versions of the same features. Consequently, they had to go back to the same features repeatedly to redo work and fix bugs. According to Rick Gessner, after the Xena project expanded to include a rearchitecting of the entire Communicator product, Netscape managers realized that they could not afford to continue two major projects (5.0 and 6.0) working in parallel on what was essentially only one product. Lou Montulli described the problems of parallel development, noting that Microsoft faced them as well but had the advantage of more people:

> Working on the next version is a very difficult thing to do at this pace of change. Microsoft has, as far as I can see, been able to do it to some degree

by having such a large amount of people. They have a huge team working here and a huge team working there. But even they have been getting caught up in this, you have to go back and do all the features that the other team did while shaking out all the bugs, et cetera, et cetera. When you're moving forward in a code base and you have all the bugs fixed, you can move forward again so you're jumping off a well-known stable base rather than jumping from this shaky base to this shaky base. [When] you had to do the code cutoff to start working on version 9 while you're still working on version 8, and you haven't fixed any of the bugs from version 8, the people working on the code aren't sure if anything is working.

Another form of parallel development came in feature teams that worked independently and then folded their work into particular releases when it was ready. Mail and news, which shipped in the Communicator 4.0 release; Netcaster, which shipped in the 4.0 and 4.01 releases; and Roaming Access (location independence), which shipped in the 4.5 release, were examples of this type of parallel development. Netscape probably would have done more of this kind of work if the client code had been more modular and if the company had not been so short of engineers.

We also saw Netscape use smaller parallel teams for server development, as in the cases of SuiteSpot 3.0, 3.5, and 4.0. Joy Lenz, who headed server QA in 1997 to 1998 before moving to the Netcenter division, came to Netscape after working as a systems engineer in EDS and test manager at Borland. She described the parallel efforts as "pseudo-parallel teams": "We call them a pseudo-parallel team mostly because it's not a complete team. It's a handful of engineers. It's between five to ten that, while we're working on the current version, will be working on a separate project to be looking at whatever new technologies are coming up or where they think our product should be heading one generation out." As the parallel group finished some of its work, a couple of testers would join the developers. For example, in August 1997, Lenz moved two testers into the parallel Enterprise (Web) Server group that was working on the 4.0 release. Part of their responsibility was to do test planning and determine whether the automated test tools used on the previous version would be adequate for the next version, or how they needed to change the tools for the future release. Some of the parallel project work in servers also aimed at rearchitecting code and incorporating new standards. Bill Turpin commented on his philosophy:

We have gone parallel. The Web [Enterprise] Server . . . had 10 guys working on 4.0 before 3.0 was out. [We] had some people working on Admin

Server 4.0 before 3.0 went out. The other thing we are trying to do is be a half-generation ahead. Like the Directory Server is used now in all the other servers. The 3.0 Directory Server is going to ship this fall and then will become part of SuiteSpot in the spring. And we are trying to do the same with the Admin Server and the Certificate Server and other things that are foundation pieces for the rest of the product line.

Parallel Development through Mozilla.org

The use of standard Internet interfaces also made it possible for Netscape to leverage the efforts of developers outside the company and have them work in parallel on features or bug fixes. This opportunity persuaded Netscape to give away the client source code for the 5.0 release. As we noted in chapter 3, to manage the process of incorporating outside work, Netscape set up an internal team called Mozilla and posted its source code on the Mozilla.org Web site.[17] In mid-1998, the group consisted of eight engineers (six developers, one IT person, and one tester) and one customer support person. Veteran developer Tom Paquin, who had worked at IBM Research and Silicon Graphics before joining Netscape as employee number 7 in 1994, headed the group.

Mozilla maintained a separate source code "tree" as well as "branches" that allowed outside developers to check-in new pieces of code or bug fixes. The tree and branch system kept the check-ins separate from the main code base until Paquin's team decided to merge the outside code with Netscape's. The Mozilla team did not evaluate the check-ins on their own, however. Most contributions from outside developers were features or bug fixes that touched on existing features. In those cases, the Mozilla team tried to go back to the original Netscape developer who had produced the code or the current Netscape person overseeing that area, and they worked with that person to make a decision on the check-in. Netscape also required that all code added to the Mozilla base be cross-platform. Three senior developers on the Mozilla team made most of the final decisions on whether or not to accept an outside contribution to the code. In the case of a dispute, Paquin explained, "I have set myself up as a court of appeal."

The initial Mozilla release on March 31, 1998, was about 1.5 million lines of code, mainly in C and C++. This was about half the size of the Communicator 4.0 release. Netscape did not initially post large chunks of code, including the Java virtual machine (Sun owned the license to this and would not allow Netscape to distribute the source code on its site), the electronic mail code, and security code. (U.S. government regulations for export control prevented Netscape from making the cryptography technology publicly available at that time.) Paquin expected outside developers to add pieces and eventually improve the product, though Netscape would play a critical role in making sure that the pieces worked together. He described the logic behind putting an incomplete product out on the Internet: "To some degree, rather than putting out a chicken, we put out an egg. And the Net is not going to turn it into a chicken. They need Netscape to do that. Once we make it into a chicken, they will go off and add extra wings and then better feet."

Netscape developers initially worried that the relative lack of modularity in the client code base would make it difficult for outside developers to make additions to the product. For example, Paquin did not expect the source code to build (i.e., compile and link). He was surprised that it worked and that outside developers did not complain too much about the old architecture: "I expected, in order to make 3/31 [the release deadline], the stuff would barely build, if it built. I did not expect it to build on a Mac at all. The client team really pulled together and pulled off a small miracle. . . . It crashes sort of, but this is pretty good. . . . I also thought they would give us a hard time about the four-year-old been-through-its-phases architecture."

It turned out that the client code was in good enough shape to allow outside developers to understand and work on it. Andreessen commented on this pleasant surprise in our May 1998 interview: "People who have worked on the code base . . . tend to have a mentality that it's just a disaster, and it's not. And the reason I know it's not is because we cleaned it up and put it on the Net. People have been able to download it and make all kinds of changes to it. And if it were as much of a mess as we thought it was, that wouldn't be the case." According to Paquin, the pattern of initial check-ins indicated that outside developers were not trying to untangle the entire client code base. They were picking at parts of it and understanding at least those parts successfully. Nonetheless, Netscape was working on a better "component model" or way of breaking up the code into modules that were small and worked across different operating system platforms.

Overall, Mozilla seemed to be headed for success. Developers were downloading the Windows version most often, followed by the Macintosh and then the UNIX versions.[18] Bob Lisbonne called the Mozilla decision the biggest change in Netscape's development strategy since 1997: "What it really reflects is this change in the development model that we've been moving toward, which is Net-based development or open source development. If you look at the success of products like Linux and Apache, that's clearly the way they have worked. . . . If you want to look at our development strategy, clearly the biggest change from last fall is posting the source code and now reorienting ourselves to be working in concert with the Net to do these products." Initial response to the open source code was so strong (250,000 or so downloads within the first month) that Lisbonne believed Netscape would release 5.0 by the end of 1998 just to meet the demands of developers, who wanted to see their features deployed more broadly and integrated into the Netscape client. This new date was sooner than planned because Netscape had scheduled the enterprise version of 4.5 for release in the fall of 1998. Lisbonne continued his comments on Mozilla:

> The response has been, frankly, overwhelming. People are already cranking out useful derivative works and contributing back a lot of bugs, bug fixes, and a lot of features. And what that told us was that moving to Net development was going to happen faster than we once planned. What that means in terms of product timing is that 5.0, which at one point we thought might follow by six months the 4.5 release, I think is actually going to happen faster because the Net won't wait. So we're gearing up to do a Navigator by the end of this year and that's based principally on the fact that I think six to eight months from now the Net will just literally be demanding such a thing because they will have been working at our code base and wanting to see the fruits of their efforts get out the door. This is really an interesting and in many ways uncharted set of waters we've navigated into because at least, to the best of our knowledge, there's not a precedent for a large commercial software company with a product as widely used as ours engaging the Net in this style of development. And so we have a lot of challenges ahead of us in defining and implementing policies to make that work.

In addition to losing some control over the schedule, giving away the client source code created two other potential problems. One was "balkanization," which occurred previously with UNIX. That is, different versions of the Netscape browser could proliferate if companies began to build their own components outside of Netscape's attempts to control this process. In particular, if outside companies and individual developers did not like Netscape's decisions over what changes to incorporate, some outside group or groups could try to take control over the future evolution of the browser. Paquin and Andreessen both worried about this problem. They believed, however, that most outside companies and developers did not want to be in the browser maintenance business and would have great incentives to create features or suggest changes in a way that allowed them to go back to the mainline code base, which Netscape would maintain.

The other potential problem was that Netscape was giving away its innovations—its crown jewels. Anyone could freely download, license, and then incorporate Netscape code, or at least learn from its designs. This would make it difficult for Netscape to reestablish or maintain any kind of technical edge in the client. Paquin did not see things this way, however. In his mind, if Microsoft decided to incorporate Netscape code, it would mean that Microsoft was abandoning at least partially its strategy to optimize for Windows. Paquin did not think that Microsoft would do this, but he believed that any decrease in Microsoft's control over standards was good for Netscape:

> If Netscape DNA infiltrates the Microsoft platform, I am happy. If they take our layout engine and NSPR [Netscape Portable Runtime layer] and God knows what else, I view that as a good thing. I do not think they are going to go there. I don't think this is a battle of clever ideas. I think this is a battle of what is the platform DNA, the lowest common thing people are writing against. . . . If . . . we can make sure this thing turns into something usable, not just simple tack-on software, the world is populated with what the world wants, not what Microsoft tells them. . . . I still believe if it comes from Netscape, if it comes from Mozilla, if it comes from XYZ code, who ships a Mozilla derivative product, if the DNA is everywhere and the world has control of what the DNA really does, we all win. Netscape can take advantage of that and XYZ can take advantage of that. Sure, Microsoft can try to take advantage of that. But if it does not lock the world into unpublished data formats and single-vendor tools, we win.

In many ways, with the Mozilla release, product design and innovation strategy at Netscape had now come full circle. The core team of browser engineers had started out in college by developing a cross-platform browser—Mosaic. Anyone was free to download this from the Internet, and later it was possible to license and modify the source code. After Clark and Andreessen founded Netscape, they concluded that cross-platform browsers and servers were the key to achieving strategic leverage vis-à-vis Microsoft. Mozilla merely continued this tradition on the browser side. To get to the point of the Mozilla release in mid-1998, however, Netscape engineers had to overcome far more technical challenges than anyone in the company had anticipated.

Figuring out how to minimize performance penalties with cross-platform designs after products had become rich in features was only the first problem. Netscape engineers handled this difficulty through a set of design techniques, shared components, and the decision to write more platform-specific code whenever product performance demanded it. A more serious challenge was to recover from two interrelated decisions involving the aborted 6.0 project that exposed the over-enthusiasm of Netscape executives and senior engineers for new Internet technologies and their own capabilities. One decision was to try to use Java extensively in a new version of Navigator and then the entire Communicator applications suite. This technology would have simplified cross-platform design, had Java worked as intended. It did not at this time. The other decision was to undertake a massive rearchitecting of the Communicator code in order to make it more modular. This initiative would have made component teams faster and more flexible because they would have been more autonomous. At the same time, Netscape had to deal with internal political issues, such as where to build common components and how to allocate responsibilities and scarce resources across the client, server, and core technologies divisions.

As we look back over 1994 to 1998, it is true that Netscape failed to rearchitect Communicator and build a Java browser. But we must also conclude that key technologies (such as the next-generation browser layout engine and modularization approaches) survived. More important, Netscape managers and engineers showed considerable skill and flexibility as they reorganized projects and set simpler design objectives and moved back to the Net for assistance in product innovation. In chapter 5, we now turn to Netscape's strategy for managing new projects as well as the details of software development and testing.

Chapter Five

DEVELOPMENT STRATEGY

Flexible, Fast, and "Slightly out of Control"

IN ADDITION TO design strategy, a firm can increase the ability of its engineering organization to be flexible, as well as fast and innovative, by using particular processes for creating, testing, and utilizing new software products. This chapter examines the development strategies that Netscape employed to be a better judo player. We also examine how management priorities helped to set the direction and culture of the engineering organization, and how these priorities had to change as markets and customers changed.

As late as 1997, Netscape managers hoped that being "slightly out of control" would enhance their ability to be flexible and creative. Michael Toy, release manager for the client products, put it this way: "Control is a bad thing. If you control something too much, you get predictable results. It's much better to get to just be slightly out of control, and then you get unpredictable and great results." But as the Internet software market moved from individual leading-edge consumers to enterprise sales for corporations, Netscape managers and engineers had to treat product stability as an important measure of quality and pay less attention to delivering innovative new features as fast as possible. Product teams still needed to be creative as well as flexible in planning new products and features because the market continued to change rapidly. Accordingly, Netscape teams allowed feature sets to evolve during development, but they controlled the iterations through tools and techniques that frequently synchronized design changes and bug fixes. Periodically, the development teams also stopped and "stabilized" the features that they had completed.

This iterative or incremental approach to software development closely resembles the "synchronize-and-stabilize" process that Microsoft has been employing since the late 1980s. Similar to Microsoft, Netscape's teams went through a daily exercise of integrating component design changes and then frequently testing and retesting components as they evolved. In addition, to increase speed as well as flexibility and efficiency in this testing process, Netscape was automating more testing, though with somewhat mixed success. (Test automation is a difficult problem to solve when engineers revise components and user interface designs so often.) Perhaps most notably, though, Netscape probably revolutionized the idea of beta testing in the way it distributed millions of early copies of its products over the Internet and then got nearly instantaneous feedback. Company employees also used products internally to get firsthand knowledge on features and quality. We believe that the following principles characterize Netscape's process for software development as well as basic elements of Microsoft's approach since the late 1980s:

- *Adapt development priorities as products, markets, and customers change.*
- *Allow features to evolve but with frequent synchronizations and periodic stabilizations.*
- *Automate as much testing as possible.*
- *Use beta testing, internal product usage, and other measures to improve product and process quality.*

Our comments in this chapter primarily describe practices that characterized Netscape's client and server development groups between July 1997 and July 1998. While we were writing this book, Netscape was continually reshuffling divisions and personnel and continually evolving both the structure of its development organization (such as moving the entire client division to the Web site division) and the processes used in the development and QA groups. Describing a moving target is difficult. Nonetheless, we tried to analyze the major practices as well as the most important process changes that we observed.

We spent much less time studying Netscape's Web site and application products groups since they were still so new in 1997–1998. Netscape was moving people from the client and server divisions to these new areas of the company. As a result, we saw some convergence in practices and expect to see more convergence in the future. Nonetheless, Netscape's various divisions all had somewhat different priorities, and these of necessity affected development practices. For example, the Web site division had to continue experimenting with new features that might attract individuals and corporate users. Not surprisingly, it was rolling out new versions of Netcenter every few months and using a very loosely defined design and development process. The applications products division was pioneering a new market for Web-based electronic commerce and had to experiment extensively as well. The server products division was more concerned with product stability and performance rather than fast release cycles and innovative features, and it was moving more quickly than the Web site or the client division toward formalizing its practices in product design and testing. Meanwhile, the client division had to keep pace with Netcenter but also release stable products for enterprise customers. It fell somewhere in between the extremes of Netcenter and the server division.

Because of these differences, we found it difficult and unwise to generalize too broadly about "Netscape practices" in software development and testing. What we were able to do instead is describe common practices and highlight major differences between the client and server divisions. One further caveat: Netscape did not always implement the principles we identified perfectly or even as well as the more experienced Microsoft teams. For example, Microsoft had tighter project controls, more layers of automated testing, and more bodies for manual testing as well as automated test preparation. Nonetheless, Netscape adopted very similar processes for software development, and Netscape especially resembled Microsoft's more flexible Internet groups. This resemblance encourages us to believe that we have identified effective principles for flexible, as well as innovative and fast, software product development.

PRINCIPLE *Adapt development priorities as products, markets, and customers change.*

Evolution in Process Priorities

Netscape managers and engineers talked about four priorities for product development that they emphasized at different times between 1994 and 1998. The apparent need to change priorities reflected both the relative stabilization of some areas of the technology as well as Netscape's strategic decision to move into different market segments, where customers had different requirements:

- *Follow short development cycles in the start-up phase* to make sure product teams ship something to customers, get feedback early, establish a market position, and keep the technology quickly moving forward, without waiting to create the "perfect" product.
- *Avoid "rocket science"* as a mantra to encourage groups not to tackle too much complexity and unnecessary invention in any one product cycle.
- *Try to ship products within three-month windows* to encourage teams to

stop changing designs and ship something to market but within a flexible time frame.

- *Shift the emphasis gradually to quality more than features or time to market* in order to create products more appropriate for the enterprise
market and to introduce change at a more palatable rate.

Short Development Cycles in the Start-up Phase. When Netscape started,
Marc Andreessen made it clear that one of the first things he wanted to do
was avoid multiyear development cycles. He did not want to spend years
trying to create the "perfect" product before shipping anything. He
adopted this philosophy after observing several other companies that had
failed to deliver on innovative technologies. In his 1996 talk at MIT,
Andreessen claimed he experienced this problem firsthand while working
as a student intern for IBM:

> When we came into this, our starting assumption was that many of the
> companies that were doing software development in the Valley were doing
> it wrong. That is the General Magic/Kaleida/Taligent model of taking four
> or five years to do something, or Apple, or any of these others. These huge
> monolithic multiyear projects were the wrong way. . . . You try to do the
> perfect product, and you spend years and years and years doing it, versus
> rip something out there into the market that is imperfect and may not even
> be commercially viable, but get feedback on it. . . . We operated almost
> entirely on the basis of counterexamples, actually, when we first started the
> company. I was at IBM as a co-op student in 1990 and 1991. I was on a
> project there, which was the classic example of the project dragging on and
> on and on, and it would constantly miss its milestones and its goals. And so
> they would constantly reset the schedule, but they would never reset it to
> give you enough time to ever do it. You were in constant crisis mode. So,
> every six months you would have to completely reset, and you were never
> doing anything that would ever allow you to actually ship the product. You
> were just trying to patch the piece of shit that you'd gotten from the last
> time you screwed it up.[1]

Michael Toy pointed out another advantage of the short development
cycles. They minimized potential scheduling errors, at least in terms of
total calendar time: "The advantage of having short development cycles is
that you can't be very far off. Right? You know if it's not running. We have
some rules of thumb that we've developed. If it's not running on a platform on a certain day, then we know it's not going to be running on all
platforms until n days and it's not going to be ship-able for features
of size." Yet even Netscape faced limits on its ability to accelerate the

development process. With the existing allocation of between two and three developers per tester in 1997 in the client division, Toy believed that Netscape could not realistically shorten cycles to less than nine months. This was the minimal amount of time he felt they needed to create and stabilize enough features to constitute a new release: "It's completely a function of the people we have in the building, the way the organizations are working together. That could all change. If I had a different QA organization, I could make that six [months]. But I don't own the QA organization, and so it's nine."

Short cycles also usually meant that teams had to ship something before the product was "perfect." The purpose here was to get feedback from customers before spending too much time on features and then have many chances to improve the product. Andreessen focused on this point as a key driver at the company: "Kick the product out the door as quickly as possible. It doesn't even matter if it's done or doesn't really matter if it does even 20 percent of what the full expression of it is." Debby Meredith, who headed client development and the strategic technologies and products division before taking over customer support, wanted early and frequent beta releases so projects could get feedback on features and usability:

> From a project point of view, we try to get early feedback from customers. We try to put a beta out there. In classic software engineering before the Net, you had things like a system-test checkpoint, and there was an alpha-test checkpoint, where you were typically feature-complete, and then beta test, where you went to customers the first time and you kind of thought your product was ready to go. And then maybe you had a beta update, and then you shipped. When we do our first public beta, we've never been feature-complete, ever. The product is stable for some definition of stable in the features that are out there. But it is never functionally complete. We do that on purpose to get something out there, sometimes to blunt the competition or get ahead of the competition, and also to get early feedback. . . . When I put a beta up there now, 20 million people or so download it within the first couple of weeks. So each one is like a mini-release—a forcing function of stabilizing the software and taking it through a set of test cycles and kind of a tapping down on the level of bugs that we want to fix for that milestone checkpoint. Those have been ways in which we're able to respond quickly because we get stuff out there and we find out that, wow, customers need to have this to deploy or folks aren't liking the UI [user interface], even though we did usability testing on the tool bar.

Netscape's most extreme examples of this idea of not waiting for the perfect product and getting early customer feedback were the first few versions of Navigator. Jon Mittelhauser, speaking in our July 1997 interview, recalled his early days as a developer and product manager on Navigator 1.0 and 2.0:

> The precedent we set with 1.0 . . . in terms of development speed has been very significant. . . . The things we did brand new to us seemed logical since we'd done them before—releasing betas to the network and speeding up your development cycle by being able to put a beta out. Within six hours of putting the beta out I have my top ten bugs, as opposed to cutting CDs and shipping them out and six weeks later hearing my first feedback. . . . The speed of that development cycle and what enabled us to attain that speed are really what fundamentally changed the way things worked around here. I think it's carrying over to other places. . . . We sort of rewrote the book on how you do development. . . . I think Microsoft is working this way as we are moving to another phase where the concept is less hard releases and more of the subscription quarterly type basis.

Mittelhauser described other benefits of having short cycles and lots of releases. One was that this approach put less pressure on developers to get *their* features into a *particular* release because there would be another version coming out soon. Releasing many betas into the marketplace also gave the company an advance boost in market awareness:

> There're a lot of things you get that are very positive out of having a short development cycle and a continual one. When you have a product that's only shipping every two years, your feature, your little pet feature, to the in-the-trenches engineer, becomes ever so much more important for you because, if you don't get it in, you're not going to see it for two years. It's a lot easier to cut a feature if you can tell the person, "Fine, we're going to ship it in the next rev." . . . [But] it leads you to worry about burnout and things more than I would think you do in a two-year release cycle. . . . [On]1.0, it seems like we released betas every other day. I'd say we did on the order of eight, if I had to pick a number. . . . Marketing and sales realized that, by releasing the betas to the Net, not only can you speed up the engineering cycle, but you gain very positive credibility. And you can almost start to sell the product months before it's done because people can see what it is and want it. . . . We actually sell product before we release it. It gives you strong credibility. You also get, potentially, a closer customer relationship. . . . They can give feedback during a development cycle and potentially get in their features. Again, that quick turnaround is a positive.

Netscape continued this practice of frequent beta releases for Navigator 2.0 and 3.0. On 3.0, for example, Netscape started the project around

FIGURE 5.1

Netscape Project Plan for Navigator 3.0 (1996)

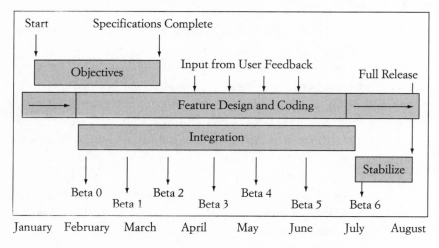

Source: Marco Iansiti and Alan MacCormack, "Developing Products on Internet Time," *Harvard Business Review,* September–October 1997, p. 112.

January 1996 and posted a beta version on an intranet Web site for internal use in February. It then posted a public beta version in March. Netscape continued to post new beta versions every two to three weeks through June, before shipping the final release in August (see Figure 5.1). As we discuss later in this chapter, Netscape has stepped back a bit from this practice. With 4.0, the first Communicator product, Netscape decided to target corporations and intranet applications. Enterprise features usually took more time to design, debug, and stabilize because they had to be easy to use and rock-solid reliable. Since the Communicator 4.0 project, Netscape managers have preferred no more than two or three betas for each product release—one after each two- or three-month period of development work. This schedule still called for more frequent releases than older approaches of shipping only one or two betas *after* completing all the product's features.

"No Rocket Science." Another of Andreessen's beliefs supported the idea of working in short development cycles and trying to avoid building a product that is too complex to explain easily (such as Lotus Notes when it first came out) or inventing the next greatest technology every time in every project. Andreessen called this "no rocket science." His ideal here was the simplicity of the old Ford Motor Company and the Model T:

A lot of other companies . . . start and they try to do rocket science. They try to do something new and very innovative that nobody has ever heard of before, and it could take a long time to explain it. It's very complicated. Those types of things are very hard to sell. It's very hard to get it out there and present it to someone in a way that they want to buy it, particularly if they don't understand it. The really big opportunities, I think, are ones where it's solving a very simple problem lots of people know they have. It doesn't matter what the problem is necessarily. It doesn't matter how good the market is. The story of Ford Motor Company is people thought they needed cars at that point in time. Of course, they were invented already but Ford was the first person to solve that basic problem and start shipping them out the door. So [we want] a real tight focus on simplicity and a real tight focus on not necessarily doing invention, really not necessarily something very new or innovative in computer science or rocket science or anything else.[2]

Bill Gates generally followed the same philosophy, especially in Microsoft's formative years. He avoided trying to invent new technologies unnecessarily and exploited innovations first introduced at other companies, beginning with his first product, a PC version of the Basic programming language (invented earlier for larger computers). Other Microsoft examples included graphical user interfaces adapted from Xerox and Apple; word-processing features from WordStar and WordPerfect; spreadsheet features from Lotus 1-2-3; a variety of operating system and networking features from Digital Research, IBM, and Novell; and groupware features from Lotus Notes.[3] And, of course, the most famous recent example was the Internet browser, which was invented at a European research lab and commercialized by Netscape and some two dozen other companies during 1993 to 1995, before Microsoft added this component to Windows 95.

The problem is that avoiding rocket science often becomes harder over time. Companies in high-tech markets can easily get into a race with competitors to introduce new features to encourage customers to upgrade or stay ahead of the competition, or to move quickly into new market segments (like a good judo player) to maintain high growth rates. Andreessen argued that Microsoft strayed from its usual approach when it was not under competitive pressure. He gave the example of Exchange, a complex product that Microsoft shipped with its operating systems to add server functions such as e-mail and groupware features. Microsoft kept redefining and expanding Exchange and consequently took years to ship a stable product:

I think they [Microsoft] still do that [try to avoid rocket science] when they're under pressure. But what I think they've showed over the last few years is that, when they're not under direct immediate competitive pressure, they don't do that. Exchange was the classic example where they broke their own rules. . . . They took literally six years to get the thing out. They kept resetting the goals. . . . You know, first it's going to be the Notes killer, and then it's going to be a great e-mail product, and then it's going to be Internet-based. It requires a lot of vigilance to continually do the iterative approach.

As we saw in chapter 4, though, Netscape itself fell into the trap of tackling too much at one time. In Communicator 4.0, Netscape tried to add on a broad range of groupware components to the browser as well as new features such as Netcaster, while using unproven technologies such as Java and JavaScript. Netscape then undertook a major technological challenge in the 6.0 project when it tried and failed to rewrite the code base in much tighter modules, making extensive use of a still-unstable Java. The Communicator 4.0 and 6.0 projects turned out to be Netscape's equivalent of rocket science.

Pressure to Ship within Three-Month Windows. Various Netscape managers talked about setting tighter deadlines for projects, although this idea really translated into three-month windows as target periods for releasing new products. This gave everybody some leeway. If the engineers fell behind, project managers would tend to cut features rather than extend the project too much or add lots of people. Meredith explained: "In software engineering, there are three variables. There are schedules, features, and resources. . . . You can hold any two constant but not the third. . . . You can play with [quality]. It's never a good idea, but I can't say we've never done that. Our overriding variable tends to be schedule. . . . We want to do a release in Q1 or Q2 or something. We certainly add people, but features are more where we trade off. So we will, in general, pick a time frame for a release."

Microsoft and most other PC software companies also selected specific periods for releasing a new product and then cut low-priority features to make those dates. Some companies added people to late projects. But, as Frederick Brooks observed after heading IBM's OS/360 project, adding people to a late software project often makes it later. This is because of the time required to train and coordinate additional staff.[4] One difference at Microsoft in scheduling, however, was that, at least internally, product unit managers chose *specific* dates, such as August 24, 1995, to put extra pressure on teams to finish. Microsoft also included *buffer time*—often from 20 to 50 percent of an entire development schedule—to allow people to make unplanned changes or deal with unforeseen problems and still make those dates. Of course, Microsoft managers would often change dates, especially in product areas like operating systems, where product reliability was far more important than time to market, but only after reviewing progress at specific milestones and "beating up" individuals and teams that missed their estimates.[5]

Gradual Shift to Quality More Than Features or Time to Market. Getting simple products out fast, incorporating feedback quickly, and then releasing improved versions in multiple iterations was how many PC software company executives preferred to develop new products, especially for the Internet. Another issue that concerned Andreessen, however, was the difficulty of trying to compress product development and release times too much. Software engineers can design and test only so fast, given the current state of the technology. Even if they could work faster, Andreessen felt that companies like Netscape could expect to sell new versions of their products only so often. In particular, enterprise customers will adopt new products or versions only when the quality is very high and the new features are compelling. He admitted that these basic factors slowed down the ability and the need of any software company to keep accelerating product release cycles:

> I'd identify three cycles that we're tied to, just like any other software company. One is the software product development life cycle, which, just due to modern technology, seems to be inherently of certain fixed aspects that are hard to get around. Second is the sales cycle, especially as we sell to businesses, which is where all the money is. And the third is the customer deployment cycle, which is the customer's ability to accept and deploy and integrate new technologies. Again, especially on the business side, it's hard to compress those. It's extremely difficult for reasons that have very little to do with what *you* want to do and have more to do with what people on the outside of your company are doing.

Accordingly, as products matured and became more widely used in the corporate market, Netscape executives and engineers began placing more emphasis on a different priority—quality. They were not overly anxious to make this shift: Testing software was far less exciting than writing software, and with tight budgets, managers were very reluctant to hire testers.

But during 1997 to 1998, we saw Netscape learn how to pay more attention to process issues in planning, development, and testing, and we saw the company elevate customer satisfaction and technical support to a much higher level than it had been in the past. Andreessen also felt that, with the limited rate at which customers could deploy new technology, Netscape was about "as fast as we need to be" in product development. He preferred to devote company resources to growing the sales force rather than investing more heavily in engineering and making only small improvements in speed. Andreessen described the changes that Netscape had to make as its products and customers matured:

> Our reality has been, for the last three years, that we believed strongly in the quality-feature-time triangle, where you get two out of three on a good day. You're always shooting for three out of three in some way. But we have, historically, definitely prioritized features over time and time over quality. We did that because worse is better for us. It's the iterative approach—kick it out into the market and get the feedback. And for a 1.0 or 2.0 product, I believe very strongly that's the right thing to do. It has the highest chance of success. But . . . for a 3.0, 4.0, 5.0, 6.0 product that's being sold into businesses, at some point you have to stop and you have to say, "Wait a minute, reset. Quality over time over features." And it's not just quality, by the way. A lot of it is also deployability and manageability and scaleability. It's the "ilities." But it's not that it's significantly more difficult to do those things with this smart team of people. People just have to know what is expected of them. If you start a design review meeting going through the list of features and then you look at the schedule and then you say, "All right, are we going to get any quality out of this?" And they say "No," and you say, "Oh, that's fine. Do it anyway." Then they know what you want out of them. And if you do exactly the opposite, then they also know what you want.

We can observe this slowing down in the release cycles for the client and some server products both at Netscape and at Microsoft. As shown in Table 5.1, both companies had similarly short intervals between major browser releases in the early years. These periods ranged between three and nine months for versions 1.0 through 3.0 of Navigator or Internet Explorer. In contrast, for Communicator 5.0, Netscape planned a cycle of about 18 months, counting from the release of 4.0. (In the meantime, Netscape was shipping a lot of "maintenance" releases for the client—mostly bug fixes and some minor enhancements that enterprise customers wanted—every three months or so. The company also planned to introduce release 4.5 in the fall of 1998). Microsoft was planning an interval of

TABLE 5.1

Intervals Between Major Browser and Server Releases

Netscape			Microsoft		
BROWSER CLIENTS					
Navigator 1.0 ⟶		(12/94)			
Navigator 1.1/1.2 ⟶	6 months	(6/95)	IE 1.0 ⟶		(8/95)
Navigator 2.0 ⟶	8 months	(2/96)	IE 2.0 ⟶	3 months	(11/95)
Navigator 3.0 ⟶	6 months	(8/96)	IE 3.0 ⟶	9 months	(8/96)
Communicator 4.0 ⟶	10 months	(6/97)	IE 4.0 ⟶	13 months	(9/97)
Communicator 4.5 ⟶	14 months	(9/98)*	IE 5.0 ⟶	16 months	(12/98)
Communicator 5.0 ⟶	18 months	(12/98)*			
SERVERS					
Communications ⟶		(12/94)	IIS 1.0 ⟶		(2/96)
Commerce ⟶		(12/94)	IIS 2.0 ⟶	6 months	(8/96)
SuiteSpot 2.0 ⟶	18 months	(6/96)	IIS 3.0 ⟶	4 months	(12/96)
SuiteSpot 3.0 ⟶	12 months	(6/97)	IIS 4.0 ⟶	12 months	(12/97)
SuiteSpot 3.5 ⟶	8 months	(2/98)			

*Planned; dates are from 4.0 release

Notes: IIS = Internet Information Server. This is Microsoft's Web server, which runs on top of Windows NT and is bundled into the NT price.

These dates indicate *intervals* between product releases, not necessarily the length of projects. Some projects overlapped with the previous projects, and others did not start immediately after the prior release. IE 3.0, for example, started in June 1995, overlapping with IE 2.0.

Sources: Compiled from various sources, including trade journals, wire service stories, and press releases. Some of the Microsoft dates from the Ben Slivka interview.

16 months between IE 4.0 and 5.0. On the server side, Microsoft released the first three versions of Internet Information Server (IIS) at four- to six-month intervals. IIS 4.0, however, came out 12 months after the previous version. Netscape was somewhere between 12- and 18-month intervals for SuiteSpot, with some intermediate products (such as version 3.5) released more quickly.

Even with the slowdown, the cycles between major releases of these Internet software products were much shorter than the two- to almost five-year intervals between releases of the Windows operating system (see

TABLE 5.2

Intervals Between Windows and NT Operating System Releases

Windows 1.03 —————————→	(11/85)	NT 3.0 —————————→	(8/93)
Windows 2.0 ————→ 25 months	(11/87)	NT 4.0 ——→ 36 months	(8/96)
Windows 3.0 ————→ 31 months	(5/90)		
Windows 3.1 ————→ 24 months	(4/92)		
Windows 95 ——→ 41/55* months	(8/95)		
Windows 98 ————→ 34 months	(5/98)		

*55 months, dated from release of 3.0

Notes: Windows 3.1 was a relatively major upgrade over version 3.0 in terms of product stability, not features, and it was the first truly successful release of Windows. We could consider a five-year gap between major releases of Windows (1990 to 1995), although Microsoft did release two incremental versions, Windows for Workgroups 3.1 (April 1993) and 3.11 (October 1993).

   Windows NT began with release 3.0. It also had an incremental release, NT 3.5, in fall 1994. NT 5.0 is likely to appear in 1999.

Source: Compiled from various public sources.

Table 5.2). Of course, operating systems are larger and more mature products than browsers and perform "mission-critical" functions in many organizations. They take longer to build, test, and debug, even with hundreds of developers and testers working on them. Windows 95 and recent versions of NT, for example, contained somewhere between 10 and 15 million lines of code, depending on which subsystems and features (such as code from Microsoft Network) the numbers include. Windows 98 and NT 5.0 size estimates *begin* at 15 to 25 million lines of code! In contrast, Communicator 4.0 was about 3 million lines of code. There is also much less demand from operating system customers for frequent innovations or changes because most features in the product are relatively transparent to users. The priorities for an operating system, like a server, usually are product reliability and performance, such as running speed.

From the "Hacker" Culture to Enterprise Software

The slowing down of release cycles gave Netscape managers an opportunity to shift the engineering organization toward quality as a higher priority. This was not such an easy transition to make, however, given that the company had been successful because of its innovative and flexible environment. In 1998, Netscape was still between two worlds: the "hacker" culture of the Internet programmer and the professional engineering culture of the enterprise software company. There was no strong tradition of tight controls on projects, as was typical of the hacker mentality. In the PC and Internet software worlds, this approach has often resulted in innovations. Unfortunately, it has also resulted in late and buggy products. The trick, then, is to balance the two cultures, which Netscape was trying to do in 1997 to 1998.

Much of the informal style that we saw at Netscape also resulted from the company's relative youth and small size. In mid-1998, Netscape had around 2,400 employees, compared to some 30,000 at Microsoft. Netscape was also just a few years old, while Microsoft had been in business for 23 years. Over time, Netscape was becoming more systematic, but the company still relied heavily on individuals—usually developers or executives like Marc Andreessen—coming up with great product ideas. Marketing was only beginning to take a more formal role in analyzing market opportunities and generating product ideas. Alex Edelstein, who had worked as a program manager on Microsoft Exchange before joining Netscape, reflected on the differences between the two companies in our July 1997 interview:

> A lot of the distinction between the two you could account for from relatively conventional differences in the size of a company. Microsoft has a more formal way of planning products, establishing strategy, and getting consensus for major decisions. Netscape has a less formal process, and Netscape's process has gotten more formal over the two years I've been there. So, to some extent, the distinction between the two companies is really just that simple. . . . [But] Netscape gives a little more leeway to someone with a really great idea who wants to push it. Microsoft, by the time I got there, had sufficient entrenched interests—that's not really the best way to put it—had *complexity* of interests that made it very difficult for an innovative idea to be quickly brought to market.

Lloyd Tabb, a senior developer who joined Netscape from Borland in spring 1995, is a good example of a person who bridged the hacker culture and the professional engineering discipline. On the one hand, he emphasized the importance of software "heroes" and insisted that people with a vision had to lead product development at Netscape. On the other hand, he built source-code management tools that enabled the individual developers in the client division to work as a team: "Really great software is built by heroes—people who champion, people who believe that, if they build this thing, they're going to be doing right, Netscape is going to succeed. . . . I believe that, in order for Netscape to succeed, I had to get 120 people working together in a way that they weren't going to kill each other . . . You have to let the engineers succeed. You have to let the guy with the vision build it."

Netscape employees, especially people who joined in the first year or two of the company, also drew on a strong sense of pride and mission to keep motivated. This feeling came from having pioneered much of the mass-market Internet and World Wide Web technology. Lou Montulli, who clearly felt this way, was particularly proud that the Netscape browser was "the most used PC application in the world." He also wanted feedback from users whether it was good or bad: "The worst thing that could possibly happen is you release a beta and you don't hear anything. You want to hear something good or something bad. At least you know somebody is using it."

But maintaining such high levels of motivation proved more difficult for Netscape as the battle with Microsoft wore on and as many newcomers joined Netscape's now-wealthy pioneers. Aleks Totic, one of the original members of the Mosaic development team, admitted that he no longer worked as hard as he once had: "I used to really kill myself. Now when I'm tired, I don't drink three Cokes. I go to sleep. Because there're so many people, I don't feel that working ridiculously hard hours is going to make Netscape a lot better company." Michael Toy confided in our July 1997 interview that, although "my highest goal is to make software . . . not to make the analysts happy," he was really at Netscape to make money:

> I'm at Netscape to play start-up bingo. I'm not at Netscape because I'm in love with Internet technology. . . . I didn't believe for a micro-second that Web browsers were going to take over the universe. I was very skeptical. I'm not a brilliant visionary. What I am is a bright person who fanatically holds on to the idea that the highest value is that the engineers are happy with what they're working on. And then everything else falls out of there. . . . In order to make Netscape successful, my strongest contribution was to not write code but to take some management responsibility. So I stopped writing code. . . . My highest goal is to get rich.

But Toy also described himself on his business card as a "Defender of the Faith." He felt he was "in charge of morale" and needed to create a buffer between engineering and marketing to help people do "crazy, insane, great things":

> One of the things that makes Netscape successful is the engineers believe it's their product. They are not implementing marketing's feature list. They are writing *their* browser, *their* editor; it's *theirs*. In some sense, I'm a shield

between them and marketing because marketing wants to believe that they tell engineering what to make. . . . You can't let marketing not believe that because marketing needs to be successful, too. But in order for engineering to be successful, they need to believe it's *their* product. And so I am in charge of helping them keep ownership of the product. It was easy when there were 13 engineers and one marketing person. He couldn't keep up with us. Now there're enough marketing people to keep up with us and it takes a concerted effort. And there's a culture . . . that seems to want marketing to dictate what engineering should do and just shut up and implement it. It's incredibly demoralizing. When people are demoralized, they don't do crazy, insane, great things. So I'm in charge of morale, not just for the stupid reason that when people are really psyched then they do insanely great things and if they're not really psyched then you get a workmanlike effort instead of an incredibly great effort. There is a sense of, "This is something worth really working for." I own that and, when that gets damaged, I own fixing it.

Eric Hahn, when serving as Netscape's chief technology officer, provided a more sobering view of the company and how well it was managing the evolution from an innovative hacker culture to an enterprise software company. He believed that the emphasis on fast cycles and creativity had built Netscape's reputation and was the main source of its success. But in our November 1997 interview, he also acknowledged there was a "seedy underbelly" to this story:

I will speak very candidly. I think our self-assessment is that we have put, historically, a phenomenal premium on time to market and leading-edge feature-technology innovation. Those have been the driving forces. If you ask the engineers, as you have, they feel probably more than anything the schedule pressure to ship and an incredible abundance of technology to create at the same time. Sometimes we are the very first commercial implementation in the whole Java bet, and there are lots and lots of examples of that. The good news is that those two factors have conspired to build a great early Netscape—brand awareness, market share, and perception of technology leadership. The seedy underbelly of that is probably not so hard to see. With the short product cycles and lots of innovation, we have had challenges maintaining product quality. We have had morale challenges inside the company. You probably detected some of that. The burnout factor is probably higher here even than other start-ups. And we do run the risk of compromising customer satisfaction, particularly as people move from a browser deployment of two years ago to a mission-critical enterprise application infrastructure, whether running a line of business apps or running their messaging system on it. So the backdrop is that, as Marc says, we shouldn't be surprised. We are where we wanted to be. We pushed these things.

John Paul took over from Hahn as senior VP and head of the server division during July 1997. He admitted in our March 1998 interview that Netscape had been slow to make some of the investments necessary to support an enterprise strategy, although the company was correcting this in 1998:

> I'd say we didn't invest enough in support, the whole product infrastructure to create an enterprise software company. Our technical support systems are not up to what it takes to support an enterprise customer. But these are some things we're changing. Let's take sustaining engineering [product maintenance] versus building the next product and what [features] to add on. Of those 200 engineers in SPD [server products division], how many were dedicated to fixing problems and existing products? There were four. So we've upped that to 20 percent of that 200 . . . So, again, the rush for functionality in the early days led us to have lots of engineers and little else, and now the transition to quality says less engineers and more of the other.

One example of this shift in priorities was Barksdale's decision in February 1998 to appoint Debby Meredith as the new senior vice president of customer satisfaction, reporting directly to the CEO. This new position involved taking charge of all customer technical support and service as well as developer support engineering. To put some "teeth" into this position, Barksdale gave Meredith a vote on the bonuses of the engineers in the server products division, based on how well they met certain quality objectives. In addition, Meredith asked product specialists from technical support who sat with the development groups to keep statistics on top features to address: bugs, customer perceptions of new products, and other issues. (Microsoft has been doing this for years.)[6] Rick Schell had this to say about Meredith's new position: "I think it's a very important move. Elevating that to Barksdale's level and putting somebody in charge who has run a big organization I think is critical. . . . I don't know if it's too little, too late. I hope it's not."

We concluded that Netscape was still in the middle of this transition from the hacker to the enterprise software worlds, although it clearly had made progress toward becoming a more professional software organization even during the year we observed the company. But senior VP Bob Lisbonne, who took over the client division after Schell and Meredith, pointed out another potential difficulty for Netscape in light of the enthusiastic reception that Internet developers were giving to Netscape's Mozilla source-code release. Enterprise customers did not want new versions of Netscape products very frequently because they could absorb new technology only so fast. Internet developers, in contrast, wanted new releases as frequently as possible so they could incorporate the latest new features and technologies into their source code. Netscape will probably have to make the Internet developers wait, rather than risk the release of unstable code and take a step backward in quality. Lisbonne, however, was contemplating a technical solution that consisted of more automated or "transparent" updating of the client code over the Web. This would enable customers to download new versions at their own pace:

> What will be interesting over the next six to 12 months is how we resolve the tension between enterprise customers who want releases in a more measured pace and the Net developers who, I think, will be an ongoing pressure for rapid development. It may be that we have different flavors of the product. We may have different release schedules for enterprise customers and others. But in the long term, what I'd like to do is just make it a nonissue by making updating of software a transparent operation. . . . We still have . . . maintenance releases. We do them every three months. And they are date-driven. . . . But what we've learned is that it is not always the case that the time-to-market dimension is the dominant one.

PRINCIPLE   *Allow features to evolve but with frequent synchronizations and periodic stabilizations.*

PC software developers, especially those working on Internet products, need to use much more flexible and less bureaucratic development techniques than software engineers working in companies where product cycles are longer and the technology is more stable. Consequently, we see at Microsoft, Netscape, and many other PC software firms techniques that consciously depart from the sequential or "waterfall" style of product development followed at older mainframe, minicomputer, and workstation software producers and at many other companies in different industries. Microsoft began refining this alternative style of development in the late 1980s and early 1990s. The authors of *Microsoft Secrets* labeled this approach the "synchronize-and-stabilize" process because it enabled relatively autonomous small teams to frequently synchronize and then periodically stabilize their design changes or feature innovations. The objective was to balance hacker-type flexibility with professional engineering discipline so that many small teams could effectively act as one large team and build large-scale products relatively quickly and efficiently. Table 5.3 summarizes the basic differences between the synchronize-and-stabilize and waterfall approaches to managing software product development. Figure 5.2 illustrates graphically what the synchronize-and-stabilize process looks like in Internet projects that ship beta releases after each milestone stabilization.

In the waterfall model, project teams attempt to "freeze" a product specification, create a functional design specification, build components, and then merge these components together, primarily at the end of the project in one large integration and testing phase. This sequential approach was common in the 1970s and 1980s for large-scale projects.[7] It has also remained a basic model for project planning in many industries.[8] The waterfall model gradually lost favor among fast-paced software companies as managers and engineers realized they could build better products if they rapidly incorporated feedback from customers during a project, changed designs in response to feedback as well as to changes in

TABLE 5.3

Synchronize and Stabilize versus Sequential Waterfall Process

Synchronize and Stabilize	Sequential Waterfall
Specification, Development, Testing in Parallel	Separate Phases in "Waterfall" Sequence
Vision Statement & Evolving Specification (specification = output, not input)	"Complete" Specification Document & Detailed Design Before Coding
Prioritized Features Built in 3 or 4 Milestones	All Pieces of a Product Built Simultaneously
Frequent Synchs (Daily Builds) & Intermediate Stabilizations (Milestones)	One "Late & Large" Integration & Test Phase at Project End
"Fixed" Ship Dates & Multiple Release Cycles	Attempt to Achieve Feature & Product "Perfection"
Customer Feedback During Development	Feedback as Input for Future Projects
Large Teams Work Like Small Teams, Even in Large Projects	Many Individuals Work in Large Functional Groups to Scale-Up Projects

Source: Cusumano and Selby, *Microsoft Secrets* (1995), p. 407.

FIGURE 5.2

Synchronize and Stabilize Development Process Model

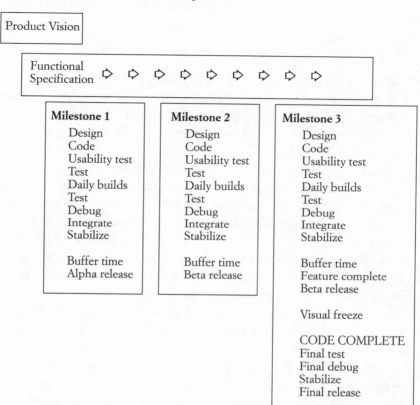

the competitive environment, and continually integrated and tested components as the product was evolving.[9]

In 1997 to 1998, Netscape's client and server divisions appeared less structured and consistent in their approaches to product development than at Microsoft, except perhaps in some of Microsoft's small Internet project teams. What we saw at Netscape was not unexpected for a relatively new company that had relied mainly on development speed and innovation to win customers. From a distance, though, we can also say that both Netscape and Microsoft of necessity rejected the sequential waterfall process as much too inflexible and slow for Internet software, and too removed from customers. Not surprisingly, the steps that Netscape went through very much resembled what Microsoft has been doing in its projects for years, with some modifications that may increase flexibility and speed (but not quality). In order to understand Netscape's version of the synchronize-and-stabilize idea, it will be useful to outline the basic Microsoft process. We will also point out some adaptations that Microsoft's Internet groups have made to increase speed and flexibility.

Synchronize and Stabilize at Microsoft

Microsoft projects built in flexibility throughout the entire development cycle, from the initial generation of product requirements through to the final ship date. In the beginning, product managers did not try to write a complete specification that locked the developers into creating a fixed set of features. Rather, Microsoft teams generally started a project by creating a "vision statement." Team members would usually gather off-site and define the goals for a new product. They would also work with customer data to prioritize features that they wanted to create. In the more established groups, such as Office, product managers took charge of writing up the vision statement, in consultation with program managers and developers. Program managers then compiled a functional specification of the product, which they continued to refine as developers wrote and changed features. The functional specification was never complete until the project ended. Before the project moved into high gear, however, program managers and developers had to outline the most important product features in sufficient depth to allow the managers to create schedules and organize feature teams. Then, during the development phase, Microsoft team members would evolve the feature set and feature details as they learned more about what should be in the product. The feature set in a Microsoft specification document might change by 30 percent or more by the end of the project.

Once product managers had prepared a vision statement, project managers divided the work among small feature teams of three to eight developers, with a parallel team of testers. They usually broke the schedule into three or four "milestone" subprojects that represented completion or stabilization points for major groups of features. Each feature team went through a complete cycle of development, feature integration, testing, and problem fixing in each milestone subproject. Moreover, throughout the project, feature teams or individual engineers synchronized their work by building the product, and by finding and fixing errors, on a daily basis. At the end of a milestone subproject, the developers fixed major errors and "stabilized" the product by agreeing not to make any more changes in particular features or to make them only very carefully. Teams also issued alpha (internal) releases and then beta (external) releases of their evolving products at the milestone junctures. The development teams proceeded from milestone to milestone and, eventually, to the ship date, continuously integrating components, incorporating feedback from external as well as internal users, and finding and fixing major bugs as they went along.

Microsoft also added buffer time (20 to 50 percent of total allotted time) at the end of each milestone to allow team members time to respond to unexpected difficulties or delays, or to add features during the project. This time, as well as the concept of an evolving specification that the team could change as they went along in a project, left developers and program managers room to innovate or adapt to unforeseen competitive opportunities and threats. In addition, most products had modular architectures that allowed teams to add features incrementally or combine them relatively easily. In the more experienced product units, Microsoft managers also tried to "fix" project resources by limiting the number of people they allocated to any one project. They usually limited the time projects could have as well, especially in applications like Office. Managers did this by setting specific ship dates, attaching years to product names (Office 97 and Windows 98, for example), and pushing teams to delete features if they fell too far behind the schedule.

In addition, product units established multiyear product plans so that marketing and engineering did not try to force all the features they wanted into any one particular release of a product. Senior managers like CEO Bill Gates and other members of Microsoft's executive committee closely followed key projects by attending program reviews held every three months or so. In addition, project managers submitted monthly project status reports, and executives checked progress relative to three-year product plans from the divisions. Most projects had considerable independence, however, and close to unlimited resources to hire as many developers and testers as the project leaders felt they needed. The absence of any practical financial limits was particularly important for new product experiments, such as Internet Explorer. (Ben Slivka, for example, admitted to us that, "I had no budget constraint" when he was the project manager for Microsoft's first three Internet Explorer products.)

For the most part, the process for developing Internet products at Microsoft followed the synchronize-and-stabilize pattern described in *Microsoft Secrets*. As Microsoft president Steve Ballmer put it to us, "Software is software." Microsoft also kept to three-year planning horizons, as we discussed in chapter 2. This was true even for the Internet groups, though managers subjected the plans to more frequent scrutiny. Slivka, for example, completed a road map for browser development in May 1995.

This document described feature plans that Microsoft ended up tackling in the first three versions of IE, which came out between August 1995 and August 1996. There were some differences, however, in how Microsoft's Internet groups organized themselves and some of the details of the development process.

One difference, as we noted earlier in this chapter, was that the time between product releases was shorter in the early days of the Internet products. A second difference was that some Internet groups adopted the practice of doing more code reviews to catch bugs early, even before going through the daily build. In fact, for IE 1.0, 2.0, and 3.0, according to Slivka, Microsoft developers held code reviews for *every* check-in to encourage people to write better code (because they knew someone else would be looking at it right away), as well as to spread knowledge around the group with regard to the code base as well as more general techniques such as coding style.[10]

Related to this change in practice was a third difference: the greater use of external design reviews and intensive work with a select group of customers in order to get deeper feedback early in the requirements generation process and in the testing phase. Slivka noted that "external design reviews were the thing that we did a lot of in IE 3.0 that were very valuable. . . . We invited key ISVs and corporate programmers and tools vendors several times in the fall of '95 to review our architecture for IE 3.0." Ballmer also commented on Microsoft's intensive efforts to get customers involved earlier in development as well as testing:

> [Microsoft] Exchange literally took 50 customers or something in the tent and made them part of the development process, gave them offices here, really worked with them on early deployment, really used them as part of the development and test process. That worked very well. Right now, we have on NT 5 what we call a set of 30 or 40—maybe it's even 50 by now— RDP rapid deployment customers. They're already part, not just of the beta, but really of the test phase and the whole thinking about the way the product rolls out. Same thing with SQL Server 7. We've brought, in that case, more typically ISVs [independent software vendors], but also a few traditional customers into the main line of our development and testing process. That's different for us. That is a change. I can't tell you it's an Internet-motivated change. . . . But it's been a very smart change. Our Exchange team pioneered that around here. . . . You have to get the depth of feedback. You can't just get, "Hey, man, the screen didn't repaint right there." That doesn't help you with Exchange or SQL Server or NT 5. Part of what we're talking about is broadly the question of flexibility, whether

it's Internet or not, because I think we're trying to make the argument that this has become more important for everybody. The Internet is just the leading edge.

Synchronize and Stabilize at Netscape

Table 5.4 sketches out key steps in Netscape's development process. This is a simplification of phases that groups in both the client and the server products division generally followed during 1997 to 1998, as described to us by people in product marketing, development, testing, product support, and the executive staff. One difference between client and server development, for example, was that Netscape's server groups were moving away from large-scale and frequent public betas in favor of intensive "field tests" or limited beta releases at a smaller number of user sites.

Similar to Microsoft, Netscape projects usually began with an informal meeting or a series of meetings among core team members from development and marketing. At some point, the product teams would hold a meeting, usually called the "advance planning meeting" (APM). Next, product management created a product requirements document (PRD) that resembled Microsoft's vision statements, laying out product themes and priorities for the next release or for a new product. Again, as at Microsoft, Netscape teams expected the product specification to evolve and had a specific process in place to manage this evolution. Then the teams set a rough schedule, organized around product features or subsystems. Product teams also broke the schedule into milestones—target dates by which they expected to complete certain features or degrees of functionality and release beta or field test versions. Netscape teams generated daily builds of the evolving products and tested as they went along. In addition, Netscape projects incorporated feedback from users during development, from beta or field testing as well as from some usability testing and other customer contacts.

The differences between Netscape and Microsoft were in both process implementation and functional roles. For example, Netscape did not have formal program managers who, in Microsoft, took responsibility for writing functional specifications, managing the design process, and serving as a buffer between marketing and engineering. Instead, Netscape developers generally wrote both the functional specification and the product code. The client division had release managers or directors of the divlets (product or release teams within the divisions) to coordinate projects. Netscape did not seem to coordinate features, feature teams, and mile-

TABLE 5.4

Overview of Netscape's Planning and Development Process

Step 1: Product Requirements and Project Proposal

- Advance Planning Meeting (APM) to brainstorm ideas (marketing, development, executives).

- Product vision generated. Initially done by senior engineers, now mainly by product managers.

- Engineers do some design and coding to explore alternative technologies or feature ideas.

- Product requirements document compiled by product managers, with help from developers.

- Informal review of this preliminary specification by engineers.

- Engineers begin writing functional specification, sometimes with assistance from product managers.

- Schedule and budget plan compiled by marketing and engineering, and informally discussed with executives.

Step 2: First Executive Review

- Executives review product requirements document as well as schedule and budget proposal.

- Adjustments to plan as necessary.

Step 3: Start of Development Phase

- Design and coding of features, and architecture work as necessary.

- Daily integration of components as they are created and checked in (builds).

- Bug lists generated and fixes initiated.

Step 4: Interim Executive Review (If Necessary)

- Functional specification almost complete at this point.

- Mid-course corrections in specification or project resources, as necessary.

- Coordination issues with other products or projects discussed, as necessary.
- Development continues.

Step 5: First Internal (Alpha) Release (Approximately 6 Weeks Long)

- Development stops temporarily.
- Intensive debugging and testing of existing code.
- Alpha release for internal feedback (or possibly a developer's release).
- Development continues.
- User feedback incorporated.
- Feature complete target (rarely met, though servers especially try to be as complete as possible).
- One week to stabilize beta release.

Step 6: Public Beta 1 or Field Test 1 (Approximately 6 Weeks Long)

- Repeat development and testing steps as in Step 5.
- Server groups were moving to "field tests" with limited customers rather than public betas.

Step 7: Public Beta 2 and 3 (Each Beta Approximately 6 Weeks Long)

- Repeat development steps as in Step 5.
- UI freeze milestone.
- Feature complete "mandatory," though some minor changes still allowed.

Step 8: Code Complete

- No more code added except to fix bugs; features are functionally complete.

Step 9: Final Testing and Release

- Final debugging and stabilization of release candidate.
- Certification meeting(s) with senior executives for ship decision.
- Release to manufacturing (RTM) and commercial release.

stones as neatly as Microsoft did in its more experienced groups. Microsoft made more use of scheduled buffer time to keep to the project deadlines. Netscape, in contrast, did not use formal buffer time but was more flexible in setting ship dates within three-month windows. As we will discuss later in this chapter, Netscape developers also did not themselves conduct tests on each daily build in addition to testing done by a separate build team. Netscape appeared as well to be less intensive and systematic in incorporating user feedback during development.

In short, Netscape followed the same basic pattern in product development as Microsoft, with some variations. The following discussion highlights several of the key activities and mechanisms that Netscape used to manage its version of the synchronize-and-stabilize approach, with comparisons where appropriate to Microsoft groups. We also point out some modifications that Netscape was making to enhance quality assurance, particularly for enterprise customers.

Comparison of Functional Roles and Head Count. Table 5.5 presents an estimate of the functional breakdown of personnel in Netscape's client and server divisions as of July 1998. The client product division contained approximately 240 people. This number included some 110 developers (software engineers), 50 testers (QA engineers), and 50 product managers (marketing specialists who work on product requirements and feature proposals). The server products division had about 400 people, including approximately 200 developers, 80 testers, and 42 product managers. The actual sizes of these divisions were continually changing. The numbers in this table, however, are useful to indicate the relative sizes and allocation of resources across development, testing, and product marketing.

The functional ratios and the organization of personnel within the divisions also reflected an underlying organizational philosophy: Operate as much as possible in small units and avoid adding too many people in testing. Netscape's approach to functional hiring and team organization was especially important because it had to make the most of its relatively limited resources. At Microsoft, for example, the personal and business operating systems division, which built Windows 98, Internet Explorer, and Windows NT, had more than a thousand people in 1998. The desktop applications division, which built the Office suite and other products, had several hundred people. Netscape's divisions were smaller than the units within Microsoft divisions responsible for products like Windows 98, Windows NT, and Office (which Microsoft broke down further into the Word, Excel, PowerPoint, and Access product units). Each of the major product units had between 300 and 450 or so people. These numbers

TABLE 5.5

Netscape's Client and Server Development Staff, Mid-1998

	Software Engineering	Testing (QA)	Product Management	Subtotal	Other	TOTAL
Client product division	110	50	50	210	30	240
Server products division	200	80	42	322	98	420
Totals	310	130	92	532	128	660

Notes: "Other" includes activities such as documentation, user interface design, OEM porting, internationalization and localization, and some special product support. These groups are particularly large in the server division.

Source: These numbers are estimates based on Netscape internal sources, as of July 1998.

included product planners (product managers from marketing who usually worked on product vision statements and long-term release planning), program managers (who worked with product planners on vision statements, took responsibility for writing down functional specifications that they created with developers, and coordinated projects), developers (who designed and wrote code and did technical testing), and testers (who usually paired one-to-one with developers and focused on more user-oriented testing, somewhat like an advance "army" of beta testers).

After Microsoft decided to enter the Internet arena, it gradually applied more and more manpower resources to creating a browser and various complementary features, to creating new Web servers, and then to adapting products such as Office, Windows NT, and Exchange for the Internet. In comparison, Netscape generally had fewer people in its individual product teams. The actual efforts (number of engineers and time spent) put into Internet Explorer and Netscape Communicator or the server products are difficult to compare directly. Each company built some components in different groups (such as security components) or in parallel projects, and they carried over code from previous projects or other organizations. Different product versions and teams also overlapped in time at both companies (the parallel development strategy we described in chapter 4). Nonetheless, the number of developers working on core browser features like the HTML engine seems to have been comparable at Netscape and Microsoft, and the two companies required similar amounts of time to create similar features.[11] This observation suggests that developer productivity was probably comparable at the two companies. Netscape's performance was especially impressive since Microsoft used at least twice as many testers as Netscape did. At times, Microsoft also used larger teams of developers than Netscape did to help it catch up and add more features.

Netscape took some shortcuts, however. Managers saved some numbers in headcount by having fewer testers and not hiring a whole category of people that Microsoft employed—program managers.[12] Alex Edelstein spoke about the negative side of not having program managers, based on his experience as a Microsoft program manager before joining Netscape:

> The disadvantage is that it's very valuable to have these people who are astride marketing and engineering, who free up the developers from having to spend any more time than they want to engage in figuring out what to build, and free up the product managers from spending any more time than they want to in figuring out how this stuff is actually going to end up looking and working. . . . Another advantage of the program manager is that it created this cadre within Microsoft who had this wonderful focus on shipping. They had no vested interest in the code and they had no vested interest in the customer. . . . We always described ourselves as, "My job is to get the product shipped." And when you don't have a program manager doing that, that job falls to some combination of a product manager and a development lead. And to the extent that they're engaged in communicating well and have the right focus, they can do just as good a job. But they're not as focused. They have a lot of other things pulling at them. . . . If I had my druthers, I would hire a bunch of program managers.

Microsoft also had variations in its product units, especially within the Internet groups. If managers of new projects wanted to move really fast—for example, on the early versions of Internet Explorer and NetMeeting, which initially shipped with Internet Explorer—developers usually took the lead in proposing features and writing up outlines of specifications. In these cases, Microsoft program managers came onboard later and worked mainly on managing project schedules, writing up test cases with testers, working with interface or Web page designers, and building relationships with outside partners and customers. Product managers in such projects played less of a role and mainly worked with customers or prepared for the sales effort.[13]

At least two factors seemed behind Netscape's decision not to have program managers. One was the desire to keep headcount low. The program manager was yet another role that Netscape would have had to recruit for and staff. (Microsoft traditionally averaged about one program manager for every five or so developers.)[14] Another factor seems to have been the desire to streamline communication between marketing and engineering. Edelstein continued his commentary: "I like the program manager concept and I think it works very well. It is very expensive, and that's one of the reasons why most companies don't do it. It's costly because it's not a zero-sum game. If you want to have a program manager, you're not going to be able to fire either a development manager or a product manager. You have to add someone—come up with the budget and add them."

To be fair to Netscape, most PC software companies did not have Microsoft-style program managers. They tended to have only product managers and to have them focus on product plans, theme statements, and feature proposals for product releases. The product managers might work with developers to put together feature lists and brief functional descriptions, though not a complete functional specification like Microsoft program managers created, usually by working side-by-side with developers. In addition, many software companies had separate project managers or at least "release managers" (like Netscape's Michael Toy) to oversee schedules and monitor progress of the different functional groups and teams.

Product Planning and Executive Reviews. Like Microsoft, Netscape evolved its process for product planning and development in stages, as it became increasingly important for projects to be more systematic and predictable. In the company's first two years, Marc Andreessen, later joined by Mike McCue and a few other engineers working in his technology group, was the primary driver of the vision for both the client and server products. Andreessen was particularly active in generating themes and feature suggestions for the early server products. Bill Turpin, formerly the VP in charge of server product development and in 1998 head of Web site development, recalled the way things were back around 1996:

> The original way we came up with the product ideas was that Marc Andreessen was sort of our product marketing guy. He went out and met with lots of customers. He would meet with analysts. He would see what other new companies were doing. In that period of time, he would come back and synthesize that. He figured out where he thought the market was going and what interesting new products we could do. And there was a period of time where, late at night, he would write these white papers about new products he wanted us to do in the server group, especially. This was in the summer of 1996. He even wrote code names for us. He named

the projects by code name and laid out three or four new servers that we needed to do. We then took that and product marketing and engineering changed it around a little bit but basically we took his vision. We staffed up some new teams and out of that came the Directory Server, Certificate Server, Catalog Server, and the next version of the Enterprise Server, which came to be known as the Web Server. So he, initially, was the marketing strategist who would define what new projects we should do.

Between 1996 and 1998, Netscape also built up its product management staff located in the product teams (as opposed to corporate marketing, which worked with the sales organization). This group gradually took on more of the responsibility for drafting initial product requirements. At the same time, however, senior Netscape developers had the freedom to form their own teams and move certain "pet" features into a new release when the technologies were ready. The developers could also exercise veto power on technical grounds, such as to say, "This feature is impossible to build." (Microsoft worked the same way, with developers having veto power, although program managers generally had more technical backgrounds than product managers and often were more adept at negotiating with developers.)

The advance planning meetings were useful to bring executives, engineers, and marketing people together to begin brainstorming features and release plans for each new product. Netscape divisions held these meetings at least once a quarter because of the number of different products and versions. Executive reviews generally followed the APMs within a month to kick off projects more formally. Then, after several months, depending on the length of the project, executives held an interim review before the first public beta to check on progress. Bill Turpin described the scheduling and review process:

> We try to have a fairly good bottom-up schedule with a features in-and-out list, estimates on how long it is going to take, names of the people on the project, plus openings we have to fill. So this is where you get a fairly realistic idea of what the project is going to be. And then you get marketing and engineering in there together agreeing on, "Yes, if we build this it will be a great product, and here is how we are going to build it." And we have [interim] executive reviews if we feel the project is in trouble or if they need to make a mid-course correction, or anything like that. So, any major change in a project, we try to have one of these executive reviews.

Unlike Bill Gates, who regularly attended reviews of major products, Netscape CEO Jim Barksdale typically did not attend executive reviews.

He left these to Andreessen and other executives responsible for product development. Barksdale, however, did at times contribute to setting product themes and objectives.

After drafting the product requirements document and receiving approval for a new project, developers typically shared their design ideas and preliminary design documents with colleagues and their managers as part of an informal review process. Developers sometimes created more formal design documents and held face-to-face meetings to discuss these prior to the mid-course executive review. How much to formalize the design documents or reviews, however, seemed up to the individual engineer or team leader. According to Jon Mittelhauser, any part of a feature with a user interface went through a relatively formalized design and review process. Netscape also relied on a separate UI group that put out a written spec to make sure that the user interface was the same across the different platform versions. The affected groups needed to review features that touched on other features, such as the new Roaming Access feature under development in 1997 and 1998, which affected security and privacy components. Again, the developers responsible for the features took the lead in scheduling these meetings. (In Microsoft, program managers often did this job of coordinating requirements and scheduling reviews to free up more time for the developers to write code.)

Netscape clearly did not engage in too much planning and formal reviewing. Managers and engineers openly adopted the philosophy that, in the rapidly changing world of the Internet, it was not possible to specify in advance of starting the coding process—the components construction phase—everything that should go into a new product or a new release. At the same time, managers and engineers clearly believed that some planning was necessary to build complex products. David Stryker, who was in charge of building shared components from 1996 to 1997, outlined the thinking that seemed to prevail at Netscape as well as at other PC software firms such as Microsoft:

> A classic statement from a gunslinger engineer is, "Do you want me to plan or do you want me to build it because, after all, if I plan it, then at the end of it you have a plan. If I build it, you have a product. Now, which do you want at the end of the process?" This is sheer bullshit, right? The way you get places, the way you hit the bull's-eye the first time, is by planning things. . . . [But] you can't plan everything down to the atoms. That just doesn't work. The art of planning is articulating your goals and nongoals really clearly and picking out the things that have to be planned down to the atoms because some things do. . . . So we make a pretty big deal of

goals and nongoals of projects. We try to make the goals measurable and concrete. The nongoals are more important than the goals because, when you're doing mid-course correction, which you do on a 72-hour basis, the best guidance you can get is to remember what you *weren't* trying to do.

The length and intensity of the planning phase varied by the complexity of the product. For some new server products, Netscape spent as long as nine months simply generating requirements and planning the product. Servers also required extra time for cross-product coordination, an area that Netscape probably needed to improve. For example, Greg Sands, the head of SuiteSpot product marketing, estimated that 60 percent of the features in the recent version of SuiteSpot were specific to individual servers and as many as 40 percent were cross-product features. In early versions, very few features were cross-product.

Probably the most important mid-project change to a PC software product in recent years was Microsoft's decision to add a browser to Windows 95 in April 1994. The product had already been under development since Windows 3.1 shipped in 1992. The decision to add the browser dramatically changed the direction of Windows and Microsoft more broadly as Office and other product groups added Internet features. We saw some major mid-project shifts at Netscape as well, such as to cancel the 6.0 rearchitecture effort and most of the Java initiatives and then reorganize the client engineers into the 4.5 and 5.0 projects. Several managers also talked about the addition of Netcaster to Communicator 4.0, which shipped in June 1997, as a good example of Netscape's flexibility. This technology responded to what became Microsoft's Active Channels in Internet Explorer 4.0. Neither feature proved to be successful commercially, and the Netcaster feature performed extremely poorly in its first implementation. Nonetheless, it gave Netscape a position and some experience in the new push technology. Debby Meredith commented in our July 1997 interview:

> Three-quarters of the way through the Communicator [4.0] development process, we decided we were going to add the Netcaster component. It was never planned to be in Communicator, never in any specs. To this date, it's not in any Communicator specs because we didn't rev it. But it was a separate project that was on a different release schedule. It was more of, we started off doing this technology, weren't really sure when it was going to hook up to one of these trains, and then we just sensed that the world was right for push technology. Microsoft was thinking about similar things. We wanted to preempt them.

Web-Based Electronic Product Documentation. To save time, Netscape's product requirements document was usually short (five pages or so) for a new product release, at least for the client. Once engineers and executives "bought off" on this document in the executive review, the developers, sometimes with the help of product managers, started to evolve this document into a rough functional specification. This spec then continued to change through at least halfway and two-thirds of the way through a project.

Some features (like Netcaster) might ship with the product and never even make it into the written specification, as Meredith admitted. This is *not* a good practice in general, however. It can confuse developers whose features interact with the undocumented new feature and make it very difficult to test the new feature. Unlike in the classic waterfall model of software development, however, most PC and Internet software companies will tolerate a lack of documentation because they put a premium on creating code, not documents. (Microsoft program managers helped in this area, too, by relieving developers of having to write a lot of functional specifications.)

The arrival of the Internet also brought some changes in documentation. Netscape and Microsoft both created electronic documents that were extremely easy to modify and structure with different layers. The new product specs were mostly HTML pages posted on internal Web sites, with indexes of features and hot links to different documents, such as API specifications. This was a major departure from the days before the Web. Edelstein recalled the huge paper documents he used to create at Microsoft in the early 1990s:

> As a program manager, I used to compile these huge documents. And we used to spend hours after hours changing them, updating them, distributing them, making sure that everyone got them, making sure they had the right version, changing all these pictures that we had done in bitmaps to reflect the new changes. That takes a huge amount of time, and a lot of bodies. And if you look at them, that's why you find 25 program managers on something like Excel. Netscape does things more efficiently.

Relatively "Loose" Project Management and Scheduling. Because it did not have much in the way of a strong tradition or orientation process that emphasized tight project management, Netscape relied heavily on strong personalities to "manage" the developers. This was especially apparent on the client side of the company, where Netscape used experienced and respected engineers to serve in the role as release manager or project manager. For Navigator 1.0, this was Tom Paquin, who joined Netscape in April 1994 after working at IBM Research and Silicon Graphics. For most of the later versions, Michael Toy, who had also worked as a developer at Silicon Graphics, played this role. In the server area, Netscape used a structure of directors, development managers, and test managers to over-see development in the smaller product teams (divlets).

The client release manager or team director took charge of the software development process, rather than coordinating other parts of the release effort, such as documentation, packaging, or marketing. Toy described his role: "I am in charge of the actual development of the software bits for the client. I draw that line because there's a whole class of things like what's in the box, what the quick reference card looks like, what the channel part-ners are concerned about, that I choose not to pay attention to." Lloyd Tabb described Toy's approach to managing the client engineers for Com-municator 4.0: "Michael Toy is the czar of the project. He was the release manager. With 120 engineers doing code, you've basically got to trust that people who are working in their areas are doing the right thing. Managers in those areas who are senior enough to know what the right thing is are doing their part. . . . Michael is in charge of coordinating the dance."

Generating a schedule for this "dance" usually began in the product marketing group. Marketing proposed a date to introduce a new product or version. Engineers sat down in each group and tried to figure out what features they could complete in that amount of time. Marketing next helped establish what were the highest priority items. The release then went out when teams finished or were close to finishing at least the top-priority features. Less important features could fall off the feature list—"miss the train"—but they often became part of the next release. Mittelhauser explained the flexible estimating and scheduling process in the client division:

> We have a date in mind that we want to hit, usually for external reasons. We don't want to leave it too long before we have a new cycle. We don't want to wait two years until we release something. So it's usually a six- or nine-month type of cycle. We set a rough date. Then the project manager for the product, such as for 5.0, basically will sit down with the functional areas and go, "Okay, mail and news, what do you think you're going to get done in this time?" I sat down with those constraints and met with market-ing and said, "Okay we've got X weeks of development. Prioritize these things and I'll commit to this and I'll try to get these two done." And so "commit to it" means they can start telling customers and writing docu-mentation sheets around these two and hint that we're hoping to have

them. . . . We set the date and then we say, "Okay, there're three to five features that are must-ship, must-have to ship. Even if the date slips two months, if these aren't there, we're going to slip the date and everything else just missed the train. You're on the next one." The group usually has enough personally invested that they want to get it out.

Toy tried to combine flexibility and realism with a gentle push in his schedules. Rather than give engineers deadlines, he asked them to estimate how much code they needed to write for particular small chunks of the product, such as features or identifiable subsystems. He let developers adjust for the complexity of a feature (how time-consuming it might be to create) as well as how self-contained it was (how much time they might spend coordinating with another group). Some engineers added a "fudge factor" for debugging time. Finally, they added time for beta testing. Toy described his approach to scheduling and interacting with marketing:

There will be a piece of software and, whatever that is, marketing is going to hype it as the next logical step in the evolution of mankind. We need to just figure out [what] we can do by then. So there are people who are thinking globally about what features do we need to do over time. And some features miss the next boat. There's no way they're going to be done in that time. And they go off and do that. The complete rewrite of mail and news that is in 4.0 completely missed 3.0. That effort was going on in parallel with 3.0 happening, just as an example. . . . We have this big dance we do with marketing and sales about features they wish they had and which ones are hard and which ones are easy. We spin on that and, at this point, marketing is asking for schedules for everything that they want. What they want is hard data so, if I want this feature, I want to know who's working on it. This is where I try not to let them get that. I get rough guesses about how big things are, but I try not to let any schedules get done. So we do this dance until we're done. Then we think that we have a feature set that we can live with and a rough time frame. We haven't actually tried to pack the blocks together very well yet, but we've at least put them on a scale. . . . We'll say, "This is a two-week thing. Does this have a big cross-platform component, little cross-platform component?" So we're asking global questions. And we know that the numbers are pretty meaningless but in some cases it doesn't matter that they're [almost] meaningless. It simplifies the universe and things would simplify even if they're not correct or useful because it allows you to get focused.

Netscape's process for estimating schedules remained loose at least in part because the developers paid relatively little attention to formal time estimates. Developers viewed the date that marketing set as the "official" schedule, but this was no more than a rough target. They made up their own estimates of how long they thought the plans would really take to implement. Even the developers' estimates were no more than rough guesses because software development, especially for the Internet, required a mixture of art, engineering, and invention. People also worked at different paces. Consequently, the developers had no problem going past the official ship date if the quality or features were not there. Mittelhauser reflected the attitude of many PC software engineers toward deadlines:

> I don't think you ever want to put anything too much in stone. I think we do that when we do the initial planning and we try to say, "Okay, we want to have this next release be in six months or nine months" or whatever the time frame is. There's often marketing or sales factors that influence that. Then, from an engineering standpoint, we go back and say, "Okay, what of this big feature plan we have? Can we get done in that time and what are we going to have to push to the release after that?" We have tended recently for the initial plan for a product to be date-driven and then, as it finishes up, we won't hold to the date to the point of putting stuff out that's absolutely miserable. But we'll try to hold to that date.

Aleks Totic claimed that the software engineers' schedules were more accurate than the official schedules: "I've learned not to fully trust our official schedule. It's like Wall Street. There's an official projection, then there's the number that gets floated around by analysts. The engineers also have the number, which is when they expect the next release to come out, considering how much stuff we have to do. So I usually use that number in my mind. And it seems to be pretty precise. We're usually off the release date by two months at most." The developers clearly used "fudge factors" to make their estimates more accurate, although Toy did not like applying buffer time or "multipliers" to individuals. He wanted more aggressive schedules:

> It's easy to make schedules that you can make. What's hard to do is to make aggressive schedules that are predictable. *That's* almost impossible. If you beat up on everybody and let them know that everyone needs to make their schedules, then everyone starts pulling up their own. Fred says it takes two months and he's times two. Bill said it would take a week and he's times four. And you get big bloated schedules where I can't push. I can't reach in here and say, "No, no, you can't do that because there's all of my slack in there." . . . I want to invent a culture where people understand and make

their own commitments and grow up in their own ability to make estimates. And so what I say over and over again is that, if we're shipping on Thursday, I don't care what it is you tell me you can do by Thursday. If all you can do by Thursday is count the napkins in your drawer, that's fine. Just tell me the real thing that you can do by Thursday that will be done. And so I'm really trying to get down to the actual person who's doing the work so that there's not this magical buffer zone between me, who's overseeing the whole project, and the person who's actually doing the work. . . . If the engineer said he'd be done by Thursday and his manager said he'll be done in November, when the engineer is late, I don't know about it. I want to know when the engineer is late because that engineer's morale is important to me. It's part of what makes the system work. And when he starts feeling late, he stops being as productive. And so, if I get rid of that buffer zone, then I know when that happened.

As a result of this development environment, as we discussed earlier, Netscape teams tended to focus not on specific target dates for shipping (as Microsoft did) but on three-month windows, mapping to the financial quarters. One reason they could be lax about ship dates was the use of the Internet for product distribution. As a result of this innovation in distribution technology, which Netscape largely pioneered for the commercial software market with Navigator 1.0, the engineers did not need extra time to ship products in boxes. Mittelhauser explained:

I don't think there's any product I've worked on that we've picked a particular date. . . . Most of our stuff, since we're just releasing it by putting it up on the Net, is not really [affected by] outside factors. Communicator [4.0] . . . was probably the hardest [target] we set and that was set basically for revenue purposes. We had to ship it in the middle of Q2 so that we could get revenue from it for Q2. That was a new thing for me to comprehend. . . . We usually say we're going to ship it in this quarter. And we target the beginning of the quarter understanding that we may slip a few weeks. But we've had product that we've slipped a whole quarter and usually it's because, midway through, we decided that a feature we had said was critical—there's normally three or four features that we determine are critical—isn't going to happen. We have to reevaluate if this is really critical. If it is, then we just keep slipping, and we keep trying to throw resources at it and pray.

Managers in the client division did not use any unusual planning tools to help create schedules, but they used the Web technology very effectively. Product teams first sketched out plans (feature lists and proposed

schedules) on a white board (and tried not to erase it). There was no formal analysis of critical paths or interdependencies, although managers
tried to identify potential roadblocks in the schedules. Later, managers
posted schedules on an intranet (rather than just sharing schedules and
progress reports periodically over e-mail, which many companies did in
earlier years). Intranets were an easy way to allow everyone—managers
and engineers—to check on the status of the daily builds for each platform
whenever they wanted and see which modules worked and which did not.

The server teams made more use of formal scheduling tools and put
more effort into standardizing release cycles so that Netscape could ship
SuiteSpot with updated versions of each server coming together at the
same time. As a result, the estimation process was somewhat more formalized, not only to coordinate requirements for the server suite but also to
make sure there was enough time for testing. Turpin also posted a master
schedule on the intranet called the "Plan of Record." This tracked the
progress of the different projects and included "Web agents" that automatically notified people of changes as they occurred:

> I have got agents on this so, whenever this changes, it sends out e-mail to
> a mailing list, anyone who wants to track Plan of Record changes. Also,
> I have this version on there using a feature in the product so that I can
> compare one version to another version to see specifically what has
> changed. . . . It is a living Web document. It's hot-linked into a lot of inter-
> esting things as well. At the bottom of the document there . . . is a link that
> shows anything that we've shipped. . . . That gives us some historical data
> to go back in and analyze from time to time.

The inputs for the Plan of Record came from the more detailed database that was part of the Signpost project management tool. This tool
helped Netscape teams identify and follow good practices. Ben Horowitz,
a VP who headed the Mission Control divlet (product line) and a veteran
of the cc:Mail and Notes divisions at Lotus before joining Netscape in
1995, described how Signpost worked:

> We've got an internal tool called Signpost, which is basically all the many
> tasks that you have to complete in order to get credit for the next mile-
> stone. Those are stored in the central database and accessible over the
> Web, so that all the divlet managers and the general manager can look at
> the project and see if the team has done the requisite things in order to
> meet the appropriate quality level. . . . The Plan of Record is generated out
> of Signpost. Signpost . . . requires about 800 different tasks to be com-
> pleted in order to meet all the milestones and it spits out a plan of refer-

ence, but it's a process management tool. We developed it internally. Basically, what we did is, we accumulated all the knowledge that we had built up over the years and assembled it and then added the new initiatives that we were doing in order to meet the quality goals and put them into Signpost.

Frequent Component Integration through Daily Builds. At the level of writing code, Netscape, like Microsoft and a growing number of other software producers, used the daily build process to coordinate the work of developers, rather than relying on detailed planning and controls to supervise the work of the engineers. Conceptually, the idea of a software build is similar to creating and evolving a working prototype that the team eventually ships to customers. But the build process quickly becomes complicated in software when there are many components, many simultaneous versions of the code (for example, UNIX versions one through nine, as well as the new Windows, the old Windows, and the Macintosh version of the browser), and many engineers who all need to work with the same components.

We can understand why the build process might become complicated by using the example of writing a report with coauthors using common word-processor files, such as one for each chapter. If all the coauthors—the development team—can make changes to the same files, then the team quickly becomes entangled in a mess of different versions existing simultaneously. One way to solve this problem is to use a tool that "locks" a file when someone is using it (i.e., when someone is writing), and then "opens" the file to changes only when the last user has changed and saved the file. This approach prevents the problem of having simultaneous multiple versions, although it is not very efficient. Some team members will almost always be sitting around waiting for a particular file (such as the one that holds a particular chapter or section of the report) to become open again.

Another approach is what PC software companies like Microsoft and Netscape do. They allow many people to work on the same files but "force" the team members to synchronize their changes as frequently as possible. If the developers have to work separately for a period of time, then they might get their own "branch" or version of the code, which extends from the main set of files or the source-code "tree." But the developers still have to merge or synchronize their branches relatively frequently or they risk creating components that do not work with other components. In a browser, for example, developers can create features in separate teams. But functions such as the bookmark feature have to work with the file management feature and the Web browsing feature; otherwise, users cannot save their favorite bookmarks and locate the addresses they want. The product is not very useful if key features do not evolve together.

Lloyd Tabb took on the role of helping to define a daily build process for the client, following practices that his previous employer, Borland, had used in its dBase group. He also led the effort to customize tools needed to make a daily build work with a relatively large number of people. Tabb described his role and showed us the build tools during our July 1997 interview, when Netscape was still finishing Communicator 4.0. He referred to this project by the code name Dogbert:

> I basically build technology to help us ship. . . . My title during Dogbert was the sheriff. . . . We had to train people to be accountable for what they did. In order to do that, you had to set laws and then not arrest people for what they did wrong but actually go discuss with them. . . . I usually ride a unicycle around here, and the fire-breathing unicycle on the Web page is me because I would ride into somebody's office and say, "Look, you checked in, you broke the build, and didn't fix the build. That's a very bad thing because you're stopping everybody else from working." We have this stable of machines that are continuously building. You check in source code into the source tree. Your obligation then is to go immediately and look at the source tree and find out, if the build stopped working, if it was you. And there were all these tools to track down who that was. They'll figure out who it was that broke the tree and then fix it as soon as possible. The problems are when your train wrecks because you have somebody checking in something very early in the build . . . and there are three things that are broken after and it masks the further breakage.

Netscape used a modified version of a source-code control tool that was freely available on the Internet called CVS. (This is also the basis for the tool that Microsoft originally used for its build process.) CVS was not particularly advanced and had limitations for managing the concurrent development of large, complex systems with many components, such as Communicator had become with version 4.0. Nonetheless, it was useful for a multiplatform company like Netscape because it ran on the Windows, Macintosh, and UNIX operating systems. Many hackers and computer science majors from college also were familiar with the tool, and developers could easily use a modem with CVS to send in or download files. Tabb and other engineers added some tools to the CVS system called

Tinderbox and Bonsai to automate the check-in and tracking process for the Communicator projects.

CVS worked by comparing new and old versions of files being checked in and then creating "patches" for the changed code when the developer asked for an update. It then kept track of these changes and allowed the developer to back up to previous files, if necessary. The Tinderbox extension to CVS was primarily an HTML page generator that showed the status of all the builds going on in the company, for all platforms, and who was checking in which components. When a build "broke," this meant that files didn't compile or link properly, or they failed a quick acceptance test. A red box appeared, and the transgressor was likely to be the person who most recently checked into that build. Netscape also added a local newsgroup feature to post all the check-in information. Developers and testers could view this information through their browsers.

Most developers need to synchronize their components with other components or incorporate other pieces of the system into the parts they are building. As a result, Netscape had to rely on a sense of obligation among the engineers to make sure the pieces they checked in worked and did not "break the build." In Microsoft, there was no rule on how often developers should check in; there was only the rule that each project had to create a build at least daily, and developers who checked in code that broke the build had to fix their code immediately and face penalties (such as become the build master for the next day, wear a dunce cap, or pay a small fine). As a result of these simple rules, Microsoft developers tended to check in and synchronize their code about twice a week on average, and at least daily in the latter stages of a project, when there were lots of bugs to fix.[15] Netscape developers also worked this way, checking in more frequently as a project moved on and often once a day or more toward the end of a project.

The Netscape client team relied on another extension to CVS and Tinderbox to keep track of who checked in and alert people to problems. What developers referred to as the "Bonsai hook" consisted of e-mail notices automatically sent to individuals who had checked in code since the last successful build. Developers were in essence "on call" until someone fixed the problem. Bonsai, in combination with CVS/Tinderbox, made it possible for a relatively large team to integrate their components in just two or so hours, on average, rather than in days or weeks. Tabb gave this account of how Bonsai worked:

> There is a dynamic mailing list of everybody who has checked in during the day. It's called the Bonsai hook. You're on the hook until you've been

cleared. . . . If you pull a build and it's not working, you can e-mail the hook and say, "Hey, what we've built today is a piece of garbage. Could anybody have broken this?" And the mail will go out to only the people who are interested parties and that list grows until the following day when the hook is cleared. . . . It's hard enough getting five people not to break the build. When you have 120 people, unless you're all building together, it's my belief that you don't ship software on time. If you have an integration step that takes a week, then your cycle time is a week. Our cycle time was hours. It had pain. You'll find around here that it was a painful thing for the developers. But it also allowed us to have our ship time very short.

Tabb and other engineers in the client division first instituted Bonsai on top of CVS in mid-1996 to get the daily builds working and to keep track of who might have broken the build. After they got this system working, they added Tinderbox a few months later to keep track of the separate builds for different versions and components. They put the new system "online" in November of 1996. By 1998, CVS/Tinderbox had become standard throughout Netscape's client and server development groups, even though many engineers recognized that it was not a state-of-the-art source-code control tool (such as ClearCase, used at many other software firms) but more of a "hacker's" system. The Bonsai hook also required considerable discipline and even a "sheriff" to keep the engineers on call. We did not see Netscape using the Bonsai hook outside the main Navigator development team. Tabb also admitted that teams building small components or features separate from the main product did not use either tool or daily builds necessarily until they merged their work. Despite these exceptions that Netscape tolerated, Tabb talked about the benefits of the continuous builds:

> The continuous builds are to make sure developers aren't stopped. In other words, the worst thing that could happen is that a developer's time is wasted. So what ends up happening is that, if you're a developer and you want to update your tree, if you update to the tip of the tree [i.e., the last point where all the checked-in components worked in the build], there's a good chance you'll be broken because somebody could have made a mistake. If you go to the continuous build page and you look for a green square [the point at which the build was still working] at a particular time, you can update . . . to the last known good thing, so that you can segregate your bugs or your build problems. . . . You can believe it built right for the continuous build so why isn't it building for me? It must be something I've done. What ends up happening is that engineers lose the accountability when they believe it might be somebody else's fault. They stop looking. If

you ever get to a point where it could be somebody else's fault, then all accountability is lost and people just throw up their arms. So what you have to do is give them a way to get to something that they know is good.

Testing and Reviewing the Builds. Although Netscape and Microsoft both used daily builds to integrate components continuously, there were important differences in how each company tested the builds. Microsoft developers generally created a build and "private release" for themselves and their buddy testers. Then they ran a quick "regression" test that checked whether existing functions continued to work after adding new code. (Some engineers called this a "smoke" test.) Next, they had their buddy testers test their code, usually from a user's perspective. Microsoft developers and testers normally went through this set of procedures *before* developers checked their code into the project build. After developers checked in to the project build, the build master or build team ran the quick regression test again. Then the testing team ran more extensive tests periodically to make sure the features were working properly and to identify problems.[16] Because of this extra layer of automated and manual testing, Microsoft projects were more likely than Netscape's to catch and correct technical errors and some usability problems before the projects did the required daily builds.

A major complicating factor for Netscape in development as well as in testing was its support for so many operating system platforms. Cross-platform products provided strategic leverage, though at a cost to development and testing productivity. Keeping so many versions of the code working on the daily builds was difficult. Tabb counted about 20 operating system versions on which they had to test the client. In addition, Netscape generally had two teams working on the same code base in parallel, such as the client 4.5 and 5.0 teams. To handle these different versions, as well as to keep the beta releases separate, Netscape had to use CVS to create different branches of the tree for the same product. (Netscape also used separate branches to build foreign language versions of its products, though separate teams handled this "localization" process.)

Netscape groups building servers and shared components also created frequent builds, at least once a week and usually daily. But their rules and tools varied somewhat from the client product division. First, there was no daily or even weekly build of SuiteSpot, even though Netscape sold this as one product. SuiteSpot was really a collection of separate server products. Instead, server QA teams did spot checking to make sure that components in the different servers worked together as well as with the client. There was also a small test group in server marketing that tested the common

install features for SuiteSpot. Second, some individual server teams preferred not to build every day because of the overhead involved. Nor did
they use tools like Bonsai to keep people who might have broken the build
"on the hook," though they did use CVS/Tinderbox to track check-ins
and notify people of problems.

Code reviews are another very useful way to find bugs before checking
changes or fixes into the builds. Netscape had no set policy with regard
to how often or how intensively developers should inspect their code or
their designs. Some components received very light reviews, while others
received fairly intensive scrutiny. It depended on the project and the manager. Dave Stryker recalled that, for shared components when he was in
charge, the reviews varied from "a two-hour session to reading every line of
code in a group of ten people around the table, each of them looking at listings saying, 'Oh, between line three and line four there might be a problem.'" Microsoft was only a little better at this: Shared components got
reviewed at the design and coding phases, and most code went through at
least a "buddy review" by one other person. But the intensity varied by
project.[17] As Ben Slivka described, however, the early Internet Explorer
groups used code reviews much more extensively—at each code check-in.

By the time teams were working on the last beta, Netscape conventions
generally required that one or two senior developers review every change
in the code and that the project or release manager also approve every
change. In addition, Netscape managers expected developers to add comments to their code noting who reviewed it and when. For bug fixes, a
tracking tool tagged each bug with a number and kept records of changes
made to the code and who checked it in and when.

Some Leeway in Milestones. Milestones were important stabilization
points as well as good indicators of how a project was progressing. For
client development, Michael Toy focused on two targets: the first alpha
(internal beta) release and the first public beta. At the beginning of a project, managers tried to determine roughly when they wanted to have the
first public beta. Then, Toy noted, they worked backward to fix other key
milestones:

> In the past, the milestones have been appearance of the first public beta
> and back before that [the alpha release]. . . . Those are the two interesting
> milestones that tell you if you're doomed. . . . We back-compute those
> days. The way that usually goes is, we pick the day we're shipping and then
> we have some experience which tells us when we know we have a feature-
> complete beta, a UI-complete beta, and another beta after that . . . and

then the final release. . . . Then, when we know what the feature-complete beta is, now we know how much time we have for feature development. For example, there's going to be two months of feature development. Now we say, "All right, in order for us to be successful in these two months, we will need one milestone build that we can aim for in the middle of that." Or, if it's three months, then we'll need two. And if it's four months, then we'll need four. That depends more on what features are coming in, and how many milestone builds there are. So there's that main development time. You're going to pick some small number of milestone builds in the middle, and maybe you will pick one or two of those to show to people.

Though Netscape projects usually had a "feature-complete" milestone scheduled along with the first or second beta release, this milestone was not rigid. Jon Mittelhauser admitted to frequent slips: "There're some hard milestones: betas, UI freezes. And usually the milestones are calendar-based. So you try to map like, 'I want to be feature-complete by the first beta or by the second beta because then it's going to give me this stretch to do bug fixes.' But those tend to shift as you go along. When we start a cycle, we say we're going to be entirely feature-complete by beta one and it hasn't happened yet here in four releases." Toy explained why Netscape was so flexible with its milestones: "You can't ship a release out this building without features getting added, no matter how fascist you try to be about saying, 'We're feature-complete, darn-it!' Again, we're responding to things on the Internet. And so, suddenly, something which didn't look like it was going to be important for another six to nine months becomes important yesterday. You've got to have a response to it."

Netscape, like Microsoft and other companies competing in PC software markets, thus chose to allow their feature sets to evolve and milestones to slip because the competition, the technology, and the market required this. There was no point shipping a product on time if it was obsolete or contained the wrong features. Conventional thinking about good practice in software engineering, however, generally preferred a more disciplined process and schedules less subject to change so that managers could plan adequately for market analysis, design and development, testing and debugging, documentation, and other activities that enterprise customers liked. Bob Lisbonne contrasted traditional software development (along the waterfall model) with the faster-paced requirements of the Internet world:

Traditionally, you have this market requirements document that's quite complete and is a research project in and of itself that's handed off or negotiated with developers to do a product requirements document or product

specification, which is then implemented according to a bottom-up schedule, a big project-management task. That just doesn't work in the Internet
world. There are too many bends in the road. . . . That is particularly true
now, when products are coming more quickly and changes are happening
more quickly. So we pretty deliberately have adopted a modus operandi
whereby we pursue several of the milestones in parallel. That is to say,
there's almost an alpha and a beta of the marketing requirements, and
developers are working on specs well before a final marketing requirements document is done. Likewise, developers are implementing features
well in advance of formal schedules being built for every piece of the product. And part of Netscape's success, or its nimbleness, which I think is part
of its success in the market, is because we approach product development
in that fashion. We are open and receptive to considering course corrections or other changes midstream.

Netscape's server groups made mid-project changes in their feature sets
and objectives as well, although these were generally minor changes or
decisions to spend more time on optimizing performance. Too many
major feature changes could destabilize a server product and make it difficult to sell to enterprise customers. Nor did the server groups have an
alpha release milestone because Netscape's internal information systems
(IS) organization would not use a new server product until it was further
along in development. Joy Lenz, the former head of server QA and now in
the Netcenter division, described the situation: "It's harder for the server
because, until we can prove that the stability is there, our IS group won't
deploy. . . . So, normally, it's like we're treating our IS group as a beta
group." But, at least in 1997, the server groups did try to schedule two six-
week periods in which they released public betas or field test betas and got
specific feedback from customers. In 1998, the philosophy was to rely less
on broad public betas and more on intensive field tests. Ben Horowitz
described the shift in thinking and noted that field tests were an adaptation to reduced pressures to ship products quickly and the need to place
greater emphasis on quality:

> We have pretty strict rules about not shipping the products until we have
> been through a multistage field testing and then come back and requalify
> the final fixes with our full regression suite and with our system test, which
> is quite a bit different than we used to test in the past. One, it makes the
> product cycle a bit longer, and the other is that, as a matter of policy, we
> just won't ship a product that has major known defects or really any known
> defects, which is also different. We have the luxury of doing that. We don't
> have the same kinds of market pressure that we had in the very, very early

days. . . . The connotation for beta was that we put it on the Internet and we forget about it but we field the bugs and that's it. . . . [Now] we're not allowed to go hit our next milestone until we have field testers identified and ready to go.

Multiple Efforts to Stabilize the Final Product. Shipping the final version of a software product requires tracking down, prioritizing, and fixing as many serious bugs as possible without introducing more bugs with each line of changed code. Many PC software engineers and testers, including people at Netscape and Microsoft, call this final debugging a "stabilization" phase. This term recognizes the reality that, given the freedom of developers to make so many late changes in a project, it is generally impossible to eliminate all bugs. But it is possible to reduce major bugs to a low and stable level before making the decision to ship.

In the client area, Netscape managers did not allow much time for final stabilization. They relied on the daily builds, multiple beta releases, and internal QA testing to find bugs and expected developers to fix problems as they surfaced. (Microsoft did the same thing.) Netscape's client QA team developed plans for functional testing along with the beta release plans and generally allowed about one week to stabilize each release. Mark Tompkins, a 20-year veteran of IBM and Tandem who headed client QA before moving to the applications products division in May 1998, stated that it took two to three days to test the client on one platform, such as Windows. Because they released on UNIX as well as the Mac, managers allotted a week to the functional testing process. After the code-complete milestone, the client division then allocated two weeks of final testing—running the functional tests as well as regression tests on bug fixes to make sure the fixes worked and did not break existing functionality. Then they would ship the last beta and repeat the process for the final release. Tompkins briefly outlined the steps toward final stabilization:

> There's a feature-complete date that precedes . . . the beta one schedule. . . . We're testing before feature-complete also, so we're testing in parallel here and our testing is causing bugs to be found. . . . We get to a time frame here which is a couple weeks before beta, where we really tighten the screws down and we really look at every fix we've put in because this is our stabilization period. . . . We will continue to take fixes but we'll take fewer fixes because we don't want to destabilize. . . . That's our [ideal] process: feature-complete, no new features, fix as many bugs as possible, tighten down within two weeks, only fix the most significant bugs with the objective of not destabilizing it.

To aid in the stabilization process, development and QA engineers tracked basic bug statistics such as the number of new bugs opened, bug close rates, fix versus invalid rates (some bugs they declare to be invalid or "nonbugs"), won't-fix numbers, and the number of bug fixes verified by QA. Most groups used the commercial Scopus tool for tracking bug data (this also monitored customer calls to technical support) and modified the tool as necessary. Netscape groups identified five categories of bugs—critical, major, normal, minor, and trivial. (The client and server groups followed the same scale, although server groups generally merged the minor and trivial categories.) Engineers (usually from QA) who found the bugs classified them initially and entered them into the database. In the client division, marketing also kept a separate list of its "top 10 bugs" as reported by customers and passed this data over to QA. In the ship-decision meetings at the end of a project, called "certification meetings" in some groups, Tompkins (or his counterparts in the server division) went over these bug statistics and trend lines with senior executives. They debated whether or not the product was ready to go to manufacturing (creation of diskettes or CDs, or certified electronic copies for Web-based distribution). It was usually the case that groups stabilized a release for one platform first (such as Windows or UNIX) and then shipped the versions for the other platforms within a month.

In the last days of a project, the team leaders held bug meetings or bug councils once a day and sometimes twice a day to prioritize bugs and make decisions on what to fix. Earlier in a project, groups tended to have these meetings about once a week after they moved into the development phase. The project or release manager generally led these meetings, which brought together representatives from development, QA, and marketing. Tompkins, who normally only attended the final ship-decision meetings, spoke about adaptations he had made given the faster pace of development at Netscape:

> Speed is very, very important in this market. I'd say my own personal opinion is, I'm adapting to some of the things that are done here that I'm not used to but that I think are good for this company and for this market. . . . I'm changing and also I'm instituting change . . . twice-a-day meetings and the decisions that get made very quickly, the empowerment at the lower levels. . . . I guess one of the areas where I am adapting would be, you go to a meeting, an issue gets raised, and if they can't decide in that meeting, they'll decide to have another meeting as part of that meeting. And it's held and somehow you've got to find out about it if you weren't there. So this is part of where speed is causing me to adapt when, in other companies, if an

issue came up, they would say, "Ok, Mark, you're responsible for setting up a meeting to go discuss this issue." Well, three days later that meeting would get set up. You'd have the right people and you would discuss that issue and you would make a decision. Well, three days went by. At Netscape, they decide in that meeting to have another one. They schedule it and they say get the word out—get the right people there. They have it. They make a decision. Now, if you don't make that meeting, that decision gets made anyway without you. But where I'm adapting is I'm learning how to find out about those meetings and get there, and make those decisions. So it's very, very quick. It almost spins your head on how quick it can be.

The decision making on the final release thus combined a number of factors. There was usually pressure to ship as well as pressure not to ship buggy products. Compared to Microsoft, Netscape managers did not have much historical data such as on expected bug rates or bug trends given certain size systems or likely areas of problems in the code. And, of course, late feature additions got much less testing than features built in the early stages of a project. These problems were common in new software companies, especially those racing on Internet time to get new products and technologies to market.

PRINCIPLE   *Automate as much testing as possible.*

The Debate over Tester-Developer Ratios

Software products need continual testing because developers continuously make changes in their code. This was especially true in companies such as Netscape and Microsoft, where developers had a lot of freedom to respond to user feedback or moves of competitors. Microsoft's strategy was to hire, on average, one tester for every developer so that it could maintain a continuous high level of automated and manual testing.[18] Netscape was at a disadvantage here because of its limited financial resources and the company policy not to hire so many testers. We can see these numbers in Table 5.3. Netscape's two main development divisions in July 1998 had about one tester (QA engineer) for every 2.4 or so developers. Although these numbers were low compared to Microsoft, Netscape had a better ratio in 1998 than the one tester for every four or five developers that the company had in 1994 and 1995. (Individual groups in Netscape might have different ratios. For example, the Mission Control Desktop divlet in the client product division had 15 testers and 11 developers in July 1998.)

Microsoft was unusual in the PC or workstation software industry. It was more common for companies to have one tester for every three, four, or even five developers.[19] Mainframe software divisions in companies like IBM provide even more of a contrast: They might have only one dedicated tester for every 10 or so developers because features and user interfaces change relatively slowly, which makes it possible to automate more testing. Like Netscape, however, Microsoft was also flexible in the tester-to-developer ratios. Some Internet groups started quickly and were slow to find good testers. Instead, they sometimes relied more on outside beta testers for feedback. As project teams ramped up, they generally came close to Microsoft's historical one-to-one ratio. For example, Ben Slivka recalled that IE 1.0 initially had very few testers. By the end of the project, he had six developers, one program manager, and five testers. The total team ended up as 12 people. (Netscape, in contrast, had 10 developers and no more than two dedicated testers on Navigator 1.0.) On some other projects, such as Exchange, Microsoft employed more than one tester per developer in an attempt to move faster and find more bugs. Microsoft also appeared to concentrate more testers on products that were critical to businesses and IT managers. Steve Ballmer, in our January 1998 interview, commented on Microsoft's testing philosophy:

> We probably have close to as many testers as we have developers, and developers probably spend about half their time in testing. So what are we? We're 75 percent a test company. . . . In some groups, I think it's more testers now than developers. And in other groups, I think it's still less. . . . I know it is more than one tester per developer in Exchange. . . . The Internet products are all over the map. The character of IE is quite different from the character of IIS [Internet Information Server]. The character of IIS is quite different from the character of the Commerce product. . . . To be fair, the next release of Office publishes and saves everything in HTML format. So what is an Internet product is a tougher discussion. It's more distinguished by technology as opposed to by audience type. The products which are more interesting to consumers than businesses have a little bit different philosophy than those products which are more interesting to IT managers or developers.

Netscape's Testing Strategy

Netscape managers did have a strategy to counter Microsoft's manpower in testing, and that was to *increase automation*. John Paul, head of the server division, commented in March 1998 on his shortage of QA personnel: "Our QA-engineer ratio is way off. Our automation in the QA side is off. . . . I don't know if the [optimal] ratio is one to one, but clearly automation is your way out of this problem." Mark Tompkins, while head of the client division's QA group, was clear about his strategy in our August 1997 interview: "Essentially, the strategy for QA here at Netscape is automation." Michael Toy, speaking in July 1997, echoed this sentiment. He especially wanted more automated testing as a safety valve for the client developers:

> I would get a stronger focus on automation. . . . Our biggest problem in going so fast is that we don't have time to identify all the dependencies. . . . So what we need is a good rear guard to pick us up when we screw up. And the closer that rear guard is to us, the more efficient we're going to be. . . . The QA organization is growing up like the rest of our organization. When we started out, our QA was one person who had done professional QA and eight people we pulled off of the community college campus who had sat in front of a computer before. And we shipped two releases of software to 20 million people with that as our QA team. . . . We need more testing.

Despite adding many testers after 1995, Netscape executives remained opposed to committing as many bodies to testing as Microsoft did. Rick Schell, when still head of client engineering in July 1997, openly criticized Microsoft's approach as too labor intensive:

> I think that the PC industry norm of one-to-one [testers to developers] is counterproductive. It was based on a very labor-intensive model of people having to do a lot of testing by hand, as well as test development. So you have people who do test development, you have people who do the test plans, you have the people who just do testing. And even though people are automating, it isn't happening as fast as it can. We want to keep the number of people doing testing—actually doing testing—down to the bare minimum. . . . I want to automate everything. So that's a piece of it. You still have to develop tests. But the next thing you've got to do is figure out how to develop test automation. There are techniques for doing that, too. But try to think out-of-the-box on that stuff. . . . The other thing is stop testing the hell out of the products. Don't do it that way. And this is something that we have to get better at, but do more design up front, and do different kinds of development. We're moving to component-based development, so that we can do earlier quality assurance.

Whatever the product, most software QA managers prefer a high degree of automation. Automation is especially useful for rapid judo-type movements and Internet time because it brings, potentially, speed *and* efficiency. This is because manual testing is slow, it requires bodies, and it is not necessarily systematic. The problem that Netscape as well as Microsoft and other PC software companies faced, however, is that test automation is hard to do when product components and user interfaces change so frequently. Writing automated tests also requires QA engineers to have some programming skills to write and revise the automated tests. As a result, Netscape made only limited progress in its strategy during 1997 to 1998 to improve test automation, although the client and server divisions both appeared to improve their testing processes more generally.

Overview of Client Testing

When Mark Tompkins arrived in January 1997 from Tandem Computer, Netscape was finishing the Communicator 4.0 product and still struggling to improve client testing. Client QA was understaffed, and testing was almost entirely manual until the last stages of the project. He recalled in our first meeting in August 1997: "Not much testing was automated. There really was no certification process. We instituted that for the client right away. . . . So I formalized the certification process, focused on automation, and also am focusing more on doing QA earlier on as opposed to just at the backend testing." Tompkins explained the two-part QA process that he was trying to introduce:

> There are essentially two parts—what I call QA upfront and then QA backend. QA upfront is where we bring in programming-skilled people who are in my organization, the QA organization, to sit down, review the designs, review the code, do code coverage analysis, try to design in hooks that will allow testing in the backend to be done in a more automated way. So I essentially have, if you will, two teams. One team that is essentially as skilled as the developers, with the focus of defect removal, defect prevention, whatever you want to call it at the design time. . . . Then, from the standpoint of the backend, which is where we focused mostly on 4.0 . . . that's traditional testing. We came up with a master test strategy which, in the case of 4.0, was we needed to have complete functional tests and we needed to have a quick beta test that was about one week in length. And we needed to have build tests. So we've come up with a strategy on how we're going to pull the project together because there're multiple components. And there're multiple teams, so we need to have a unifying approach to our testing. Then each team, as they are organized, builds its own test plans against the functions that are being developed for that release. We write those test plans. We write the tests. In the past, they have been manual.

With 5.0 and 6.0 [later changed to 4.5 and 5.0], and at the end of 4.0, we started to develop automated tests. So we now have an automation framework that will allow automation to be done for [4.5 and 5.0] pretty much across the board.

The backend QA relied on three types of tests. First was the automated regression, or smoke test, run by the client build team every day as a simple acceptance test. In summer 1997, this test took about an hour to set up and run. It was 100 percent automated in 1998 and included 10 test cases covering basic functions, such as opening up a Web page, or sending and receiving an e-mail message. The test results determined whether or not basic functions in the evolving product worked—whether or not the code, in Tompkins's words, was "dead on arrival."

Second, the client QA team created a set of functional tests designed to exercise all the new features that developers were building as well as carried-over features. Netscape targeted only about 20 percent of these tests for automation in summer 1997 and raised this target to 80 percent a year later, according to Tompkins. The other 20 percent of the tests required some manual exercising of different features in the product, according to scripts usually written in HTML with Navigator Composer. If there were four weeks allotted for testing prior to a beta release, QA might take at least two and as many as three of those weeks to run through all the tests. QA engineers also enhanced the tests for each beta release as well as for final testing.

Third, the client QA team created a special beta-release test that was a subset of the functional tests. QA usually ran this for about one week in order to stabilize the product. The objective was to test more extensively the most critical features planned for the release and repeat these tests quickly as developers added bug fixes. This test suite was also partially manual and time-consuming to set up, though the goal was to automate 100 percent of the beta-release tests for Communicator 5.0. In addition to the test scripts, QA engineers did some unstructured or ad hoc testing to "play around" and see how well features worked. Product management also ran "bug-arama" sessions that simulated novice users trying a new piece of software.

Initially, Tompkins wanted to hire more testers with enough programming skills to write automated test scripts and possibly review code. He was unable to get significant resources to add people. Nonetheless, Tompkins did organize a team of six to seven skilled test engineers, later called the tools and automation group, that worked during 1997 to 1998 on providing automated tests for other testers as well as on tools, metrics, and performance data analysis. Netscape's client division used QA Partner, a commercial product sold by Segue Corporation, as its main automation tool. This provided a framework and scripting language for creating test cases and running them automatically by simulating keystrokes on a keyboard or mouse clicks. In addition, an in-house tool called Beaker served as a repository for the client test cases and their different versions as well as kept track of pass-fail statistics and historical data based on the test results. Tompkins described the division's progress on test automation between August 1997 and July 1998:

> My strategy was to get everyone to start writing automated tests. . . . I had a lot of manual testers who didn't have programming abilities. . . . I wanted to hire programmers to complement the manual testers and I did. But our hiring was very minimal through the months, so I didn't get to hire too many. As a result of not being able to hire enough people with programming skills, I needed to train and use the people I had. And it became obvious to me that, in the environment where we're shipping product all the time, rapidly—beta releases, internal releases, and regular releases—the manual testers were fully consumed at testing. And when I was reviewing status reports, it was becoming obvious to me we're not making progress in the area of automation. It's not a tools problem anymore. . . . The tests weren't getting automated because I tracked the status every week. How many tests do we have, how many are manual, how many are automated? The manual was going up but the automation was not going up. The problem was the investment in time a manual tester would have to make to learn the scripting language. They just couldn't do it. So . . . I turned to my separate department that I had created earlier . . . the tools and automation group . . . and requested their help to accelerate our automation efforts. We set up a system where the manual test groups would put the test descriptions into our test case repository, Beaker. The tools and automation team would then pull them out and start automating them. After automation was complete, they returned the tests to the manual test groups to run and maintain.

QA Partner was useful, especially with a library of test cases, although it was not as effective as some engineers wanted it to be and not all client test engineers used the tool consistently. On the positive side, it ran on different operating systems, which was important for Netscape, though not on all versions of UNIX. On the negative side, the scripting language essentially required programming skills and was not so easy to learn. In addition, the automated test scripts did not work if developers changed the graphical user interfaces without changing the test scripts in parallel.

Therefore, even the automated tests required lots of manual labor to keep updated, and Netscape did not have anywhere near enough manpower. For stable features, however, QA and development could run the automated tests over and over again to make sure changes did not cause bugs in existing functions. Tompkins commented on the limitations and strengths of QA Partner in our July 1998 meeting:

> I wouldn't say there's anything wrong with the tool. What's wrong with the idea of automating tests against a graphical user interface is, when the user interface changes, it breaks. So you've got to go in and maintain your automated tests. The weakness of any and all tools is, the more you change the user interface, the more you've got to maintain the test, and so you have to account for a lot more maintenance. And if you were doing it manually, you might be able to visually look at the difference and do it a little faster. But if you had to do it 10 times over and over, you're going to lose that efficiency.

It was also impossible to automate usability testing, which required manual effort from users in addition to laboratory staff and developers to understand the results of the tests. This type of testing provided early indications of user responses to a product and helped developers make adjustments in their designs during a project, rather than in the next release of a product. It was a major part of the development process in Microsoft, where developers regularly ran their features through usability labs with one-way mirrors and video cameras. The challenge was to see how many novice users hired "off the street" could get the features to work without assistance.[20] Netscape had similar labs but used them less intensively. For example, it was not a regular step for developers to take their features to the labs and try them with novice users, though some developers did this. Rather, Netscape had a separate UI group that mostly used the labs to test the user-interface designs.

Overview of Server Testing

Netscape managed server testing somewhat differently from client testing because of higher reliability requirements as well as a longer history of having dispersed development groups. The server products division divided up server QA engineers by products, with the developers. Then managers broke down the server QA groups further by subsystems or functional areas within each product and, more recently, into functional types of testing. Testers assigned to a particular subsystem or area tested that function for all server versions. Client testing was more centralized, even after a May 1998 reorganization that broke up QA into the several client divlets, because Netscape tested and then shipped Communicator as one product.

As on the client side, Netscape's server QA teams generally were short-handed. Consequently, they had to limit their involvement mostly to what Tompkins called the backend of testing, rather than getting involved much in the design phase, such as by participating in design and code reviews. As in client testing, after server developers mapped out the functionality they expected to build by certain milestones in a project, QA began working on test plans and writing test cases to exercise those features by the estimated completion dates. QA also worked with development to set up criteria for the functional tests.

To compensate for the relatively low number of testers relative to developers, one change that we saw between summer 1997 and summer 1998 was the decision, at least in some groups, to ask developers to do more of their own testing. In particular, unit and functional testing were now the responsibility of at least some developers. In these cases, server QA focused on more intensive system testing in the latter stages of a project as well as managing the field testing or beta testing process. Ben Horowitz described the changes for the Mission Control divlet (which built Directory Server and the shared security components) in our July 1998 interview. He also noted that all new hires went into QA rather than into development:

> We moved unit and functional test responsibility over to development. . . .
> Our ratio of developers to QA was, at its peak, probably four to one or
> something like that, which was too high to accomplish what we wanted
> to accomplish. Now, understand at the same time that, overall, the head-
> count in the company and growth, due to the rapid decline in browser rev-
> enues, had slowed down. We could have reassigned developers to QA.
> That turns out to be a fairly difficult thing to pull off. Generally, people
> quit. We could have said the heck with profitability and just hired a lot of
> QA engineers, although that probably wouldn't have had the greatest
> results. Or, we could have done what we did, which was all new hires were
> QA. So with the growth we had and with the replacement headcount that
> we had, we hired strictly QA and have been doing that for the last three
> quarters, which has made our ratio much better. For example, in the Mes-
> saging divlet, we're at two to one now, and we're improving on that. But
> the other thing that we did, which is probably as significant, is we took the
> bulk of what our QA organization used to do, which is really functional
> and unit tests, and we moved that into development. . . . If you're not hir-
> ing and you've got a 4 to 1 ratio, what do you do?

To make testing in the development stage more efficient and automated, managers in some of the server groups assigned "buddies" to each developer from among the other developers. (These were different from orientation "buddies.") The buddy developers then had the responsibility of writing automated tests for the features that their buddies were developing. This solved the problem of developers not being good testers, at least of their own code. QA also inherited these tests and used them in system testing, along with other tests to "stress" the product. Horowitz explained the new practice in his group:

> Every developer now has a buddy. So, if you develop, for example, a replication code, your buddy will develop an automated test for the basic functions of that code. Both of them are placed in the systems test framework, which the system test engineering has access to and runs. And they use it to do very heavy stress testing and system testing and negative testing and some of the other things that you need a lot more sophistication to do. . . . They don't test their own code but they test their buddy's code. . . . This does a couple of things. One, it develops an automated suite without either reassigning developers to QA . . . or hiring, tripling the size of the QA organization. . . . The other thing is that the development engineers are a very tight peer group, so it has made them much more conscious of quality in that their peers are now writing the automated suites for their code. Passing those tests becomes very important. . . . What QA or what we call systems test engineering gets now is much, much higher quality than it was in the past.

The various server development groups also had their own build teams that ran an automated acceptance test on the builds to check basic functionality. As in the client area, QA engineers built the tests, and the build teams were responsible for running them. If the build worked, developers were free to download the code. If the build failed, a red light went off and developers who had just checked in code got e-mail notices via the CVS/Tinderbox system. Netscape also seemed to be increasing the thoroughness of this testing. For example, to test the Enterprise Server, in July 1997, the acceptance test had about 800 test scripts and took 20 minutes to run and about twice this long to set up. To test Directory Server and various security components, as of July 1998, the build acceptance test had several times this number of test cases and took several hours to run.

Because of the high reliability requirements, the server QA teams generally took one of the builds done during the week and ran a more extensive set of automated tests on the code. The Enterprise Server group called the result its "weekly QA build" and put this together either on a Tuesday or Thursday morning. This weekly QA build test in July 1997 had about 3,000 test cases and took an hour to run and two hours to set up (a somewhat tedious manual process that was more automated in 1998). Finally, QA teams ran an extensive set of system tests before shipping a product. These tests usually took about three days to set up and run. The key objective here was to simulate thousands of users and millions of database "hits."

Server groups automated the build acceptance tests but still used some manual testing for the functional and system tests. According to Horowitz, in 1998 about 70 percent of the functional tests and a lower percentage of the system tests were automated. QA engineers in the server division usually had programming skills and they wrote and ran their own tests (in contrast to the client division). The server QA groups, therefore, did not have separate teams to write automated tests, though some testers specialized in automation tasks. To write the automated tests, some engineers were using an automated framework tool called TET, which came from the Open Software Foundation. This tool was better suited to testing protocols and APIs than QA Partner, which the client groups used. Server testers did use QA Partner for UI testing and wrote other test cases from scratch in C, Java, the Python scripting language for UNIX, and Perl for CGI (Common Gateway Interface) scripts.

The Illusive Goal of Test Automation

The above overviews indicate that Netscape was only partially successful in implementing its goal of test automation. A lot of the testing and stabilization work remained manual, and it was likely to require lots of people for many years to come. We might even say that complete test automation in software is another rocket science–type of idea: great in theory, important to pursue as far as possible, but hard to do completely.

In large part, necessity rather than theory drove Netscape's strategy of test automation: Most groups chose to allocate scarce engineering dollars in favor of hiring developers. This decision made sense strategically in the first two years or so, but not when Netscape pursued the enterprise market. Managers were left to find a way out of this problem. As Netscape managers found out, however, the test automation strategy still required lots of investment in people to create and update the automated tests. Netscape did not allocate enough people to QA in order to be a leader among PC software companies in test automation. (Ironically, by virtue of having so many testing personnel to do both manual testing and write automated test suites, Microsoft seemed far more advanced in applying automated tests, such as the quick regression tests that developers ran on their code before checking into the project builds.)

To be fair to Netscape and, especially, to its client division, automating a large part of the regression testing for relatively mature consumer products such as Microsoft Office or operating systems and servers in their Nth versions was easier than automating testing for new features or constantly changing user interfaces in the client. Systems and server software components mostly talked to other pieces of software and communicated through standard protocols and interfaces. The user interfaces were relatively simple and did not change as frequently. It was, though, *very* difficult to automate the network setup for testing servers or networked operating systems. As a result, even server and operating systems testing continued to depend on people.

The nearly infinite number of potential combinations of usage patterns, software applications, and hardware platforms, and the unpredictability of user behavior with new products and features, were the reasons why Microsoft relied so heavily on manual testing (both structured and unstructured) as well as automated testing and other techniques also used at Netscape, such as beta releases and internal usage of products before commercial release.[21] And, despite its investments and obvious progress in quality, Microsoft still struggled to eliminate bugs and get products out when promised, at least in part because teams continually changed product designs until the last days of a project. The bottom line: Automated testing did not fully substitute for bodies in testing. Tompkins, speaking in our August 1997 interview, felt he could *never* have enough QA people:

> There's never been enough QA. I think you can always have more QA and, at some point in time, you have to make a business decision on how much resource you have. . . . I would agree there wasn't enough QA to do everything that we wanted to do. And I'm not sure that statement will ever change. . . . You could build quality upfront where you don't need to test as many of the areas because, supposedly, they are defect free or have fewer defects. But . . . I would say there wasn't enough QA. And, if you came back a year from now, I would probably say the same thing.

We did come back a year later and Tompkins did say the same thing. He complained that he *had not* received significant more dollars to hire QA people. Testers in 1998 still felt overworked because they had to test so many beta and point releases for so many different platforms and they didn't have time to upgrade their skills, such as to learn automation techniques. Tompkins updated us in our July 1998 meeting:

> There're 21 operating systems that we try to test and that we release on. And in my previous company, the [tester to developer] ratio was one to three for one operating system. It seems really interesting that we're about . . . one to two and a half, depending on how you round, almost one to three, and yet we're testing 21 releases. That makes it real difficult. And especially the fact that we are doing a lot of manual testing still instead of automated testing makes it tough. I think that's one reason that a lot of people work a lot of hours, long hours. They work hard here. There is no nine-to-five attitude here at all. I think that's because the workload is just so great that there's no way you could ever do that. So my feeling on ratios is, I don't know exactly how to calculate them. All I can say is, do we, the QA folks and the QA management team, feel that we're doing the job or that we really are satisfied? And the answer is no because we're working harder than we think we should be working. . . . The manual testers had no time to learn automation skills, and they'd like to do that. So that kind of gives you the indication that we're probably understaffed according to the things that we'd like to do.

PRINCIPLE *Use beta testing, internal product usage, and other measures to improve product and process quality.*

In addition to formal testing, Netscape, again like Microsoft, took full advantage of different methods to find bugs in products as well as to learn about how to improve product features and development processes. One area stands out: Netscape's use of beta testing over the Internet (although this also had limitations). In addition, Netscape employees made extensive use of products internally (a practice they called "eating your own dog food," which Microsoft has also been doing for years). Netscape employees also learned from customer-calls data and project postmortems and was making some progress in capturing good practices and incorporating these into training and knowledge sharing for new testers.

Netscape's Beta Testing Revolution

As we discussed in chapter 2, Netscape probably revolutionized the use of beta testing with its early Navigator products. Software producers have used beta testing or field testing of their products in some form since the beginning of the computer industry. Beta tests are important because actual users will find bugs or design problems that testers in a laboratory or software company employees cannot find because they are not average users. But Netscape took the concept a step further. It released betas extremely frequently in its early years and took full advantage of the Internet as a mechanism to deliver these betas at the rate of between 100,000 and 200,000 a day by 1997. The delivery and the user feedback both were nearly instantaneous because of the electronic nature of the Internet.

Before the Internet, most software companies shipped betas in a time-consuming process of producing and then distributing computer tapes, diskettes, or CD-ROMs. To avoid duplicating this expense too often, companies would usually wait until the product was feature-complete and tested thoroughly in-house. One or two beta releases provided additional real-life feedback before the final commercial release. It is true that, in the PC industry, some Microsoft groups released frequent and early betas before the arrival of the World Wide Web, such as for MS-DOS and Windows NT during 1992 to 1994. Microsoft sent out diskettes by mail and used CompuServe connections for electronic feedback. But the time and expense of the old beta process led even Microsoft to limit its beta releases to small numbers of people, though these numbers had increased significantly by 1995. (Beta users rose from 7,000 on MS-DOS 6.0 to 400,000 for Windows 95.)[22] Alex Edelstein compared the philosophy toward beta releases that he saw while in the Microsoft Exchange group during the early 1990s versus the practices at Netscape in 1997:

> Microsoft, I think, still has a culture of, "You have to have the product mostly done by the time you go into beta." We really felt that beta was like, once you've completely internally tested it, then you can put it into beta, whereas Netscape from day one really saw the beta process as this interactive thing. We throw stuff out there that [Microsoft] never would have put out there. And we [Netscape] are also much more relaxed about changing stuff once it's there. Microsoft, I think, over time has become somewhat scarred and somewhat cognizant of all the customers it has to please. It's a little more reluctant to do massive changes of things because, when it does change things, it tends to catch a lot of flak.

We found Netscape customers who did not feel the company handled the beta process very well, especially in the early days. Some customers complained that Netscape had *too many* releases, which frustrated users who wanted more stable products. Netscape did not appear to have enough people and processes to digest the flood of responses and suggestions, and it did not always do a good job producing patches or bug fixes. Lots of beta releases also brought lots of attention, and this was both good and bad. Dave Stryker stated the problem simply: "We're always in the spotlight because we're always in beta test." Nonetheless, in developing the Navigator and Communicator products, Netscape's frequent and early release of betas provided useful feedback not only on bugs but also on designs and usability. In other words, the betas were early enough to influence developers' design decisions during a project, rather than just accumulating information to fix bugs for the final release and perhaps influence concepts for the next version of the product. Lou Montulli spoke about the benefits of the short and frequent beta cycles:

> Our beta cycles are a couple of weeks long. That's unheard of. We get amazing amounts of feedback from millions of people and shake out all these bugs very quickly and turn it around. . . . We accept these schedules where we ought to be feature-complete, and we just keep adding more features because they're interesting things to do. . . . So we've never had a beta where we've reached feature-complete. We've added major features after the last beta. . . . I don't think that's necessarily bad. I don't know that we could keep our rapid pace of change if that wasn't the case because, when you go into a beta cycle, you typically have areas of downtime for engineers because bug fixing is not a full-time activity.

Montulli also described how developers used beta releases, e-mail, and newsgroups to interact with large numbers of customers quickly. He even preferred this mode of communication to "human contact":

> It happens through the miracle of the Internet here. Ever since the beginning, we release our betas out on the Net and then our forums are direct e-mail. A large part of it is Usenet News. There're these Internet newsgroups people are posting to. We read those and we find out bugs that way. We find out what people are irked by or really like about the product. You can tell the positive or negative feedback of a particular feature by how long the thread lasts. If it's 50 or 60 messages, you know somebody really cares a lot about it. And you go read them. Everyone has an issue with something. We understand that; you're never going to make everyone happy. But you can see the issues play out through the discussions of other people. You can also figure out things that you might not have thought. . . . Our technical support people actually meet with physical companies, but our engineers here are almost entirely Web-based communication and it's much more efficient than human contact in general.

Microsoft distributed a much smaller percentage of its products over the Internet because of its enormous OEM sales through computer hardware vendors. Nonetheless, Microsoft adapted its practices to the Internet and, since the arrival of Internet Explorer, it has released beta versions earlier than it once did. For complex products such as Exchange, however, some managers preferred to bring customers in to Microsoft to help in designing features, finding bugs, and providing direct feedback on usability *before* the beta release process started. Netscape was doing some of this, too—bringing customers in to help design and test, as well as testing complex products such as servers in the field before or in place of broader public betas. Edelstein reflected on the gradual convergence in practices at the two companies:

> [Microsoft] adapted to these newer techniques, and now they put stuff out there much earlier than they would normally have. I still think that, if you really put the products side by side, they work longer on it internally, do more internal testing, before they're willing to go beta. They try to make up for that by bringing in the customer separately, by spending the money to fly the customers in and show them stuff before it goes into beta. We find it more efficient to kind of blast it out to the world, although there's more convergence than divergence. We, too, have begun councils where we bring in top customers and focus on that, whereas, in the very first version, we just didn't have anyone to do that. We would just put the beta out there and see what happened. Now, there are factions within Netscape that pay attention to the top direct sales accounts, and there are factions that pay attention to the needs of the value-added resellers. So there are people to take better care of specific segments of customers. We're starting to look more like Microsoft. At the same time, they're trying to evolve to be like us.

Diminishing Returns of Too Many Beta Releases

Managers at both Netscape and Microsoft also recognized that there were diminishing returns in beta testing. Microsoft's Steve Ballmer, who once managed the Windows beta releases, told us in January 1998 that he was not a big fan of beta releases: "Beta testers don't turn in a high percentage—never have—of the problems and bugs that we find preship." Ballmer's claim seemed particularly true for products like operating systems and servers, which companies had to deploy on their networks to create a real-life testing environment. In contrast, individuals could test applications like browsers or word-processing programs and not have to worry about hundreds or thousands of people being inconvenienced if the beta product crashed.

It may be the case that Netscape overdid the betas in its early years and should have focused on producing fewer and more stable releases of its products. We can see the extremely high frequency of beta releases in the first few Navigator and Communicator products. As illustrated earlier in Figure 5.1, Navigator 3.0 had six beta releases—about one a month. This was typical of the client products through Communicator 4.0. Development plans after 4.0 reduced the planned number of client betas to no more than three. Debby Meredith spoke about the decision to cut down in our July 1997 interview: "With 4.0, I think we had six public betas. We're kind of thinking that's a bit much. We think probably three real betas and maybe a verification beta might be the right way to go." Mark Tompkins, speaking in August 1997 about Communicator 4.0, explained why he disliked having too many betas:

> About March or April, when I was into my third or fourth beta, I went to the project lead and I said, "Why are we doing so many betas?" There's a set of fixed costs whenever you release something, right? And I think we've decided that maybe it's been two too many and we can optimize. We will always have a beta process because we find that very valuable to get our product out into the hands of users. But I don't know if we need as many. It's the fixed cost. . . . All the testing of all the builds that has to be done. All the documentation that has to be done in support of the beta. All the resources that are brought to bear to put a public release on the FTP site. A project manager has to be involved, marketing has to be involved, they have to put announcements on our Web site. There's just a tremendous cost involved in doing this. I think that cost is okay in a fewer amount. We have a good return on investment for the right amount of betas. And my gut says three is probably the right amount instead of five, or six, or seven.

The effort required to put out so many betas was not worth it, in Tompkins's view, because he agreed with Steve Ballmer that beta users found only a limited number of problems. On the other hand, he did feel that early beta releases were good public relations and effective rallying points for the development team. Tompkins commented in July 1998:

> The QA people are going to be killed because of all those releases going on simultaneously. . . . Because you're trying to test the browser in 4.5, you're trying to test early browser stuff in 5.0, and you've got 4.06 or 4.07, so you may have three simultaneous releases or three releases that are very close to each other. You've got to have a breather once in a while, and there is none. And that's for development as well. . . . So, even though they're spreading out the big releases, there's still a lot of parallel activity going on that's pretty hard on some of the folks. . . . [Betas] don't augment [testing] as much as I think we'd like them to. And, I think it's because, if I go back and look at the

problems that are found by the people who are using it, by the time they find it, we already know about them. . . . [But] it's good PR as far as what's happening. It shows reality in our product development schedules. It is a way of rallying a milestone, getting all the troops to move forward toward a certain release date. I think that's valuable as far as the process goes.

With the release of the Communicator 4.5 beta in July 1998, we did see a change in process at Netscape that leveraged the Internet technology and should make beta testing more effective. With the 4.5 beta, Netscape decided to include a new tool that it licensed from Full Circle Software, Inc., called Full Circle Talkback. (Other companies, including Microsoft with Windows NT, have also adopted this or similar tools for their beta products.) When the beta version crashed, the tool automatically captured system data at that exact point in the form of a "black box" report. If the user agreed, Talkback automatically sent the data back to Netscape. Users could add their own comments as well to the report. Netscape data in July 1998 indicated that between 10,000 and 13,000 beta users a day were activating the tool. The client product marketing group, led by Todd Goldman, a veteran of Hewlett-Packard and IBM, collected the data and transferred it (manually) to the Bug Splat database used by the QA team. Goldman gave us this commentary on Talkback, along with a demo:

> You can see the numbers going up and that's because you're getting more and more people running it. . . . We know there's this crash on exit all the time that seems to be happening. So there's a number of different reports. What Talkback does is it collects these black boxes that come in, it analyzes them, and it categorizes them. So it can, by looking at the stack signature, analyze that signature and determine whether a problem from one person is the same problem as another person. . . . What we're doing is we're turning all these into Bug Splat bugs. So the engineers actually go off and fix these. And so in the next version of beta, we're going to go back and take a look and make sure that these aren't happening again, and that, hopefully, we have a different set of problems that are occurring. The count number should, by the time we get to beta 2, be down in the hundreds number. And each time we should be driving that number down to the point where it becomes statistically insignificant for us.

The use of betas on the server side in Netscape was more restrained, again, because of the higher reliability requirements for these products. John Paul believed in working closely with a select group of customers to test new products in the field, rather than investing too heavily in internal testing or putting out public beta releases too early. As a result, the server division was placing more emphasis on limited betas or field tests that resembled acceptance tests. In our July 1998 interview, Ben Horowitz described the change in process:

> We used to do something called a "public beta," which is similar to what we did on a client—basically, put the servers on the Net and have people download them. What we found from early experiences is that, for servers, we got very little useful feedback from public betas. So we shifted from the public beta model to something that we call a "field test." The way the field test works is we start off with an internal deployment, and that happens sometimes before the first functionally complete beta, where we deploy it inside Netscape. We're now 2,400 or 2,500 employees, so that turns out to be a pretty interesting real-world test. Once we get through a system test and internal deployment, we move out to about 10 to 15 very committed betas . . . companies [that] have committed to testing a product. We send engineers on site to help them get up and running with it, and we are much more extensive in the field test. These tests in the field tend not to be like ours in that they're not on production systems for the most part because, with Web servers . . . [and especially] things like Directory, people aren't generally willing to go production off of beta. But they do conduct very heavy acceptance testing of it and they simulate their environment, so they do a pretty robust pilot. We go through a couple of iterations of that field test.

Feedback from Using Company Products Internally

The most obvious and rapid source of feedback and new ideas that Netscape employees got on their own products was from using them in-house before and after releasing them to the public. We saw many examples where Netscape people had beta versions of new products running while we visited them in their offices. Lou Montulli pointed this out: "All of our servers here are Netscape servers. We put the betas up immediately and everyone here is using betas of the client. So we're all using beta software. Eat our own dog food, so to speak. Get things going, make sure there's not a problem." Using products internally also aided beta testing, beginning with the first internal releases. This was true for servers as well as for the client and other applications. Debby Meredith talked about the client product: "Internally, our IS department doesn't roll it out to the whole corporation until we ship. They are just like a customer. But development has development servers where we post internal builds and people typically jump all over those internal builds." Bill Turpin gave an example of the Enterprise 4.0 server, which he was using while it was still in beta release:

> I'll install betas on my machine. Engineering is obviously running even more raw things than that. Our Enterprise 4.0 project, which isn't scheduled to ship for a long time, is already running the Enterprise 4 server on their home page. . . . They've got their own proof of concept running there. Our e-mail team uses the Messaging Server just as soon as it is available. So we have a philosophy of we eat our own dog food. We're committed to using our servers before we ship them to our customers. And that is particularly true with our Messaging Server. A lot of people view messaging as a mission-critical thing, so they are not going to take one of our beta servers and install it. They want a finished server. We find that, if we don't use it ourselves, there are not a whole lot of people who will use it in a production environment. So we switch over and run them in production here before we ship the final bits.

Then there were tools that we described earlier—such as Tinderbox and Bonsai for managing source code and the build process (which used dynamic e-mail lists and HTML pages, accessed through browsers and running on Web servers), or the server division's project tracking system (which used Web agents). These are all relatively simple illustrations of how to use the Web technology. David Stryker added this observation about Tinderbox as a Web application: "Tinderbox . . . is a wonderful thing. It's an example of how this Internet technology is revolutionizing people's thoughts about application building. . . . This phrase 'eating your own dog food.' It's not just that, obviously, we use browsers and our own e-mail and our own servers all the time. It's things like Tinderbox, where the technique we use to solve our problems is based in a really deep way on the technology we're providing to our customers to solve problems."

The other major area where Netscape learned from the technology it was creating was in its internal information systems. We noted in chapter 2 that one of the principles Jim Barksdale and other executives followed in scaling up Netscape was to create an infrastructure that would not hinder the growth of the company. Much of that infrastructure depended on information technology. Netscape experimented with and introduced state-of-the-art systems. Larry Geisel was the senior VP in charge of information systems when we met in August 1997. He spoke about Netscape's position at the "bleeding edge" of the technology:

> One of the advantages in having a CEO who was previously a CIO [Chief Information Officer] is they appreciate the value of information technology

to growing the business. . . . If we're all about moving the company forward at Net speed, I kind of feel like the minister of transportation. I'm trying to build the infrastructure to help us get there. And in a software company, it's particularly acute because you have so many opportunities to take advantage of IT. . . . But to try to go from zero to a half-billion-dollar-a-year run rate in two-years-plus and try to position yourself such that your own infrastructure is never an obstacle to growth is yet a whole other issue. . . . We're right on the bleeding edge. . . . We are customer zero. We're the alpha test site. We deploy everything we build internally before we foist it on our customers. . . . So, in that sense, we're almost an extension of product development. . . . Nobody knew the fact that I was running a handful of my Web site servers on SuiteSpot 3.0 before it was out there and that's the reason why it was a good solid product when it came out the door. We really worked it over hard.

Netscape also made extensive use of its own technology in company intranets. In our first interview with her, Debby Meredith boasted that, "We have one of the biggest corporate intranets." And as far as we could see, Netscape did. The company had placed as many of its internal systems as possible on intranets, rather than using conventional paper documents and filing cabinets. For example, Mike Major, director of HR operations, stated this objective in our July 1997 interview: "Our longer term goal is to get to a totally paperless self-serve HR environment worldwide. It will take us a while to get there, so what we've been doing is phasing into that." Most HRM systems (compensation information, benefits checklist and registration, new employee information, job descriptions, employee surveys, interviewing guidelines) were on intranet sites. Netscape also used digital signatures in place of passwords for some systems to control employee access.

We saw other intranet examples as well. Marketing, engineering, QA, and customer support all had Web sites posting information that each group frequently accessed. Meredith explained: "We use all our products to run our business. We've got a Web site set up for every project where the marketing information is there, the engineering schedules, the specs, the results of the usability tests, a big hyperlink document if you will, with all the information, and then down to who does what." Julie Herendeen found the intranet postings useful to understand what groups outside of her department (client product marketing) were doing:

Everything gets posted on internal Web sites. My group builds its own Web site, where we post all of our information about the products. So we definitely use the technology and it does facilitate the communication, particularly when you're growing so rapidly. I'm constantly thinking, "God, what are those people doing?" They're over in this other building now, and they're doing one thing with administration, and I'm doing another. And I'll check on the Web site, and I can get a pretty good snapshot in terms of where they are.

Netscape also used intranets and Web agents to coordinate across the client and server teams. This coordination was becoming increasingly important as the company tried to leverage and tie together different features in its products as well as sell bundles to intranet, extranet, and electronic commerce customers. Netscape made extensive and growing use, as well, of extranets to service customers and partners. As we explained in chapter 2, these are like intranets in that they use the basic Internet protocols and browser-server-Web-page structure. Rather than allowing access only to people within an organization, however, the extranets provide a secure connection from the inside to certain outside customers or partners. The secure connection then makes it possible for outsiders to access product information (specifications, price lists, bug lists, case studies, product update information, evaluation forms) as well as technical information (such as for product support or electronic help) and actual products (downloads of daily builds, beta releases, QA patches, new product versions, feature updates, and the like).

Netscape called the extranet for customers and partners "Netscape Insight." This had about 6,000 users in mid-1998, including 200 to 300 members who purchased Netscape's premium support package and got special access privileges as a result. Netscape called the extranet for software developers "DevEdge OnLine." This had about 50,000 users. The Netscape staff that ran these two systems consisted of about 20 people in marketing and three to four in engineering. The most important components that Netscape used in the extranets were its own Internet directory (Lightweight Directory Access Protocol, or LDAP) and security technology (Secure Sockets Layer, or SSL). These two technologies, in combination with Netscape servers and applications, allowed the company to create and manage access to a secure network for customers. Larry Geisel commented on Netscape's use of its own products and technologies:

We're providing the container, the vehicle, including the secure encrypted delivery of content outside the firewall, with dynamic updates. . . . These kinds of things don't make sense to the general public but, for a select clientele, you want to open up a lot more of what you have inside externally. To help do that, we're using our own products index, our intranet assets, originally a Catalog Server and now a beta version of the new

Compass [Server], which includes some intelligent agents, and, of course, all of our other various push mechanisms, in part based on the Marimba technology and part based on Inbox Direct. There are some unique features, which we generally label under universal registration. It means, once you register with us and you establish a digital certification, we know who you are. We can now send you encrypted information with very simplified sign up for a variety of services. . . . We're making available to a secure pipe access to select information internally, which we're managing via an LDAP directory using digital certs encryption and this universal registration notion to bind it all together.

Netscape's new Web site, Netcenter, was another example of how the company has been trying to leverage technologies developed in-house in other operations and in other parts of the business. In this case, Netscape's Netcenter affected more than customer service and the marketing of the company image. As we discussed in chapters 2 and 3, Netcenter has also become an essential mechanism to generate new revenues. Netscape was using the Web site to offer a variety of products and services with a growing number of partners, such as Excite, which managed significant portions of Netcenter's content and advertising. In addition, Netscape had extended certain features in the browser and tied these to Netcenter as a way to draw more "eyeballs" to its Web site and to keep more people using new versions of Navigator or Communicator.

Other Product and Process Improvement Initiatives

In addition to the product redesign efforts we described in chapter 4, another way to improve products was to capture and analyze information from customers outside of the beta or field tests. We saw Netscape doing this in several ways. One was through customer support's call tracking system. (This was similar to the process used at Microsoft and many other first-tier software companies.) In 1997, according to Bill Gargiulo, then the head of North American customer support, Netscape received about 90,000 phone calls a month, or about 350,000 calls per quarter. These were in addition to about 25 million "hits" per quarter on Netscape's Help Web site and 3 million hits on the KnowledgeBase site. The number of calls was relatively few given the fact that Netscape had perhaps 70 million customers. (Microsoft, by comparison, if we extrapolate from daily numbers, had about 600,000 phone calls to customer support each month in 1995 as well as 5 million electronic queries per quarter. Microsoft supported some 200 products, however, and had several times more customers than Netscape had.)[23]

The phone calls reflected some continuing problems with Netscape products, but they also constituted an enormous database on potential areas to improve. And, in fact, Netscape had a relatively sophisticated process in place to do just that. Customer support used the Scopus tool to classify incoming phone calls by product, customer, and severity of the problem. Periodically, support staff summarized the data and sent it over to engineering. Bugs found through tech support then went into engineering's bug-tracking systems. Development and QA engineers used the data to help them make decisions on what bugs or design issues to work on in the current project or the next release. In late spring 1997, Netscape also instituted a system whereby engineering had a set number of hours to respond to problems sent over from customer support, depending on the customer and the severity of the problem.

Netscape used other processes to capture different kinds of information from customers. For example, customer support organized Internet newsgroups through which customers could send in requests for enhancements or new features. Netscape also had a small team of product specialists (approximately eight) assigned to the product teams from customer support. They analyzed this data and worked with engineers from the design phase through beta and commercial release of the product on what issues to deal with in the current project and in the next release. Special extranet connections to customers and developers provided another means of detailed feedback.

On the process side, an important way to improve techniques was to have product team members from marketing, development, and QA review what went well in a project, what went poorly, and what they should do next time. Most software companies that went through this type of three-step self-critiquing exercise called the result a "postmortem." Some companies even wrote and circulated formal reports. Microsoft, which was a leader in this kind of activity, had product teams that began writing postmortem reports in 1986. These self-critiques were essential to formulating the synchronize-and-stabilize approach and other process improvements.[24]

Netscape teams also adopted the practice of doing postmortems, even though the company was so new and focused on getting innovative products to market. Julie Herendeen claimed that the client team started doing postmortems, led by the engineers, around June 1995, shortly after she joined Netscape. She described the output: "It results in a written document that's usually sent around via e-mail. Usually the outcome of it is the summary of the pluses and the minuses that the team went through in the course of development, and then also objectives for what we need to change or what we need to do differently in the next generation." Not everyone was enthusiastic, however. Aleks Totic, for example, found post-mortems useful to reflect on the process but not so useful when people were tired after just shipping a product: "You just want to go on vacation instead." Mark Tompkins, however, practically glowed when we asked about postmortems in our August 1997 interview:

> We just did a postmortem to go through some of the things on how we can get better. This is one thing I like about Netscape. They're a three-year-old company, but they're interested in improving from their previous experiences. We just had a postmortem. I wasn't even sure they'd do those kinds of things at Netscape, but they do. Talked about tighter specs, tighter feature-complete dates, better scheduling, scheduling the most critical items to be done first so that if you have to cut, cut the least critical items at the end. So we're learning how to improve our processes, and I'd say we're learning rapidly. The state of change here is just incredible.

We found that at least some of Netscape's server groups did post-mortems as well. According to Tim Howes, these exercises also focused on "what went right or what went wrong and what we need to improve upon." Rather than written reports, as in Microsoft or Netscape's client division, the server groups held meetings and circulated notes by e-mail.

In general, though, process was less important at Netscape than delivering products quickly. The development groups had no specific rules such as to define development practices, coding styles, frequency or mode of design and code reviews, or what tools to use. The company objective was to maintain flexibility and enhance speed and efficiency when possible. A quality process in the classic software engineering sense (such as standardized good practices and tight controls on designs and changes, with every design and piece of code carefully reviewed in formal meetings)[25] was a secondary, though gradually rising, consideration. Debby Meredith gave this response when we asked if Netscape had a written set of steps that developers were supposed to follow in development:

> We're thinking about it. But we don't—and that is what I think is part of what keeps us flexible. There's no book. We were joking because IBM has something called the Red Book. It's all the steps that you have to do to get a project approved or moved from here to there. It's pretty much the amalgamation of everything that went wrong in all IBM projects and a remedy

like, "Oops, we didn't have resources at the right time. So what's a cure? To do that? Let's add that to the book." We're much more nimble. . . . We do the code reviews. But it's not formalized, like, all code has to go through this process. . . . And we do classic software engineering stuff. At the tail end of a project, any check-in that's made to the source tree . . . in the last couple of weeks of the process . . . gets reviewed by one or two people. So you have to, before you check in your code, have someone review it, and you try to pick someone who would be a tough reviewer of your area. Fixing a bug is good, but introducing three at that time is not the right thing to be doing.

Besides lacking standard processes, most groups had few or only brief architectural documents to help newcomers along; managers expected new hires to jump in and work. Mittelhauser described what new developers faced: "Throw them on the fire. It's one of our problems. Somebody coming in is just handed this chunk of spaghetti code and is expected to solve it. There's really nothing. It's word of mouth." This lack of process was not unusual in PC software companies, where product designs changed frequently. But it became a problem in the client area after Netscape developers wrote the early Navigator products quickly and did not structure the code very well. Newer groups in the client division, like the mail and news teams, tended to have more structure and formalism. The browser group, however, remained quite informal, since most of the senior developers were old friends and had worked together for years.

Testing was an area where companies could accumulate a lot of knowledge to share, such as in the form of written guidelines or checklists. Prior to the fall of 1997, however, neither the client nor the server division spent much time developing these kinds of testing aids or formally training new people. Managers for the different testing areas simply gave new hires suggestions on what they needed to learn and what intranet or Internet links to use for particular information. Netscape did, however, assign mentors or buddies to each new tester (which Microsoft did as well for all developers, testers, program managers, and product managers). The buddies helped newcomers with basics like learning the terminology used in the different groups (such as what an "acceptance test" meant or what a "release candidate" was). In addition, the testing groups circulated test plan templates.

For the most part, Netscape got by with very informal practices because it hired a lot of experienced engineers. Orientation, training, and knowledge sharing depended heavily on the individual manager. Mark

Tompkins worked particularly hard in the client area trying to upgrade his division's testing practices. He gave us this update in July 1998:

> We put together QA processes and we put together QA templates. So we were starting to systematize how QA was done at Netscape based on my previous experience with other companies. . . . Instead of creating a document like we would have done at other companies, we actually created HTML online information, which you could click to and then read the text of how to do QA within Client. What are the build processes, what's a build acceptance test and why do we do it, how do you write a test plan, why do you write a test plan? And then if you want to write a test plan, click on this link and you'll get a template that describes what one should look like. So that was a concerted effort. . . . I had a group of 50 and I pulled various people out of those groups and formed little mini-work-groups to put that together. . . . The templates were done roughly in the August/September [1997] time frame. The process document wasn't done until about March [1998].

Overall, we cannot say that Netscape was unique or particularly refined in its development practices. We can say that the company was effective and efficient, despite or perhaps because of its informality and occasional lack of discipline. Netscape's product teams did what they had to do in order to deliver complex software products and services to new markets. They were flexible as well as fast and innovative when these characteristics were important to success, and they paid more attention to quality when this became a more important goal for enterprise customers.

As one of the very first Internet software companies, Netscape also provides an opportunity to reflect on the difficulties of developing software on Internet time. We learned, for example, that a Microsoft-style synchronize-and-stabilize process worked well for the Internet's very fast cycle times. This development approach, aided by some homegrown tools, gave Netscape (and Microsoft) engineers an effective mechanism to coordinate large numbers of people and still retain the nimbleness of small teams. It also provided great flexibility in controlling design changes even during the latter stages of a project. Netscape's loose attitude toward project milestones such as feature-complete and beta deadlines provided flexibility when changing features or project goals.

We also saw that flexibility had some costs: Being "slightly out of control" strained testers and the testing process, and probably strained technical support and customer patience as well. More progress in test automation, a major goal of the company in 1997 and 1998, could provide Netscape engineers with more flexibility and speed, as well as efficiency, in the future. It is apparent, though, that the goal of complete test automation was illusive because automation required lots of bodies to write and rewrite tests. Netscape probably made the biggest mark on software development strategy with its early and frequent use of beta releases, which it distributed to millions of users electronically over the Internet. We learned, however, that beta releases also had a cost in terms of testing and preparation, and that too many were not so valuable because of diminishing returns in the number of new bugs identified from the later tests. In chapter 6, the conclusion to this book, we reflect more broadly on these and other lessons from Netscape's experiences as well as from the continuing battle with Microsoft.

Chapter Six

COMPETING
ON INTERNET TIME
Lessons from Netscape and Microsoft

NETSCAPE BROUGHT the concept of *competing* on Internet time to life. In the 18 months following its birth, Netscape introduced new products and technologies at breathtaking speeds. After Microsoft joined the race at the end of 1995, both companies began refining the principles for *winning* on Internet time. Neither has been completely successful; both companies have done many things right and some things wrong. Yet together, they have redefined the nature of competition for the Internet age.

Both Netscape and Microsoft have changed dramatically over the past four years. When Jim Clark and Marc Andreessen started Netscape, it quickly emerged as *the* browser company. In rapid succession, Netscape developed into an intranet company, an extranet company, and, finally, an enterprise software and Web portal company. By the middle of 1998, Netscape had built a half-billion-dollar software business that bore little resemblance to the start-up of 1994. Similarly, Microsoft supposedly ignored the Internet for too long and seemed like a dinosaur to many industry observers in the fall of 1995. In three short years, Microsoft grabbed half the browser market from Netscape, integrated Internet technology into nearly all its products, and evolved into one of the kings of the World Wide Web. Microsoft has become so successful, so feared, and so dominating in this new arena that the Department of Justice has felt compelled to try to slow Microsoft down.

Netscape and Microsoft have been making extraordinary changes with extraordinary speed. We believe that both companies will continue to compete and live on Internet time for the foreseeable future. In the "old" pre-Internet world, PC software companies had the luxury of 24- to 36-

month development cycles for major products like operating systems. (This was still at least twice as fast as IBM had previously replaced its mainframe operating systems.) Microsoft, for example, delivered a new version of Windows roughly every three years. In the more "mature" segments of the Internet market, such as browsers and Web servers, where release cycles have begun to slow, Netscape and Microsoft planned to introduce new products roughly every 18 months. But in emerging fields, such as electronic commerce and Web portal sites, competing on Internet time continued to demand significant product and feature changes every three to six months.

We believe that firms operating in Internet markets will face a similar mix of maturing product cycles and emerging growth cycles as we enter the next millenium. The Internet has come a long way since 1993, but we are still in the early phases of its evolution. Consider the implications of growing communications capacity and exploding processing power. The opportunities to do new things on the Internet will multiply again as more broadband capabilities appear over the next decade. Today, most consumers still use relatively slow telephone modems to connect to the Internet. Yet new options, such as superfast cable modems and new telephone connections (xDSL), as well as direct broadcast satellite, are rapidly becoming available. By the middle of the next decade, today's Internet will feel like an old black-and-white television without a remote control. Just as the browser revolutionized the ability of the average consumer to get access to information, true broadband will revolutionize the form and use of digital content on the World Wide Web.

In addition, Moore's Law (Intel founder Gordon Moore's prediction that the number of transistors on an integrated circuit would double every 18 to 24 months) guarantees that enormous processing power will become available in the next decade. In 1998, a standard desktop computer ran at roughly 150 million instructions per second. By the year 2010 or 2011, computers and other Internet access devices should have the capability to process 100 billion instructions per second! This explosion of processing power will be the engine driving voice recognition, powerful visualization, and other Star Trek–like capabilities.

No one can be certain about the future of any company in this type of environment. The only certainty is more rapid change. But even amid this turbulence, firms can manage better. In this chapter, we offer a few key lessons about what to do, and what not to do, when competing on Internet time. Netscape and Microsoft were two of the most prominent companies on the Internet because they learned how to *move rapidly* to new products and markets; how to *be flexible* in strategy, structure, and operations; and how to *exploit* all points of leverage for competitive advantage. In this book, we described this combination of movement, flexibility, and leverage as the techniques of judo strategy.

It was Netscape's ability to move quickly, for example, that allowed the company to jump on the Internet bandwagon ahead of the masses. Both Netscape and Microsoft also cultivated flexibility as a core skill. At the level of competitive strategy, this translated into a willingness to "embrace and extend" each other's technologies and the critical standards of the Internet. In development strategies, both companies enhanced flexibility by using nonsequential development methods and increasing product modularity. Finally, the strategic successes and failures of both companies came from leverage. Netscape gained leverage from its ability to capitalize on open standards and cross-platform technologies. These sources of leverage gave the company significant advantages in its competition with Microsoft. At the same time, Microsoft found a point of leverage by giving Internet products away for free.

Neither Netscape nor Microsoft enjoyed complete success. In part, of course, this was due to each company's efforts to thwart its rival. And in part, it was due to failures in execution. In reviewing the negative side of the performance record, we discuss some of the tradeoffs that judo strategy involves and suggest a number of "don'ts" for competing on Internet time. For example, the experiences of Microsoft and Netscape teach us that managers should avoid proclaiming the revolution before its time. They should also be wary of underestimating the importance of quality and service for enterprise customers in the race for greater speed.

To close the book, we speculate about the likely future of Netscape. We believe that Netscape has transformed itself over the past four years into a company that can survive and potentially thrive, despite competition from Microsoft and IBM—to name just two determined opponents. Real challenges remain, including questions of leadership and the possibility of defeat in the browser wars over the next several years. Nonetheless, Netscape has built a strong brand name, a productive and innovative engineering organization, an effective electronic distribution mechanism, and a large installed base of users who could provide the basis for a healthy and prosperous future.

JUDO TECHNIQUE #1:
MOVE RAPIDLY TO NEW PRODUCTS AND MARKETS

The landscape of the Internet changes so quickly that firms must have the capability to move rapidly. Yet the organizational and operational challenges of rapid movement are daunting. Netscape and Microsoft conquered many of these challenges with combinations of vision, strategy, and development techniques to navigate through the fog of technical possibilities and deliver new products and broad product portfolios at incredible speeds.

Strategy and Tactics

From Vision to Action. Some people argue that visions of the future are irrelevant because the pace of change is so great that companies need to be adaptive, not necessarily proactive, in a world of constant change.[1] We believe that the experiences of Netscape and Microsoft prove the opposite: These companies have been two of the most successful enterprises on the Internet precisely because senior executives communicated clear, compelling visions of their future that had immediate ramifications for company action.

Netscape's vision was the brainchild of cofounder Marc Andreessen. He and Jim Clark clearly deserved credit for seeing the importance of the browser and the Internet, long before Bill Gates. Andreessen was also fairly quick to recognize that companies could use Internet technology to organize their businesses (intranets), build relationships with customers (extranets), and leverage the World Wide Web to do both (Netcenter). We spent less time on Microsoft's vision of the future. However, vision was as critical in Redmond as in Mountain View. Bill Gates's understanding of the "Internet tidal wave" led to a stunning turnaround at the end of 1995, as Microsoft became a "hard-core" Internet player. Once Microsoft's transformation was under way, Gates also demonstrated a characteristically clear grasp of the network dynamics that would ultimately yield a single winner in the browser wars. Without this very precise vision about the role of the browser and how the market was likely to evolve, Microsoft would never have moved so quickly and decisively.

Rapid Movement to Uncontested Ground. Rapid movement to uncontested ground was a central principle guiding the implementation of Netscape's vision. As Jim Barksdale liked to say, "If Microsoft is a shark, we strive to be a bear and make sure the battle takes place not in the ocean but in the jungle."[2] In the first round of the browser wars, Netscape moved to shift the battle from traditional retail and PC manufacturer (OEM) channels onto the World Wide Web. Later, with Microsoft and IBM in hot pursuit, Netscape moved the focus of the struggle from the Internet to the intranet and the extranet, where its cross-platform commitment gave it a natural edge. Finally, in 1998, it moved into the thinly settled territory of electronic commerce, hoping to exploit synergies between content and software on the Web. With each of these moves, Netscape found numerous opportunities to change the competition from big versus small to quick and nimble versus slow and lumbering. Yet it was rarely able to exploit uncontested terrain for long. Despite its size, Microsoft proved to be surprisingly agile and kept Netscape on the move. It took Microsoft less than a year to develop a browser and Web server that essentially eliminated Netscape's technological lead. Microsoft also moved quickly to capture momentum in the intranet market with its messaging server, Exchange.

Acquisitions to Gain Experience and Expertise Quickly. In order to drive faster into new markets, both companies made aggressive use of high-flying stock to swallow companies, people, and technology in a single gulp. Acquisitions allowed the two rivals to build management depth and product portfolios at Internet speed. Between 1995 and 1998, Netscape bought eight companies, in areas ranging from groupware to electronic commerce. Microsoft made a number of highly visible acquisitions as well, including WebTV and free Internet e-mail provider HotMail. As Steve Ballmer, the president of Microsoft, told us in March 1998:

> We've had to step up and either make or not make big investments on Internet time. Like WebTV. Like HotMail. Some of them, I think, will prove smart. Maybe some of them won't prove smart. But they're not huge decisions. We have a currency [with our stock price] that makes them relatively small decisions. These deals [WebTV and HotMail] were both done for stock. I still think it's real money, whatever it is—$400 million or so per acquisition. But I can stop and say, "OK, that's half of one percent of Microsoft." That's probably a reasonable insurance policy to pay.

Whereas Netscape's emphasis in acquisitions was to add experienced staff to its management and development teams, Microsoft gave greater priority to technology and market position. In this area, Netscape might have benefited from taking a page from Microsoft's book. Buying great people *and* technology or market positions can rapidly accelerate movement to a new competitive position. As Netscape learned from the acquisition of Collabra, without *both* management *and* technology, acquisitions can slow a company down.

Implementation

Tapping External Resources. To implement its strategy, Netscape drew heavily on resources external to the company. For example, PC software companies would normally hire legions of QA engineers and deliver beta versions of software on diskettes or CD-ROMs *after* engineers had finished most of the design and testing work. Netscape, instead, turned to the community of the Web, with a beta release policy that enrolled millions of users in the search for bugs and design suggestions. Netscape received immediate user feedback from its virtual workforce, which allowed the engineers to improve product designs continuously. Similarly, Netscape exploited public relations and the press to build a virtual marketing organization. Netscape generated unprecedented attention from business and technical reporters, which bolstered its fame as well as its credibility. Lastly, both Netscape and Microsoft courted independent software vendors, independent content producers, and various distribution channels, such as PC makers and Internet service providers. The strength of both companies' products depended on achieving a critical mass of applications and users as quickly as possible.

Components That Multiple Teams Can Share. Netscape and Microsoft also adopted a range of product design and development techniques that enhanced speed. Both companies sought to make their engineering organizations faster and more nimble by creating common components that different product groups could share. Microsoft's depth of experience gave it an advantage in this field. It had already learned that an effective way to share technologies was to assign the development task to the product team that had the greatest expertise in a particular area. In contrast, during 1996 and 1997, Netscape tried to centralize the creation of common components before moving the task back to individual product teams. In addition, the need to design components that worked well across more than a dozen platforms complicated the job confronting Netscape engineers, while Microsoft teams built primarily for Windows.

Parallel Development. Managers at Netscape and Microsoft emphasized parallelism in product design as well as in project management and scheduling. For example, two teams would start and work simultaneously on different versions of the same product—the next and the next-plus-one release. Small groups of engineers also developed individual features independent of particular projects but in parallel and then merged their code when it was ready. This approach worked, though resource constraints sometimes got in the way at Netscape. Parallel development allowed both companies to explore new technological directions as well as shorten development times and intervals between product releases by overlapping engineering work.

Testing Automation. It is important when competing on Internet time to allow engineers to make lots of changes in product designs. To keep products stable, however, projects must continually test the changes, find and fix bugs, and then test again. An efficient way to test continually is to automate. Then engineers only have to rerun the automated tests to make sure that the changes they made to the product do not create other problems or cause the product to fail. Both Netscape and Microsoft pursued the strategy of automating testing at different points—for the check-ins to their daily builds as well as throughout a project and before major milestone points, such as beta releases. Both companies illustrate, however, that test automation does not eliminate the need for manual test engineers. Someone has to write and update the automated tests. In addition, manual testing is necessary to supplement automated testing because there generally is not enough time to create updated tests to cover last-minute design changes. It is also impossible to automate some key aspects of the product, such as network setup, user interface design, and usability.

"Eating Your Own Dog Food." Finally, employees at both companies used products under development internally in order to get immediate and intimate feedback, even before they publicly released beta versions. At Netscape, for example, numerous company operations ran on homegrown intranets, Web-based software tools, and Web-based applications. All the customer support and marketing operations relied on extranets that Netscape built on top of its client, servers, and security technology. In addition, Netscape ran large-scale transaction processes through Netcenter using its application servers.

JUDO TECHNIQUE #2:
BE FLEXIBLE IN STRATEGY AND IMPLEMENTATION

Success in fast-changing markets requires flexibility on many levels. On the strategic level, managers must be flexible about when they go head-to-head with a competitor and when they give way. If you have the strength to overpower your opponent, you can abandon judo techniques and face your opponent head-on. In this type of sumo competition, the biggest, strongest players generally win. If, however, you cannot overpower your competitor with sheer strength, then you have to learn how to give way to frontal attacks and avoid potentially fatal blows. Strategic flexibility also requires organizational flexibility and the ability to make changes in structure that are consistent with shifts in strategy. Finally, even the strongest players have to be operationally flexible and give their managers and employees the leeway to respond to constant change.

Strategy and Tactics

Sumo Strategy. Judo strategy is not always the right answer for competing on Internet time. If you have a very strong position, deep pockets, excellent distribution, and great products and technology, the best approach may be to attack your opponents directly. Rather than judo, your model is sumo, where players try to win by throwing their competitors out of the ring. For Internet start-ups, such as Netscape, this approach is obviously foolhardy. Netscape could not win in a sumo competition with Microsoft or IBM. But established competitors like Microsoft can often win a pure sumo match. Indeed, much of Microsoft's later success came from implementing a sumo-type strategy. Once it had narrowed the product gap with Netscape, Microsoft tried to go head-to-head with Netscape as often as possible. In a direct contest between the two companies, Microsoft would offer anything and everything to win—and usually it did.

Giving Way to Superior Force. For the smaller company, the challenge is to avoid sumo competitions through deft, rapid moves, and turn the match back to judo. Quickness and agility, however, are not always enough. As Netscape discovered, no matter how quickly you move, sometimes you will encounter a direct assault. When this occurs, you must be strategically flexible to survive. As Aesop's fable of the oak and the reeds suggests, if you do not bend to superior force, you can break.

Netscape was highly flexible at the tactical level. Managers made frequent adjustments in directions and product plans in response to competitive challenges. In mid-1997, for example, Netscape responded to Microsoft's announcements about push technology by reshuffling its development schedule to add a push component to Communicator. A few months later, Netscape management responded to deteriorating financial results by moving quickly to find new revenue sources in areas such as electronic commerce and the Netcenter Web site. Even former employees who were otherwise critical of the company marveled at Netscape management's ability to make quick, effective decisions. Karen Richardson, former VP of strategic accounts, noted:

> Netscape tended to be really good, in general, about making tough technology decisions and quickly acting on those decisions. In 1997, the sales

force was talking about the brutal competition to sell the current server products. We said that we needed to do some other things. And if you really look at the amount of time it took from those clamorings to making decisions, it is only a few months before the executive committee and the engineering groups did the analysis and figured out that we ought to buy a company. We found Kiva and we bought it. Despite its size, Netscape was willing to spend that kind of money and take those kinds of technology risks.

While Netscape was good at tactical adjustments, Microsoft was the master of strategic flexibility. If we define strategic flexibility as a willingness to bend and give way to superior force, it was Bill Gates who understood that you should not stand stiffly in a gale-force wind. By the time Microsoft discovered the importance of the Internet, Netscape already had 80 percent of the browser market and many Web masters were building their sites around the standards Netscape had helped to define. Microsoft management recognized that it was too late to replace the Internet's standards with its own. Instead, Gates chose to "embrace and extend" Internet protocols and Netscape technologies. The Microsoft strategy was classic judo: Accept Netscape's success, take its best ideas, incorporate those ideas, and try to improve upon them. Fighting the dominant player in the market on its turf when you only have a trivial market share in browsers would have been a losing proposition for Microsoft.

Meshing Strategic Plans with Tactical Adjustments. Microsoft illustrates another important lesson about tactical flexibility: Making adjustments is compatible with making longer-term strategic plans. The joke in Silicon Valley likens competing on Internet time to leading a dog's life—compressing seven years into one. But this does not mean that companies should plan on seven-week cycles. At Microsoft, for example, a three-year planning horizon allowed the company to mesh its short-run tactical plans with a broader strategic view of how to win the war. As Steve Ballmer asserted, the Internet had not required a fundamental change in process:

[At Microsoft], we do a mid-year review. We gestate on it. We then do a three-year outlook. We do an executive review. And then we have all that input and take a look at macro sales, marketing investments, and product plans. This hasn't changed. . . . The fact of the matter is that customers can't take cataclysmic change every three months. The organization also can't. You can ship products quickly. But you can't say, "Oh, we have a radically new strategy" every three months. You can say, "We have a new product, we have a new this, a new that." And most of the stuff we do for the Internet today fits into our broader strategy.

Microsoft demonstrated that planning on Internet time is more about the ability to make quick adjustments in response to new competitive forces than about shortening the planning horizon. By flexibly engaging issues as they arose, or using "pulses," in Ballmer's words, Microsoft executives identified competitive threats. Then they set deadlines for public events, in order to force the organization to commit to a new path. Ballmer felt that these pulses made Microsoft, with almost 30,000 employees, as nimble as a start-up:

> We have learned how to set seminal events for ourselves that really help drive a consensus and action on issues. . . . Making internal events never seems to really help companies as much as you might think. The only consensus that locks people in is when you commit to your customers. You've got to force yourself—maybe quicker than a lot of companies feel comfortable with—to articulate your decisions, because that helps to make them stick.

Implementation

Building Internal Resources for a Large but Flexible Organization. Executives at both Netscape and Microsoft made conscious efforts to maximize flexibility within their organizations. At Netscape, Jim Barksdale worked hard to introduce large-company systems without the bureaucracy and agony of large-company rules. Barksdale also emphasized the importance of pushing responsibility down throughout the company's ranks. In practice, this meant relying on small teams of experienced people who focused on specific products rather than on compartmentalized functional roles. While both companies organized this way, teams were generally smaller at Netscape than at Microsoft. Netscape executives and engineering managers made it a high priority to keep the number of engineers low, break teams up into small divlets, maintain relatively few controls on features and deadlines, and institute a very informal culture that extended from project management to hiring. Netscape also tried to mix experienced people and Internet specialists who could serve as product champions—what one employee referred to as "software heroes." These practices allowed the company to meld small, flexible teams with a sharp product focus.

Investing in Modular Product Architectures. Flexibility was also an important goal in product design. Software developers *should* be able to make changes, even very late in projects, in order to respond to feedback from customers or competitor moves. Creating modular architectures is one of the best mechanisms for building this kind of flexibility into product designs. Modularity allows individual groups of engineers to design and test their components relatively independently, thereby simplifying the process of incorporating new features and technologies. In addition, a modular architecture makes it easier for OEMs, such as AOL, Intuit, and Lotus, to take core software components and customize the user interfaces around their own brands.

The problem with modular architectures is that lasting designs usually require extra time upfront to create. As Netscape engineers rushed products to market from 1994 to 1996, they did not have the time to design for the future. Microsoft engineers, on the other hand, were playing catch-up. They licensed the original Mosaic browser technology from Spyglass, learned from Netscape's designs, and took advantage of their extensive experience with modular designs for PC software products like Windows and Office. This experience helped Microsoft's technical leaders realize that they had to pause and make sure their Internet products were sufficiently modular to handle new features and technologies quickly and easily. Accordingly, Microsoft redesigned its browser in the IE 3.0 project between December 1995 and August 1996 when the code base was still small and manageable.

Adapting Development Priorities to Target Customers. An important part of operational flexibility was the ability to change priorities as customers and technologies changed. In the beginning of the Internet browser wars, Netscape put a premium on time to market and innovation; these goals suited the Internet "hacker" culture perfectly as well as leading-edge users. As target customers increasingly became corporations interested in using browsers as well as servers for intranets, and then extranets, and eventually electronic commerce, Netscape had to redraw its priorities and its culture to become more focused on quality and support for enterprise customers. Microsoft had to do the same thing with its Internet groups, although the company already had experience making this transition with its operating systems (Windows and Windows NT) and desktop applications (Office).

Evolving Features with a Synchronize-and-Stabilize Process. Both companies further promoted flexibility by using a "synchronize-and-stabilize" process for product development. Although Microsoft and other PC software companies pioneered this approach, Netscape mastered the same basic techniques. The synchronize-and-stabilize philosophy enabled development teams at both companies to invent as they designed, incorporate feedback from users during a project, and make late changes that reflected this learning. Key to the process was the use of "daily builds" of the evolving product to synchronize many design changes continuously. Relatively large teams (numbering a hundred or more developers) could then coordinate their efforts easily and work more effectively. The team members also periodically stopped and stabilized features to make sure they worked and then showed their work-in-progress to internal and external users, such as through alpha and beta releases.

Using these techniques, Netscape and Microsoft remained very flexible on feature sets and project plans. Both companies had milestones such as the first public beta and the "feature-complete" date. But nothing was sacrosanct; all dates were subject to revision because changes in market needs, technology evolution, and competitor behavior were not really predictable more than six months to a year in advance. At the same time, successful projects built products incrementally to avoid spinning out of control. They prioritized feature suggestions in the planning process and tried to complete the most important ones first. They divided work into chunks or subsets of features and did not try to do everything at once. At key milestone junctures, they took time to reflect on what they were doing and make mid-course changes. "Synchronize and stabilize" was, no doubt, the best way to develop new products when companies cannot accurately determine when they start a project exactly what features they should build or how customers and competitors would respond.

JUDO TECHNIQUE #3:
EXPLOIT ALL POINTS OF LEVERAGE

Leverage is the third and, in some senses, the most important technique of judo strategy. In this case, leverage has a specific meaning: Turn your opponent's strength into weakness. Use your competitor's size, installed base, and revenue streams as the basis for moves that make it painful to respond. When used effectively, leverage can cause opponents to become immobilized by the fear of undermining their own success. While movement and flexibility are strategic mechanisms for getting out of the way of larger, stronger competitors, leverage is what gives you a chance to win!

The idea behind leverage is particularly powerful for competing on Internet time. In industry after industry, the Internet is changing the rules of the game. This creates openings for new, innovative firms to take on well-established players who are weighed down by their success in the bricks-and-mortar world. If you are Barnes & Noble, for example, and you have a huge fixed investment in real estate and physical infrastructure, you might be slow in responding to competition from Amazon.com. The cannibalization of moving a large percentage of your sales to the Internet at lower prices could have a devastating impact on your existing business. Yet, if you are competing on Internet time, slowness to respond can be deadly. Give Amazon.com a year or two to build traffic, a brand, and a loyal following, and it might be hard (and extremely costly) to catch up.

Strategy and Tactics

Exploiting the Weight and Strategy of Opponents. Leverage offers special promise to the relatively weak. Not surprisingly, this was an area in which Netscape outperformed Microsoft, at least early on. Finding leverage against Microsoft might have seemed tricky, but Microsoft was actually a company with a great of deal of weight on its shoulders. Microsoft's business model has depended—and still depends today—on controlling the Windows operating system, continuously getting the installed base of Windows users to upgrade their operating systems, and killing alternative operating systems and applications, especially UNIX in the corporate server market.

Netscape's first point of leverage was to offer browsers and servers for more than a dozen operating platforms, including Microsoft's entire installed base. By supporting the heterogeneous computing environment that exists in most corporations, Netscape staked out a market position that Microsoft could not match without undercutting the strategy that had brought it success in the past. The majority of Netscape's customer sales came from corporations that did not want to become captive to Microsoft.

Netscape found a second point of leverage in Microsoft's reliance on proprietary software to drive the company's enormous profitability. Microsoft's revenue streams depended to a considerable extent on its ability to lock in customers who used its operating systems and applications. In contrast, Netscape promoted its support for open standards as a victory for consumer choice. Netscape designed its "open, but not open" technology strategy (i.e., more open than Microsoft, but not 100 percent open) to keep Microsoft on the defensive while allowing Netscape to reap the benefits of its innovations. In 1998, this policy culminated in Netscape's decision to give away the source code for its browser—a move that Microsoft, which had integrated its browser into Windows 98, was unlikely ever to imitate.

Finally, Netscape sought to leverage the opposition to Microsoft that had emerged within the computer industry as a byproduct of Bill Gates's success. Netscape formed partnerships with a number of companies, including Oracle, Sun, and IBM, that felt threatened by Microsoft's still growing dominance in a range of fields. These partnerships focused on potential challenges such as the Java programming language and network computers. In addition, Netscape often sought support from the ABM (Anyone But Microsoft) contingent in battles over technology standards. Netscape's partnership strategy was, at best, a partial success. Its aims, however, were fully in line with the thinking behind judo strategy.

We must also note that, as a strategy, leverage may seem better suited to Netscape, the small, flexible start-up going up against an industry giant. But as Netscape became increasingly successful, Microsoft found leverage points of its own. Notably, Microsoft was able to use Netscape's browser revenue stream to paralyze the smaller company for more than two years. Microsoft's decision to give its browser away for free was a move that Netscape was highly reluctant to match—even as its lead in the browser market dwindled away.

Implementation

Cross-Platform Product Design. Netscape's technological ace in the hole has been cross-platform design—the ability to create products that run on any PC or workstation operating system. To implement this strategy, Netscape engineers avoided using all but a few features, interfaces, or programming conventions that were specific to particular hardware and operating system platforms. They also created a special layer to isolate Netscape's browser and server products from the different operating systems and shared core technologies that made it easier to develop cross-platform products. These and other design strategies allowed Netscape to deliver products for multiple markets simultaneously and dominate enterprise accounts that were heavily weighted with UNIX servers or a mixture of machines and operating systems—UNIX, Windows 3.1, Windows 95, Windows 98, Windows NT, and Macintosh.

Leverage from cross-platform designs came with some costs, however. Cross-platform products took longer to design than products built just for one platform, such as Windows or UNIX. Thoroughly testing the different browser and server versions on many different operating systems also proved to be very time-consuming and tedious, though necessary to produce quality products. Netscape also failed in its efforts to use the Java programming language as a grand solution to cross-platform design. It learned through this experience the pitfalls of trying to build complex products and features with a new, evolving technology. In addition, cross-platform products did not always perform as well as products optimized for particular operating systems. As a result, rather than adhere blindly to the cross-platform strategy, Netscape engineers learned to select where they would use cross-platform components and where they would not. Netscape had to continue balancing platform-specific with cross-platform designs to make sure its products remained competitive.

WHAT *NOT* TO DO
WHEN COMPETING ON INTERNET TIME

Judo strategy provides a strategic, organizational, and technological framework for competing on Internet time. Yet judo strategy alone does not guarantee success. The history of Netscape's battle with Microsoft makes this clear. By 1998, the browser wars had taken a serious toll on Netscape. Some of the damage, of course, was inevitable. Microsoft is one of the toughest competitors in the world, with one of the strongest competitive positions in the history of information technology. Not even IBM in its heyday during the 1960s could claim the same level of dominance that Microsoft has exhibited since the mid-1990s. But both Netscape and Microsoft have made mistakes. The Internet is a new medium, and companies have to experiment. No matter how good you are, lots of experiments are going to fail. When Microsoft makes mistakes, however, it has certain luxuries that are not available to most companies in the world. As Steve Ballmer told us, "When we make mistakes, you won't see it in our revenue for three or four years!" For Netscape and most other companies competing on Internet time, mistakes can become evident in days or weeks.

The principles we have laid out in this book suggest effective ways to compete in fast-changing markets. To draw additional lessons from our story, we believe that it is also important to suggest a few lessons from the Netscape and Microsoft experiences about what companies should *not* do when trying to compete on Internet time.

Don't Depend on the Revolution Coming Tomorrow

Overestimating the pace of change is the risk most directly associated with an emphasis on movement and speed. Netscape started a revolution by popularizing the Internet. For years, the name "Netscape" was virtually synonymous with the impending IT revolution. But revolutions do not happen overnight in information technology, even when the technology is the Internet. As Netscape has discovered, the tyranny of the installed base is real. Early adopters become excited by new technologies and often assume that the rest of the world will follow their lead. They often forget that there are roughly 300 million operating PCs in the world today and it takes a long time to change the behavior of 300 million users.

The last two revolutions in information technology are good examples. We had a revolution in the mainframe world when IBM introduced the System 360 in the 1960s. That revolution took more than two decades to unfold. Steve Jobs then started the PC revolution in 1977. This revolution took a decade and a half to bring about fundamental changes in user behavior. Not until the late 1980s did minicomputer and mainframe customers and vendors begin to feel the heat. The Internet revolution is undoubtedly moving much faster than any previous revolution, but it will probably be five to ten years before the impact diffuses more fully to the mass market.

Many of Netscape's problems in execution came from broad technical and product visions that assumed the revolution was upon us already. If you believe the revolution is coming tomorrow, you can fall into several traps. One trap, as Marc Andreessen admitted, is creating a strategy "to take all products into all markets."[3] Netscape is relatively focused today. In the earlier years, however, it tried to offer products in every important Internet and intranet client and server category and to cover every possible computing platform, regardless of the revenue potential. The sheer breadth of its product portfolio and ambition *slowed* Netscape down. Rather than have a few truly great products, where it could compete with the best vendors in the world, it divided scarce resources across too many products and markets. By 1997, Netscape had a huge product portfolio. They were good products, but not all were great products. And customers noticed.

A second trap of prematurely proclaiming the revolution is doing "rocket science" to accelerate solutions and solve hard technical problems. Despite Andreessen's deep concern that Netscape should avoid overly complex projects, the demands of the revolution led the engineers down several technical dead ends. These ranged from trying to rearchitect the browser client while adding complex new features like Netcaster and doing both the redesign and the innovation with still-evolving technologies like Java and JavaScript. Netscape also wasted time and money working on its own Java components as well as trying to build "Javagator," the 100 percent Java version of Navigator.

Don't Underestimate the Importance of Quality and Process

A preoccupation with speed and flexibility can also lead companies to trade off quality and process to an excessive degree. Companies need to keep these goals front and center, even when they are racing to introduce new products and technologies on Internet time. This is especially true when trying to reach enterprise customers. No product will gain acceptance in the mainstream unless it is reliable and supported. We recognize that it is difficult to build and support new products when engineers can change designs at the last minute and live in almost constant "beta release mode." There is little time left for testing, documentation, or design rework to prepare better for the future. But to live on Internet time, companies have to cultivate seemingly contradictory skills: They have to be flexible in design and promote constant innovation, but still retain control over schedules and quality. They must invent new features, but they must also test them—continuously and repeatedly, with manual and automated techniques. Netscape in particular looked for shortcuts here, as Microsoft used to do and sometimes still does with new products. In the long run, however, there are no real shortcuts in quality where enterprise customers are concerned.

Netscape's engineers wrote code very fast and created numerous innovative features. Early on, the company skimped on in-house testing in order to rush a flurry of beta versions of Navigator out the door. To its credit, Netscape did not let these weaknesses go without addressing them. During 1997 and 1998, we could see changes emerging. Netscape was reducing the number of planned beta releases to give projects more time to stabilize the code. Engineers were focusing more effort on raising quality levels in both the client and server products. Some server developers were even writing automated tests for each other's code to make up for the shortage of dedicated test engineers. In October 1997, Netscape executives made customer satisfaction a top priority. By 1998, these efforts were paying off: An independent survey found Netscape's server software outperformed Microsoft on product quality, reliability, and support.[4]

The fundamental struggle within Netscape has been to find the right balance between speed and quality, given limited financial and human resources and the pressures of competing on Internet time. Mark Tompkins, who headed QA in the client product division before moving to another division, captured the dilemma: "The right amount of process is important. I'm still wrestling with whether we have the right amount or not. But too much is very stifling, and I've been there. I've seen it at larger companies. And so you've got to have the right amount of process for meeting your goals of speed as well as quality."

The tradeoffs are especially complex when the pace of competition and innovation is so fast. But we have also argued in this book that *Internet time does not last forever.* At some point, companies must invest as much in improving product architectures, testing, and process control as they do in generating new features, sales, and additions to the product portfolio. Achieving the right balance is also important because perhaps the biggest problem new companies face is *customer perception,* not even reality. If a company gains a reputation for shipping buggy products and letting customers suffer the consequences, then this image is hard to overcome in corporate procurement offices. To compensate for its past reputation and quality problems, Microsoft has probably spent billions of dollars in testing. We even quoted Steve Ballmer as saying that *75 percent of the company is testing.* Yet Microsoft continues to struggle with the perception that it is, underneath the surface, still dominated by "hacker" software developers who are content to ship late and buggy products. At Netscape, Jim Barksdale was deeply concerned about the image and long-term viability of his company. In our May 1998 meeting, he announced that, "Netscape has only two goals this year. One, to improve customer satisfaction as measured by external surveys. . . . The second one is improved revenue per employee." He then expanded on the goal of improving customer satisfaction:

> There are many ways to do that, one of which is product quality. The other is Debby Meredith's function of tech support and much better focus now on tech support's translation of escalating product problems to the engineering staff. We are also taking a large part of tech support out of tech support and putting it into engineering and QA, with people who've been on the front line. We want to sustain engineering now away from the regular engineering so we do a better job on maintenance. Those are efforts—outward, visible signs of our effort to do that. And we're making much more commitment financially to the QA function than we've ever had before, relative to the total product. We're getting external surveys from realistic evaluators of our products, our customers, of the product characteristics and then measuring, which is exactly what we did at Federal Express to improve enough to win the Baldridge Award. And every quarter you test against your customers' perceptions—not people who want to write about your doom and decide do they like the dog food or don't they and what do they like or not like. . . . But we've got to do that, or we'll never get there.

In other words, Netscape has started to change reality by changing its priorities. Now it has to change perceptions—an even harder task.

Don't "Moon the Giant"

Movement and flexibility are not the only elements of judo strategy that involve tradeoffs. Leverage also has a potential downside. When leverage is used effectively, it tends to target sensitive areas of the rival's business. Especially in a world of increasing returns, where network externalities drive many segments to winner-take-all outcomes, how can you prevent the dominant players from responding to a potential threat to their core business? The first answer, in the words of Netscape's former head of OEM sales, Ram Shriram, is that you don't "moon the giant." Telling the (much larger, more powerful) enemy that you are going to kill him is likely to have one predictable outcome: a lethal response. Mike Homer's self-confessed obsession with beating Microsoft, Jim Clark's public proclamation of Microsoft as the "Death Star," and Marc Andreessen's repeated predictions that Windows would become irrelevant could only antagonize the entire Microsoft corporation.

The better approach is to take a page from Greek mythology and learn from the lessons of the Trojan horse. Imagine a strategy where you begin by giving your product away for free, just like the Trojan horse. Next, you allow your customers to enjoy the product and integrate it into their daily work or routines. All the while, you want your competitors and customers to be lulled into a false sense of security. Finally, by the time they wake up and realize they are locked in to your solution, it is too late. The market has tipped in your favor.

Trojan horse strategies have been at the core of the most enduring franchises in information technology in the past three decades. When Intel started to sell its microprocessors aggressively in the late 1970s and Microsoft offered very favorable terms on its operating system, DOS, in the early 1980s, few people really understood what they were buying. Had IBM understood, it had the resources and capabilities to respond effectively. The company owned a large share of Intel, which it could have expanded, and it could have bought a significant share of Microsoft or extracted different terms in its operating system license. Yet IBM and others failed to see the Trojan horse, and neither Intel nor Microsoft told them! We can also see this phenomenon of lock-in in other industries that depend on standards and complementary products, ranging from video recorders to instant cameras and refillable razors, though these cases may have been more obvious to consumers.

There are two important lessons from the Trojan horse. First, if you are a customer, "beware of information technology companies bearing gifts." Second, if you are a company employing Trojan horse strategies, avoid "mooning the giant." Trojan horse strategies depend on the enemy being asleep. If you moon the giant or awaken the enemy, you might get burned. Netscape did a brilliant job of building a Trojan horse (Navigator), getting inside the walls (80-plus percent market share), and creating the foundation for a new platform that might ultimately have replaced Windows as the universal user interface. Maybe with an extra year or two, Navigator might have become so deeply entrenched that it would have been extraordinarily difficult to displace. Yet Netscape management, especially Andreessen and Homer, got carried away. On the one hand, managers always want to tout their company and create momentum behind their products. Public relations was indeed one of Netscape's strongest competencies. But repeatedly telling the world that Microsoft's operating system would become nothing more than "a mundane collection of not entirely debugged device drivers"[5] got Bill Gates's attention. And once the enemy was awake, the soldiers in the horse became vulnerable. Awaken a sleeping giant, and you put your life at risk.

Don't be Afraid of Cannibalization

All three of judo strategy's techniques—movement, flexibility, and leverage—involve tradeoffs that require careful management. Perhaps the biggest strategic dilemma for judo strategy is, the more prosperous you become, the more history, installed base, and baggage you carry. In other words, the greater your success, the greater your weight, and the more vulnerable you become to someone else using judo strategy against you! In the browser wars, Microsoft looked at Netscape in 1996 and found that as Netscape grew bigger, it, too, became weighed down by its history, revenue streams, and installed base. Netscape's biggest burden was its pricing model. By the end of 1996, revenues from *"not* free" browsers represented the lion's share of Netscape's sales and profits. Once Microsoft gave the browser away, Netscape was in a quandary: How could it afford to support ongoing development and maintain its revenues and stock price when a competing product was available at no cost? Just as Netscape froze its competitors by its initial "free, but not free" policy, Microsoft's strategy of offering the product for free froze Netscape. Microsoft's strategy worked: It took the loss of 30 market-share points in browsers before Netscape management became unstuck.

The only way to successfully fight such a judo attack is to accept the inevitability of cannibalization and cannibalize your own business. Bill Gates realized that browsers might replace alternative interfaces, perhaps even Windows. In addition, the Internet would kill alternative technologies for aggregating content, such as proprietary online services. Rather than allow someone else to do it, Gates chose to risk cannibalizing his own business. In 1995, Microsoft had made public commitments to an array of strategies for competing online, including proprietary technologies, such as ActiveX and Blackbird, as well as a proprietary online service, Microsoft Network (MSN). Microsoft sank hundreds of millions of dollars into MSN before the Internet moved to the top of Gates's agenda. But rather than allow these commitments to slow Microsoft down, Gates was willing to do everything and anything to get share for Internet Explorer. Doing everything and anything included transferring control of some proprietary software to an industry group (ActiveX), abandoning other investments (Blackbird), and even undermining MSN. To promote Internet Explorer market share, Microsoft was even willing to give some of the most valuable real estate in the world (a piece of the Windows desktop) to AOL and other online services and Internet service providers. Gates knew this would eliminate MSN's most significant competitive advantage— being the sole icon for online content and Internet access on the Windows 95 desktop. But for the long run, it was worth the price.

Don't Be Too Greedy

Finally, Netscape and Microsoft both have been guilty of simply being too greedy. Netscape was too greedy for cash, and Microsoft was too greedy for market share. Some greed is good. After all, you have to be tough to win business in an epic battle like Netscape versus Microsoft. Greed and toughness also drive the organization to perform. But too much greed is bad—very bad. If you are too tough with your customers or partners, you risk alienation, retaliation, and government intervention. Put another way, you should be "greedy, but not too greedy" and "tough, but not too tough."

In Netscape's case, there was excessive enthusiasm for extracting cash from every relationship and excessive enthusiasm for pleasing Wall Street. Gaining and maintaining market share remains the most important strategic imperative in a networked world. As Andreessen recognized from the beginning, firms earn long-run profits by getting customers hooked on their solution. If getting share necessitates making short-run financial sacrifices, that is the cost of success. But within months of launching Navigator, Netscape managers took every opportunity to raise revenues and profits and, even worse, they raised revenue and profit expectations. In the rush to go public and demonstrate their success, they were willing to lose market share, delay important strategic decisions (such as reducing the price of the browser), and weaken potentially valuable long-term relationships (with content companies like CNET) to satisfy Wall Street.

The contrast between Netscape's behavior prior to 1998 and Microsoft's is startling. Microsoft's near-monopoly position in operating systems gave it luxuries that few firms could afford. Microsoft was rarely greedy for cash. In fact, Microsoft usually tried to reduce Wall Street expectations and spend its cash. Financial considerations never seemed to dominate Microsoft's decision making. But Gates and company were too greedy and too tough when it came to winning market share in the browser wars. In winner-take-all environments, firms can gain so much market power and market share that they have special obligations under antitrust laws. It is perfectly legal to win a near-monopoly through good business practices. But once you have a dominant position, special rules apply. You can be a tough competitor, but you cannot use your monopoly power to hurt a competitor in another market. Regardless of the legal issues, exclusive bundling deals, leveraging your monopoly into related products, or threatening to cut off your largest customer (i.e., Compaq) from Windows if it uses a competitor's product might be going over the line. Strategically, you invite government intervention and customer retaliation. Microsoft's take-no-prisoners strategy might have been fine, if it had been anyone but Microsoft.

NETSCAPE AND THE FUTURE

Netscape will face many challenges in 1999 and beyond. At the broadest level, the company will have to address questions of leadership and execution. Managing in rapidly changing environments can be difficult under the best of conditions. But competing on Internet time greatly exacerbates the trials of management and leadership. Senior managers constantly face tough choices among competing technologies, competing market opportunities, and even competing business models. Making these judgments requires a deep understanding of technology and the capabilities of the engineering organization as well as a good feel for the competition and a great sense of the customers. Ultimately, to provide effective leadership, the person at the top should make the final decisions.

While Jim Barksdale clearly has a great sense of the customer and a good feel for the competition, he has to rely on others for judgments about technology and engineering. Critical pieces of strategy and operations, in other words, are not in the hands of the CEO. Barksdale is highly charismatic and intelligent. He inspires people. But Barksdale is a nontechnical general manager who is resting a big part of Netscape's future on the maturing technical and operational judgments of Marc Andreessen and the aggressiveness and ability to execute of Mike Homer. In addition, Barksdale's consensus management and conflict-avoidance style will continue to be a challenge. Most successful high-technology companies encourage constructive confrontation at the top to ensure that managers hear all points of view, debate contrary positions, and do not bury good ideas.[6] Consensus management can work well in relatively stable environments, but trying to avoid conflict, rather than resolving the fundamental problems behind it, can be dangerous in the midst of constant turmoil.

Netscape's second major challenge is implementing a corporate strategy that is far more complex than anything it has attempted before. In its first four years, Netscape focused on a number of different markets in turn. Today, Netscape is a diversified software company that provides products and services to the entire spectrum of customers, from individual consumers to the world's largest enterprises. This corporate strategy requires Netscape to battle on three fronts. In the browser wars, Netscape remains pitted directly against Microsoft. In the server wars, in addition to Microsoft, Netscape's opponents include IBM and Oracle, two large and very successful companies that have been delivering products and services to enterprise customers for many years. In the Web portal wars, Netscape faces off against Microsoft (again) and companies like Yahoo!, AOL, and Excite, which have earned sky-high valuations by focusing intensely on providing information and services primarily to mass-market consumers.

The challenges of managing a multibusiness enterprise while fighting an intense, multifront war raise an obvious question: Can a diversified Netscape deliver better products and services than Microsoft and a host of strong, focused competitors? The answer, of course, is *maybe*. Diversification always creates problems of coordination, management distraction, overhead costs, and the alignment of incentives in different marketplaces. In addition, the human and material costs of fighting a three-front war loom large for a company of Netscape's size. Yet Netscape has a rare combination of assets that could create advantages most competitors would find difficult—or impossible—to match. Potentially, there could be powerful synergies with the dominant Web browser, one of the world's most heavily visited Web sites, and a half-billion-dollar enterprise business. Successfully exploiting those synergies will not be an easy feat. At stake is the viability of the Internet's first great success story. While no one can accurately predict the future of Netscape, we can speculate on the likely outcomes of the three major struggles in which it is now engaged.

The Browser Wars

Many people have already pronounced Microsoft the winner of the browser wars. At the time of this writing, Microsoft has momentum, close to 50 percent of the total market, and a more modular and flexible product that will be easier to adapt and evolve over time. We do not think it is that simple, however. Netscape remains a very innovative company in the browser space. In the middle of 1998, it introduced the beta version of its next-generation Communicator product and pioneered new ground. We can see potentially compelling features such as Smart Browsing, which makes it easier for everyday users to find things on the Internet. In addition, Netscape's Mozilla.org strategy, which has delivered a quarter of a million browser source-code files in its first four months, could generate a new swell of creativity. This virtual workforce is huge and far exceeds Microsoft's cast of developers. In theory, the community of Internet developers could create enormous leverage for Netscape in the coming months and years.

Last, but certainly not least, Netscape continues to control slightly more than half the browser market. And switching browsers, especially in the corporate market, will not happen overnight. The technical switching costs of changing from Navigator to Internet Explorer are low, but there is definitely some "stickiness." Out of habit or taste, some consumers simply like Navigator better. In addition, other individuals who adopted Navigator in the early years are reluctant to switch because they have to transfer things like bookmarks (which users can move, but with some effort) and customized interfaces. Companies who adopted Navigator during the early years are reluctant to switch for these and other reasons. IT managers need a compelling reason to retrain staff and reconfigure computer desktops. When Netscape was charging $49 for the product, and Microsoft was giving it away for free, IT managers had their compelling reason. But today, if people in an organization are comfortable using a particular browser, there simply is no good reason to switch.

The logic of increasing returns and network effects, however, suggests that ultimately, there will be *one dominant* player in this market. Over time, maybe over four or five years, Web masters will increasingly choose between optimizing for Internet Explorer or Netscape Navigator, but not both. Today, Web masters have little choice. With the market split roughly equally, they must make their Web sites browser-neutral or optimize for both browsers. If you choose one, you face the possibility of losing half your potential market. Yet the current 50-50 division of the market is unstable. The two products will coexist only if they can remain close to 100 percent compatible. Today, for example, there are only small differences between Navigator and Internet Explorer. But one survey estimated that it was costing Web masters as much as 25 percent of the total expense of creating a Web site just to accommodate those minor variances.[7] We believe that over the next several years, either Microsoft, or Netscape, or both will inevitably try to differentiate their browsers and drive an even greater wedge between the two products. When that occurs, the market will tip. The one with greater share, more momentum, and a stronger perception of long-term viability is likely to win.

As more and more Web masters optimize for a single browser, the consumer will choose a winner by default. The market tipped in favor of VHS over Betamax after OEM licensing deals and video rentals on the shelves tipped toward VHS.[8] The market tipped in favor of Windows over the Macintosh as Apple machines became too expensive and fewer and fewer applications were available for the Mac. Similarly, the browser market will gravitate naturally toward the standard that has the most Web sites and the most content. The "loser" may still keep 10 or 15 percent share from users in niche markets. But there will probably be one dominant player by the middle of the next decade.

The wild card on whether or not this market will tip is the U.S. Department of Justice. Joel Klein wants to preserve competition. If he wins his case quickly and requires Microsoft to distribute Navigator with new versions of Windows, then Microsoft's greatest advantage will dwindle and the market might not tip for some time. Moreover, one of the purposes of the antitrust case against Microsoft is to prevent Microsoft from bundling its browser with the operating system and prohibiting computer manufacturers from customizing their first screens. If computer companies have the option to include a free Navigator in place of a free Internet Explorer, at least some will do so to differentiate their machines. Therefore, we can say that *if* Klein wins, and *if* Microsoft chooses to avoid a long appeals process, and *if* many computer companies opt for Netscape, *then* the perception of momentum could reverse.

Netscape's dilemma, of course, is that there are too many "ifs" to be

optimistic. Despite Netscape's current strength and hopes for future innovation, Microsoft is the most likely winner of the browser wars. Microsoft
can and will copy virtually any innovation that Netscape devises. Microsoft also can and does pour enormous resources into product testing,
customer support, and partner relations. As long as consumers and Web
masters believe that Microsoft will match Netscape's innovations as well
as deliver and support quality products as far into the future as the eye
can see, then Netscape's creativity or speed is no guarantee of success. In
addition, unless the DOJ and Joel Klein achieve a very quick victory,
Microsoft will continue to offer advantages that Netscape can never
match. Microsoft has the world's best distribution channel (integrated
with the Windows desktop). Microsoft gives the computer OEM a comparable browser at no charge and with no added labor (which OEMs need
to install Navigator). It also gives the ultimate consumer a comparable
browser that is well integrated into the operating system and other
Microsoft applications. Netscape can bargain with OEMs, by asking, for
example, to be loaded with Windows in exchange for advertising their
product on a vehicle like Netcenter. This approach may indeed guarantee
Netscape some market share in browsers for years to come. We also think
that the browser will become a universal interface, as Andreessen once
predicted. Most browsers in the future, however, will probably carry the
label "Internet Explorer."

The Server Wars

The good news for Netscape is that its revenue model no longer depends
directly on browsers. While Navigator is still a critical strategic complement to its server and Web site businesses, the ultimate success of Netscape will depend on its performance in enterprise software, especially
servers, and on Netcenter.

Netscape will face increasingly tough competition in the server wars.
Since June 1998, Netscape's goal has been to become an Enterprise Service Provider. The objective is to offer large companies scalable systems
that take advantage of the Internet, intranets, and extranets and link them
all together. This strategy demands that Netscape compete directly with
IBM, Microsoft, Oracle, and thousands of other hardware, software, and
service providers. In addition, Netscape will have to compete against freeware, such as Apache, the market-leading Web server.

Netscape has a very compelling portfolio of product offerings to deliver
on this strategy. The first offering is its "Mission Control" software, which

includes technology that Netscape has been developing from the early days of the company, including its Directory Server and security components. The second is Netscape's Application Server (which came with the purchase of Kiva). This product is pioneering a new layer of Internet application servers that is highly scalable to thousands or millions of users. The third is electronic commerce (which came with the buyout of Actra). Here Netscape offers a full range of software that can help companies replace or extend their legacy electronic data interchange (EDI) and enterprise resource-planning systems. And the fourth is Netscape's Web site and Internet online service, Netcenter, which Netscape can use to drive consumers to its server customers as well as to generate transaction and advertising revenues.

Unlike the browser wars, the server wars are unlikely to end with one or even two winners dominating the market. This is very good news for Netscape. Corporate IT infrastructures are extremely heterogeneous, and the demands of corporate customers are highly diverse. These are also huge markets (Barksdale predicted they will reach $30 billion by 2001), where multiple standards and multiple solutions can thrive. In this type of space, Netscape brings some real advantages over Microsoft and IBM.

The first advantage is Netscape's true cross-platform support. For companies that are unwilling to commit 100 percent to any single vendor, such as Microsoft or IBM, Netscape remains one of the few credible companies that support UNIX, NT, and disparate environments. Surveys of IT managers suggest that NT has two or more product generations to go before it matches UNIX in performance. This means that Netscape has at least two NT product cycles—perhaps six years—to try to lock up corporate accounts. Second, Netscape has early mover advantages in some of these technologies. As Barksdale told us in May 1998, Netscape is significantly ahead of its biggest competitors. He noted that "there are very few products from IBM which have multihosting capability and scaling capability like our products. Oracle is still a year or so away. Microsoft's directory product is two years away, and it's proprietary. They have very immature e-commerce products." A third potential advantage over IBM and Oracle (less so Microsoft) is the Web site. The sheer traffic currently generated by the Netscape default home page makes it an attractive asset for large corporations like Citibank, which want to use the Internet to build a new model for acquiring customers.

Netscape's challenge is that great technology and first mover advantages are not enough. There are huge scale economies in this business, especially in sales and service, that favor IBM, Microsoft, Oracle, and others. The numbers are straightforward: Netscape is currently generating revenues at a run rate of about $500 million per year in the corporate market. Netscape has roughly 200 to 300 salespeople in the field. By comparison, Netscape's direct competitors in this marketplace—IBM, Microsoft, and Oracle—have much larger revenues, far larger sales forces, and significantly lower costs per salesperson. They can also offer much more sales support and technical expertise. In addition, corporate enterprise solutions require long sales cycles and long deployment cycles. The key to achieving significant returns in these markets is ensuring that customers deploy and use the technology and then charging for upgrades and support over time.

We believe that Netscape's vision of this market is more or less on target, but it has a relatively small number of large enterprise customers today who have fully deployed Netscape's solutions. It will take time (probably years) to build a significant installed base of corporate accounts. Finally, Netscape must appear stable and viable over the long run to be successful. Continuation of its recent turmoil will be deadly. The last thing corporate IT managers want to do is bet on a dying horse.

Ultimately, we believe that Netscape can be a viable player in the server wars, but it may take some time. Part of the delay is that some of these markets, like e-commerce and application servers, are at the early stages of growth. Netscape needs time to achieve critical mass and gain the economies of scale to compete effectively. It also has to gain the confidence of more large customers. If these businesses take off, then supplying software and services for e-commerce and Internet/intranet infrastructures could be a very big and profitable business. The server strategy will require the company to execute its technology strategy extremely well, but Netscape is a much better and more focused organization today than it was in mid-1997, when we started this book. The big problem in the future will be generating enough positive cash flow to build credibility in the corporate IT world, fund ongoing research and development, and generate scale economies in sales and support. In the short and medium run, Netscape's future will depend on its performance in the portal wars. Without revenues and profits from browsers, winning a big piece of the portal wars will be critical for getting Netscape over the hump.

The Portal Wars

If the browser wars will be a winner-take-all struggle and the server wars will be a long drawn-out battle among several large competitors, then what is the likely outcome of the portal wars? We believe that the portal wars will have yet another character, more like a two-stage race. We are already in the first stage. Competitors today are scrambling to grab as many "eyeballs" as they can. The winners, however, will emerge in the second stage of the race when they successfully hook (through personalization, virtual communities, and specialized content) as many consumers as they can.

Netscape just entered this fray in the spring of 1998. Netscape enters, though, with a strong position and a number of big advantages. The most obvious advantage is that Netscape has one of the strongest brand names on the Internet and one of the most heavily trafficked sites on the Web. Despite underestimating the value of the Web site for almost four years, Netscape has a large installed base of users who come to the site by default. So far, it has grabbed a large number of eyeballs, but not yet hooked and reeled them in. This will be a highly competitive market in the next few years as Netscape competes with Yahoo!, AOL, Excite, Snap, Lycos, Microsoft's Start page, and numerous others who want to be every consumer's first location on the Internet.

The economics of the portal wars are also fundamentally different from the economics of the server wars and the browser wars. The good news for Netscape is that the Web site has been very profitable and should remain so for at least another 12 to 24 months. As Mike Homer told us in May of 1998, "Our Web site is the best money machine on the Internet. Last year [1997], we did $108 million in revenue, with more than 50 percent bottom-line profits. The Web site has been a magical subsidy for the entire move into the enterprise business." Netscape's Web site has been so profitable because more than half the browsers in the world automatically take people to Netcenter. This has allowed, and should continue to allow, Netscape to charge significant fees for retailers, advertisers, search engines, and other content providers who want access to Netscape's customers. Netscape has also been the low-cost provider of Web services. Yahoo! and Excite have each hired more than 400 people to run their Web sites, while Netscape (partly out of neglect) had only 40 people in 1997, ramping to 180 permanent employees in 1998. Excite's willingness to pay $70 million dollars to have a preferred position with Netscape for two years is testimony to the value of Netscape's asset.

Netscape has one significant advantage in the portal wars that only Microsoft shares. It can build functionality into its browser that could make Netcenter easier to use and better than most of its portal competitors. Netscape has already added to Communicator 4.5 features in the Navigator browser that take you to your customized home page, help you search for related items on the Internet, or allow you to synchronize personal information (like e-mail, addresses, or bookmarks) on different computing devices from any location. Over time, Netscape plans to add more features that will "hook" the consumer. Microsoft, of course, can imitate or even improve on Netscape's features, given enough time, and Microsoft will invent some new features of its own to tie browser users into its Web site. But, in this battle, Netscape has huge potential advantages over other competitors, including portal "giants" such as Yahoo! and AOL.

This means that Netscape is in yet another race. If we are right and Netscape loses the browser wars in the next five or so years and draws even in the server wars, then it has to build a strong, self-standing Web site that can compete on its own merits without the advantages of a customized browser. For the next few years, it will be a race among Yahoo!, AOL, Netscape, Microsoft, and all the other portal wannabes to build great Web sites that pull in eyeballs and hook consumers. Netscape's complex challenge will be to build a compelling Web portal that exploits a strong competitive asset (the browser) that will go away.

Executing the portal strategy will not be easy. For most of its history, Netscape has been a software company. Even during the early browser days when Netscape targeted consumers, its forte was not Web services. The company's distinctive competencies have been in building and shipping Internet-based software products. For Netscape to succeed in the portal space, the company will have to develop a new set of competencies that are closer to a Disney than to an IBM. Netscape will also have the burden of managing and paying for a browser development organization—a burden not shared by other (non-Microsoft) portals. In addition, Jim Barksdale and other executives will have to learn how to manage a software conglomerate with a wide range of products and services. The tasks ahead for Netscape are daunting. Microsoft is the best model, but Gates has spent more than a billion dollars on media-related Web services, with only modest success. Can Netscape create the culture and environment of Yahoo! or CNN on one side of the company while building the enterprise culture of IBM or Oracle on the other side? This will be difficult, though not impossible to do.

Netscape's ultimate advantage in these battles may be its experience. The company has weathered many bumps in the Internet road. It has matured and become more focused as we approach the next millennium. The management team has successfully ramped up the company, figured out how to control exponential growth, streamlined the technology organization, and improved product development and testing. In the process, Jim Barksdale, Marc Andreessen, and Netscape's other senior managers and engineers have created an entity that is accustomed to handling rapid change and continuous evolution as well as wrestling with giants. They have proven their ability to adapt in the past; we think they can adapt in the future. Netscape has also taught us much about competing on Internet time. At the very least, it has surely given Microsoft a run for its money. Not many companies can make that claim.

Appendix One

Netscape's Chronology

1994

April 4	Jim Clark and Marc Andreessen found Mosaic Communications Corp.
August 24	The University of Illinois at Urbana-Champaign announces a master-license agreement assigning all future commercial licensing rights for NCSA Mosaic to Spyglass, Inc.
October 13	Beta release of Navigator 1.0.
November 14	Mosaic changes name to Netscape Communications Corp.
November 21	MCI chooses Netscape client and server software as the basis of its new internetMCI service.
November 29	Digital Equipment Corp. becomes the first reseller of Netscape server products.
December 15	Netscape ships Navigator 1.0, Communications Server 1.0, and Commerce Server 1.0.
December 21	Netscape reaches a settlement with the University of Illinois at Urbana-Champaign, leaving it free to market its products without a license.

1995

January 11	Jim Barksdale becomes Netscape's president and CEO.
January 24	Silicon Graphics agrees to resell Netscape products.
February 6	Novell agrees to resell Netscape products.
February 8	Delphi Internet Services licenses Netscape client and server software.
March 6	Beta release of Navigator 1.1.
March 22	Netscape opens a subsidiary in Japan.

March 27	Netscape announces Communications Server 1.1, Commerce Server 1.1, News Server, Proxy Server, and Integrated Applications (Merchant System, Community System, Publishing System, IStore).
April 7	Six publishing and high-technology companies invest in Netscape.
May 23	Netscape licenses Java from Sun Microsystems, Inc.
June 20	Beta release of Navigator 1.2.
August 9	Netscape's initial public offering values the company at $2.2 billion.
August 15	AT&T WorldNet Services licenses Navigator.
August 24	Microsoft ships Windows 95, Microsoft Network, and Internet Explorer 1.0.
September 18	Netscape announces Navigator 2.0 and Navigator Gold 2.0. The Gold editions of Navigator incorporate WYSIWYG (What-You-See-Is-What-You-Get) tools for editing in HTML.
September 21	Netscape acquires Collabra Software for 1.85 million shares, then valued at $109 million. Forty-seven Collabra employees, including CEO Eric Hahn, join Netscape.
October 2	Netscape opens subsidiaries in the United Kingdom, France, and Germany.
October 10	Beta release of Navigator 2.0.
October 31	IBM agrees to resell Netscape products.
November 27	Netscape announces Mail Server.
December 6	Netscape's share price reaches an all-time high of $174.
December 7	Microsoft unveils its Internet strategy.
December 13	Netscape announces its products are used by 70 percent of the Global Fortune 100.

1996

January 23	Netscape stockholders approve a two-for-one stock split.
January 29	Beta release of Navigator Gold 2.0.
January 31	Netscape acquires InSoft and its 71 employees for 1.96 million shares, then valued at $161 million.
February 5	Netscape ships Navigator 2.0.
February 12	Microsoft ships Internet Information Server 1.0.
February 12	Netscape acquires Paper Software and its 12 employees for an undisclosed sum.
February 15	Beta release of Navigator 2.0 in French, German, and Japanese.
February 20	Microsoft creates the Internet Platform & Tools Division.
March 4	Netscape acquires Netcode. The terms of the deal are not disclosed.
March 5	Netscape announces FastTrack Server, Enterprise Server 2.0, and SuiteSpot at its first Internet Developers Conference.

March 11	America Online licenses Navigator.
March 12	America Online makes Internet Explorer its default browser.
April 2	Microsoft ships Exchange Server.
April 10	Netscape and General Electric Information Services announce the formation of Actra.
April 22	Netscape joins more than 40 other companies in endorsing the Lightweight Directory Access Protocol.
April 23	Microsoft ships Internet Explorer 2.0 for Macintosh.
April 29	Beta release of Navigator 3.0.
April 30	Microsoft ships Internet Explorer 2.0 for Windows 3.1.
May 8	Beta release of Navigator 2.0 in Brazilian, Dutch, Italian, Korean, Portuguese, Spanish, and Swedish.
May 28	Beta release of Internet Explorer 3.0.
June 12	Netscape announces that its products are used by 92 of the Fortune 100.
June 19	Netscape announces that Navigator has become the world's most popular personal computer application, with more than 38 million users.
July 29	Netscape announces the Netscape ONE development environment.
August 12	Netscape sends a letter to the U.S. Department of Justice (DOJ), charging Microsoft with anticompetitive practices.
August 12	Microsoft ships Internet Explorer 3.0.
August 19	Netscape ships Navigator 3.0.
August 20	Netscape invests in the Java Fund, a $100 million fund run by Kleiner Perkins Caufield & Byer to support start-ups developing Java-based Internet software.
August 29	Netscape joins six other companies to form Navio Communications, with the goal of adapting Netscape's software for use on set-top boxes, cellular phones, and similar devices.
September 20	The Justice Department renews its probe into Microsoft's business practices.
October 15	Netscape introduces Communicator 4.0 and SuiteSpot 3.0 at its second Internet Developers Conference; it also announces plans to "embrace and integrate" Microsoft technologies and products.
October 30	Netscape files for a secondary offering of 5 million shares.
December 9	Microsoft ships Internet Explorer 3.0 for Windows 3.1.
December 23	Beta release of Communicator 4.0.

1997

| January 8 | Microsoft ships Internet Explorer 3.0 for Macintosh. |
| January 13 | Netscape announces that it delivered more than 1 million servers in 1996. |

March 19	Netscape announces an agreement allowing Yahoo! to manage a guide to Web sites located on the Netscape site. The deal is reported to be worth $30 million to Netscape over two years.
April 1	Netscape announces Visual JavaScript, its first full-fledged development tool.
April 8	Beta release of Internet Explorer 4.0.
April 29	Barksdale announces that he will forgo his salary in 1997.
April 30	Netscape acquires DigitalStyle Corp. and Portola Communications Inc. In order to finance the acquisitions, Netscape issues 2.08 million shares, then valued at $56 million.
May 19	Navio merges with Network Computer Inc., a subsidiary of Oracle Corp.
June 2	Netscape announces Mission Control.
June 11	Netscape ships Communicator 4.0 and SuiteSpot 3.0 at its third Internet Developers Conference. It also announces that a "100 percent pure" Java version of Communicator will be released in 1998.
June 11	Netscape posts an open letter on its Web site, promising to support all open standards.
July 8	Netscape announces more than 200 "design wins"—deployment of at least 500 seats of Netscape software by enterprise customers and large organizations.
August 6	Microsoft invests $150 million in Apple Computer.
August 15	Netscape ships Netcaster.
August 18	Netscape offers a stand-alone browser, Navigator 4.0, and announces the "Netscape Everywhere" initiative to distribute client software.
September 3	Netscape relaunches its Web site as Netcenter.
September 30	Microsoft ships Internet Explorer 4.0.
October 20	The U.S. Department of Justice (DOJ) charges Microsoft with violating a 1995 consent decree.
November 7	Netscape buys back GEIS's interest in Actra for 1.7 million shares, then valued at $56 million.
November 24	Netscape acquires Kiva Software for 6.3 million shares, then valued at $180 million.
November 24	Netscape launches Netscape Business Journal by Individual, a personalized business news service, on Netcenter.
December 11	Netscape launches Marketplace, an online shopping site, on Netcenter.
December 11	Judge Thomas Penfield Jackson issues a temporary order forbidding Microsoft to require licensees of Windows 95 to install Internet Explorer.

1998

January 9	Microsoft ships Internet Explorer 4.0 for Macintosh.
January 21	Microsoft ships Internet Explorer 4.0 for Windows 3.1 and Windows NT 3.51.

January 22	Netscape makes Navigator and Communicator available for free; in addition, it announces that the source code for Communicator 5.0 will be available for free licensing on the Internet.
January 26	Netscape launches Netcenter Travel by Travelocity, an online travel reservations service.
January 27	Netscape announces a loss of $88.3 million for the fourth quarter of 1997; it also announces 300 employees will be laid off.
February 3	Netscape ships Application Server 2.0.
February 24	Microsoft releases IE 4.0 for Solaris and three other versions of UNIX.
February 26	Netscape confirms that the all-Java browser project is on hold.
March 1	Microsoft announces that it has loosened some restrictions in contracts with Internet service providers.
March 3	The Senate Judiciary Committee holds a hearing on competition in the computer industry.
March 25	Netscape creates a new division focused on Netcenter.
March 31	Netscape posts the source code for Communicator 5.0 on mozilla.org.
April 22	Netscape announces "Project 60," a 60-day campaign to strengthen Netcenter. Features to be added to the site include free e-mail and a Netscape-branded search engine.
May 4	Netscape chooses Excite to operate its search engine; the deal is estimated to be worth between $70 million and $100 million to Netscape over two years.
May 6	Netscape announces that it will release the source code for its Directory Software Developer's Kit.
May 12	Netscape announces that it will release the source code for the Messenger component of Communicator 5.0.
May 13	Netscape releases BuyerXpert 1.0, the last remaining piece of the CommerceXpert electronic commerce suite, which it acquired with Actra.
May 18	The Justice Department and 20 state attorneys general file antitrust suits against Microsoft focusing on the company's strategy in the browser market.
May 27	Netscape announces a loss of $54.2 million for the month of January and net income of $8,000 for the three months ending April 30.
June 4	Netscape unveils a new strategy focusing on enterprise software, electronic commerce software, and Netcenter.
June 17	Netscape announces Communicator 4.5.
June 23	The U.S. Court of Appeals for the District of Columbia overturns the preliminary injunction issued in December 1997.
June 25	Microsoft ships Windows 98.
June 30	Netscape launches Netcenter 2.0.

July 15   Beta release of Communicator 4.5.

August 18   Netscape announces net income of $100,000 for the three months ending
               July 31.

Netscape's Products

Clients

Navigator	Stand-alone browser, includes Netcaster; provides Web access to basic e-mail and calendaring when used with Netscape servers
Communicator (Standard)	
Navigator	Browser
Messenger	E-mail client
Collabra	Discussion group client
Composer	Creates and publishes HTML documents
Netcaster	Delivers information to the desktop through "push" channels
Conference	Supports real-time multimedia communications (conference calls, e.g.)
AOL Instant Messenger	Informs users if friends are online and supports instant message exchange
Communicator (Professional)	Standard Edition plus:
Calendar	Scheduling client
AutoAdmin	Supports centralized management and updating of Communicator
IBM Host On-Demand	Provides access to applications and data on IBM host systems
Communicator Internet Access Edition	Navigator plus basic Internet tools, including Internet connection software and automatic Internet account creation
Communicator Deluxe Edition	Communicator Internet Access Edition plus Norton AntiVirus Internet Scanner and 15 additional utilities and plug-ins

| Publishing Suite | Communicator plus NetObjects Fusion PE and other tools for creating and publishing Web sites |
| Mission Control Desktop | Centralizes customization and deployment of Communicator |

Servers

FastTrack Server	Entry-level Web server
SuiteSpot Standard Edition	
Communicator Standard Edition	Client suite
Enterprise Server	"Enterprise-strength" Web server
Messaging Server	Supports enterprise e-mail
Calendar Server	Supports individual and group scheduling
Collabra Server	Supports secure, online discussion groups
Directory Server	Centralizes directory administration across multiple Internet applications
SuiteSpot Professional Standard Edition:	Standard plus:
Communicator Professional	Enhanced client suite
Mission Control Desktop	Centralizes customization and deployment of Communicator
Compass Server	Creates, catalogs, and manages an online catalog of intranet and Internet documents
Certificate Server	Issues and manages authorized user certificates for intranets and extranets
Proxy Server	Replicates and filters Web content to improve security and performance
SuiteSpot Housing Edition	A version of SuiteSpot designed for Internet service providers and telecommunications companies
Application Server	Supports large-scale, business-critical Internet and extranet applications

Commerce Applications

ECXpert	Business-to-business electronic commerce system
SellerXpert	Internet order-taking and transaction-processing system
BuyerXpert	Internet-based purchasing system
PublishingXpert	Commercial Internet publishing system
MerchantXpert	Internet-based retailing system

Development Tools

SuiteTools

Component Builder	Enables developers to create reusable components in Java, JavaScript, and CORBA; includes Component Developer's Kit, JavaScript Debugger, Symantec Visual Café for Java Professional Development Edition, and NetObjects JavaScript Bean Builder
Visual JavaScript Pro	Speeds up the development of Web-based applications using JavaBean, JavaScriptBean, and CORBA components; includes Visual JavaScript, Enterprise Server, and an Oracle Lite database

Interviews

Note: All interviews are with Netscape employees unless otherwise noted.

	Recent Position	Date of Interview(s)
Marc Andreessen	Executive Vice President, Products and Marketing	November 10, 1997; May 21, 1998
Jennifer Bailey	Senior Vice President, Strategic Development and Marketing, Netcenter Division	March 25, 1998
Steve Ballmer	President, Microsoft	March 23, 1998
Jim Barksdale	President and CEO	July 31, 1997; May 21, 1998
Carl Cargill*	Program Manager, Standards	August 25, 1997
Desmond Chan*	QA Manager, Proxy Server	May 12, 1998
Michael Dell	Chairman and CEO, Dell Computer	March 30, 1998
John Doerr	Partner, Kleiner Perkins Caufield & Byers and Director, Netscape	September 18, 1997; November 12, 1997
Alex Edelstein*	Assistant to Jim Barksdale	July 30, 1997; January 20, 1998
Bill Gargiulo*	Director, North American Technical Support	November 10, 1997
Larry Geisel*	Senior Vice President, Information Systems	August 28, 1997
Rick Gessner	Director of Engineering, Client Product Division	September 8, 1998

*No longer with the company

	Recent Position	Date of Interview(s)
Skip Glass	Vice President, Strategic Partnerships and Developer Relations	June 29, 1998
Todd Goldman	Group Product Manager, Client Product Division	July 22, 1998
Andy Grove	Chairman, Intel	February 24, 1998
Eric Hahn*	Executive Vice President, Chief Technology Officer	November 10, 1997
Julie Herendeen	Group Product Manager, Client Product Division	July 31, 1997
Mike Homer	Executive Vice President and General Manager, Netcenter Division	May 21, 1998
Ben Horowitz	Vice President and General Manager, Mission Control Business Unit, Server Products Division	July 29, 1998
Tim Howes	Chief Technical Adviser, Server Products Division	August 28, 1997
Jerril Jimerson	Director, Web Site Marketing, Netcenter Division	March 25, 1998
Roberta Katz	Senior Vice President, Secretary and General Counsel	July 28–29, 1997; August 25, 1997; June 11, 1998
Joel Klein	Assistant Attorney General, Antitrust Division, U.S. Department of Justice	July 14, 1998
Joy Lenz	Director of QA, Netcenter Division	July 28, 1997
Anton LeRoy	Vice President, Deutsche Bank Securities	June 17, 1998
Bob Lisbonne	Vice President, Client Product Division	August 2, 1997; April 14, 1998
Mike Major	Director, HR Operations	July 29, 1997
Kandis Malefyt	Senior Vice President, Human Resources	July 29, 1997

	Recent Position	Date of Interview(s)
Mike McCue	Director of Technology, Corporate Staff	August 26, 1997
Debby Meredith	Senior Vice President, Customer Satisfaction	July 29, 1997; March 25, 1998
Halsey Minor	Chairman and CEO, CNET	September 15, 1997; May 19, 1998
Lori Mirek	Senior Vice President, Worldwide Marketing	July 20, 1998
Jon Mittelhauser*	Developer, Client Product Division	July 28, 1997
Lou Montulli	Developer, Client Product Division	July 19, 1997
David Moore*	Director of Development, Microsoft	April 13, 1998
Max Morris	Program Manager, Internet Applications and Client Division, Microsoft	October 31, 1997
Tom Paquin	Fellow and Manager, Mozilla.org	May 22, 1998
John Paul	Senior Vice President and General Manager, Server Products Division	March 26, 1998
Karen Richardson*	Vice President, Strategic Accounts	June 16, 1998
Todd Rulon-Miller*	Senior Vice President, Sales and Field Operations	March 24, 1998; May 8, 1998; May 11, 1998
Greg Sands	Group Product Manager, SuiteSpot Product Marketing, Server Products Division	August 26, 1997
Steve Savignano	Senior Vice President and General Manager, Applications Products Division	May 22, 1998
Rick Schell*	Senior Vice President, Client Product Division	July 30, 1997; March 26, 1998
Danny Shader*	Vice President, Partner and Developer Relations	June 15, 1998
Sharmila Shahani	Vice President, Application Server Marketing, Applications Products Division	May 21, 1998
Ram Shriram*	Vice President, OEM and Web Site Sales	August 26, 1997; November 10, 1997; June 7, 1998

	Recent Position	Date of Interview(s)
Ben Slivka	General Manager, Windows User Interface Group, Microsoft	April 30, 1998
David Stryker*	Vice President, Core Technologies Division	August 26, 1997
Rob Sullivan	Director, Content Technologies, Intel	August 27, 1997
Lloyd Tabb	Developer, Client Product Division	July 29, 1997
Mark Tompkins	Director of Engineering Services and E-Commerce, Applications Products Division	August 27, 1997; July 21, 1998
Aleks Totic	Developer, Client Product Division	July 29, 1997
Michael Toy	Release Manager, Client Product Division	July 30, 1997
Jeff Treuhaft	Director, Extranet Marketing, Netcenter Division	March 25, 1998
Bill Turpin	VP, Web Site Product Development, Netcenter Division	August 25, 1997

Notes

Chapter One. Introduction

1. A basic introduction to the technology behind the Internet is Preston Gralla, *How the Internet Works* (Emeryville, CA: Ziff-Davis Press, 1996).
2. A useful history of the Web and the Internet is contained in Robert H. Reid, *Architects of the Web: 1,000 Days That Built the Future of Business* (New York: Wiley, 1997).
3. Nua Internet Surveys, July 1998: http://www.nua.ie/surveys/how_many_online/index.html.
4. Peter Coy, "You Ain't Seen Nothin' Yet," *Business Week,* 22 June 1998.
5. W. Brian Arthur, *Increasing Returns and Path Dependence in the Economy* (Ann Arbor: University of Michigan Press, 1994).
6. Metcalfe's Law was described in *Forbes* magazine, http://www.global.forbes.com/tool/html/98/jun/0615/feat.htm.
7. Netscape was initially incorporated as Electric Media before taking the name Mosaic Communications Corp. in May 1994. After the University of Illinois challenged Clark and Andreessen's appropriation of the "Mosaic" name, the company was renamed Netscape in November 1994.
8. See Michael A. Cusumano and Richard W. Selby, *Microsoft Secrets: How the World's Most Powerful Software Company Creates Technology, Shapes Markets, and Manages People* (New York: The Free Press/Simon & Schuster, 1995), for a discussion of Microsoft and its strategy through mid-1995. The original Windows product specification created in 1992 said nothing about browsing the Internet. Later, Microsoft planned to incorporate basic Internet access and file transfer capabilities into the Windows 95 operating system, and it did license Mosaic's browser technology in December 1994. Microsoft made the decision to create and add a browser to Windows 95, however, relatively late in the planning and development cycle for this product. For an account of this story, see Kathy Rebello, "Inside Microsoft: The Untold Story of How the Internet Forced Bill Gates to Reverse Course," *Business Week,* 15 July 1996.
9. Joshua Cooper Ramo, "Winner Take All," *Time,* 16 September 1996: http://www.pathfinder.com/time/magazine/archive/1996/dom/960916/cover.html.

Chapter Two. Creating the Company

1. Christopher J. Alden, "Bill Gates with a College Degree," *Red Herring Online,* January 1996: http://www.redherring.com/mag/issue27/degree.html.

2. Andrew Grove, *Only the Paranoid Survive* (New York: Doubleday, 1996), 83.
3. "Playboy Interview: Bill Gates," *Playboy,* July 1994, 63.
4. "Smithsonian Institution Oral and Video Histories: Marc Andreessen," June 1995: http://www.si.edu/resource/tours/comphist/ma1.html#starting.
5. Marc Andreessen and the Netscape Product Team, "The Networked Enterprise: Netscape Enterprise Vision and Product Roadmap," http://home.netscape.com/comprod/at_work/white_paper/vision/print.html.
6. Robert H. Reid, *Architects of the Web: 1,000 Days That Built the Future of Business* (New York: Wiley, 1997), 31.
7. W. Brian Arthur, *Increasing Returns and Path Dependence in the World Economy* (Ann Arbor: University of Michigan Press, 1994).
8. Alex X. Vieux, "The Once and Future Kings," *The Red Herring Online,* November 1995, http://www.redherring.com/mag/issue25/once.html.
9. Transcript of Marc Andreessen's remarks at MIT, 14 November 1996.
10. John Markoff, "New Venture in Cyberspace by Silicon Graphics Founder," *The New York Times,* 7 May 1994.
11. Amy Harmon, "Now You Don't Have to Be a Geek to Use the Net," *Los Angeles Times,* 13 November 1994.
12. Louise Kehoe, "US Groups in Internet Commerce Agreement," *Financial Times,* 3 November 1994.
13. David Bank, "Programmer Re-creating Internet Life," *The Orlando Sentinel,* 15 June 1994.
14. While Netscape sold a great deal of server software for online malls and publishing in 1996, many of those systems were not fully deployed by customers. Like many early technology products, customers had trouble making them work, which created some problems for follow-on sales in those accounts in 1997 and 1998. Interviews with Ram Shriram and Karen Richardson, 1998.
15. Amy Cortese, "Here Comes the Intranet," *Business Week,* 26 February 1996
16. Zona Research Inc., cited in Cortese, "Here Comes the Intranet."
17. Marc Andreessen and the Netscape Product Team, "The Netscape Intranet Vision and Product Roadmap," revised 16 July 1996: http://www.home.netscape.com/comprod/at_work/white_paper/intranet/vision.html.
18. Ira Sager, "The Race Is On to Simplify," *Business Week,* 24 June 1996.
19. Frank Gens, "Why the PC Business Is Becoming Obsolete," *IDC Executive Insights*: http://www.idc.com/F/Ei/gens14.htm.
20. Netscape press releases, 12 June 1996, 10 October 1996.
21. Mark Halper, "So Does Your Web site Pay?" *Forbes ASAP,* 25 August 1997.
22. "Gartner Group's Conference, Focused on Intranets and Extranets, Attracts 4,000 Senior Managers," *Business Wire,* 26 September 1997.
23. Marc Andreessen and the Netscape Product Team, "The Networked Enterprise: Netscape Enterprise Vision and Product Roadmap," http://home.netscape.com/comprod/at_work/white_paper/vision/print.html.
24. "Netscape Breaks Free," *The Economist,* 28 March 1998.
25. The mozilla.org site has published http://www.search.netscape.com/comprod/at_work/white_paper/intranet/vision.html. An annotated version of the Netscape Public License, which gives this explanation of what types of changes developers must make publicly available: "If you change anything within one of the files contained in the Source Code, that is a Modification, and it must be made publicly available in source code form. If you take code out of one of the files contained in the Source Code and place it in a new file, whether you add new code or not, that is a Modification, and it must be made publicly available in source code form. If you rename a file or combine two or more files contained in the Source Code, that is a Modification, and it must be

made publicly available in source code form. However, if you add a new file that does not contain any of the Original Code or subsequent Modified Code, it is not a Modification, and need not be made publicly available in source code form. This remains true even if the new file is called or referenced by changes you made in the Source Code, though those changes do constitute a Modification and must be made publicly available in source code form."

26. "Netscape Wants to Be Media Firm," *CNET NEWS.COM*, 24 April 1998: http://www.news.com/News/Item/0,4,21475,00.html.

27. Paul Festa and Dawn Kawamoto, "Netscape Extends Search Contracts," *CNET NEWS.COM*, 30 April 1990: http://www.news.com/News/Item/0,4,21662,00.html.

28. Ultimately, the Netscape Guide by Yahoo! generated less revenue than either partner had expected. In August 1997, the terms of the deal were renegotiated to reduce Yahoo's first-year payments to Netscape. In May 1998, the two companies agreed to terminate the agreement.

29. Margie Wylie, "Down Home with Jim Barksdale," *CNET NEWS.COM*, October 1996: http://www.news.com/Newsmakers/Barksdale/barksdale.html.

30. Tim Clark, "Online Ad Spending to Skyrocket," *CNET NEWS.COM*, 14 August 1997: http://www.news.com/News/Item/0,4,13365,00.html.

31. Alex Lash, "Netscape Late to Leverage Traffic," *CNET NEWS.COM*, 30 December 1997: http://www.news.com/News/Item/0,4,17688,00.html.

32. RelevantKnowledge press release, 9 June 1998.

33. Bob Metcalfe, "From the Ether: Without Case of Vapors, Netscape's Tools Will Give Blackbird Reason to Squawk," *InfoWorld*, 18 September 1995; Peter Huber, "Reno Rewrites Your Operating System," *Forbes*, 1 December 1997.

34. The average age for Microsoft employees in 1997 is for U.S. employees only. "Microsoft Fast Facts," http://www.microsoft.com/prespass/fastfacts.htm. The Intel number is worldwide.

35. John Markoff, "New Venture in Cyberspace by Silicon Graphics Founder."

36. John Heilemann, "The Networker," *The New Yorker*, 11 August 1997.

37. "John Doerr: The Coach:" http://www.edge.org/digerati/doerr/.

38. Michael S. Malone, "John Doerr's Startup Manual," *Fast Company*, October–November 1996: http://www.fastcompany.com/07/082doerr.html.

39. Doerr also recruited Jim Sha, another very senior engineering manager to work with Rick Schell.

40. Joshua Cooper Ramo, "Winner Take All," *Time*, 16 September 1996.

41. David B. Yoffie and Tarun Khanna, "Microsoft 1995," HBS no. 795–147, 18.

42. Carol Sliwa, "Roller Hockey, Junk Food and Futons: Growing up Netscape-style," http://www-gsb.stanford.edu/~roxyhart/case/sandsart.htm.

43. Transcript of Marc Andreessen's remarks at MIT, 14 November 1996.

44. Reid, *Architects of the Web*, 24.

45. Transcript of Marc Andreessen's remarks at MIT, 14 November 1996.

46. Reid, *Architects of the Web*, 24.

47. "The 25 Most Intriguing People in '94," *People*, 26 December 1994/2 January 1995.

48. David van Biema, "A New Generation of Leaders," *Time*, 5 December 1994.

49. Transcript of Marc Andreessen's remarks at MIT, 14 November 1996.

50. Molly Baker, "Netscape's IPO Gets an Explosive Welcome," *The Wall Street Journal*, 9 August 1995.

51. "Beyond Browsing," *Computer Business Review*, 1 December 1994.

52. Transcript of Marc Andreessen's remarks at MIT, 14 November 1996.

53. Andreessen and Meredith took a very different view of Collabra. Andreessen told us, "The decision to buy Collabra was brilliant, in terms of improving the management team dramatically. From a product/technology standpoint, it's been virtually mean-

ingless. That acquisition was a success purely on the basis of the management team, which is in large part the Netscape management team." Debby Meredith pointed out that Collabra's team was "the nucleus and brains behind Messenger," the mail component of Communicator 4.0.

54. Netscape press release, 19 October 1995.
55. AppFoundry never materialized into a significant program. According to Microsoft executive Ben Slivka, however, Microsoft believed that AppFoundry could have been a real threat, and was "shell shocked at the time." Slivka felt that Netscape "over-promised and under-delivered."
56. Transcript of Marc Andreessen's remarks at MIT, 14 November 1996.
57. Peter H. Lewis, "Through the Internet with a Pair of Rival Guides: Why Not Hire Both?" *The New York Times,* 27 August 1996.
58. According to Desmond Chan, who tested Netscape's servers, there was a big downside to the DEC contract. Chan noted it was "a multiyear contract with DEC [and] . . . there were very few server sales on Digital Alpha NT and Digital UNIX, but because of the contract with DEC, every server had to be supported. It was such a waste of manpower and resources on a platform that had next to zero sales." E-mail from Chan, 10 August 1998.
59. Nick Wingfield, "Battle for Developers' Hearts, Minds," *CNET NEWS.COM,* 18 March 1996: http://www.news.com/News/Item/0,4,928,00.html.
60. Transcript of Marc Andreessen's remarks at MIT, 14 November 1996.
61. E-mail from Ram Shriram, 8 August 1998.

Chapter Three. Competitive Strategy

1. Charles Yerkow, *Modern Judo: The Complete Ju-Jutsu Library* (Harrisburg, PA: The Military Service Publishing Co., 1942), 15; "Judo," *Britannica Online* : http://www.eb.com:180/cgi-bin/g?DocF=micro/307/70.html.
2. Judith R. Gelman and Steven C. Salop, "Judo Economics: Capacity Limitation and Coupon Competition," *Rand Journal of Economics.* 14:2 (Autumn 1983), 315–325.
3. Adam M. Brandenburger and Harborne W. Stuart, Jr., "Value-Based Business Strategy," *Journal of Economics and Management Strategy* 5:1 (Spring 1996), 5–24; Eric K. Clemons, David C. Croson, and Bruce W. Weber, "Market Dominance as a Precursor of a Firm's Failure: Emerging Technologies and the Competitive Advantage of New Entrants," *Journal of Management Information Systems* 13:2 (Fall 1996), 59–75; Peter F. Drucker, "Entrepreneurial Strategies," *California Management Review* 27:2 (Winter 1985), 9–25; Joseph Farrell and C. Shapiro, "Dynamic Competition with Switching Costs," *Rand Journal of Economics* 19:1 (1988), 123–137; Drew Fudenberg and Jean Tirole, "The Fat-Cat Effect, the Puppy-Dog Ploy, and the Lean and Hungry Look," *American Economic Review* 74:2 (May 1984) 361–366; Carmen Matutes and Pierre Regibeau, "Standardization Across Markets and Entry," *Journal of Industrial Economics* 37:4 (1989), 359–371; Richard Schmalansee, "Advertising and Entry Deterrence: An Exploratory Model," *Journal of Political Economy* 91:4 (1983), 636–653; Lars Sørgard, "Judo Economics Reconsidered: Capacity Limitation, Entry, and Collusion," *International Journal of Industrial Organization* 15 (1995), 349–368.
4. Jonathan B. Baker, "Fringe Firms and Incentives to Innovate," *Antitrust Law Journal* 63 (1995), 621–641.
5. *Aviation Week & Space Technology,* 5 October 1992, 44–45.
6. Andrea Rothman et al., "The Season of Upstart Startups," *Business Week,* 31 August 1992. In the end, Kiwi's judo strategy did not succeed in heading off retaliation. A number of airlines (American, Continental, United) moved to match its low fares, but

they only did so for a small number of seats on each flight and imposed restrictive conditions on these tickets. Nonetheless, Kiwi initially enjoyed significant growth. Between 1992 and 1996, Kiwi grew to operate as many as 76 flights a day. However, after intense retaliation by Continental, and considerable internal disarray, Kiwi filed for chapter 11 and temporarily shut down operations. Four months later, Kiwi returned to service in early 1997 and is still operating today, serving Atlanta, Chicago, Newark, Orlando, San Juan, and West Palm Beach. In 1997, Zagat's Survey ranked Kiwi as the sixth best airline in the United States.

7. Adam M. Brandenburger and Barry J. Nalebuff, *Co-opetition* (New York: Currency/Doubleday, 1996), 114, 237–242.

8. Gary Hamel and C.K. Prahalad, *Competing for the Future* (Boston: Harvard Business School Press, 1994); Dorothy Leonard Barton, *Wellsprings of Knowledge: Building and Sustaining the Sources of Innovation* (Boston: Harvard Business School Press, 1995).

9. David W. Fuller, "The Man with the Slingshot," *Costco Magazines,* August 1997: http://www.costco.com/pcc/cover.story/9708cs1.htm.

10. "Growing Mozilla," *Network World Fusion,* 22 September 1997: http://www.nwfusion.com/intranet/0922view.html.

11. Ibid.

12. Matthew Gray of the Massachusetts Institute of Technology, "Web Growth Summary," 1996: http://www.mit.edu/people/mkgray/net/Web-growth-summary.html.

13. Tim Stevens, "NCSA: National Center for Supercomputing Applications," *Industry Week,* 19 December 1994.

14. Michael Krantz, "Toward a More Gorgeous Mosaic," *Mediaweek,* 8 August 1994.

15. Gary Wolf, "The (Second Phase of the) Revolution Has Begun," *Wired,* October 1994.

16. "Beyond Browsing," *Computer Business Review,* 1 December 1994.

17. Rick Ayre and Kevin Reichard, "The Web Untangled," *PC Magazine,* 7 February 1995.

18. Peter H. Lewis, "Cruising the Web with a Browser," *The New York Times,* 7 February 1995; Zona Research press release, 21 May 1996.

19. Rick Ayre and Kevin Reichard, "The Web Untangled," *PC Magazine,* 7 February 1995; Barry Gerber, "Browsers on the Wild, Wild Web," *Network Computing,* 1 April 1995; Peter Kent, "Browser Shootout," *Internet World,* April 1995.

20. "Smithsonian Institution Oral and Video Histories: Marc Andreessen," June 1995: http://www.si.edu/resource/tours/comphist/ma1.html#starting.

21. Nick Wingfield, "Netscape Ponders the Price of Its Strategy for Growth," *The Wall Street Journal Interactive Edition,* 28 January 1998.

22. Data from IDC, cited in Laura DiDio, "The Future of Networking," *Computerworld,* 13 January 1997.

23. Owen Thomas, "Actra Returns to the Fold," *The Red Herring Online,* 11 November 1997: http://www.redherring.com/insider/1997/1111/actra.html.

24. E-mail from Russell Siegelman, 12 August 1998, commenting on an early draft of this manuscript.

25. Andreessen quoted in Bob Metcalfe, "From the Ether: Without Case of Vapors, Netscape's Tools Will Give Blackbird Reason to Squawk," *InfoWorld,* 18 September 1995.

26. *Aesop's Fables* (Cleveland: The World Publishing Co., 1965), 112.

27. The term "sumo strategy" was suggested by our colleagues in a presentation at Harvard Business School in February 1998.

28. Kozo Hikoyama, *SUMO: Japanese Wrestling* (Tokyo: Board of Tourist Industry, 1940), 1; Marc Schilling, *Sumo: A Fan's Guide* (Tokyo: The Japan Times, 1994), 72.

29. George Gilder, "The Coming Software Shift," *Forbes ASAP,* 28 August 1995.

30. Bill Gates, "The Internet Tidal Wave," Microsoft internal memo, May 1995.

31. Transcript of Bill Gates's remarks at Microsoft's December 7, 1995, Internet strategy briefing.

32. Interview of Russell Siegelman in February 1996 for the Harvard Business School case study of MSN. See David B. Yoffie, "Microsoft Goes Online: MSN 1996," HBS no. 797–088.

33. David B. Yoffie, "Microsoft Goes Online: MSN 1996," HBS no. 797–088.

34. Microsoft estimated its acquisition costs at roughly $15 per customer, which included limited advertising and other channel incentives. Ibid.

35. Interview with Bill Gates, 10 April 1996, for David B. Yoffie, "Microsoft Goes Online: MSN 1996," HBS no. 797–088.

36. Reid, *Architects of the Web*, 22.

37. Alex Lash, "Homer's Run," *Industry Standard*, 27 July 1998, 34.

38. Ibid., 33.

39. Kara Swisher, "How Steve Case Bought a Browser and Changed the World (Wide Web)," *Industry Standard*, 25 June 1998: http://www.thestandard.net/articles/news_display/0,1270,817,00.html.

40. Marc Andreessen, "ONE for All," *TechVision*, 1 August 1996: http://www.netscape.com/comprod/columns/techvision/one.html.

41. E-mail exchange with Ben Slivka, commenting on early versions of the manuscript, 12 August 1998.

42. Dana Gardner, "Netscape Aims for Secular Audience," *InfoWorld*, 27 April 1998.

43. Chris Jennewein, vice president/technology operations for Knight-Ridder New Media Services, quoted in Michael Moeller, "Netscape Opening Up to Windows," *PC Week Online*, 16 February 1998: http://www.zdnet.com/pcweek/news/0216/16kiva.html.

44. Yerkow, *Modern Judo*, 21.

45. This strategy of blurring the distinction among systems, applications, and networking software was something Microsoft has been doing for years, as it added more and more functions to Windows. See Cusumano and Selby, *Microsoft Secrets*, chapters 3 and 7.

46. Datamonitor, *Servers and the Internet: Executive Summary*, 1998, 1.

47. *InformationWeek*, 21 October 1996: http://techWeb.cmp.com/iw/602/andrees.htm.

48. Frank Gens, "IDC Web Mindshare Monitor: Microsoft Stalls, IBM Surges, Customers Balk," *IDC Executive Insights*, 1998: http://www.idc.com/F/ei/gens18.htm.

49. Ibid.

50. Mike Homer, "Netscape Open Standards Guarantee," 11 June 1997: http://search.netscape.com/zh/tw/comprod/columns/intranet/open_standards.html.

51. Ibid.

52. Carl Shapiro and Hal R. Varian, *Information Rules: A Strategic Guide to the Network Economy* (Boston: Harvard Business School Press, 1998).

53. Reid, *Architects of the Web*, 59.

54. James Glave, "Netscape Loses Inside Track on HTML Standard," *Wired News*, 18 December 1997: http://www.wired.com/news/news/technology/story/9283.html.

55. Nick Wingfield, "Marc Andreessen Tackles Internet Issues for IT Managers," *InfoWorld*, 23 October 1995.

56. Erica Rex, "Exclusive Interview: Andreessen Warns of Attempt to 'Rehighjack the Hearts & Minds of Content Developers,'" *Netscape World*, July 1997: http://www.netscapeworld.com/netscapeworld/nw-07-1997/nw-07-Andreessen.t.html.

57. Netscape press release, 22 January 1998: http://www.netscape.com/newsref/pr/newsrelease558.html?cp=new01flh1.

58. While Microsoft would not open its browser source code, it did have a more flexible, modular architecture, which allowed other developers to customize IE. This flexibility neutralized some of Netscape's potential advantages with Mozilla.

59. While Linux and Apache were freeware, they were closer to "free, but not free." Most corporations had to pay for third-party support.

60. John McCarthy of Forester Research commented, "A lot of large corporations have no problem working with Netscape, but they don't necessarily want to swap their groupware or e-mail products." Nick Wingfield, "Netscape to Offer New Internet Software in Bid to Head Off Inroads by Microsoft," *The Wall Street Journal,* 18 August 1997.

61. Chris DeVoney, "Browsers Go Head to Head," *Computerworld,* 15 December 1997; David Haskin, "Netscape Communicator Pro 4.0: Still the Champ of the Internet," *Computer Shopper,* October 1997; Jason Levitt, "Browsers Display Clear Differences—Choice Between Microsoft and Netscape Depends on Your Enterprise Environment," *InformationWeek,* 20 October 1997.

62. Yerkow, *Modern Judo,* 21.

63. John Wilke, "U.S. Closes in on New Microsoft Case," *The Wall Street Journal,* 6 April 1998, A3.

64. Dan Goodin, "DOJ, States File Suits," *CNET NEWS.COM,* 18 May 1998: http://www.news.com/News/Item/0,4,22201,00.html

65. James Daly, "The Robin Hood of the Rich," *Wired,* August 1997: http://www.wired.com/wired/5.08/ reback.html.

66. Gary Reback's Letter to the Justice Department, 12 August 1996, provided by Netscape.

67. Nick Wingfield, "DOJ Fight Hits Fever Pitch," *CNET NEWS.COM,* 22 August 1996: http://www.news.com/News/Item/0,4,2259,00.html.

Chapter Four. Design Strategy

1. Michael A. Cusumano and Richard W. Selby, *Microsoft Secrets* (New York: Free Press/ Simon & Schuster, 1995), 150–151.

2. E-mail correspondence from Peter MacDonald, Netscape Communications Corporation, Server Product Marketing, 9 April 1998.

3. Jim Rapoza, "Communicator Still Has Java Jitters," *PC Week,* 13 April 1998, 38.

4. Michael Moeller, "Netscape Chasing 'Network of Eyeballs' and E-Commerce," *PC Week,* 13 April 1998 (http://www.zdnet.com/pcweek).

5. Michael Moeller, "Plug-in Updates Java VMs," *PC Week,* May 1998; Dana Gardner and Niall McKay, "Netscape Drops Development of Java Virtual Machines," *InfoWorld Electric* (http://www.infoworld.com), 2 July 1998.

6. Wylie Wong, "Andreessen: Netscape's Javagator Is Dead," *Computer Reseller News* (http://www.crn./com), 1 July 1998.

7. Michael Moeller and Mary Jo Foley, "Browser Battle Picks Up Steam," *PC Week,* 8 June 1998, 1.

8. See *Microsoft Secrets,* 236–243, 384–397; Helen Custer, *Inside Windows NT* (Redmond, WA: Microsoft Press, 1993), 25–27.

9. Mary Jo Foley and Michael Moeller, "IE 5.0 Components Will Add to Sum of Browser," *PC Week,* 27 April 1998, 17.

10. See Andy Eddy and John Cox, "Navigator to Lose Win 98 Speed War," *Network World,* 4 May 1998, (http://www.networkworld.com).

11. See Stephen H. Wildstrom, "Build Your Own Browser," *Business Week,* 20 July 1998, 17.

12. We can assume that developers numbered only about 60 percent of total staffing resources (person-months) at Netscape (see chapter 5, Table 5.3). Therefore, the 1,400 lines of code per person-month that Netscape averaged from Navigator 1.0 through Communicator 4.0 drops to about 800 lines of code per month or 10,000 per

year, if we include rough estimates for product management and testing. This adjusted figure is about average for a sample of high-performing U.S. and Japanese software projects, according to data published in 1990. For these data, see Michael A. Cusumano, *Japan's Software Factories* (New York: Oxford University Press, 1991), 459. The original reference for the study is Michael A. Cusumano and Chris F. Kemerer, "A Quantitative Analysis of U.S. and Japanese Practice and Performance in Software Development," *Management Science,* 36, 11, November 1990.

13. Michael A. Cusumano and Kentaro Nobeoka, *Thinking Beyond Lean* (New York: Free Press/Simon & Schuster, 1998), as well as M. Meyer and A. Lehnerd, *The Power of Product Platforms* (New York: Free Press/Simon & Schuster, 1997).

14. *Microsoft Secrets,* 384–397.

15. Japanese software factories faced similar issues and solved them in various ways. See in particular the discussion of Toshiba in *Japan's Software Factories.*

16. Steve Hamm, "The Education of Marc Andreessen," *Business Week,* 13 April 1998, 84–92.

17. Netscape Communications Corp., "Netscape Accelerates Communicator Evolution with First Release of Next-Generation Communicator Source Code to Developer Community via Mozilla.org," press release available on Netscape Web site, posted ca. 31 March 1998.

18. Connie Guglielmo, "Netscape Says Source Code Giveaway Has Been a Hit," *ZDNET/ Interactive Week Online* (http://www.zdnet.com /intweek/>inter@ctive week online), 13 July 1998.

Chapter Five. Development Strategy

1. Transcript of Marc Andreessen's remarks at MIT, 14 November 1996.

2. Ibid.

3. See Michael A. Cusumano and Richard W. Selby, *Microsoft Secrets* (New York: Free Press/Simon & Schuster, 1995), 127–186.

4. Frederick Brooks, *The Mythical Man-Month.* (Reading, MA: Addison-Wesley, 1975).

5. *Microsoft Secrets,* 251–259.

6. Ibid., 370–373.

7. See Winston W. Royce, "Managing the Development of Large Software Systems," *Proceedings of IEEE WESCON,* August 1970, 1–9.

8. Steven Wheelwright and Kim Clark, *Revolutionizing Product Development* (New York: Free Press/Simon & Schuster, 1992); Glen. L. Urban and John. R. Hauser, *Design and Marketing of New Products* (Englewood Cliffs, NJ: Prentice Hall, 1993); and Karl Ulrich and Steven Eppinger, *Product Design and Development* (New York: McGraw-Hill, 1995).

9. For alternatives to the waterfall process outside of Microsoft, see articles such as Victor R. Basili and Albert J. Turner, "Iterative Enhancement: A Practical Technique for Software Development," *IEEE Transactions on Software Engineering,* vol. SE-1, no. 4 (December 1975); Barry W. Boehm, "A Spiral Model of Software Development and Enhancement," *IEEE Computer,* May 1988. Also see Nancy Staudenmayer and Michael Cusumano, "Alternative Designs for Product Component Integration," MIT Sloan School of Management Working Paper #4016 (April 1998).

10. E-mail from Ben Slivka, 11 August 1998.

11. This is also the conclusion of our colleagues Alan MacCormack and Marco Iansiti at Harvard Business School, and Roberto Verganti at Milan Polytechnic, who have been collecting data on various Internet software projects. For an early summary of their research, see "R. Verganti, A. MacCormack, and M. Iansiti, "Rapid Learning and

Adaptation in Product Development: An Empirical Study of the Internet Software Industry," *Proceedings of the 5th International Product Development Management Conference,* Como, Italy, 25–26 May 1998, vol. 2, 1063–1080.

12. See *Microsoft Secrets,* chapters 2 and 4, for detailed discussions on the role of program managers.

13. Interview with Max Morris, Program Manager, Internet Applications and Client Division, Microsoft, 31 October 1997. Discussions on changes in Microsoft's development practices during 1995–1997 also benefited from our interview with David Moore, former director of development, Microsoft, 13 April 1998.

14. See *Microsoft Secrets,* 51.

15. See, for example, Ibid., 270–274.

16. For a detailed discussion of testing at Microsoft, see Ibid., chapter 5.

17. See Ibid., 302–303, 430–431.

18. See Ibid., especially 51.

19. Desmond Chan, "The Design of a Software Company in the Internet Age," Cambridge, MA, Unpublished Master's Thesis, MIT Management of Technology Program, June 1998, 45.

20. See *Microsoft Secrets,* 304–307, 375–384.

21. See Ibid., 295–315.

22. See Ibid., 310.

23. See Ibid., 365.

24. See Ibid., 330–339, as well as Jim McCarthy, *Dynamics of Software Development* (Redmond, WA: Microsoft Press, 1995); and Steve McConnell, *Rapid Development: Taming Wild Software Schedules* (Redmond, WA: Microsoft Press, 1996).

25. See, for example, Watts Humprey, *Managing the Software Process* (Reading, MA: Addison-Wesley, 1989).

Chapter Six. Competing on Internet Time

1. Shona M. Brown and Kathleen M. Eisenhardt, *Competing on the Edge: Strategy as Structured Chaos* (Boston: Harvard Business School Press, 1998).

2. "Growing Mozilla," *Network World Fusion,* 22 September 1997: http://www.nwfusion.com/intranet/0922view.html.

3. Andreessen quoted in Elizabeth Corcoran, "Netscape Details Shift in Strategy," *Washington Post,* 6 June 1998, E2.

4. Jacqueline Henry, "Netscape Solid in Server Software," *Computer Reseller News,* http://www.crn.com/sections/supplement/794/794cc45.asp.

5. Andreessen quoted in Bob Metcalfe, "From the Ether: Without Case of Vapors, Netscape's Tools Will Give Blackbird Reason to Squawk," *InfoWorld,* 18 September 1995.

6. The term "constructive confrontation" is used by Intel to describe its management system. Since a large number of Silicon Valley managers spent time at Intel, it is an approach that has been adopted fairly widely. It would also be a good description of Microsoft's senior management style.

7. Chris Oakes, "Group Out to Set a New Standard," *Wired News,* 10 August 1998.

8. See Michael A. Cusumano, Yiorgos Mylonadis, and Richard S. Rosenbloom, "Strategic Maneuvering and Mass-Market Dynamics: The Triumph of VHS Over Beta," *Business History Review,* Spring 1992.

Index

About the Authors

MICHAEL A. CUSUMANO, co-author of the recently published *Thinking Beyond Lean* and the international bestseller *Microsoft Secrets,* is the Sloan Distinguished Professor of Management at MIT's Sloan School of Management. A leading expert on technology management and software development, Professor Cusumano consults widely with major corporations throughout the world. He is also the author of *The Japanese Automobile Industry* and *Japan's Software Factories.*

DAVID B. YOFFIE is the Max and Doris Starr Professor of International Business Administration and co-chair of the Competition and Strategy Department at the Harvard Business School. A leading authority on competitive strategy and international competition, Professor Yoffie is a member of the Board of Directors of Intel Corporation and several other high-tech companies. He is editor of *Competing in the Age of Digital Convergence* and author of *Strategic Management in Information Technology.*